W9-BYZ-064

ALSO BY ROBERT GOTTLIEB

Sarah: The Life of Sarah Bernhardt

George Balanchine: The Ballet Maker

Reading Dance (editor)

Reading Lyrics (editor, with Robert Kimball)

Reading Jazz (editor)

Everyman's Library *Collected Stories* of Rudyard Kipling (editor)

The Journals of John Cheever (editor)

A Certain Style: The Art of the Plastic Handbag, 1949–59

Lives and Letters

Lives

and

Letters

Robert Gottlieb

Farrar, Straus and Giroux   New York

Farrar, Straus and Giroux
18 West 18th Street, New York 10011

These essays originally appeared in somewhat different form in the following pub-
lications: *The New Republic, The New York Observer, The New York Review of Books, The New
York Times Book Review, The New Yorker, Vanity Fair,* and the Everyman's Library edition of
Rudyard Kipling's *Collected Stories* (Random House, Inc.).

Grateful acknowledgment is made to Photofest for the images of Tallulah Bankhead,
Bing Crosby, Judy Garland, Lillian Gish, Katharine Hepburn, Porfirio Rubirosa, Diana
Vreeland, Mae West, and the Windsors, and the movie still from *Devotion*; to Dominique
Nabokov for the image of Elia Kazan; to Gamma-Rapho for the image of Minou Drouet;
to the Alexander Liberman Trust for the image of Francine du Plessix Gray and her
parents; to Keith Money for the image of Margot Fonteyn; and to the Marjorie Kinnan
Rawlings Collection, Department of Special and Area Studies Collections, George A.
Smathers Libraries, University of Florida, Gainesville, for the image of Marjorie Kinnan
Rawlings.

Grateful acknowledgment is made for permission to reprint lyrics from "Wintergreen
for President," music and lyrics by George Gershwin and Ira Gershwin, copyright ©
1933 (renewed) by New World Music for the United States; Chappell & Co. and New
World Music Company (Ltd.) administered by WB Music Corp. for all British
Reversionary Territories; New World Music Company (Ltd.), administered by WB
Music Corp. for all other countries.

Library of Congress Cataloging-in-Publication Data
Gottlieb, Robert, 1931–
    Lives and letters / Robert Gottlieb.— 1st ed.
        p.   cm.
    ISBN 978-0-374-29882-1 (alk. paper)
    I. Title.

AC8 .G813 2011
081—dc22
                                        2010038530

www.fsgbooks.com

For my daughter,
Elizabeth Gottlieb Young—Lizzie

Contents

Preface

The pieces in this collection fall mainly into two categories: Lives and Letters—hence the title. The first considers the histories of a group of remarkable men and women; the second is more concerned with literary phenomena, although the essays on Dickens and Thurber and Steinbeck might just as well have found themselves in the first category. All these pieces were commissioned—I didn't proceed from a personal agenda or with a formal purpose—but I can see now that they all reflect the two things I most care about: what happens to people, and writing.

Some of these lives are great success stories: Sarah Bernhardt, Lillian Gish, Elia Kazan all surmounted early obstacles and survived emotional hardships; their energy, their talent, their canniness, their good luck—and most of all, their implacable willpower—saw them through. Others—Isadora Duncan, Judy Garland, Tallulah Bankhead—crashed and burned. Charles Dickens, Eleonora Duse, Bruno Bettelheim, James Thurber led conflicted and painful lives despite their extraordinary accomplishments. Each of these histories has its unique trajectory, and what could be more interesting than tracking them and trying to understand what went right here, what went wrong there?

Some of these figures I had always been fascinated by—Isadora, for instance. We all know that her astonishing life, so crucial to the history of dance, ended in disaster. But why? Was it historical circumstance? Some fatal flaw in her temperament or character or intelligence? There isn't a simple answer, but after spending months grappling with the extensive Duncan literature, I felt that I had begun to understand what she had been and what her story had to tell us. So for me, writing about her was a happy ending, however unhappy her own ending had been.

Other figures were significant names in our culture but not part of the furniture of my mind. I knew relatively little about Douglas Fairbanks, probably the biggest male movie star of the silent screen (yes, even bigger than Chaplin); about Joseph Jefferson, the most beloved stage actor of the second half of the nineteenth century—he played Rip Van Winkle more than five thousand times—and, indeed, about the whole saga of the American theater of that period; about Freud's interactions with the poet H.D. and the novelist known as Bryher.

By accident I stumbled on two subjects about which I knew absolutely nothing and which came to engross me. One was the pathetic, ultimately inspiring history of the eight-year-old poet Minou Drouet, who galvanized France in the 1950s and eventually, against the odds, survived her harrowing start in life. The other was the horrifying Scott Peterson murder case, about which I became curious when three books about him reached the top of the bestseller list almost simultaneously. I had heard his name, but didn't even know whether he was the murderer or the victim. I found out soon enough, and was quickly struck by the uncanny connection between him and Clyde Griffiths, the central character of Dreiser's 1925 *An American Tragedy*. Here was life imitating art—except that Dreiser had a real-life model for Clyde. This was actually life imitating art imitating life.

One advantage to writing for more than one publication is the range of opportunity the various editors provide. Not every subject that interests them is necessarily tragic, triumphant, harrowing, or illuminating—but who could resist the fun of spending time with the Royals or the Mitfords? Or the adventures of Porfirio Rubirosa, the greatest playboy of the century? (He married the two richest heiresses of his day, Barbara Hutton and Doris Duke, but the love of his life was a heroine of my own, Zsa Zsa Gabor.) Or *Sex and Shopping*, the autobiography of Judith Krantz? (She and I went to the same bizarre Manhattan private school.) And then there's been the fun of comparing all the inadequate film versions of *Vanity Fair*, and parsing the movies' ludicrous attempts to explain the creative genius of Shakespeare, Molière, Austen. (They all loved . . . and lost.)

As it happens, a number of the people I've written about I had encountered in real life, either glancingly (Lillian Gish) or professionally. As a young editor at Simon and Schuster, I dealt for a while with Thurber. I spent fifteen or more years working with the New York City Ballet and

George Balanchine. I edited books by, and knew with varying degrees of closeness, Elia Kazan, Bruno Bettelheim, Margot Fonteyn, Diana Vreeland, Jessica Mitford, and Katharine Hepburn, which is why there's so much of me as participant or direct observer in this collection. (In other cases I name myself only in the cause of full disclosure.) The only pieces in which I'm at ease being present are the three grouped in the coda.

It was an impersonal curiosity that led me to consider the work of two important but controversial writers. Why does a wildly uneven novelist like John Steinbeck, who has been generally ignored by serious critics for at least the past half century, have everything—including his weakest and most obscure books—in print? I felt that by reading and reporting on all of them, I was performing a public service: No one will have to do *that* again. Yet at his best Steinbeck is a strong presence—and another conflicted man. On the other hand, I felt no ambivalence about the work of Rudyard Kipling, whose stories I was invited to collect and introduce for the Everyman's Library; reading all two hundred or so of them only confirmed my view of his genius. Kipling's reputation rises and falls, but his sheer brilliance and fluency—and, yes, depth—place him with Dickens as one of the greatest of English storytellers. T. S. Eliot, George Orwell, Angus Wilson, Randall Jarrell, among many other distinguished critics, have all borne witness to his tremendous talent, yet every generation has to be reminded of it: A dead white male—and one (unfairly) perceived as an apologist for imperialism—doesn't fit easily into today's agenda-ridden canon.

Finally, two essays that had particular meaning for me, the first an account of the reissue, in the early 1960s, of F. R. Leavis's groundbreaking and vastly influential critical quarterly, *Scrutiny.* The magazine lasted for twenty years, and the twenty volumes of its reissue were priced at $100— more money than I could possibly have afforded back in 1963. *The New Republic* not only acquired the set for me but paid me something like $75 to spend my summer reading through it and wrestling it to the ground. It's time, almost fifty years later, to remind people of just how important *Scrutiny* was, as it certainly was to me in my formative years.

And then there's the history of Maxwell Perkins and his author Marjorie Kinnan Rawlings. (Her Pulitzer Prize–winning novel, *The Yearling*, was the biggest bestseller of 1938.) Perkins was and is the hero of all American fiction editors, but although the correspondence between him and Rawlings is largely about editing, it's also a moving chronicle of a professional relationship that grew into a deep friendship between two diffident and guarded people.

In the case of Perkins and Rawlings, the boundary between Lives and Letters blurs. But when dealing with writers, is it really possible to keep them apart for long?

Lives and Letters

Dah-ling

Most famous stage actors tactfully fade away. Who today is interested in Katharine Cornell, that First Lady of the American Theater? Or that other First Lady, Helen Hayes? Or that First among Firsts, Ethel Barrymore? (Well, yes, she was the great-aunt of Drew.) Of the theatrical greats of their day, only Tallulah Bankhead, who died in 1968, has not gone gentle into oblivion. Since her death, there have been seven biographies, the latest, *Tallulah! The Life and Times of a Leading Lady*, by Joel Lobenthal, published only recently. And her own book, *Tallulah*, the number-five nonfiction bestseller of 1952 (number one was the Revised Standard Version of the Bible; Whittaker Chambers's *Witness* was number nine), is recently back in print.

Not many people remember Tallulah's stage performances, and not many more see her few movies, yet here she is again, hectoring, demanding attention, catastrophically self-destructive; a star more than an actress, a personality more than a star, a celebrity before the phenomenon of celebrity had been identified. How appropriate that her final public appearance was on *The Tonight Show* (where she chatted with Paul McCartney and John Lennon). And what a complicated professional trajectory that suggests, given that her first real success—in London in 1923, forty years before the Beatles—was opposite Sir Gerald du Maurier, then the British theater's leading matinee idol. ("Daddy," his daughter Daphne exclaimed, the first time she encountered Tallulah, "that's the most beautiful girl I've ever seen in my life.")

Tallulah, with her signature "dah-ling"s and her notorious peccadilloes and her endlessly caricaturized baritonal gurgle of a voice—a voice that the actor-writer Emlyn Williams said was "steeped as deep in sex as the human voice can go without drowning"—would be easy to dismiss as a joke if she hadn't also been a woman of outsize capacities. As it is, the story of her messy life reaches beyond gossip and approaches tragedy.

Tragedy, in fact, struck at the beginning. Her twenty-one-year-old mother—"the most beautiful thing that ever lived"—died of complications following Tallulah's birth, leaving her father, Will, so grief-stricken that he collapsed into a pattern of alcoholism, self-pity, and absence which lasted for years. The Bankheads of Alabama weren't rich, but they were aristocracy—Will Bankhead's father and brother were both United States senators—and the motherless Tallulah and her sister, Eugenia, were reared by their grandparents and aunts with strict guidelines (which they ignored) and a strong sense of privilege (which they indulged). Once Will pulled himself together, he went on to become a successful politician, ending as a much-admired Speaker of the House under Roosevelt. Tallulah, in turn, was a lifelong passionate Democrat, and took credit—some of it deserved—for helping elect both Truman and Kennedy.

Politics was not the only passion that Tallulah inherited from her father—as a very young man, he had gone to Boston to try his luck as an actor. (He was hauled back home by a no-nonsense letter from his mother.) Even as a little girl, Tallulah was crazy to perform, and frequently when Will, somewhat the worse for drink, drifted home with his pals, he would lift her up onto the dining-room table and have her entertain the boys with risqué songs. She reveled in it. A plump child with startlingly gold hair, Tallulah was an exhibitionist from the beginning.

Another side of her dramatic temperament expressed itself in wild tantrums when she didn't get her way. ("To deny me anything only inflames my desire.") She would throw herself down, beat the floor, grow purple in the face, scream bloody murder. Her sister would hide in the closet, but her commonsensical grandmother would simply fling a bucket of water in her face.

There were attempts at conventional education for the Bankhead girls. Eugenia, however, eloped in her debutante year with a boy she had met that day. As for Tallulah, at fifteen she convinced her family that she was born to be an actress, and her senatorial grandfather staked her to an assault on Broadway. Chaperoned by her Aunt Louise, she found herself living at the Algonquin Hotel in its early palmy days, and there she encountered the greats of the theatrical profession, including John Barrymore, who, true to form, tried to seduce her in his dressing room. She had

no schooling as an actress and she lacked discipline, but she had vivid charm and looks, and she was absolutely determined to prevail. "I was consumed by a fever to be famous, even infamous," she wrote.

In her desperation to be noticed, she experimented with alcohol and cocaine, but her main shock tactics involved sex. Apparently, her first affair was with the celebrated actress Eva Le Gallienne, three years her senior, but although she liked to boast about her irregular love life—"I'm a lesbian," she announced to a stranger at a party. "What do you do?"— she also told a friend, "I could never become a lesbian, because they have no sense of humor!" Perhaps she found later women friends like Billie Holiday funnier than Le Gallienne. On the whole, though, her taste was for men, and early on she met the man she undoubtedly cared for longest and most deeply, "Naps" Alington—Napier George Henry Sturt Alington—the third Alington baron—who was, in the words of Lee Israel, her

most perceptive biographer, "a soft-spoken, blond tubercular—well cultivated, bisexual, with sensuous, meaty lips, a distant, antic charm, a history of mysterious disappearances, and a streak of cruelty."

Tallulah was generally out of funds, scrounging meals and running
up bills at the Algonquin, whose long-suffering owner, Frank Case, announced at one point, "I can either run this hotel or look after Tallulah
Bankhead. I can't do both." Although she was slowly progressing from
walk-ons and small parts to leads in undistinguished plays, after some five
years in New York the big breakthrough hadn't come, and she was frus-
trated, anxious, and broke. When the chance came to play opposite du
Maurier in London, she leaped at what she saw as an opportunity to conquer the West End. (Hadn't a fashionable astrologer told her that her future lay across the Atlantic? "Go if you have to swim.") The play was
called *The Dancers*, and she was Maxine, a Canadian saloon dancer who
eventually marries Tony the bartender, who turns out to be the Earl of
Chively. With her glorious hair, her unique voice and accent, her unrestrained dancing and cartwheeling (during her English career, she cart-
wheeled whenever the script allowed, and sometimes when it didn't), she
did indeed conquer the West End.

Throughout the ten-month run of *The Dancers*, a group of rabid young
women gathered nightly up in the gallery to express their love for their
heroine by screaming, stomping, throwing flowers. Within three years,
she had attracted the most loyal and vociferous following in London. Observing this phenomenon, Arnold Bennett noted, "Ordinary stars get
'hands.' If Tallulah gets a 'hand' it is not heard. What is heard is a terrific,
wild, passionate, hysterical roar and shriek. Only the phrase of the Psalm-
ist can describe it: 'God is gone up with a shout.'" She informed a reporter
from New York, "Over here they like me to 'Tallulah.' You know—dance
and sing and romp and fluff my hair and play reckless parts." She had
become a verb!

During her London years, Tallulah appeared in sixteen plays, ranging
from outright junk (*Conchita*, *The Creaking Chair*, *Mud and Treacle*) to the
Pulitzer Prize–winning *They Knew What They Wanted*. She missed playing
Sadie Thompson in Somerset Maugham's *Rain* when Maugham nixed her
at the last minute, making her so despondent that she thought she'd give
suicide a try, and, according to Lobenthal, "swallowed twenty aspirins,
scribbled a suicide note—'It ain't goin' to rain no moh'—and lay down on

her intended bier." The next morning, feeling fine, she was wakened by a phone call begging her to step into a leading role in Noël Coward's *Fallen Angels.*

Her life in London was hardly restricted to work. She was as famous for her shenanigans offstage as for her flamboyant performances. In her autobiography, she confides, "Have I darkly hinted that for eight years I cut a great swath in London? Well I damned well did, and it was all a spur to my ego, electrifying! London beaux clamored for my company." Her highly publicized flings extended from the tennis champion Jean Borotra to Lord Birkenhead to a fraudulent Italian aristocrat whom she almost married. And, of course, Napier Alington was always on her mind and often in her bed.

But as the decade drew to a close she decided that it was time to go home: She was approaching thirty, Naps was marrying the daughter of an earl, and she was out of money, since she always spent everything she earned, and then some. And suddenly the way was open to her, via an extraordinary offer from Paramount, beginning at $5,000 a week. This was the moment when, with the recent coming of sound, Hollywood was signing up every attractive stage star it could find, and the exotic Tallulah, with her husky seductive voice, could well prove to be the next Garbo, the next Dietrich. "Hollywood for me I'm afraid," she wrote to her father and, in January 1931, embarked for New York.

In a year and a half, Bankhead made six feature films (and a lot of money), but none of them really worked. It didn't matter whether she was leaping off a balcony rather than go back to her blind husband, escaping from a submarine that her crazed husband had sabotaged, or going on the streets to procure money for the medicine needed by her desperately ill husband—reviewers said either that she was wasted on such clichéd vehicles or that she didn't live up to the better of them. The bottom line is that audiences just didn't take to her. George Cukor, who directed her once, concluded that she wasn't naturally photogenic: "On the screen she had beautiful bones, but her eyes were not eyes for movies. They looked somehow hooded and dead." The reality was that she was first and always a creature of the stage, all about projecting her larger-than-life personality at an audience, never about allowing a camera to explore her face and reveal her feelings. The movies caged and suppressed her. (They did the same thing to another stage phenomenon, Ethel Merman.) Bette Davis, who clearly had benefited from studying her speech patterns and vocal mannerisms, burned up the screen; Tallulah doused it.

She did, however, have a good time in Hollywood, what with her Rolls, her suntan, and her nonstop parties. Joan Crawford reminisced, "We all adored her. We were fascinated by her, but we were scared to death of her, too. . . . She had such authority, as if she ruled the earth, as if she was the first woman on the moon." There were the usual sexual escapades, including an encounter with Johnny (Tarzan) Weissmuller in the Garden of Allah pool, about which she reported that she had been "a very satisfied Jane." Yet the biggest scandal she created was a remark she tossed off in an interview: "I haven't had an *affaire* for six months. Six months! Too long. . . . I WANT A MAN." This was not the kind of publicity the studios—or the production code—could condone, and it helped send her back to Broadway (with her earnings of $200,000).

For half a dozen years, she failed at everything she tried on the stage, most spectacularly in 1937, when she had the calamitous misjudgment to take on *Antony and Cleopatra*: She had no classical technique, and she refused to be coached. The text was butchered, too—in the climactic scene, for instance, the deaths of Cleopatra's handmaidens were eliminated ("Because, of course, darling, we only want one death in that scene!"). One critic wrote that she was "more a serpent of the Swanee than of the Nile"; another famously quipped, "Tallulah Bankhead barged down the Nile last night as Cleopatra—and sank."

Also trapped in this disaster was a second-rank actor named John Emery, whom Tallulah had picked up on the summer circuit and, rather casually, married. Emery was good-looking, capable, and amiable. Best of all, he bore a marked resemblance to John Barrymore, and not only in profile: Years earlier, when Barrymore revealed himself to her in his dressing room, Tallulah had sworn to herself (and anyone within earshot) never to sleep with any man who wasn't "hung like Barrymore," and went on to claim that she had stuck to her word. (Since she also claimed five hundred or more conquests, perhaps she wasn't always so picky.) One of Tallulah's party tricks was to escort guests to the master bedroom, fling back the covers from the bed in which Emery was sleeping, and crow, "Did you ever see a prick as big as that before?" So size mattered, but eventually, in his case, not enough. Soon she was telling people, "Well, darling, the weapon may be of admirable proportions, but the shot is indescribably weak." Within a few years, the marriage, such as it was, was over.

During the thirties, Tallulah had entered the hospital for what was announced as an "abdominal tumor" but was actually a case of gonorrhea—contracted, she was to say, from George Raft—so violent it brought her close to death. It led to a five-hour radical hysterectomy, and by the time she left the hospital she was down to seventy pounds. Undaunted, she announced to her doctor, "Don't think this has taught me a lesson!" The hysterectomy left her not only psychologically shaky but erotically diminished—again and again, she testified to her lack of physical pleasure, telling Tennessee Williams's friend Sandy Campbell, for instance, that she couldn't reach an orgasm with any man she was in love with. (She gave as an example the multimillionaire Jock Whitney.) Louise Brooks reported to Kenneth Tynan, "I always guessed that she wasn't as interested in bed as everyone thought." Apparently, Tallulah cared more about the act of conquest than about the sexual act itself.

Another aspect of her pathology was her unrestrained exhibitionism. She was famous for throwing off her clothes at parties, for leaving her bathroom door open, for working without panties on. When she was performing in Thornton Wilder's *The Skin of Our Teeth*, so many people in the audience complained that Actors' Equity had to order her to wear underpants onstage. When she was making *Lifeboat*, Alfred Hitchcock, as Lobenthal puts it, fielded complaints "with his much-quoted deliberation about whether the matter needed to be referred to the makeup or the hairdressing department."

In the late thirties, after the failure of her vigorous campaign to secure the role of Scarlett in *Gone with the Wind*, her luck changed. Her commanding performance in Lillian Hellman's *The Little Foxes*, as a malevolent Southern matron who stands by coldly while her husband dies, riveted Broadway. A month after the opening, in March 1939, she was on the cover of *Life*, and the text of the accompanying story was unambiguous: "Somehow it seemed impossible to find adequate parts for this strange electric woman with the languid eyes, the panther's step and the siren's husky voice. But now . . . she fills, for the first time, a role carved big and fierce enough for her talent." Her triumph was unalloyed, except for the fury and chagrin she felt at losing the film version to Bette Davis.

Late in 1942, she opened in the allegorical *Skin of Our Teeth*, playing the immortal temptress Sabina in the various guises of housemaid, beauty-contest winner, and camp follower. This demanding role gave her a chance to display her rollicking humor and her allure and gave her a second Broadway triumph. And soon she was playing a famous journalist in that claustrophobic wartime drama *Lifeboat.* "It was the most oblique, incongruous bit of casting I could think of," Hitchcock later said. "Isn't a lifeboat in the middle of the Atlantic the last place one would expect Tallulah?" Yes. But she carried it off (if somewhat heavily), and was rewarded by the New York Film Critics Circle, which named her Best Actress of 1944. There was only one more important film, a year later—*A Royal Scandal,* which sank under the weight of Otto Preminger's direction and her own somewhat labored performance as Catherine the Great.

These years that established her as a major force on Broadway also saw the development of Tallulah's serious interest in politics and world affairs. At the time of Dunkirk, she swore not to have another drink until the Allies were back in Paris, and she more or less kept her word. On the home front, she campaigned for every Democrat in sight and helped her friend Eleanor Roosevelt set up the Washington branch of the Stage Door Canteen. In the early fifties, at the height of Joseph McCarthy's influence, she pulled no punches about her loathing of him: "I think Senator McCarthy of Wisconsin is a disgrace to the nation." She was also a passionate anti-Communist.

From the start, her political mentor had been her father—he died in 1940—but although she always claimed that he was the most important figure in her life, the reality is that they never were comfortable with each other and spent almost no time together. Lobenthal is convincing when he says that the "paper trail records her attempts to put definite boundaries around their relationship. . . . Yet when she did write, her invariable recitation of only good news also tells us how much she sought his approval." Nor were her relationships with the rest of her family any less complicated.

Now, however, she found a new family. A young actress named Eugenia Rawls, who was playing her daughter in *The Little Foxes,* became an integral part of her life. She made Rawls's husband her lawyer (he won her a large settlement when she sued the makers of Prell shampoo for presuming to use the name Tallulah in an advertising jingle), and stood as godmother to the couple's two children, eventually leaving each of them a quarter of her (large) estate. In an affecting book, Rawls demonstrates that she both loved and understood the older woman: "Tallulah could be savage, her appetites of mind and body wild and sometimes gross, as if everything had to be possessed and devoured and destroyed. And none of this mattered. It was as though all dross burned away, leaving someone frail and loyal, eager to please."

In 1948, Tallulah turned up on Broadway in a revival of Noël Coward's *Private Lives*, which over the years she had been playing in summer stock, and which she went on playing, across the country, until 1950. This was the one stage performance of hers I saw, and she put on quite a show. It wasn't Noël Coward's show but her own outrageous, rampageous eruption of high camp and low comedy. Audiences ate it up—Coward, predictably, didn't—and it made her a fortune, but it was her last hit in the theater. (Let's pass over a series of insignificant comedies and the disaster of Cocteau's *The Eagle Has Two Heads*, from which she had the young Marlon Brando fired, and the debacle of her revival of *A Streetcar Named Desire*.) There were several inconclusive cabaret engagements and countless radio and TV appearances, but it was all small potatoes compared with her glory days. In her final eighteen years—and she was only sixty-six when she died—she had only two real successes, both in the early fifties, and neither was on the stage or the screen.

In 1950, Tallulah ushered out commercial radio with a bang as the MC of a weekly hour-and-a-half extravaganza called *The Big Show*. To everybody's surprise, including her own, it not only was hailed by critics as the potential savior of radio but was an immediate hit. (A friend of mine says it awakened his "sequin gene.") Listening to air checks of *The Big Show* today is like slipping through a crack in time: Ethel Merman is plugging *Call Me Madam* and trading insults with "Tallu"; beloved Jimmy Durante is making a hash of his lines; Groucho Marx is singing "Some Enchanted Evening" with a Yiddish accent; Bob Hope is cracking Jack Benny jokes; Tallulah is cracking Bette Davis jokes when she isn't reciting Dorothy Parker monologues. You rise to her generosity, her sense of fun, her self-deprecation, her giggle—and her unerring timing. This was a deserved but short-lived success, as radio inevitably lost out to television.

And then, in 1952, came her book. Prickly, honest (for its day), and amusing, it made a sensation. Who else would have written about her marriage, "My interests and enthusiasms are too random for sustained devotion, if you know what I mean. . . . I had roamed the range too long to be haltered." She had help putting the book together from tapes, but its manic, bravura style is pure Tallulah.

As she passed the age of fifty, her demons grew stronger. She had always been a heavy drinker; now she was consuming a quart of bourbon a day, together with a dangerous mixture of Tuinal, Benzedrine, Dexedrine, Dexamyl, and morphine. She had always been insomniac; now she was frantic for sleep—as far back as 1948 she had been observed knocking back five Seconals and a brandy chaser after a night of drinking. She couldn't bear to be alone: Friends, colleagues, servants, and the young men she attached to her and whom she called her "caddies" would be wheedled or ordered to sit on her bed (or lie in her bed) all night while she struggled for sleep. She couldn't stop talking—someone followed her around one day and claimed that she had racked up seventy thousand words, the length of a novel. (No wonder the songwriter Howard Dietz commented, "A day away from Tallulah is like a month in the country.") Lobenthal writes of "bills for rolls and rolls of three-inch adhesive tape" observed in her hotel suite. It turned out that her maid was taping her wrists together at night to keep her from taking more pills during her intervals of wakefulness. One night, a colleague saw her in a hotel hallway, "a wild woman, like a caged chimp." Lobenthal continues: "Stragglehaired, barely wrapped in a thin robe, she flailed at the walls, sputtering 'Where am I?'" There were serious accidents and psychotic episodes; she was violent under sedation.

Orson Welles called her "the most sensational case of the aging process being unkind. I'll never forget how awful she looked at the end and how beautiful she looked at the beginning." At least her sense of humor didn't desert her: When people on the street asked, "Aren't you Tallulah Bankhead?," she'd answer, "I'm what's left of her, darling."

For years, she had insisted that she wanted to die. Once, playing the Truth Game with Tennessee Williams, she confessed, "I'm fifty-four, and I wish always, always, for death. I've always wanted death. Nothing else do I want more." It was a dozen years later, in 1968, that she finally got her way, quickly succumbing to double pneumonia. Her last words were "codeine—bourbon."

Not one of Tallulah's most important rivals crashed and burned the way she did; even the alcoholic Laurette Taylor redeemed her lost decades with her unforgettably great performance in *The Glass Menagerie*.

But then the others—Katharine Cornell, Helen Hayes, Ethel Barrymore, Lynn Fontanne, Eva Le Gallienne—were first and foremost actresses. They obsessed over their craft; they led relatively regular lives, conserving their energy for their work. Tallulah substituted personality for technique and eccentricity for effort, wasting her abundant talent—the predictable result of ignored guidelines and an indulged sense of privilege. And since she was intelligent, she must have been aware of the waste. No wonder she despaired.

So what is left to us of this "Humphrey Bogart in silk panties," this "most thoroughgoing libertine and free-swinging flapper of the age"? *The Little Foxes*, to theater buffs; *Lifeboat*, to film buffs; a faint memory of a rowdy life and a purring drawl of a voice. Joel Lobenthal doesn't really make her come alive, but he cares for her, defends her talent, sympathizes rather than condemns. Surely now it's time to let her rest.

May 16, 2005

The Drama of Sarah Bernhardt

Sarah Bernhardt won't go away. She was born in 1844 and died in 1923, well past her glory days and well out of our reach. Her few silent films are awkward and off-putting. Yet she remains the most famous actress the world has ever known. Books about her, films, plays, dance works, documentaries, exhibitions, merchandise—they keep on coming. Only last year (2006), a big new biography was published in France—respectable, but essentially going over the same old ground. Also last year, the Jewish Museum in New York staged an exemplary Bernhardt exhibition, which demonstrated, among other things, why Bernhardt was the priestess of art nouveau, with her elaborately rich costumes, her splendid ornaments of gem-studded precious metals, and—obvious in the portraits, the photographs, the caricatures—the way she almost always stood and sat: in a pure art nouveau spiral.

Among the scores of books on Bernhardt, there have been two major biographies in English: *Being Divine* by Ruth Brandon (1991), particularly perceptive on Sarah's emotional life, and *The Divine Sarah* by Robert Fizdale and Arthur Gold (also 1991), brilliant on her artistic and social surround. And let's at least acknowledge Françoise Sagan's bizarre contribution, *Dear Sarah Bernhardt* (1988), a fictional exchange of letters between Sagan and the long-gone Sarah. (It turns out they had a lot to say to each other.)

Other fiction? At least a dozen novels, beginning in the nineteenth century with Edmond de Goncourt's mean-spirited *La Faustin*, Félicien Champsaur's *Dinah Samuel* (Sarah as lesbian), and the sensational roman à clef *Les Mémoires de Sarah Barnum* by her onetime intimate Marie Colombier. And, as recently as 2004, Adam Braver's *Divine Sarah*, a confused fantasy of Bernhardt doing drugs in L.A.

Sarah Bernhardt as Phèdre

The movie *The Incredible Sarah* starring Glenda Jackson? Flee it. The French TV documentary with English voice-over by Susan Sontag? Not very illuminating. Jacqulyn Buglisi's modern-dance work *Against All Odds*? Unconvincing. On the other hand, totally unlikely and highly amusing: her star turn in one of the "Lucky Luke" books (like *Tintin* and *Astérix*, a hugely successful French series of graphic novels for kids). Sarah is setting out on the Wild West leg of her first American tour and President Rutherford B. Hayes entrusts her safety to Cowboy Luke.

And then there's her presence in various Hollywood movies, from Marilyn Monroe in *The Seven Year Itch* ("Every time I show my teeth on television, I'm appearing before more people than Sarah Bernhardt appeared before in her whole career") to Judy Garland in *Babes on Broadway* to an aging Ginger Rogers as a very young Sarah, intoning "La Marseillaise" in *The Barkleys of Broadway.*

Merchandise? eBay has provided me with the 1986 "Dame aux Camélias" memorial plate (Limoges), one of several available embroidery patterns based on the famous art nouveau posters by Mucha (stich your own Gismonda), and a 1973 Mexican comic book called *Sara, la Artista Dramática Más Famosa en la Historia del Teatro.* So far I've resisted the book of Sarah Bernhardt paper dolls, the Madame Alexander Sarah Bernhardt doll, the "asymmetrical" Sarah Bernhardt earrings, and the "Heirloom" Sarah Bernhardt peony.

Why this ongoing attention to a French theatrical star of the distant past? You can ascribe it to Sarah's rich and notorious private life, always ripe for retelling; to the central role she played in the history of the theater in particular and the culture of her time in general; to the unique way she grew into legend—morphing from a tarty little actress into the most famous French person of her century after Napoleon and the most admired Frenchwoman in history after Joan of Arc (whom she played— twice; she didn't manage Napoleon, but one of her greatest triumphs was as his doomed son, L'Aiglon).

Her undying celebrity would not have surprised her: From her earliest years she was determined to be noticed, to conquer the world, and to do it her own way. When at the age of nine she was dared to jump a ditch and broke her wrist falling into it, she cried out in rage, "Yes, yes, and I'll try it again if I'm dared to! I'm going to do exactly what I want all my life!" That's when, she claims, she decided on *"Quand même"* as her motto, and she never relinquished it. She decorated her stationery, her dishes, her silver with it; it was inscribed on the flag she flew over the little fort she bought and summered in on Belle-Île, off the Brittany coast; it was as much a part of her legend as her scrawniness, her legion of lovers, the coffin she sometimes liked to sleep in. But how to translate it? "Even so"? "No matter what"? "All the same"? "Despite everything"? "Nevertheless"? "Against all odds"? "Whatever"?

"Quand même" may not be translatable, but the message is clear: "Nothing can stop me!" And nothing did—not war, illness, scandal, bankruptcy. Sarah was not only "divine," she was indefatigable, reckless, tireless, brave, commanding. She has to reach New Orleans for a performance while floods are threatening a bridge over a swollen river? She bribes the engineer of her private train to make the desperate attempt, and moments

after they're safely across, they hear the bridge crash into the river. When she's a seventeen-year-old debutante at the Comédie-Française, she explodes when a veteran actress slaps her little sister backstage and slaps her back, refuses to apologize, and is gone from the company. Marie Colombier publishes that scandalous roman à clef? With her son, Maurice, and her current lover, she invades Marie's apartment, wreaks havoc, and slashes her with a whip. *Quand même.*

She was provocative, generous, maddening, fun to be with—and constitutionally untruthful: constantly self-dramatizing, embroidering, storytelling. That bridge on the way to New Orleans? Maybe, although in three different accounts—her own, her granddaughter's, her grandson-in-law's—it's a different river and a different destination each time. Basic facts? We can't be certain what year she was born, what street she was born on, or even who her father was—a young law student named Édouard Bernhardt (or was he her mother's brother)? A naval officer from Le Havre named Morel? Paris's Hôtel de Ville, where the relevant municipal data were kept, went up in flames during the Commune uprising of 1871. It's not even 100 percent certain that the father of her beloved Maurice (she was twenty when he was born) was the Belgian Prince de Ligne. Her story is that the prince wanted to marry her, but his stuffy aristocratic family said "*Non*"—shades of *La Dame aux Camélias*. Marie Colombier's far more likely story is that when Sarah invaded the prince's mansion in Paris with the news of her pregnancy, he showed her to the door, remarking that when you sit on a patch of thorns, you can't tell which particular thorn has scratched you.

And is it remotely possible that on her first Atlantic crossing, in 1880, she saved the life of Abraham Lincoln's widow by grabbing her when a huge wave struck the ship and Mrs. L. was about to plunge headfirst down a dangerous staircase? "A thrill of anguish ran through me," writes Sarah in her autobiography, *My Double Life*, "for I had just done this unhappy woman the only service I ought not to have done her—I had saved her from death. Her husband had been assassinated by an actor, Booth, and it was an actress who had now prevented her from joining her beloved husband. I went back to my cabin and stayed there two days."

We can turn to Dumas *fils*, author of *La Dame aux Camélias* (she played it almost three thousand times), for the ultimate word on Sarah's veracity. Referring to her notorious thinness—the physical quality that most defined her, that was endlessly derided and caricatured in her early years—he said affectionately, "You know, she's such a liar, she may even be fat!"

In regard to her childhood we have only her memoirs to go by, and though they're factually preposterous, they come across as emotionally true. Yes, her demimondaine mother, known as Youle, sent her off semi-permanently to a farm in Brittany (her first language was Breton), but did she really fall into a fire only to be saved by some neighboring peasants who threw her "all smoking, into a pail of milk"? When eventually she was brought to Paris by her nurse-turned-concierge, was she really lost to her mother, like a child in Dickens or *Les Misérables*, and only retrieved when her Aunt Rosine happened to alight from her carriage in the sordid courtyard where tiny Sarah was playing? And did she then really fling herself from a window, breaking her arm and her kneecap, to prevent Rosine from leaving without her?

Yet however fanciful her autobiography is, it has verve and charm—what Max Beerbohm called its "peculiar fire and salt . . . [its] rushing spontaneity." She's completely believable in the portrait she sketches of herself as a child installed at a fashionable convent school: turbulent, savage, imperious. (Those poor nuns!) And we sense all too keenly her anguish at having been abandoned by her adored mother: adored, but not adoring. From the first, Youle dealt with her as an impediment, not a beloved child. The favorite was Sarah's half-sister, Jeanne (father unknown), who was placid, conventionally pretty (Sarah never looked like anyone else), and easy to control. But not even the strict and withholding Youle, who on top of everything else was coldly dismissive of her acting, could control Sarah—nobody ever could.

The depth of the psychic wounds she received as a sensitive child with no father and a rejecting mother reveals itself not only in the elaborations of her memoirs but in *The Idol of Paris*, a trashy semi-autobiographical novel she produced late in life. Her heroine, Espérance, is a beautiful budding actress of genius with ideal parents: a distinguished professor of philosophy about to be inducted into the Académie Française and a loving, tender mother—they live and breathe to attend to her every whim. As a novel it's ludicrous, but as an act of wish-fulfillment it's fascinating—and saddening. Clearly, despite the unparalleled triumph of her life, she never got over having been an unwanted and unloved child.

When she was twelve, Sarah took her first communion and officially became a Catholic, despite the fact that her mother was Jewish, of German-

Dutch stock. In the convent she also learned the manners and speech of well-bred Parisians—she could pass for a lady. But she wasn't a lady, so what was she to do with her life? The turning point came when she was fifteen—out of the convent, fit for no occupation, and a drag on her mother's life and finances. The half-Jewish illegitimate daughter of a courtesan, Sarah could hardly marry into society, and she was adamant about not marrying into the dreary petit bourgeois world some of her relatives would have settled for.

Youle and her sister Rosine were comfortably established in their demimondaine world, making the rounds of Europe's fashionable spas with their wealthy "protectors," entertaining many of the great figures of the Second Empire—Rossini, Dumas *père*, Emperor Louis-Napoléon's doctor, and, most important, the Duc de Morny, one of Rosine's lovers (and probably one of Youle's as well) and the most powerful man in France apart from his half-brother, the emperor himself.

Something had to be done about Sarah, and a family conference was held to decide her fate. Among those present were her godfather; her upstairs neighbor the angelic Madame Guérard, who was to become her greatest friend and protectress; and—in attendance on Rosine—Morny, who, after endless discussion, casually remarked, "Take my advice. Send her to the Conservatoire." It was settled, and Sarah—who claims she had never been to a theater and had notions of becoming a nun (at one point she thought she'd like to be a goatherd)—was soon feverishly preparing to audition.

The outcome was never really in doubt, given Morny's influence. Even so, the audition had to proceed according to the rules. When Sarah's turn came, she was asked who was going to cue her, but no one had informed her of this requirement. "Then I'll recite La Fontaine's *Les Deux Pigeons*." Recite rather than perform a scene? Uproar! She triumphed, however, her voice so ravishing, her diction so exquisite, that, against custom, she was accepted on the spot. Her life was ready to begin.

But unlike Espérance, her alter ego, Sarah had a hard road to travel before she prevailed. She did well, though not especially so, at her studies. Her short first stay at the Comédie-Française was less than distinguished, although she was certainly noticed, if only for that notorious thinness and the uncontrollable red-blond hair. The first review she received from the all-powerful critic Francisque Sarcey, on the occasion of her debut as Racine's Iphigénie, was hardly auspicious: "Mlle. Bernhardt . . . is a tall,

attractive young woman with a slender waist and a most pleasing face. . . .
She carries herself well and pronounces her words with perfect clarity.
That is all that can be said for the moment."

Some days later, on the occasion of her appearance in *Les Femmes Sa-
vantes*, he had more to say: "That Mlle. Bernhardt is inadequate is unimportant. . . . It is natural that there are some beginners who do not
succeed."

She was gone from the Comédie-Française in a matter of months, and
for three years there was no work apart from a few scattered and frivolous
engagements. How did she live? She was on her own, with her baby, Maurice, and Madame Guérard—and a circle of affluent and influential men
whom she "entertained" and who contributed to her expenses, even club-
bing together to buy her the famous coffin she was so eager to acquire.

It was only in 1866 that she found herself back in the theatrical mainstream, offered a place at the Odéon, France's second official theater. An
affair with its young administrator, some early reversals, the growing
band of vociferous Left Bank students who made her their favorite, and
then success in Dumas *père*'s *Kean*, bigger success in François Coppée's *Le
Passant* (her first trouser role), and finally, in 1872, the first immense success of her career, in a revival of Victor Hugo's *Ruy Blas*.

The critics, led by Sarcey, were ecstatic over her nobility and beauty,
the perfection of her poetry. *Ruy Blas* had two immediate consequences.
First, a secret fling with Hugo, a mere forty-two years her senior (for a moment it even looked as if there might be a baby). And, of more consequence,
the capitulation of the Comédie-Française. There was no way that France's
most important theater could ignore France's most acclaimed young actress. Her contract with the Odéon? She broke it, paying a large fine. Ten
years after her ignominious departure from the Française, Sarah was back.
As the critic Théodore de Banville put it, "Poetry has entered the domain
of dramatic art. Or, if you like, the wolf has entered the sheepfold."

She stayed for just under eight years. At last, at the advanced age of thirty,
she played Phèdre, confirming her position as the greatest tragedienne
since Rachel. She was now the theater's biggest attraction—by the time
the company was negotiating a season in London, the English impresarios
refused to proceed unless she was part of the deal. And in London she

carried everything before her. "It would require some ingenuity," wrote Henry James,

> to give an idea of the intensity, the ecstasy, the insanity as some people would say, of curiosity and enthusiasm provoked by Mlle. Bernhardt. . . . I strongly suspect that she will find a triumphant career in the Western world. She is too American not to succeed in America. The people who have brought to the highest development the arts and graces of publicity will recognize a kindred spirit in a figure so admirably adapted for conspicuity.

(James was to use her as his model for Miriam Rooth, the heroine of *The Tragic Muse*, just as Proust would use her as his model for Berma.)

James was prophetic. Returning to Paris, Sarah found excuses for being offended by the company's management, breaking yet another contract and instantly forming her own company for a whirlwind tour of the Continent before setting out for America. The die was cast. From 1880 until her death, she remained in sole control of her career. She chose her plays, her co-actors, her managers. She ran her own theaters. She oversaw the lighting, she commissioned the scenery, the music, and the costumes, often she directed. And, perhaps not surprisingly, when she took command of her life, her previously fragile health miraculously righted itself. Only her agonizing stage fright—*le trac*—stayed with her to the end.

This American tour, the first of nine, lasted six months (short by her future standards; one world tour lasted two and a half years), and America rewarded her with money and fame. Wherever she appeared there was sensation (much of it about her exotic menagerie, which at various times included a lynx, a lion, a baby alligator that died from being fed too much champagne, and a boa constrictor which killed itself by swallowing a sofa cushion). And of course there was gossip (much of puritanical America was scandalized by her unconventional, and highly public, love life, to say nothing of her illegitimate child). In countless magazines and newspapers everything about her was both breathlessly reported and gleefully parodied. A typical verse, from *Puck*:

> *Sadie!*
> *Woman of vigorous aspirations and remarkable thinness!*

I hail you. I, Walt Whitman, son of thunder, child of the ages, I hail you.

I am the boss poet, and I recognize in you an element of bossness that approximates you to me. . . .

The Worcester *Evening Gazette* condensed *La Dame aux Camélias* for its busy readers:

ACT I—PARIS

He—You are sick. I love you.
She—Don't. You can't afford it.

ACT II—PARIS

She—I think I love you. But good-bye; the Count is coming.
He—That man? Then I see you no more. But no! An idea! Let us fly to the country.

ACT III—THE COUNTRY

His Father—You ruin my son! Leave him.
She—He loves me.
His Father—You are a good woman. I respect you. Leave him.
She—I go.

ACT IV—PARIS

She—You again? I never loved you.
He—Fly with me, or I die.
She—I love you; but good-bye now.

ACT V—PARIS

She—(Very sick.) Is it you? Is God so good?
He—Pardon me. My father sent me.
She—I pardon you. I love you. I die. [*Dies. Tears. Sensation. Curtain.*]

But the critics and the audience weren't only condemning or laughing; they also found in her acting, and celebrated, a realism, an emotional truth that was absent from the more extravagant melodramatic style of the American theater at that time.

The most telling change in Sarah's career during this period was her new repertory. At the Comédie-Française she was mostly interpreting the classics. Now she was appearing almost exclusively in what was known as boulevard drama: *Adrienne Lecouvreur, Frou-Frou, La Dame aux Camélias.* And then, in 1882, came the first of the blood-and-thunder vehicles Victorien Sardou concocted for her: *Fédora* (Russian nihilists), to be followed by *Théodora* (Byzantine empress), *La Tosca, Cléopâtre, Gismonda, La Sorcière,* in almost all of which roles she perished in the final scene. In fact, her deaths—by poison, by strangulation, by disease, by suicide—were perhaps her strongest suit: drawn out, accurately differentiated, grippingly realistic. And since the subtleties of her diction could mean little to the foreign audiences before whom she now mostly performed, she depended more and more on glamorous costumes and scenery and personal adornment, on her genius for striking gestures and poses (no wonder Edmond Rostand famously acclaimed her "*Reine de l'attitude et Princesse des gestes*"), on her projected sexuality, and of course on the famous voice—*la voix d'or*, as Hugo dubbed it—which appears in reality to have been more silvery than golden. (Rachel's had been a voice of bronze.)

Throughout her early career, it was indeed Rachel—also Jewish, and with a comparably conspicuous private life—to whom she was constantly compared, especially in regard to their highly different approaches to Phèdre. The critic for *The Times* of London clarified that difference: Rachel's Phèdre inspired awe, Sarah's inspired sympathy. Her Phèdre was a tormented woman in the throes of passion rather than a statuesque emblem of antique tragedy. As for Corneille, Rachel's favorite, he was not for Sarah. His noble heroines were too invested in *la gloire*, not enough in *l'amour.*

During the latter part of Sarah's career, it was the younger Eleonora Duse to whom she was constantly compared, but now, ironically, it was Sarah who was considered artificial, Duse the apostle of the natural. Their repertories overlapped to a certain degree, but Sarah kept away from Duse's Ibsen, Duse from Sarah's classic heroines. The critic Desmond McCarthy put it this way: "The art of Sarah Bernhardt made us first conscious of the beauty of emotions and passions, while that of Duse was a revelation of the beauty of human character." When the rival divas' paths crossed, they were scrupulously polite; in private, equally bitchy. But essentially Duse was an irrelevancy to Sarah. As Maurice Baring explained,

"She took herself for granted as being the greatest actress in the world, as Queen Victoria took for granted that she was Queen of England."

Duse, certainly, never attempted the trouser roles that Bernhardt so enjoyed. ("I don't prefer men's roles," she said; "I prefer men's minds.") Among her men: Musset's Lorenzaccio, Rostand's L'Aiglon (L'Aiglon was twenty, Sarah fifty-six), Pelléas, Werther, Judas, and most famously Hamlet. Far from being the Romantic era's indecisive weakling, her Prince of Denmark was virile and determined (not unlike Madame herself). Many critics were impressed. Not Max Beerbohm, who ended his review by saying, "Yes! the only compliment one can consciously pay her is that her Hamlet was, from first to last, *très grande dame.*"

Her progress, if that's what it was, from the classicism of the Comédie-Française to the melodrama of Sardou (or, as Shaw labeled it, Sardoodledom) can be likened to the more or less contemporaneous "progress" in operatic style from bel canto to verismo. Lytton Strachey explained her artistic choices wryly yet sympathetically:

> This extraordinary genius was really to be seen at her most characteristic in plays of inferior quality. They gave her what she wanted. She did not want—she did not understand—great drama; what she did want were opportunities for acting; and this was the combination which the *Toscas,* the *Camélias,* and the rest of them, so happily provided. In them the whole of her enormous virtuosity in the representation of passion had full play; she could contrive thrill after thrill, she could seize and tear the nerves of her audiences, she could touch, she could terrify, to the very top of her astonishing bent. In them, above all, she could ply her personality to the utmost.

As for her private life—not that it was ever very private—as a matter of course she slept with almost all her leading men, most clamorously with her male vis-à-vis at the Comédie-Française, Jean Mounet-Sully, a lion of a man. (In his old age he was to remark, "Up to the age of sixty I thought it was a bone.") He was determined to marry and "reform" her, she would have none of it, and their incendiary relationship crashed and burned. The most notorious of her leading men, whom she had turned into an actor, was the man she shocked her world by marrying—Aristides Damala, a handsome, aristocratic Greek who proved to be a disaster both as actor and husband. Congenitally unfaithful, envious of her fame, dishonest financially, abusive about her Jewishness, he was to die young of morphine addiction. Sarah mourned him, for years referring to herself as the Widow Damala.

Even so, she turned at once to new lovers, having already "entertained" such eminences as Edward, Prince of Wales; Gustave Doré (who helped her with her not inconsiderable career as a sculptor); D'Annunzio (a slap at his adoring lover Duse); Pierre Loti; the elegant Charles Haas, on whom Proust modeled Swann; and the ultra-homosexual Robert de Montesquieu, Proust's Charlus, whom she mischievously initiated into heterosexual sex, reducing him to twenty-four hours of vomiting. There had been scores—hundreds?—of others, presumably the last of whom was the beautiful young Lou Tellegen, a gift to her from her close colleague the ultra-gay Édouard de Max. Questioned about Tellegen (she was sixty-six), she replied, "To my last breath I will live as I have lived." Tellegen wrote lovingly—and discreetly—about their relationship in his autobiography, *Women Have Been Kind.*

Despite all this activity, however, until an operation in her middle years, she apparently couldn't achieve orgasm. (Marie Colombier called her "an untuned piano, an Achilles vulnerable everywhere except in the right place." Another witticism given wide currency: "She doesn't have a clitoris, she has a corn.")

Unquestionably the most important man in her life, the one she loved passionately from start to finish, was not a lover but her son, Maurice, whom she raised to be an aristocrat, a blade, and whom she spoiled, cosseted, and adored. "All I ask of him," she remarked, "is to dress well."

Her friends and acquaintances? Everyone. In America she drops in on Edison, beards Longfellow in his home. ("Can you read my poetry?" "Yes. I read your 'He-a-vatere.'" "My—Oh yes—'Hiawatha.' But you surely do not understand that?" "Yes, yes, indeed I do. *Chaque mot.*") In England she's on the best of terms with Ellen Terry, Henry Irving, and Mrs. Patrick Campbell, to whose Mélisande she played Pelléas (in French), as well as with Queen Alexandra and, later, Queen Mary. Oscar Wilde writes *Salomé* for her——the censors squelched it. As she proceeds on her ceaseless world tours she's feted by kings, czars, emperors. When she sinks to the floor in the deepest of curtsies before Czar Alexander III, he protests, "No, no, it is *We* who must bow to you."

Her admirers? To name a few: Mark Twain ("There are five kinds of actresses: bad actresses, fair actresses, good actresses, great actresses—

and then there is Sarah Bernhardt"), Freud ("After the first words of her lovely, vibrant voice I felt I had known her for years"), D. H. Lawrence ("She represents the primeval passion of woman, and she is fascinating to an extraordinary degree").

Her detractors? Chekhov, Turgenev, and most famously George Bernard Shaw, who derided what her acting had become by the time he was reviewing it, in the 1890s—"a worn out hack tragedienne"—although he later confessed, "I could never as a dramatic critic be fair to Sarah B., because she was exactly like my Aunt Georgina."

The route she traversed from scandal to national heroine—the symbol of La France—is a complicated one. In 1870, during the siege of Paris in the Franco-Prussian War, the theaters are shut down, and she turns the Odéon into a hospital for wounded soldiers, nursing the men indefatigably (and knowledgeably). She's a violent Dreyfusard, rallying to support Zola, for the only time in her life breaking with Maurice. She violently opposes capital punishment—"I hate the death penalty! It's a vestige of cowardly barbarism"—although she attends four executions, no doubt to take notes on how people die. When begged by the German ambassador to Belgium to perform in Germany—she can name her price!—the sum she names is five billion francs, the exact sum Germany extracted from France as war reparations.

In a word, she loves and identifies with France. Yet she always boasts of "my beloved blood of Israel," even though for years her Jewishness, and what was seen as her natural Jewish tendency to money-grubbing, are the objects of ugly caricature and slander. And France comes to love her. "France has only one ambassador—Sarah Bernhardt!" says the French ambassador to Russia at a formal dinner. When she dies, her funeral cortege through the streets of Paris is followed by hundreds of thousands of people.

Her bravery never faltered. In 1915, after years of agonizing pain in her knee, she decides to have her leg amputated. (She's seventy.) Firing off telegrams to her friends—"Tomorrow they're taking my leg off. Think of me, and book me some lectures for April"—she not only survives the operation, she refuses a prosthetic device (the legend of her stomping around the stage on a wooden leg is pure fable) and arranges to have herself carried everywhere in a made-to-order sedan chair. This is how she manages her final American tour—to ninety-nine towns. And this is how in 1917 she's transported to the front, in easy hearing distance of the guns, so that she can recite patriotic poetry to the troops.

To the end she goes on working. She's rehearsing a play by Sacha Guitry when she collapses from the uremia that has tormented her for years. Carried to her house, which she never leaves again, she persists with the last of her movies—they come to film her at home. Then coma, and death—in Maurice's arms.

One of the last people to interview her was Alexander Woollcott, two months before she died. She's thinking of another American tour, she tells him, but this time not a long one, since she's "much too old for such cross-country junketing. . . . Of course, I shall play Boston and New York and Philadelphia and Baltimore and Washington. And perhaps Buffalo and Cleveland and Detroit and Kansas City and St. Louis and Denver and San Francisco. . . ."

Of course. How could she stop? Like Pavlova, like Nureyev, she was a driven performer, endlessly working at her art, eternally touring. "I love, I adore my profession," she said.

> I serve it constantly. I never stop acting. I've always acted—always and everywhere, in all sorts of places, at every instant—always, always. I am my own double. I act in restaurants when I ask for more bread. I act when I ask Julia Bartet's husband how his wife is feeling. Blessed work that fills me with drunken joy and peace, how much I owe to you!

May 10, 2007

The Case of Dr. B.

Within months of his death, in 1990, the reputation of Bruno Bettelheim—the revered survivor of the camps, head of the famous Sonia Shankman Orthogenic School for troubled children at the University of Chicago, formidable educator, and author of the acclaimed *The Informed Heart, The Empty Fortress, Love Is Not Enough, The Children of the Dream*, and *The Uses of Enchantment*—appeared to be in shreds. Certain former students from the school and several of his former associates were accusing him of everything from plagiarism and lying about his past to brutality and child abuse. He was even bitterly condemned for having taken his own life. So radical and abrupt a shift in perception about a famous and admired man suggests an overpowering personality whom others had feared and resented and only now felt safe in attacking.

Indeed, Bettelheim was just such a personality—inspiring, seductive, aggressive, irascible, dismissive of fools or perceived enemies, and capable of both great kindness and great unkindness. Like other remarkable men who have been leaders, even gurus, within small, intense, contained institutions—Lee Strasberg at the Actors Studio, William Shawn at *The New Yorker*—he attracted passionate loyalty and affection but also built up suppressed (or open) resentment in certain of his disciples.

This is clearly what happened with one of Bettelheim's closest associates, Jacquelyn Sanders, who had worked side by side with him for thirteen years, left to marry, and then returned when, on his retirement, he chose her to replace him as head of the school. She told Bettelheim's relentlessly negative biographer, Richard Pollak, that, having begun in therapy "to realize the degree to which she had allowed herself to be manipulated and exploited," she grew "so angry that she not only stopped calling Bettelheim about school matters but ceased speaking to him for several years." That a serious educator/therapist could break from her former leader only by—temporarily, at least—forgetting both her professional debt to him and the sympathy due an old man who, like Lear, has surrendered his kingdom is less an indictment of Sanders than an indication of just how powerful his hold was on those around him.

Pollak's *The Creation of Dr. B*, published in 1997, is one of three extended accounts of Bettelheim's life to have appeared in the past half-dozen years. (Bettelheim steadfastly refused to write his memoirs, and throughout his writings was sparing with details of his personal life.) Pollak makes it clear at the start why he hates—not too strong a word—his subject: When he was fourteen years old, his disturbed, possibly autistic younger brother, Stephen, then eleven and home for a visit from the Orthogenic School, died in a freak accident; Pollak had been alone with him at the time. When, twenty-five years later, Pollak approached Bettelheim about his brother, Bettelheim heaped contumely on the Pollak parents, particularly the mother; insisted that young Stephen had committed suicide; and told Pollak that the school had warned the family that a visit home might lead to Stephen's harming himself, and that "despite our objection the visit took place . . . [and] the child died in a carefully contrived accident." As an older brother present at the scene of the fatal accident, Pollak might well have been left with some unacknowledged—and no doubt undeserved—guilt, but there is no hint in his account of anger at himself. Instead, his anger is directed at Bettelheim, who certainly deserves at least some of it for his callousness.

Pollak claims, and undoubtedly believes, that he has "tried to keep my personal experience of Bruno Bettelheim from unfairly darkening my portrait," but his book, despite some pro forma appreciation of Bettelheim's achievements, reads like a shout of rage. Which is unfortunate, because Pollak's bias undercuts the reliability of the charges he makes, and for which, in some cases, he offers convincing evidence.

Theron Raines's *Rising to the Light: A Portrait of Bruno Bettelheim* is uncannily opposite to Pollak's portrait. Just as Pollak had personal reasons for attacking Bettelheim, Raines has personal reasons for championing him: He was Bettelheim's literary agent for decades, and not only admired but loved him. Sometime before Bettelheim's death, Raines began interviewing him for what was at first to be a magazine profile and eventually became this book. *Rising to the Light* is a slow, earnest attempt to grasp Bettelheim's conflicted nature; to reconcile the nobility Raines found in the man with the ugly accusations that followed his death.

One biographer hates Bettelheim, the other loves him. Again we sense how powerful a psychic presence this complicated man was in the minds of those to whom he was connected. Bettelheim's view of his school, expressed frequently, was that the children represented the id, the counselors stood for the ego, and he was the superego. As such, he played both the Big Bad Wolf and Santa Claus, and as the Wolf he was there to impose order. He unquestionably succeeded in doing that. Every account of the school stresses the respect, awe, and fear in which he was held, partly through his authority, partly through his uncanny intuitions, partly through his absolute belief in his own rightness and his unswerving determination. These are clearly the qualities that made the school the success it became. When the University of Chicago prevailed on Bettelheim to take it over, it was floundering—if "not quite an orphan in 1944," says Raines, "it was surely an unwanted child."

Raines is particularly strong on the early years of the school. Although there had been modest attempts at "milieu therapy" before, there had been nothing remotely as concentrated and organized as what the Orthogenic School was to become. Central to the plan was the relationship each child was to develop with one or more loving and omnipresent caretakers. And the caretakers had to internalize one of Bettelheim's most important insights: that a disturbed child's symptoms are his way of expressing his sense of the world and of himself. "You have to understand," Bettelheim said, "that this behavior is the child's greatest achievement. To him, it is saving his life." With this understood, it was possible that—insulated from the pressures of the nuclear family, in an environment that provided structure, love, therapy, education, understanding, and discipline—a disturbed child might slowly, very slowly, abandon his symbolic behavior and achieve a more realistic relationship to the world.

That Bettelheim failed to make real headway with seriously autistic children now appears certain, but that he healed many emotionally disturbed children is equally certain. It's unfortunate that in any discussion of him today, thirteen years after his death, it seems necessary to begin by weighing the posthumous charges against him rather than by assessing his achievements and failures.

The accusations against Bettelheim fall into several categories. First, he lied; that is, he both exaggerated his successes at the school and falsified aspects of his background, claiming a more elaborate academic and psychoanalytic history in Vienna than he had actually had. There is conclusive evidence to support both charges. But is stretching the truth a defining quality, or are his lies isolated lapses that can be explained and to some extent even justified? Bettelheim began to exaggerate his professional qualifications when he first arrived in America, immediately after his release from Buchenwald. He was without a job—without, really, a profession—and desperate to gain a foothold in a new world. I suspect he simply said what he thought it was necessary to say, and was then stuck with these claims later on, when he could neither confirm them (since they were false) nor, given his pride, acknowledge that he had lied. This may be one reason why he chose to remain so private about his life.

As for his exaggerations about the rate of success at the Orthogenic School, they would have served both to attract essential financial support and to fortify his sense of self. As Nina Sutton, the most balanced and persuasive of Bettelheim's biographers, puts it in *Bettelheim: A Life and a Legacy*: "Bettelheim never saw anything wrong with being economical with the truth in order to promote a good cause." In any case, "success" in this ambiguous territory is hard to gauge. There were spectacular success stories—former students who went on to do well in the outside world, proclaiming their gratitude to Bettelheim and the school. (One remark repeated frequently is "He saved my life.") But there were also severely damaged children who were quietly dismissed from the school and placed in institutions for the incurable.

The plagiarism accusation concerns a passage in *The Uses of Enchantment* which closely echoes a passage in a more academic book on fairy tales by a clinical psychiatrist named Julius Heuscher. Undeniably, there are direct correspondences between these passages. The issue is whether they are the result of conscious plagiarism. Heuscher told Raines, "Bruno Bettelheim was a very busy gentleman, I assume, and he had, probably, some people collect material for him when he wrote. And probably somebody collected this, and he was not even aware that he was taking it from somewhere. . . . I'm sure it was not done deliberately, and I think it's ridiculous to make a thing about this." When the issue was first raised, Heuscher had said, "We all plagiarize. . . . I am only happy that I would have influenced Bruno Bettelheim."

Far more serious, and more damaging to Bettelheim's reputation, is the charge that on occasion he slapped or even beat the children in his care. While Bettelheim was alive, no word of corporal punishment leaked from the Orthogenic School, yet we know now from the testimony of many former counselors and patients that often he did strike children. The question is, for what reason? To his detractors he did so because he was a brute ("Bruno Brutalheim"). Others of his former associates and patients explain that he did so because he sensed that sometimes physical intervention was helpful therapeutically. There was a crucial difference, he insisted, between punishment, which he deplored, and discipline, which he thought essential.

For her book Nina Sutton talked with Bert Cohler, who had been a patient at the school and went on to succeed so markedly that at one point Bettelheim brought him back to run it. Cohler, she tells us, "clearly remembers the slaps he got from Dr. B one day when he returned from class with an excellent grade for a German essay. . . . When I asked him about it, [he] burst out laughing. 'Dr B knew exactly what he was doing: In my essay I attacked Arthur Schnitzler. And I knew Schnitzler was one of his favorite authors.'"

Sutton is shocked by the incident, and remarks that it took her a long time to understand it:

> Cohler had lived, until his arrival at the Orthogenic School, in constant terror of expressing even the slightest amount of anger, for he had been led to believe that if he dared to show the aggressiveness he felt toward one of his relatives, he would be killed. . . . By acknowledging the aggression implicit in Cohler's act [criticizing Schnitzler], by showing that he knew it was aimed at him, and by responding with overt violence, Dr. B was playing his role as a lightning rod, ensuring that the dangerous charge was mortal neither for its originator nor for its recipient.

Since Bettelheim did not write or speak publicly about striking the children under his care, we can be grateful to Theron Raines for eliciting his views on the subject:

> Sometimes one [child] would get so out of control, so out of bounds, that some radical measure was needed as a shortcut. It's an undesirable shortcut. It was against all my principles to hit the children, but I learned that sometimes it's a shortcut that is important for the

person—to feel that they can be controlled, because the anxiety of their getting completely out of control is very great.

Bettelheim also told Raines that restoring order in the school during a crisis was a secondary consideration, and that "the first order he wanted to reestablish was in the child's inner world."

It is hard to overcome one's revulsion at defenseless—in fact, damaged—children being struck, but although at times Bettelheim may just have lost his temper and in his talks with Raines was rationalizing his behavior, he did believe that in certain circumstances hitting was necessary. Also, of course, he came from a world and a time in which corporal punishment was an acceptable, indeed normal, aspect of child-raising.

Accusations of sexual abuse are cited by Pollak, to whom three young women, former patients, complained that Bettelheim had fondled them and performed other inappropriate acts. The sincerity and anguish with which these women spoke to Pollak, he says, "invite[s] belief. Nonetheless," he goes on,

> it is possible that they imagined he touched their breasts, or exaggerated his actions. His acts, if they did take place, had no witnesses, or none who spoke to me. Of the twenty-seven other former Orthogenic School residents I interviewed, none even hinted that Bettelheim indulged in such behavior, including several whose continuing antipathy to him is such that they would not have hesitated to reveal his sexual abuse had they known of it. No former staff member suggested that Dr. B had lost control in this way.

Pollak then remarks, "I enter these caveats in an effort to be fair, but also with a certain reluctance." Does he, then, hope these accusations are true?

It isn't difficult to understand why the attacks on Bettelheim after his death took hold with such persistence and left his admirers on the defensive. He was a man who created large constituencies of enemies: psychoanalysts who resented his fame and authority, while distrusting his credentials; Jews who fulminated at his provocative suggestions that the "ghetto thinking" of many European Jews was a decisive factor in making the Holocaust possible—people were especially enraged by his questioning the world's reverence for Otto Frank; Israelis who resented his suggesting that the communal child-rearing practiced in the kibbutz was creating a somewhat homogenized and bland generation; liberals and radicals who despised him for his increasing conservatism—his scorn for the student rebels of the sixties (he compared them to the Hitler Youth), his support for Nixon and the Vietnam War. Perhaps most of all, he has been vilified by women for his suggestions, expressed most forcefully in *Love Is Not Enough*, that coldness and unconscious hostility on the part of mothers are the likely cause of their children's autism. Yet except in politics, Bettelheim's positions were more nuanced than his critics stopped to discover (he wrote, for instance, that "fortunately, psychoanalysts are beginning to decry the haunting image of the rejecting mother"), but that did not protect him when he was no longer alive.

The antagonism of certain of his former followers was fueled by the manner of his dying. When he felt he was in danger of losing control over his body—unable to work, his wife dead, estranged from at least one of his three children—he took pills and placed a plastic bag over his head to hasten his death. No one should have been surprised—this was an act completely in line with his lifelong determination to assert control over his own fate. As Nina Sutton reminds us, almost all those who first attacked him belonged to the last generation of Orthogenic School children with whom he had worked: "Most important, it was the generation that he had abandoned by retiring." And by choosing to die.

Sutton sees Bettelheim as a flawed great man. Consider his history. To begin with, he felt a lifelong inferiority over his looks. (A traumatic event in his life was his mother's early remark, "Thank God he's a boy," which he took as a comment on his physical ugliness. At the end of his life he could say to a close friend, "I'm nothing but an ugly old Jew.") His father died after a long, debilitating, and (to Bruno) mysterious disease—it turned out to have been syphilis, a shattering discovery for the young man, who then had to abandon his advanced studies in psychology and philosophy and take up the life of a Viennese businessman, running the successful lumber business his father had co-owned. During this period, he fell in love with and married a woman who didn't love him.

In 1938, he was deported by the Germans first to Dachau, then to Buchenwald. Surviving through his determination and strong sense of self, he was rescued by the efforts of his family and friends. When he arrived in America in the spring of 1939—only four months before the outbreak of World War II—he found that his wife, Gina, who had preceded him to New York, had fallen in love with another man and wanted a divorce.

Scrambling for work, he managed to find teaching jobs at second-level women's colleges in the Midwest, then so impressed authorities at the University of Chicago that he was invited to take charge of the Orthogenic School. By that time, he had begun writing about the camps, beginning with a highly influential paper, "Individual and Mass Behavior in Extreme Situations," published in 1943, probably the earliest firsthand testimony of the horrors being committed in Germany.

The school, together with a loving second marriage, changed his life. It gave him the opportunity to develop and implement his ideas about curing emotionally damaged children, or at least relieving their anguish. And it gave him the opportunity, which he badly needed, to become a figure of authority. Totally absorbed in the school, he was an indefatigable worker—home for dinner every night but then back to the school until midnight or later, making certain the children were settled in properly, then holding intense staff meetings, conducting counseling sessions with his aides, and writing.

The range of his literary output is extraordinary: In addition to his most famous books—on the school, on autistic children, on the Holocaust, on the children of the kibbutz, and his controversial Freudian reading of fairy tales—he wrote convincingly about the failings of James Strachey's standard English translation of Freud; mounted a scathing attack in *The New Yorker* on Lina Wertmüller's popular movie about the Holocaust, *Seven Beauties*; produced a long-running popular column in the *Ladies' Home Journal*; and published a series of reflections on parenting (*The Good-Enough Parent*) as well as an original examination of circumcision (*Symbolic Wounds*), which explores men's deep envy of, and hostility toward, women, a book that might surprise Bettelheim's feminist critics.

Throughout these years, Bettelheim was also teaching regularly at the University of Chicago, attracting a large body of students who were both fascinated by him and terrified. (Theron Raines recorded his impressions of a seminar run by Dr. B.: "Sometimes he leads, sometimes he follows; his mind darts in circles like Robin Goodfellow, but he is not playing tricks. He is teaching by courting the intelligence of the young person who has come to learn from him.") Yet despite this almost obsessive expenditure of positive energy, he suffered from lifelong depression.

As he grew closer to retirement, Bettelheim seemed to become more domineering, more angry. When he left the school, he tried to stay active, particularly through writing, but his move to California was not a happy one for him, and after his wife's death, an attempt to live with their older daughter was a disaster. At his death at the age of eighty-six, he was living alone in a semiretirement community in Maryland.

Sutton's account of Bettelheim's life is both sympathetic and clear-eyed. But Raines has something to offer that neither she nor Pollak had: direct testimony. The interviews he conducted help us to catch Bettelheim's voice and follow the subtleties of his thinking. And it's impossible not to be moved by his account of Bettelheim's last days. (Raines was with him on the Saturday before he died.) I only wish that his empathy for his subject hadn't led him to imagine for us, step by step, Bettelheim's last minutes on earth.

Nothing better demonstrates Bettelheim's vulnerability and sardonic self-awareness toward the end of his life than an anecdote Raines tells of a phone call he received from his client/friend one night at home. Raines's wife, Joan, answered the phone and explained to Bettelheim that "it would take a moment for me to come to the phone because Buck [their English bulldog] was on my lap. Bruno, having met Buck, could visualize this highly domestic scene and said to Joan, 'Ohhhh, to be Buck!'"

It was through Theron Raines that, in the seventies, Bettelheim came to Knopf, where I edited a number of his books. I found him to be a man of great charm; of a very European courtesy, almost courtliness. As a writer, he was unsure of himself. Pollak cites a letter of mine to Bettelheim about *The Uses of Enchantment*, a letter "recommending a number of specific changes and in general urging him to curb his repetitiveness and his tendency to give the fairy tales simplistic, dogmatic Freudian interpretations." He finds Bettelheim's response "abject": "You are so very right with all you point out, that I am worried you did not find more to criticize." And I am urged to feel free "to rewrite it in any other and better way to meet your most justified objections. . . . Please remember my reputation was not made as a writer, but as a therapist. I need your help badly as an author." This indicates a realistic modesty about his prose: Even with all the help he received from outside collaborators before delivering manuscripts to his publishers, his English could be awkward and unclear. I don't recall this correspondence, but I do remember feeling at the time that Bettelheim held an inflated respect for "literary" people, beginning with myself. (I was both startled and embarrassed when he inserted verbatim several half-baked notions of mine into his text.) By the mid-eighties his work seemed to me to be growing less well developed and more cranky, and his courtesy somewhat eroded as my editorial comments grew more intense. Even so, I never ceased liking and admiring him.

I've recently read two extended firsthand accounts of the Orthogenic School by former students/patients there. One is a novel, *The Pelican and After*, by Tom Wallace Lyons, published almost twenty years ago. The other is a new memoir, *Not the Thing I Was*, by Stephen Eliot. Both gain credibility from the fact that they describe almost parallel experiences, as well as from the intense sincerity that informs each of them.

The Pelican and After barely bothers to disguise the school or Dr. B.—he's called Dr. V.—and indeed the book is partly dedicated to Bettelheim, who read it and congratulated Lyons on it, despite the obvious ambivalence Lyons expresses toward him. Certainly, Bettelheim's recourse to physical violence is not downplayed. Early in the book, Lyons recounts a scene in which Dr. V. confronts a youngster named Ronny who had earlier in the day accidentally hit a girl in the eye. That evening Dr. V. appears in the dorm room and stands over Ronny. "Since ven do ve hit people in zhe eye?"

When Ronny answers "I didn't *mean* to,"

Dr. V.'s left hand caught Ronny on one side of the face, then returned with a swift backhand across the other. SMACK! SMACK! SMACK! SMACK! SMACK! Dr. V.'s left hand moved quickly, methodically back and forth across Ronny's face. Then: SMACK! SMACK! SMACK! SMACK! with both hands on the back of the head as Ronny ducked forward. Dr. V. grabbed a small tuft of his hair and shook. And with both hands he caught Ronny by the shirt and hauled him halfway out of his chair.

"Vhy did you hit her in zhe eye!"

When Ronny again claims it was an accident,

Dr. V. stepped back; he watched Ronny while the latter sniffled once or twice. Suddenly he extended his hands, palms up, in grandiose gesticulation, "I didn't mean to! It vas an accident!" he shrilled mockingly. This made him appear less frightening. In his more normal, but still menacing voice, he asked, "Does zat make it feel any better?" Ronny shook his head. "All right, zhen, remember zat ven you have accidents, I vill have zem also. Is zat clear?"

"Yes," Ronny nodded.

38

It's telling that here, as in Stephen Eliot's memoir, the kids who are struck are scared but don't seem to feel resentment. "Tony"—that is, Lyons—who portrays himself as having been filled with dangerous impulses when he came to the school, reports healing conversations with Dr. V. And Dr. V. is surprisingly open-minded and understanding when Tony, a rebel, decides in his mid-teens to leave the school, not because he feels brutalized but because he feels oppressed by being treated like a child. Perhaps one key to Bettelheim's effectiveness lies in something one of Tony's counselors says to him: "Dr. V. makes you feel all the good in yourself." And, writes Lyons, "Tony felt this was true." Lyons himself went on to the Columbia School of Journalism and a career as a reporter.

Stephen Eliot's *Not the Thing I Was: Thirteen Years at Bruno Bettelheim's Orthogenic School* is the most detailed, moving, and persuasive account I've encountered about life at the school. It's also a completely believable and very touching account of the struggle of an intelligent yet seriously disturbed boy to conquer his problems and emerge into a full adult life—a struggle, Eliot tells us, that is not over yet, decades after he left the school. (A graduate of Yale and with an M.B.A. from Columbia, he became a successful investment banker.) On the one hand, *Not the Thing I Was* portrays the intense bonding between the students and their prime counselors, Dr. B.'s "reign of terror," the different kinds of troubled children and how they interacted. On the other hand, it reveals the ordinariness—games, mischief-making, kids mimicking Dr. B. (he knew), the usual teenage rivalries and friendships, the first sexual impulses. Tom Lyons's Tony is obsessed with prostitutes; the young Stephen Eliot slowly comes to terms with being gay. (He is still angry at the lack of support and understanding the Freudian-minded school provided him in this regard.)

We follow Eliot's progress from a boastful, insecure little boy isolated within his very capable brain ("My world ended at my shoes") and terrified of never having enough contact with others to make a real life possible, to a compassionate young man eagerly helping the younger children. His eventual capacity for love is suggested by his devotion as an adult to his school psychiatrist, Margaret Carey:

There was barely a month that went by that I didn't speak with her until her death, talking with her from wherever I was in the world. She delighted in getting calls from me when I was in Tokyo or Hong Kong. The last three or four years of her life, she was in a nursing home, unable to walk and, finally, unable to talk. Then I would call and ask the nurses to put the phone next to her ear, so she could hear my voice and know I hadn't forgotten her.

Eliot acknowledges that Bettelheim hit the children, but says that what he really feared and resented was Bettelheim's verbal cruelty. Once, he tells us,

I complained I would rather be at home than in this prison. True to form, Dr. B. walked in just as I said it. He hauled me out in the hall for a private conversation, which consisted of him telling me "Do you know why you are here?" I just looked down. "I'll tell you why you are here. You are here because your parents can't stand you, so don't talk about how much you like being at home."

Eliot goes on to say, "I could forgive Dr. B. much, but not that. Even now, as I write this, I remember all those years of terror—please don't humiliate me, please don't." And yet, he understands that Dr. B. was a benign genius as well as a flawed, even destructive, ultimately tragic man:

Looking back . . . I now wonder whether his death was a final cry of desperation, for despite all he had done, his life's work was fading as was his memory and one man can only do so much. In the final analysis, his work was not enough to change the world in the way he envisioned. It was, however, enough for me.

February 27, 2003

Going His Way

Four men dominate the history of popular singing in the twentieth century (if you want to double the number, throw in the Beatles). They were Al Jolson, Bing Crosby, Frank Sinatra, and Elvis Presley, and during the period of their ascendancy they not only led the way, they *were* the way. We think we know them. Jolson, the cantor's son, headlining in blackface and ushering in the era of sound; Sinatra, the tough Italian kid from Hoboken, who transformed himself into the revered Ol' Blue Eyes; Elvis, the hip-wriggling, dirt-poor truck driver from Tupelo, whose life sputtered out so stupidly. But what do we know about Crosby? Throughout his decades at the absolute pinnacle of his profession, he was just Bing—decent, casual, modest, above all normal; a guy whose baritone voice happened to be better than ours or we could have been him. (We certainly never thought we could be Jolson or Sinatra or Presley.)

His reputation hasn't fared well. Today he may be admired by singers and critics, and remembered with respect and affection by those who go back fifty years, but he's generally brushed aside by younger people, who associate him with their parents' (or grandparents') old-fashioned taste. What's left of him? "White Christmas" and "Silent Night" during the holidays. Possibly the "Road" pictures. Less likely, his Oscar-winning Father O'Malley in (ugh) *Going My Way*. Maybe *High Society*. As for his life story, if it's known at all it's because of the pathetic death of his alcoholic first wife, Dixie, and the revelations of his son Gary's book, *Going My Own Way*. The world's most successful singer, ever, is neglected as an artist, and Mr. All-Time Nice Guy has been turned into Daddy Dearest.

Years ago, the eminent jazz critic Gary Giddins set out to tell the full story of the life and to analyze and reassess the career. In 1993, he provided the introduction for a new edition of Crosby's autobiography, *Call*

Me Lucky, written forty years earlier; a publisher's note said of Giddins, "His long-awaited biography of Bing Crosby is slated for publication . . . in the fall of 1995." It took another half-dozen years for the long wait to be over—or partly over. The more than seven hundred pages of *Bing Crosby: A Pocketful of Dreams* tell only half the story, the years from 1903 to 1940—no "White Christmas," no Father O'Malley, no Frank Sinatra on the horizon. And no big dramatic crisis to neatly split the story in two. Indeed, once Crosby got rolling, there *were* no crises. He shot to the top before he was thirty, "having fallen upward every step of his career," Giddins remarks, and he stayed there until rock and roll supplanted his music and the sixties undid the America he epitomized.

Perhaps what has taken Giddins all this time—apart from working on his award-winning *Visions of Jazz* and on the Ken Burns project *Jazz*—

has been the difficulty of grappling with a subject who so successfully presented himself as simple, even transparent, yet who actually was enigmatic, even opaque. Previous biographies have been either idolatrous or (as Giddins calls one of them) "scurrilous"; this new account may at moments overinflate Crosby's significance, but when the facts are unpretty we aren't spared them. Most of all, though, Giddins is in love with Crosby the singer, and here his knowledge of popular singing gives his book the weight and value that no other account commands.

The career is unparalleled. Giddins marshals the evidence: In 1925, the twenty-two-year-old Bing, fresh from the twenties equivalent of garage bands, sets out with his even younger sidekick and partner, Al Rinker, in a legendary drive in a legendary old jalopy down from Spokane to Los Angeles, where they have no prospects and practically no connections. In less than a year, they're signed by the number-one entertainer in America, Paul Whiteman, to sing in his band and are wowing people in vaudeville and at Hollywood nightclubs. By mid-1927, Crosby's voice is heard on his first Whiteman hit, "Muddy Water." Crosby and Rinker, joined by Harry Barris, become the Rhythm Boys; hit follows hit; and in 1931 Crosby goes solo. Some forty number-one records follow (compared to twenty-four for the Beatles and eighteen for Elvis), and an unbelievable two hundred and twenty-five top-ten records. (One of these is "White Christmas," which has sold well over thirty-five million copies.) As a movie star, he tops the Quigley box-office poll for an unheard-of five years in a row. His radio shows rank among the top dozen for decades. And finally he moves into television, yet again warming America's heart with family Christmas shows. His new family, that is; Dixie is dead, their four sons are in the doghouse, but there is young, pretty wife number two, Kathryn Grant, and their three adorable kids.

Through his movies we can watch him develop from the jaunty, likable, sometimes rascally Joe College type of the thirties, to the jaunty, likable, sometimes rascally co-star, with Bob Hope and Dorothy Lamour, of the "Road" pictures, to the jaunty, likable, but never rascally priest of *Going My Way* and *The Bells of St. Mary's*. "Develop" may not be the word: He ages and he grows more proficient, but he doesn't really change.

Through his records we can follow him as he develops into a superior jazz musician—influenced, in the Whiteman band, by Bix Beiderbecke and Frankie Trumbauer—then into our most famous crooner (a word he disliked). Giddins underlines again and again that Crosby's singing is virile, not "effeminate," "effete," or "like a Floradora girl"—in other words, not like the high-pitched Irish tenors who had preceded him. And unlike imitators like Perry Como and Dick Haymes, he never lost his swing, despite the countless middle-of-the-road songs he recorded. Giddins readily acknowledges the downside of Crosby's popularity. "His major achievement was to plait the many threads of American music into a central style of universal appeal. . . . To achieve universality, he had to dilute individuality."

This is the Bing who was indiscriminately singing superior Depression-era songs like "Brother, Can You Spare a Dime?" and "Pennies from Heaven," while dabbling in faux-Hawaiian, faux-Mexican, faux-Western, plus Stephen Foster, "Ah! Sweet Mystery of Life," "When the Organ Played 'O Promise Me,'" and "Did Your Mother Come from Ireland?"—hardly the Great American Songbook. Crosby thought that his singing grew more secure through the years—that he had been sloppy in the early thirties. It didn't matter: The rich intimacy of the voice, the beautiful phrasing, the perfect elocution and pitch, and, crucially, the mastery of the microphone and of radio prevailed over carelessness and weak material. Crosby is both revolutionary, in that no earlier singer sounds anything like him, and assimilative, containing the Jewish Jolson, the African American Louis Armstrong, his own Irish musical heritage. He's both a melting pot and uniquely himself.

Crosby the man is a mix as well—of his happy-go-lucky, charming, mandolin-playing father, Harry, and his dominating, demanding, disciplinary mother, Kate, perhaps the one person of whom Bing was afraid. (At least four of his siblings admitted that "they felt no love for their mother at all. They were scared of her.") She was the kind of Irish mother who would have liked one of her boys to become a priest, and indeed Bing attended a Jesuit high school in Spokane, studying Latin and mastering the art of elocution, to which he later said he owed his remarkable phrasing, and went on to Gonzaga University, even doing a year of law. ("I studied law in college and I can truthfully say that the bar of the state of Washington is the only bar I was ever kept out of.")

In fact, Giddins sums up, this promising mirror of a rigorous Jesuit education "was slipping out of Gonzaga's grasp." He slipped fast and far. Into his mid-twenties, Bing was a love-'em-and-leave-'em Don Juan and a serious drinker. About his women he was close-mouthed—in a 1931 interview (published not long after he got married) he tactfully protests,

"They say I left a trail of broken hearts behind me. . . . Now I wouldn't do a thing like that. The fact is I left a trail of broken bottles and unpaid bills." His drinking led not only to a jail sentence for drunken driving but to increasing unreliability. The genial Paul Whiteman remarked, "No, he was never hard to handle. But sometimes he was hard to find."

And then, in the spirit of Saint Augustine (of whom Giddins reminds us a few too many times), comes reform—marriage to the starlet Dixie Lee, four kids, money piling up, work habits rigorous enough to satisfy even the Jesuits. You could say that Bing Crosby spent his life outwardly embodying the casual charm of his father while inwardly obeying the demands of his mother. It was a formula that worked: The world both loved him and approved of him.

Yet the people closest to him found him not just casual but remote, even cold. He had no talent for intimacy—almost no real friends. Dixie was left to her own devices, and to alcohol. The four boys were disciplined as harshly as he had been disciplined by Kate. He was accused of shutting people out of his life, most dramatically Al Rinker and Harry Barris, when he decided to go it alone. Yet in many ways he was generous, not least to other actors and singers, and most of all to Armstrong: "He is the beginning and the end of music in America." (Louis returned the compliment: "Ever since Bing first opened his mouth, he was the Boss of All Singers and still is.")

Crosby's modesty, his lack of vanity, were real. He insisted that his success was due to luck (*Call Me Lucky*). He knew his looks were nothing remarkable, and he never tried to glamorize himself: At Paramount, he refused to have his big ears pinned back and resented having to hide his receding hairline. Most remarkably, he insisted on the famous Crosby clause in his contracts, by which he refused to be billed alone above the picture title: Minor actresses were elevated into co-stars. This was shrewdness as well as modesty, of course; if the picture failed, it wasn't his fault alone.

By 1940, Bing had, Giddins tells us, invented his own image as "an all-American character: a plucky, eternally boyish, self-made millionaire with a common touch and uncommon voice." No wonder that in a national poll taken in the late forties, he was voted the most popular man alive. Women found him appealing, even sexy, yet unthreatening; men were drawn to what Giddins calls his "working-class man's-man insouciance." For Gary Crosby, the adulation "blurred the boundaries between

'God and dad, because everybody revered both of them.'" He was "quint-essentially American," says Giddins, "cool and upbeat, never pompous, belligerent, or saccharine, never smug or superior. He looked down on no one and up to no one." Above all, he was natural—"an extraordinary or-dinary guy." But how ordinary is a man who dominates the entertainment industry for decades, amasses a fortune, masks his ambition even from himself, and achieves universal popularity?

It's hard to think of a comparable figure. The young Bing suggests a Huck Finn who quickly turns into Tom Sawyer—it's Huck who floats down the West Coast in that jalopy, but it's Tom who immediately starts falling upward into the tremendous career. Perhaps the man who most resembles Crosby in his natural charm, his hidden strengths and ambi-tions, his boyish appeal is the equally all-American Eisenhower. Can it be accidental that the two most famous nicknames of the century were Bing and Ike? (How many people even know that Bing's real name was Harry Lillis Crosby?)

Gary Giddins has performed a great service in tracking Crosby's life and career so scrupulously. He's not only superb on the music, but he's lov-ingly considered the films of the thirties—he's particularly perceptive about the vaudevillian "Road" pictures (Crosby and Hope "are anarchists with sweet souls"). Sometimes his prose gets a touch fancy or peculiar—a song treatment is "supernally relaxed," his work "failed to sate Bing's en-ergy," Bing "had haplessly incarnated the excesses of Prohibition"—and one can argue with certain judgments: Is Crosby really a "far more impor-tant artist" than John McCormack? But these are hardly blemishes on a masterly performance. Some readers may feel that this book tells them too much. But those of us who have been waiting all these years to learn every-thing there is to know about Crosby can only be grateful for Giddins's depth of detail and soundness of judgment. Now, where is Volume Two?*

February 11, 2001

---

*Good news: It's well on its way.

The Impresario

Serge Diaghilev died in 1929. Twenty years earlier, his Ballets Russes had ignited the revival of ballet in the West when, with Pavlova, Nijinsky, and Karsavina as his stars, he took Paris by storm with a season highlighted by *Les Sylphides* and the "Polovtsian Dances" from *Prince Igor.* The next year brought *Schéhérazade*, *The Firebird*, and *Le Carnaval*, and, the following year, *Le Spectre de la Rose* and *Petrouchka*. Fokine's choreography, Stravinsky's music, the genius of Nijinsky, the lushly colorful decor by Bakst, the sensuality—the orientalism!—of it all added up to both revelation and revolution. The intellectual and social elite of London as well as of Paris responded to Diaghilev's vision of ballet as an art form that at its best could reconcile and harmonize music, choreography, narrative, and the visual arts on the highest level, and Diaghilev himself became a figure of tremendous glamour and reputation—of necessity, since he required rich and impressionable patrons to keep the Ballets Russes going. There were no government or corporate subsidies in 1909.

Through the company's two decades of existence, Diaghilev attached to it or developed in it the greatest talent of his day—"He was a fertilizer of genius" is how Marie Rambert put it. Only Pavlova went her own way—their goals were imcompatible: He was the apostle of Art, she was the apostle of Dance, as embodied in herself. He commanded the services not only of Stravinsky but of Prokofiev, Ravel, Richard Strauss, Satie, de Falla, Poulenc, Milhaud, among other composers; Picasso, Matisse, Derain, Braque, de Chirico, and Rouault among artists. The choreographers he launched or propelled to fame were Massine, Nijinsky, Nijinska, Lifar, and Balanchine. We owe to him *L'Aprés-Midi d'un Faune*, *The Rite of Spring*, *Les Noces*, *La Boutique Fantasque*, *Les Biches*, *Apollo*, and *The Prodigal Son*. And although he was a perpetually self-renewing one-man New Wave, he was also the traditionalist who restored the loftiest ideals of ballet classicism to the West with his superb if ill-fated production of *The Sleeping Beauty* in London in 1921. Finally, after his death the diaspora of his followers led to Ninette de Valois's Royal Ballet and Balanchine's New York City Ballet. It would be hard to identify another figure in ballet—in any art form— who so single-handedly and definitively transformed the art for which he labored.

Because of his extraordinary achievements, and because his personal life—in particular his sexual history with, among others, Nijinsky and Massine (both of whom "betrayed" him by marrying)—was so dramatic and so public, Diaghilev has remained a focus of attention in countless biographies and memoirs. He has even been popularized—"caricatured" is probably the more apt word—in the movies: as the impresario Lermontov in *The Red Shoes* and as himself in the potboiler *Nijinsky*. Yet he remains mysterious. We still find it hard to grasp how he did what he did—how he marshaled his resources, energized and inspired so many major artists, captured and held the imagination of so sophisticated a world for so long, maintained his standards, and deployed his unquestioned authority. And today these matters seem more urgent than ever, as the balance between quality and marketing in artistic ventures has tilted so alarmingly in the direction of the latter. Diaghilev used publicity to protect and advance his aesthetic; today, publicity more and more *is* the aesthetic.

John Drummond, in his book *Speaking of Diaghilev*, asserts that it is this crisis in the arts, and most particularly in arts management, that makes Diaghilev so important an object lesson. His observations on these matters are acute—he himself has been an important figure in the official world of British arts leadership for many years, and he knows the score. Given the overwhelming cost of running any large ballet, opera, or theater company and thus the involvement (meddling?) of arts councils and boards of directors, how could a figure like Diaghilev arise today—a man of extraordinary culture (a superb musician, deeply versed in the fine arts, and uncannily prescient in his instinct for talent in dancers) who, as Drummond puts it, "lived an entirely ad hoc existence, taking real risks and suffering occasional disasters" yet who "remained a free agent"? The closest we have come to a second Diaghilev, we are reminded, was Lincoln Kirstein, although Kirstein's main role at the New York City Ballet was to support George Balanchine's artistic decisions, not to *make* the decisions. (Is it my imagination that detects in Drummond's tone a hint of a suggestion that he himself might qualify?)

The heart of *Speaking of Diaghilev*—at least two-thirds of it—comprises twenty-two interviews with Diaghilev collaborators filmed by the author in the mid-sixties for a two-part BBC documentary that against considerable odds he succeeded in bringing to the screen. Although some of the big guns got away—Stravinsky and Balanchine the biggest—the testimony of these other witnesses is both fascinating and invaluable. To start with, we get a composite idea of the physical Diaghilev—large and handsome, with the white streak in his dark hair (he beat Susan Sontag to it), always exquisitely dressed, soft hands, with a "sort of funny rolling gait," according to Karsavina: "Rolling his head from side to side, he reminded me very much of a sea lion." (Bronislava Nijinska, in her memoirs, found his expression "at once reassuring and attractive—like a bulldog's.") To Cecil Beaton, he was more "a sort of chinchilla. . . . He had a mouth rather like a shark and a marvelous poreless complexion." All in all, Beaton found Diaghilev "very grand seigneur."

We begin to understand how he achieved his authority: implacable in his demands for perfection, austere and impersonal at times, then charming and seductive. "Frightening" is a word used over and over—yet kind, even paternal, to the fourteen-year-old Alicia Markova. The highly admired dancer (and excellent reporter) Lydia Sokolova (born Hilda Munnings) acknowledges that "he could be terrifying," yet remembers how he solemnly said to her, at a moment when she was in great difficulty, "Now, I want you to remember that I can be as a father to you, and when you are at any time in trouble, real trouble, either in the day or in the night, and you send for me, I will come." He was to keep his word, "so how could I not love anybody like that? Of course I loved him."

There is example after example of Diaghilev's always constructive attention to detail, of his intuitive understanding of what might help a dancer grasp a role, of his sure sense of what he wanted and how to get it. The musicians Ernest Ansermet, Henri Sauguet, and especially Nicolas Nabokov are completely convincing about his musicality. And we believe Sauguet when he says: "Diaghilev was the absolute master, the man who did everything and saw everything. Nothing escaped him. I have never since seen a man with such an understanding or such a sense of the science of it all, such capacity for work and at the same time a sort of grandeur and magnetism. He was a man of extraordinary allure, absolutely unique in his way."

The interviews are also valuable for what they reveal about the interviewees. Only Serge Lifar, Diaghilev's lover-protégé, with his notorious vanity and lack of delicacy, would declare, "You could say that I am his spiritual heir." And it is almost mind-boggling to hear the formidable Dame Ninette de Valois admit, "I was really always too scared of him to say that I had looked him straight in the face." Perhaps this is where she learned to scare the rest of us. (Actually, Diaghilev admired her dancing, although, we are told, he didn't admire her stage name: "Half tart, half royal family of France," he said.) Unsurprisingly, almost everyone who was there in the early years was still gripped by memories of Nijinsky more than forty-five years later; his remote, impenetrable nature, his unsurpassed talent, and his tragic fate remain the great legend of twentieth-century ballet. And fortunately Drummond asks good questions about Balanchine, so that our picture of him is amplified, as well as our sense of the choreographic procession that began with Fokine and *Les Sylphides* and led to Balanchine and *Apollo*.

These interviews don't pretend to tell the whole story. For one thing, they don't include anyone who was present at the beginning stages of Diaghilev's public life, as a functionary of the imperial theaters. His slightly older colleague Alexandre Benois tells us, in his *Reminiscences of the Russian Ballet*: "It was loathsome to see Seriozha's ingratiating manner when he approached personalities of high standing. . . . As a student, Diaghilev was never alluded to otherwise than as a terrible fop, and this reputation prevented him from being taken seriously for a considerable time." As the man closest to Diaghilev in the early years of the Ballets Russes, Benois was in a position to observe his less attractive qualities—snobbery, ingratitude, conceit, willfulness. Benois is not a disinterested reporter—his resentment of Diaghilev's success is all too apparent—yet his final judgment rings true. Commenting on the fact that Diaghilev liked to boast of his descent, *de main gauche*, from Peter the Great, he concludes: "In Diaghilev there was undoubtedly the inborn love of power, the mind that penetrated to the origins of all things (often without any actual knowledge of them), the capacity to gauge people's weaknesses and play on them, that were fundamental characteristics of the great reformer of Russia. Diaghilev was a born leader."

Mathilde Kschessinska, the prima ballerina assoluta of the Maryinsky

Theatre, where she held a privileged position as ex-mistress of the czar, had various run-ins with Diaghilev both before and after the revolution, but she came to appreciate and admire him, as she tells us in her self-glorifying yet canny memoir, *Dancing in Petersburg*. She deals with his unconventional sexuality in a particularly discreet way: "S. P. Diaghilev nearly always accompanied me home after the performance. Curiously, I have always been successful with men in whom I expected least of all to awake admiration! And yet there was nothing boyish about me." (Her czarevitch and her various grand dukes would have agreed.) Karsavina, in *Theatre Street*, fills in the picture with a charming anecdote: "I was having a bath in my dressing room after a hard evening of ballet when to my horror Diaghilev strode in. 'Tata, que vous êtes jolie,' he said, as if commenting, en passant, on a hitherto unseen frock. And then, in the same breath, 'Nous répétons demain à dix heures.'" ("Tata, how pretty you are.... Rehearsal tomorrow at ten.")

The oddest part of Drummond's book is the opening section, which atempts several things at once. To begin with, it narrates in far too great detail his travails in producing his documentary and indulges itself settling old scores with forgotten BBC functionaries of the sixties. ("Huw Wheldon . . . always behaved as if he resented my knowledge, which frankly, in a number of areas, outran his own." "Margaret Dale had absolutely no creative imagination.") Not only was he "not much taken" with the critic Richard Buckle "as a person" but he was exposed to "a not very good lunch at a restaurant in Southampton Street, the nearest to his flat." This disappointing meal, we must remember, took place in 1965!

He is also revealed as an inveterate gossip. It was said of Benois's daughter, Anne, "that her husband had shot himself after finding her in flagrante with a family friend." The dancer Anton Dolin, another Diaghilev lover-protégé, is kind enough to tell Drummond (and therefore us) that Diaghilev's sexual demands were "straightfoward, rather adolescent and did not involve any form of penetrative intercourse." Lydia Sokolova "speculated wildly" on the relationship between the dancer Idzikowski, "a tiny and brilliant technician," and the "rather larger" Madame Evina. Sokolova and another dancer "had once found some condoms in Idzi's coat pocket—'The very smallest size, dear, and you know Evina was huge—I don't know how they managed!'" No wonder that when Drummond mentioned Sokolova's name to Idzi, the tiny technician seized a chair and smashed it into pieces.

Yet despite the self-serving and catty aspects of this introductory narrative, the book has real, writerly virtues. Drummond emerges as a man in love—in love with Diaghilev, with the world as well as the accomplishments of the Ballets Russes, and with a number of the survivors. He tells us how, on his first meeting with Karsavina, whom everyone adored, they go down "to a small but charming morning room, where silver kettles, pretty cups, the thinnest cucumber sandwiches were waiting." After she asks him to choose a tea (when he picks a "highly perfumed China" variety, somehow we're not surprised), "we sipped it from the little cups. I can scarcely recall ever being so happy." This is the authentic voice of the best kind of fan—or, to put it more kindly, enthusiast. It is also the voice of a true memoirist, a judgment confirmed by his accounts of a series of remarkable encounters he had during the two years it took to complete his documentary. A demented pilgrimage to Massine's Italian island home, a riveting meeting with Stravinsky, characteristic brushes with the eccentric Sacheverell Sitwell and the "silly" Lifar are narrated with energy, color, and conviction. What does it matter that Drummond is careless about things like the date of *Prodigal Son* or that he doesn't really appreciate Margot Fonteyn? Yes, he is small-minded, but he is also large-minded, and his work in the sixties, expanded and explicated thirty years later in *Speaking of Diaghilev*, is a true contribution to dance history and a fitting tribute to a great man.

August 1, 1999

A Lost Child

If you mention the name Minou Drouet to your French friends in Paris, not many of them under the age of fifty know whom you're talking about. But older people know very well, even if they don't all know the same thing. What do they think they know? She was seven—or was it eight?—years old. She wrote some poems. She didn't write some poems. In any case, they were a hoax, *une supercherie*; it was really her mother who wrote them. She was a victim of her publisher, of the press, of her family. She was talented, but she was a flash in the pan. She had no talent at all— what was it Cocteau said about her, something witty and bitchy? And Roland Barthes, in his *Mythologies*—didn't he weigh in, too?

There's a faint sense of embarrassment when people admit that they remember her, as if they'd just as soon forget that their world made all that fuss about nothing, and they move on to more elevated subjects, like Sartre and Juliette Gréco and the nouvelle vague. Because Minou disappeared from the world stage so totally and so long ago, remembering her today reminds people that they're of a certain age. As a saleswoman in the bookstore around the corner from the Comédie-Française remarked when I asked her whether any of Minou's work was available, "Well, that question definitely dates us!"

In fact, you can't find a book by Minou Drouet in any bookstore in Paris, not even her phenomenally successful *Arbre, Mon Ami*, which was published just over fifty years ago—early in 1956—by the aggressive René Julliard, who a year earlier had scored an international triumph with Françoise Sagan's *Bonjour Tristesse*. But Sagan had been eighteen; Minou was eight.

In his introduction to *Arbre, Mon Ami*, Julliard explained that it was his friend Professor Pasteur Vallery-Radot "of the Académie Française"— the grandson of Louis Pasteur—who had first told him about Minou.

Vallery-Radot had heard about her from Lucette Descaves, of the Conservatoire de Paris, who was giving the little girl piano lessons, and who soon entrusted Julliard with a batch of letters she'd received from her pupil. "Never had I lit upon a vein of such richness," Julliard wrote. "I at once discovered a freshness and liveliness of feeling, a gift for imagery, and a power of expression that were quite exceptional—in short, a poet." Within days, he had arranged for Minou's adoptive mother to bring her to

Paris from Brittany, where they lived, and soon the Julliards, too, were receiving extraordinary letters from her. Julliard was captivated by the child and impressed by the mother. He decided to publish.

But not in the standard way. Late in September 1955, five hundred copies of a forty-eight-page sampling of Minou's poems and letters were meted out to "certain critics and amongst my friends." And at once a storm broke—a dispute that, Julliard wrote, "divided the literary and journalistic world into two houses—a sort of minor Dreyfus Affair." As *Time* put it late in November—beneath the heading RAGE OF PARIS—"In France, where literature can be a hot front-page issue, the biggest story of the week—and the year's liveliest press brawl—raged around the blonde head of an eight-year-old poetess. Was little Minou Drouet a genius or a fraud?"

Proof that *Time* wasn't exaggerating exists in a book called *L'Affaire Minou Drouet*, which was rushed out by Julliard in early January, just as he was also publishing *Arbre, Mon Ami*. The author, André Parinaud, took almost two hundred and fifty crammed pages to chronicle—in agonizing detail—the events of the few months that followed the private distribution of Julliard's pamphlet, recapitulating the vicious attacks and counterattacks in the press, interviewing various participants in the fray, and drawing solemn conclusions.

Just before the pamphlet appeared, two of Minou's poems and two of her letters had been printed in the review *Les Lettres Nouvelles*. A few days later, *L'Express* ran "Who Is Minou Drouet?" and within two weeks the entire world of French literary journalism had joined in. *L'Express* was pro-Minou, who "writes poems that would place her among our fine poets—even if she were an adult." *Combat* was anti: "A prodigy, if you like; but a prodigy not of freshness but of a precocious pedantry." *France Observateur*: "It's impossible to believe that a more expert hand didn't guide these little seven-and-a-half-year-old fingers. Rimbaud, after all, was sixteen." Rimbaud?

Le Figaro, Le Monde, L'Aurore, France-Soir, France-Dimanche, France Observateur, Franc-Tireur, Tribune de Paris, Paris-Presse, Ici-Paris—each of them took a position. But the most contentious article appeared in the popular weekly *Elle*, which sent a reporter and a photographer to spend time with Minou and her mother, and gave the story four pages and seven photographs. The story didn't actually accuse Mme. Drouet of writing her daughter's poems, but the implication was clear: At best, the mother was a domineering, interfering woman, manipulating her child's talent.

Elle's chief rival, *Paris-Match*, also printed four pages on "L'Enigme Minou Drouet." Its story was less prosecutorial and more of a cliff-hanger: "Brilliant child . . . or victim of a hoax." After three days with the Drouets, the magazine could report that it had found Minou to be "a little girl like other little girls, merry and charming, preoccupied with her toys. 'Great!' she shouted. 'No homework today!'" She's photographed at her desk, pen in hand; asleep in her bed, with her teddy bear; waking up, grinning, "with a new dream" to report—"I stepped out of the pink of my bed, and in the blue of my nightgown went out into the blackness of the garden."

Soon experts, invited and uninvited, were chiming in. A *psychotechnicienne* from Nîmes wrote to *Le Figaro*, referring to Minou as "that poor child" and stating that, in her professional opinion, a single line of Minou's—"My heart has been nothing but a stupid little mayonnaise whisk"—was enough to have her placed under observation. Minou was put to the test— to a variety of tests. Her poems and letters, of course, were handwritten, and graphologists were called in. Those hired by *Elle* were certain that the handwriting was essentially Madame's, and the magazine followed up its original, relatively cautious piece with an article forthrightly declaring that it was all "a cruel hoax"—the mother had "not only thought up all of Minou's poems but we have evidence that she also wrote them herself in pseudo-childish handwriting." The experts brought in by Minou's supporters were equally certain that she, and only she, had written the poems and the letters—including those composed long before the world had ever heard of Minou Drouet.

At the prompting of both suspicious journalists and staunch defenders, Minou was required to write poems before witnesses, one of which she produced while paying a visit, alone, to the Julliards. "Maison Plantée sur le Sable" begins:

House planted on the sand
like a pine tree in the wind
house that echoes with song
and sighs of the sea

It's a cry of longing for a small beach shack that the Drouets rented on the Atlantic coast. She asks if she can write a letter home, and in twenty minutes it's done: "Mama dear, come get me. . . . I've been so unhappy. . . . I

slide my arms around your neck, and my little heart is all clothed in sadness." Within days this letter is reprinted in *France-Soir.*

The tormenting of the child never let up. In a letter to Mme. Julliard,
Minou wrote, "Our street is vomiting journalists non-stop. It feels like
the whole world is after me. . . . I wish I were dead. They keep on and on at
me with their questions. I think the only words I can utter are fear, pain,
death." As Roland Barthes commented—and, years later, Minou quoted
him—"One can prove imposture; never authenticity."

By the time *Arbre, Mon Ami* was published, in January 1956, the publicity had been so unrelenting that within a few months the little book had
sold forty-five thousand copies. (Later, Minou said, "I believe that René
Julliard himself was at the bottom of this campaign.") The celebrated actress Madeleine Renaud recorded a group of the poems and letters. A jazz
band, Michel Attenoux et Son Orchestre, released the "Minou Drouet
Stomp"—you can find it in a recent CD collection, *Jazz in Paris.*

A month after publication, Minou was put to the severest test of all.
The February 13 issue of *Life* tells the story: To resolve the controversy,
Minou agreed to take a test for membership in the Society of Authors,
Composers, and Music Publishers. She was left alone in an office (from
which "the telephone had been removed to prevent all communication
with the outside world") and given a choice of two topics to write on: "I'm
Eight Years Old" or "Paris Sky." "My eight years were already too sad,"
she said. "I chose Paris Sky." Within twenty-five minutes she had written
a few dozen lines, and the judges, as *Life* put it, "admiringly awarded her
membership. 'I've won,' yelped Minou." *Life*'s translation, in part:

> *Paris sky*
> *secret weight,*
> *flesh which in hiccoughs*
> *spits into our faces*
> *through the open jaws of rows of houses,*
> *a stream of blood*
> *between its luminous teeth*
> *Paris sky*
> *cocktail of night and of fear*
> *which one savors with little licks of the tongue*
> *with little catches of the heart*
> *from the tip of a neon straw*

Life's heading: PROOF OF A PRODIGY. The photograph: tiny Minou—a huge bow on top of her head—with two beaming elderly gentlemen standing behind her. The caption: "Test finished, Minou hands poem to Society's judges. She sat on a pillow, kept pet dog on desk."

Minou Drouet's existence was turbulent well before she became a cause célèbre—in fact, from the very beginning. When she was a year and a half old, she was adopted by Claude Drouet, an educated woman who earned her living by coaching children at home. The story was that Minou's parents had drowned in a fishing-boat accident, but actually she was illegitimate, and her birth mother had signed away all rights to her. This fact was printed in *Elle* as proof that "The Mother" was a liar, but it's obvious that Mme. Drouet was acting to protect Minou's reputation, not her own: Bastardy would have been a serious black mark against a child in the moral climate of a small town in Brittany in the late 1940s. The editors of *Elle* must surely have known that what they printed would come to the attention of this very sensitive child.

Minou was almost blind at birth, and for three years or so lived in a semi-autistic state, unable to speak and cut off from communicating with people other than her mother and her beloved grandmother. Years later, she wrote, "Locked inside myself, I led the life of some kind of vegetable. . . . The doctors warned Mama, 'The condition of this child is desperate. We can't imagine her being cured.'" Other children were unkind to her, and her emotions were directed almost entirely to nature: to animals, birds, and especially the big tree in the garden—"*Arbre, mon ami.*"

> *Tree*
> *drawn by a clumsy child*
> *a child too poor to buy colored pencils*
> *who scrawled you with the brown left over*
> *from drawing maps at school.*
> *Tree I come to you.*
> *Console me*
> *for being only me.*

Then, when she was three, Minou heard Bach organ music on the radio, and it awakened her to the world. Music became her link to humanity, and in those early years it was music rather than writing that obsessed her. Her passion led to piano lessons from a local teacher, and her abilities led her eventually to Mme. Descaves, in Paris; if the child wasn't a miniature Mozart (any more than she was a miniature Rimbaud), she was clearly gifted.

Mme. Drouet encouraged her gifts—some would say exploited them. However devoted she was to her child, to strangers she could appear severe, controlling, overprotective. She would jump to answer questions put to Minou, declaim her poetry, boast about her talent. She was, clearly, a classic stage mother—using her child both to live out her own ambitions and to carry her and Minou onto a larger stage than was available to them in La Guerche-de-Bretagne. Minou read the situation with a cool precision: "My successes opened the door for her to opportunities that would otherwise have remained closed."

The child was firmly disciplined—kept hard at work and punished for infractions of the rules. (Minou in a letter to the famous pianist Yves Nat: "Little girls' bottoms are really a wonderful gift from heaven for calming the nerves of mothers.... It's because of you that I had my bottom spanked, because I didn't write Mr. in the address and didn't put a capital letter.")

When Minou was seven, her mother took her to a well-known ophthalmologist in Lyons, who operated successfully on the little girl's eyes, making possible the highly charged years that lay ahead. Soon after the publication of her book, Minou's life began its transformation from that of a controversial child poet to that of a full-fledged celebrity. She mixes with cabinet ministers at the Julliards'; she collaborates with famous singer-songwriters like Gilbert Bécaud; she's photographed with Maurice Chevalier (he's kissing her hand) and at the premiere of Jacques-Yves Cousteau's *The World of Silence*. (She's ten, and that big bow is still in her hair.) She stars in a movie. She launches and designs lines of children's fashions. She demonstrates her guitar playing for Andrés Segovia. Pablo Casals teaches her his "Song of the Birds." In Rome, she encounters Vittorio De Sica, and "quickly we were inseparable—we spent the entire day together."

She even wins Cocteau over. His famous comment—the one thing everyone remembers about Minou—is quoted in many versions. In her memoirs she recalls it this way: "All nine-year-olds have genius—except Minou Drouet." But one day at a book signing he came up to her and hugged her. "He was so charming that you couldn't hold anything against him."

Most impressive of all, at the age of ten she's granted a private audience with Pope Pius XII. When she and her mother arrive at the Vatican, her mother warns her to behave herself, but "I forgot all these instructions when a monsignor, dressed in a long violet soutane, came to meet us in an outer chamber. He leaned toward me in a friendly way":

"Minou Drouet, I very much like your poems."

I answered like a shot: "And I like your robe a lot too. It's really well cut!"

Maman threw me a look. A nun, standing by, sketched a smile. We followed the monsignor. In the innermost chamber a priest pointed to a massive gold throne and said, "His Holiness is going to sit here to receive you."

I looked at the throne. I raised my eyes. I pointed to a Jesus on the Cross that was hanging on the wall.

"His Holiness is going to sit on this throne? And what's the One up there going to say about that—He's only got two pieces of wood!"

A burst of laughter from behind me. Pope Pius XII had just come in. "I don't think anyone's said anything like that in the entire history of the Vatican," he remarked.

After Minou and the pope take each other's measure and discuss where she might receive her first communion, he says to her, "Come and visit me again if God so wishes it." She writes, "Impulsively, I sprang toward him and flung my arms around his neck."

The pope: "I'm going to pray that you always remain just as you are."

By this time, Minou was in rigorous training, every minute accounted for. She practiced the piano for hours every day; studied guitar and gymnastics; spent six years learning ballet. Soon she was touring France, appearing with other celebrities—pop singers and comedians—in nightclubs, theaters, arenas. Her act involved reading her poems aloud, singing to her own guitar accompaniment, playing "Claire de Lune," Handel's Passacaglia, Albinoni's Adagio on the piano. (There's a demented photograph of her standing on a piano, arching backward until her fingers are on the keyboard. She's playing upside down!) In June 1957—she's about ten— she's at the Gaumont Palace in Paris, the largest theater in Europe (six thousand seats), performing between screenings of Gary Cooper's *Friendly Persuasion*. In Brussels, she's on with Jacques Brel and Charles Aznavour. At

La Scala, she's a guest of honor at a gala for Mario del Monaco. She's thirteen when a rose is named after her.

Her mother made all the decisions, refusing to bring in a professional
manager and appearing to say yes to anything and everything . . . until,
eventually, Minou said no. Or life said it for her. Her grandmother fell
fatally ill, and Minou nursed her, and then, impulsively, decided to study
nursing: "From one day to the next in 1966 I decided to enter the universe
of the ill." She worked in a hospital for two years, caring for women giving
birth, old people, and desperately ill children. Then it was back to Paris
and the bohemian life of the Left Bank, singing and playing her guitar in
cafés and clubs, running around on her motorbike in a leather jacket, and
marrying a stand-up comedian and writer who worked with the famous
humorist Thierry Le Luron. (When you mention this to the French
they're stunned—and impressed. Although Thierry has been dead for
twenty years, his TV clips and records are still wildly popular, part of the
cultural climate. It's as if we suddenly discovered that Shirley Temple had
been close to Lenny Bruce.)

In her early twenties, Minou published some fables, a novel for children, and a novel for adults, but the irresistible impulse to write had left
her when she was fourteen: "When a bird no longer feels the desire to
sing, it stays silent." Her mother contracted Parkinson's and needed her,
her marriage petered out, and in her early thirties she retreated to La
Guerche-de-Bretagne, to the house where she had grown up. There she
cut herself off completely from her public past, making no appearances
and refusing all interviews, until 1993, when, having remarried—her husband, Jean-Paul Le Canu, is a local garageman—she published a reticent
and skimpy memoir, *Ma Vérité* (*My Truth*). But the public was indifferent.
Her celebrity, like her talent, had disappeared.

In her book, Minou acknowledged that part of her had found it hard
to give up the fame, the applause, the perks: "You amputate part of yourself." But she went on to say, "If I had the kind of child I myself was, I
would try to protect her from all the temptations and assaults of the
world. . . . Beyond the public recognition there's everything that can't be
replaced—play, friends, family, a kind of freedom. Everything I had to
live without."

Last year, I telephoned Minou Drouet from Paris, explaining my interest in her and her work, and proposing that we meet. Her voice was
soft, but her attitude was firm: It was years, she said, since she'd spoken

publicly about her early life, and she was determined to keep it that way; under no circumstances would she see me. Fair enough: Given her history, if anyone deserved privacy it was Minou Drouet. Nevertheless, I wanted to observe at first hand the world she had come from and then retreated to.

La Guerche-de-Bretagne, a half hour's drive from the substantial city of Rennes, is a small market town, almost characterless. It isn't a tourist destination; there's nothing historic or olde-timey about it. It's the equivalent of a small upstate New York town, only with a central square rather than a main street; you don't go through it, you go into it. On the Place Charles de Gaulle, there's a standard church, a jewelry store, a travel agent, one or two real estate agencies, and a restaurant with modest pretensions that at lunch was packed with people, most of them eating slabs of meat seared on an open fire. La Guerche looks as if nothing had changed there since the end of the war, just before Minou was born.

When I began asking people about her, it became clear that she was living less in privacy than in anonymity. No one in the restaurant, the travel agency, the jewelry store was aware that a once-celebrated figure named Minou Drouet had grown up in their town or lives in it today. In the one place that sells books—a large stationery store carrying magazines, computer games, maps, guidebooks, cookbooks, and a few "real" books, like *The Da Vinci Code*—the salespeople had never heard of her.

The pleasant residential street she lives on is a ten-minute walk from the center of town. The street curves, and there at the end of a row of attached brick houses is the family house that now belongs to Minou. It's set back from the others, and is larger; the Drouets were people of means. To the right and stretching out behind it is a large garden, Minou's beloved garden, and in the middle of it is a very big cedar of Lebanon—her friend the tree. There's no one on the street as I walk down it, trying to be inconspicuous; no one peering out through the immaculate lace curtains that hang in every front window. Beyond Minou's house, the street dwindles into fields. As I pass, I'm startled to see a woman emerge from the back door and step into the garden, then go back inside. She's handsome—a woman in her fifties, dressed in good country clothes, her blond hair piled up on her head. She doesn't see me, and I'm both relieved that I haven't intruded on her privacy and moved at this fortuitous sighting.

As I head back, a man who's doing something under the hood of his car looks up at me sharply. How many strangers can have strolled down this quiet street, leading nowhere, since the days when it was "vomiting jour-nalists"? It turns out this man is aware that Mme. Le Canu was once some kind of writer, although he's never read anything she wrote. "She walks past here almost every day, carrying her basket to the market," he tells me. "She's very nice, good-looking, quite friendly." And he adds, "Her hus-band is much younger than she is." He seems to feel that this is a touch a journalist would appreciate; it certainly interests him more than the idea that his nice neighbor was once a famous child poet. Which only confirms my sense that although Minou Drouet may have grown up in La Guerche, she's not to be found there today. The woman living on this street, whom I've just had a glimpse of, is Mme. Jean-Paul Le Canu.

Weeks later, I talk to the writer Jean-Max Tixier, who, in the early nineties, collaborated with Minou on *Ma Vérité*. When he first saw the manuscript, he says, it was "very thin"; "only facts"; "close to unpublish-able." You can see why: This is a book pulling in two directions at once. You feel a strong internal pressure in Minou to disgorge her "truth," but there's an equally powerful impulse toward discretion, omission, sup-pression. It doesn't require much psychological acumen to figure out that what she needed to express and what she needed to suppress are the same thing: her anger at what had been done to her. "No one protected me. Adults rode on my back to exploit me. . . . I was caught up in the gears."

And who was the person who *should* have protected her? Her mother—the one who exposed her to the world, first as a beleaguered victim, then as a performing seal. Yet it's also her mother who rescued this semi-autistic, semi-blind orphan and gave her a life. Minou is rigorously fair, fully aware of her debt to the woman who adopted and succored her. But her account has very little warmth, and it leaves out a good deal—for in-stance, that her birth mother, who she discovered lived only a few kilome-ters away, had refused to meet her. One of the oddities of *Ma Vérité* is that the text switches back and forth between Minou's cautious memories and Tixier's commentary on them. It's as if he were reviewing the very book he's helping to write: "She sidesteps, she runs away, she doesn't remember, she's lost the documents that would clarify."

M. Tixier and his wife, Monique (who, luckily for me, speaks excel-lent English), spent time in La Guerche while he worked with Minou, and he tells me that, except for one or two paintings of her as a child, there's no sign in her house of her earlier existence—no copies of her books, no scrapbooks. "She's completely confined to her current world," he says.

"She didn't keep anything of the past." Although the Tixiers say they liked her, they found her strangely distant and affectless—much the way she came across on the telephone. "When we had dinner together, she was like a little girl, not like a grown woman," Monique Tixier remarked. "She sat in her place, very proper, well behaved, and, to be frank, uninteresting. It was strange—as if she were still carrying that little girl around inside herself." Some people deal with their pain by exploring and absorbing it; that, clearly, had proved impossible for Minou Drouet. Her way was to lop it off and bury it—by burying herself in La Guerche. Which leaves only her work to reveal her to us.

Her fiction offers few clues. The tales for children are almost exclusively about sensitive, special children and their beloved animals—loving squirrels, heroic dogs, loyal falcons. Her only novel for adults, called *Donatella* in its English translation, is a strongly felt, if peculiar, book that arbitrarily shifts its center of attention from a lonely boy who suddenly goes blind to a young, attractive nurse in training who does things like crouch all night by the bedside of an Arab boy who's dying of cancer, earning the enmity of the coarser nurses but winning the heart of a handsome young doctor. When these modest books were published, they received some favorable attention, but decades of silence followed—until *Ma Vérité*, which she could hardly bring herself to write and which she refused to promote. No wonder it passed unnoticed.

That leaves the poems and the letters. The poems are what grabbed attention back in the fifties, and they're still remarkable for their combination of naïveté and richness of imagination. A passage like the following is not the typical effusion of a seven- or eight-year-old:

> *I was the clock face*
> *whose hands bite the fleeting*
> *now,*
> *then silently*
> *move on to what is*
> *already no more,*
> *and from what is already no more*
> *life is born in me.*

A child who had been mute and isolated, both burdened and blessed with overwhelming feelings that she couldn't express, is bursting out, giving us the unmediated outpourings of an over-full heart. Is it great poetry? No. But it's no *supercherie*; it's real.

And in a way Minou is even more remarkable in her letters. Whether they're addressed to Lucette Descaves ("I cover your eyes with kisses") or to the Julliards ("I love you, my Arabesque, my Sonata, you are the two who are indispensable to me"), the letters spill over with everything she's doing, thinking, feeling. Perhaps the most extraordinary are those addressed to her friend Philippe, who's fifteen and has sworn to marry her when she grows up, and with whom she's made a pact: They will always think of each other at exactly eight in the evening. This is from the last letter that appears in *Arbre, Mon Ami*:

> My darling, it's eight o'clock, our eight o'clock. You remember the night when you said to me, in our cedar, "I love you so madly that if you want I'll go and find you the moon." . . . Philippe, at the eighth stroke of eight o'clock I plunged the sliver of crystal you sent me into the sea, at the place where the moon trembles, and I held it out to you, the moon, that living petal in its crystal cage. And I threw back my head and held out my hair to you, my hair in which you so loved to bury your face, it was the color of sad water and tasted of salt, and its tendrils were saying to you: You're loved.

This is Minou Drouet before she's eight—a primitive, an ecstatic, an original. A few years later, she's become a phenomenon, a scandal, a byword. "I was a lost child," she says. "I was only a pathetic little animal," she says. "What crime did I commit to be persecuted this way?" she asks. There is no answer. That she survived at all is a testament to her strength. That she lost Minou on her way to becoming Mme. Le Canu is the price she was willing to pay.

November 6, 2006

Free Spirit

The most famous woman of the first quarter of the twentieth century may have been Mary Pickford, but the most influential, and the most notorious, was Isadora Duncan. She was the progenitor and soul of a new art form, modern dance. She was the prototype of the uninhibited young American whose freshness and originality charmed jaded old Europe. And for decades she startled respectable society—even as she helped transform it—with her flouting of conventions, both onstage and off. You would have to go back to George Sand or Byron to find a comparably galvanizing figure. Early in 1927, in the fledgling *New Yorker*, Janet Flanner identified her as "the last of the trilogy of great female personalities our century produced," along with Duse and Bernhardt. But those two supreme actresses were dead ends; no one could follow in their footsteps. Isadora's accomplishments reverberate through the history of dance to this day.

Isadora Duncan was born in San Francisco in 1877, the youngest of four children. Her father regularly made and lost fortunes, and eventually was gone from the family (he was to die in a shipwreck—nothing the Duncans did was ordinary). The children and their mother lived from hand to mouth; there is more than a touch of Micawberism in the way they got by—high spirits in the midst of semi-penury. But already Isadora was demonstrating the vigorous independence that was to carry her to world fame.

In *Isadora: A Sensational Life*, Peter Kurth traces her blazing path. From the start she was clearly the Chosen One within what the family called the Clan Duncan. At eighteen, with her mother in tow and $25 in her pocket, she started east and soon wangled a job in Chicago with Augustin Daly's prestigious stage company, spending months in various demeaning

(to her) roles and developing "a perfect nausea for the theater." She confronted Daly: "What's the good of having me here, with my genius, when you make no use of me?" By the time she was twenty-one, she was established in New York, appearing in concerts, dancing to Chopin at special matinees, providing entertainment in private salons (including Mrs. Astor's, in Newport). She was young, slender, very pretty with her vivid red hair and Irish button nose, and exceedingly charming—a Botticelli figurine. She was also highly respectable, with her formidable mother at the piano and her brothers and sister accompanying her dancing with recitations, often from *The Rubaiyat*. Yet she was already shocking people with her "unobscured limbs." And she was already lecturing—hectoring?—her audiences about The Dance.

In May 1899, after a typical Duncan calamity (a near-fatal fire in their hotel), Isadora set out for the larger opportunities of Europe. Her reputation grew as she succeeded in London, then Paris, and was sealed in Budapest in 1902—twenty sold-out performances, ovations, roses thrown at her feet. She was also no longer a virgin. Oszkar Beregi, a handsome young actor, was performing Romeo, and very quickly she was his off-stage Juliet, only without benefit of Friar Lawrence. She had waited a long while to discover sex—she was twenty-five—but she would make up for lost time.

Not for long with Beregi, however; soon he tactfully suggested that she proceed with her career, and, having fantasized about marriage, she felt as if she had "eaten bushels of broken glass." On she went, though, to Vienna and Munich, where she had an even greater triumph. It was there, Kurth tells us, that "the German 'cult of Isadora' was born, a national craze that took her beyond success and notoriety into the realms of literature, philosophy, feminism and even science ... as the realization of Darwin's dream, the 'Dancer of the Future,' whose coming proclaimed the triumph of beauty and the liberation of women in the final perfection of the race." In *My Life*, her more readable than accurate autobiography, she recalls that it was in Berlin at this time that "on my return from performances where the audience had been delirious with joy, I would sit far into the night in my white tunic, with a glass of white milk beside me, poring over the pages of Kant's 'Critique of Pure Reason.'" Her bluestocking earnestness had found its perfect match in Germanic high seriousness. It was also in Berlin that she was invited by Cosima, the Widow Wagner, to perform in the bacchanal from *Tannhäuser* at Bayreuth. This experience proved to be a mixed blessing, but a passion for Cosima's son-in-law helped distract Isadora from the loss of Oszkar.

Through these years, she was constantly studying the sources of movement and refining her own liberating approach to dance, which she claimed to have discovered in the waves breaking on California shores, in the art of ancient Greece, in the ideas of Whitman, Nietzsche, and Wagner. Wherever she went, she proclaimed her aesthetic, both from the stage and in writing. Her costumes were scant, but she was shrouded in her lofty ideas: "Art which is not religious is not art, is mere merchandise." Within a short time she was being acclaimed everywhere as a profound revolutionary spirit.

But what was her dancing really like? She never allowed herself to be filmed, so all our evidence is secondhand. In a 1992 article, Anne Hollander, having studied the numberless photographs and artistic representations that constitute the massive Duncan iconography, reported that they

> tell a fairly consistent story, showing the thrusting knee, the bowed or thrown-back head, the open arms, the whirling colored stuffs veiling the torso. None show Duncan in midair. Along with running, she seems to have done a great deal of skipping and prancing, with her bare knees pushing up through slits in the drapery, but no high or broad leaping, no extended legs. Instead, she used the floor, kneeling and reclining, collapsing and rising. The face in the pictures is always blank—attention is riveted on those flashing naked legs and feet, those sweeping bare arms, that rounded exposed throat.

In other words, throw in Isadora's radical insistence that movement must come from the solar plexus, and here is modern dance. We also know how musical she was, responding spontaneously rather than analytically to her beloved Chopin, her Gluck, her Beethoven, her Brahms, her Wagner. In this, too, she was radical—critics violently disapproved of her presumption in dancing to symphonic masterpieces.

In 1903, Isadora temporarily abandoned her career so that the Duncans could fulfill their dream of setting foot in Greece, which—in order to make the trip "as primitive as possible"—they approached in a little sailing boat, at dawn. On the beach, Isadora and her brother Raymond knelt down and kissed the soil, Raymond declaiming poetry. "The inhabitants all came down to the beach to greet us, and the first landing of Christopher Columbus in America could not have caused more astonishment among the natives." Soon the clan had rejected their already unusual garments to don "tunic and chlamys and peplum"; they had already substituted sandals for shoes. (Isadora was to dress this way for much of her life, and Raymond for all of his.) They bought land and started to erect a temple, but alas, the land they had acquired had no water within two and a half miles. Still, "we were living under the reign of Agamemnon, Menelaus and Priam." (Priam, presumably, was on a visit from Troy.) After a year of the simple life, she was touring again, to the usual acclaim.

Soon Isadora met the man who was surely the great love of her life, the avant-garde stage designer Gordon Craig, who was the illegitimate son of Ellen Terry, England's most treasured actress. Craig was handsome, he was brilliant, and he was a ruthlessly selfish womanizer. (He was not only married but was the father of eight children, only four of them with his wife.) Craig brought Isadora the sexual and intellectual companionship she craved, the satisfaction of being linked with a great man (as she and he both saw him), and her first child, Deirdre. He also brought her anguish, as their passion and their competing obsessions with their work turned them into characters out of Strindberg. (The evidence is all there in Francis Steegmuller's invaluable edition of their correspondence, *"Your Isadora."*) As usual, Isadora held nothing back: "O I tell you I have no caution or care," she wrote to him, "& if I don't see you soon I will pull myself up by the roots & throw myself in the Sea. . . . Come nice growly Tiger—Eat me up . . . Come Eat me—Put your lips to mine & begin that way." Her need to give too much had found its fatal counterpart in his bottomless need to take.

Late in 1904, in the flush of her early happiness with Craig, she arrived in St. Petersburg on her first trip to Russia—a crucial moment in ballet history, given the liberating influence her dancing was to have on the young Michel Fokine's experiments. There has been endless discussion as to exactly how great an influence this was, but according to Diaghilev, she dealt the Russian ballet "a shock from which it could never recover." Despite her animadversions against ballet—"an expression of degeneration, of living death"—she was warmly welcomed by the ballet establishment and, of course, by the public. And she made a powerful impression on Stanislavsky, who later wrote, "It became clear to me that we were looking for one and the same thing in different branches of art."

It was around this time that Isadora began her lifelong struggle to establish a school for children. The first one was in Berlin, and was run mainly by her sister, Elizabeth; there were to be others. Wherever she went, Isadora battled to convince not only rich patrons but governments to back her grandiose plans. These schools were Isadora's obsession, reflecting both her determination to spread her word—that to live was to dance—and her fierce need to mother. For years she spent the fortune in fees she was earning to support them.

In her endless pursuit of money for the Berlin school, Isadora often joked about acquiring a millionaire, and as usual she had her way. In 1909, she encountered the astonishingly rich Paris Singer, an imposing, well-educated, and generally amiable forty-year-old who was one of the heirs of the Singer Sewing Machine Company. She reports: "He entered, tall and blond, curling hair and beard. My first thought was: Lohengrin." A second thought: "I realized that this was my millionaire, for whom I had sent my brain waves seeking." Lohengrin was instantly smitten, and soon was providing jewels, yachts, a magnificent château in which she could start yet another school, and a second child, Patrick. She loved Singer, was grateful to him, and then perversely and repeatedly treated him so badly that he backed away. The last straw came in 1917 when he offered to buy her Madison Square Garden. "What do you think I am, a circus?" she snapped. "I suppose you want me to advertise prizefights with my dancing!" At that, he was finally gone.

But by then she was no longer the Isadora the world had celebrated. Four years earlier had come the great tragedy of her life. Deirdre and Patrick, six and three years old, were drowned when the car they were riding in slid down a muddy embankment and into the Seine. It was a death blow to Isadora: "When real sorrow is encountered there is for the stricken no gesture, no expression. Like Niobe turned to stone, I sat and longed for annihilation in death." She fled to Greece with her brothers and sister; to Turkey, Italy, Switzerland, Paris, back to Italy, finding solace nowhere.

What eventually brought her back to life was dancing. Her most famous work during this period was *Marseillaise*, which ended with "her left breast bared in evocation of Delacroix's 'Liberty Leading the People,'" and she was to bare her breast in Europe and across North and South America throughout World War I. Agnes de Mille, who saw her at this time, described her as a "prematurely aged and bloated woman," yet added, "Isadora wore a blood-red robe which she threw over her shoulder as she stamped to the footlights and raised her arms in the great Duncan salute. . . . This was heroic and I never forgot it. No one who saw Isadora ever forgot her."

After a period of relative calm, the final significant episode of Isadora's life began in 1921 with an extended stay in the Soviet Union, which had promised her an official school. (She now saw herself as a Communist, insisting on being called "Comrade" by the startled Russians.) This was the trip that kindled her last full-blown romantic liaison, with the gifted but dangerously unstable poet Sergei Esenin. She was forty-five when they met; he was twenty-six. It was another case of love at first sight, followed at once by every kind of trouble—yet, presumably to ensure Esenin safe passage to the West, she married him, after decades of proclaiming herself above marriage.

To call this relationship a fiasco is to fail to do it justice. Disaster? Debacle? Catastrophe? He was violent, alcoholic, and untrustworthy, but also extraordinarily talented and famous—vital for Isadora. Besides, with his baby face and golden hair he reminded her of her poor dead little Patrick. (There's a recipe for marriage!) He loved her, needed her, sponged from her, abused her. They racketed around Europe and America creating bedlam wherever they went—drunken scenes, unpaid bills. (As one observer put it, "Every intelligent person, in Moscow and everywhere else they went, from Paris to Kansas City, knew that this blind union was a disaster to them both, as well as to the hotel furniture.") She got him back to Russia, where he dumped her; she saw him only twice more. A year later, he hanged himself in a hotel room, having first slit one of his wrists so that he could write a final poem in his blood.

By then she was back in France, and for the rest of her life she lived mainly in Nice and Paris. She was in a dire state. Friends loyally denied that she was a drunk, but she was one. And she was fat. The seventeen-year-old George Balanchine had watched her perform in Petrograd in the early twenties, and, with all the heartlessness of youth, saw her as "a drunken, fat woman who for hours was rolling around like a pig." (He did add, though, "She was probably a nice juicy girl when she was young.")

She was equally far gone emotionally. She had grown sexually rapacious and undiscriminating, and was living precariously, with occasional handouts from friends and a few francs earned from makeshift performances. There were pawnshops, dispossessions; always one step ahead of the sheriff. (On a train trip to Paris—the deluxe train, of course—the porter had to pay for her dinner.) Then, flings and extravagant generosity when money came through. Economy and moderation were, needless to say, alien to her nature. In 1927, desperate for cash, she finally settled down to write her memoirs. (Her publishers had insisted that she spice them up; well, maybe they were right—*My Life* is still in print.) Her last lover in residence was a young Russian musician, but she also became involved with the notorious Mercedes de Acosta, who later took up with Garbo and Dietrich, among others. The evidence points to a passionate affair. (Until then, Isadora had presumably been too busy with men, as she lurched from the famous—Picabia, Steichen, the pianist Harold Bauer, the war ace Roland Garros, to name a very few of her scores, even hundreds, of conquests—to just plain Joes like the stoker, the boxer, and the gigolo she dallied with on the steamship that took her to South America in 1916.

By the fall of 1927 she had little to look forward to; at fifty, and given her physical condition, she could not realistically count on a dance future. The famous death came swiftly. Flirting with a young garage mechanic from Nice, she demanded that he take her out in a racing car that she announced she was thinking of buying. (Isadora had always loved fast cars.) She stepped into the car wearing a large shawl that her closest friend, Mary Desti, had designed for her. *"Adieu, mes amis, je vais à la gloire,"* she cried. The fringes of the shawl caught in the spokes of the left rear wheel, the car started forward, and within seconds Isadora's neck was broken and she was dead. Desti confessed to her son, the director-to-be Preston Sturges, who was partly raised in the Duncan circle, that "actually it was a good thing. Isadora was drinking heavily, had become as fat as a balloon and was daily destroying the legends of her past loveliness and the dignity of her great position among the artists of the world." It is certainly tempting to see her instantaneous and painless death as a merciful release.

How to make sense of this immense, complicated, beautiful, and grotesque life? Many have tried: The Isadora Duncan literature is a tidal wave of loving reminiscence, obfuscation, self-glorification, infighting, and supposition by those who knew her, followed by a series of generally worthy biographies and extended commentaries on her work. And now there is Peter Kurth, sardonic yet appreciative, neither adoring nor denigrating. Manfully confessing in his preface that when he began, dance was "a field as foreign to me as physics or stock-car racing," he has stylishly synthesized the literature to give us the fullest and most coherent account of the life to date. He is least useful, naturally, on Isadora's dancing; nor is he particularly insightful about her psychological makeup. Fortunately, these are the two areas in which Fredrika Blair's *Isadora: Portrait of the Artist as a Woman*, published in 1986, is strongest: Blair believes in, and carefully places, Duncan's work, and she points gracefully, never heavily, to what she sees as the roots of Isadora's erratic behavior.

Yet despite such excellent work as Kurth's and Blair's, we are left with questions. First, how good a dancer was she? There is so much testimony to her performing genius, her irresistible stage charisma, that they can hardly be doubted. Consider: Edith Wharton ("That first sight of Isadora's dancing was a white milestone to me. It shed a light on every kind of beauty"); Diaghilev's great ballerina Tamara Karsavina ("She moved with those wonderful steps of hers with a simplicity and detachment that could only come through the intuition of genius itself"); the authoritative music critic Ernest Newman ("The soul becomes drunk with this endless succession of beautiful lines and groupings"); Frederick Ashton ("I got an impression of enormous grace, and enormous power in her dancing—she was very serious, and held the audience and held them completely"); Serge Koussevitsky ("She incarnated music in her dance"); Ruth St. Denis ("For Isadora, I would do battle. To reject her genius is unthinkable"); Rodin ("The greatest woman I have ever known. . . . Sometimes I think she is the greatest woman the world has ever known"). If we can't trust witnesses like these, whom can we trust?

It is her life that presents the unanswerable question. Why did this glorious girl, with the world at her feet, turn into the ghastly wreck who could say toward the end, "I don't dance anymore, I only move my weight around," and "There are only two things left, a drink and a boy"? The easiest explanation is that the death of the children permanently unhinged her. But the seeds of her destruction must always have been there, and two of her early New York friends suggest what they may have been.

Arnold Genthe, who took superb pictures of her, wrote in his memoirs: "Where her work was concerned she had integrity and patience, knowing no compromise with what she felt to be the truth about beauty. In her personal life she had charm and a naïve wit. Of tact and self-control she had very little, nor did she wish to have. She was the complete and willing tool of her impulses."

And the socialist writer Max Eastman, who knew her early and intimately, confesses that "despite her beautiful and triumphant deeds," her "courage, kindness, wit and true-heartedness," he did not like her. "She had made a cult of impulse and impracticality, rapture and abandon. . . . She had confused caprice with independence, heroics with heroism, mutiny with revolution. . . . How embarrassed I always was by the admirable force of character with which Isadora insisted on being half-baked."

In other words, she demanded total, untrammeled freedom. "I am the spiritual daughter of Walt Whitman," she had declared, and indeed "Song of Myself" could stand as a motto for her entire life. She is an extreme example of the American spirit of self-reliance that believes only in itself and refuses all limits. For Isadora there were no rules, there was only the Song of Herself; she lacked the discipline, the emotional and moral resources, to keep liberty from collapsing into license.

It was this that Max Eastman grasped and deplored. Yet he could also say, "All who have escaped in any degree from the rigidity and prissiness of our once national religion of negation owe a debt to Isadora Duncan's dancing. She rode the wave of revolt against Puritanism; she rode it, and with her fame and Dionysian raptures drove it on. She was—perhaps it is simplest to say—the crest of the wave, an event not only in art but in the history of life."

Janet Flanner, who wrote while Isadora was still alive, understood it this way: "Great artists are tragic. Genius is too large; and it may have been grandeur that proved Isadora's undoing—the grandeur of permanent ideals. She is too expansive for personal salvation."

December 30, 2001

La Duse

arly romantic accounts tell us that the world-renowned actress Eleonora Duse was born, in 1858, in a train, an appropriate setting for
someone who was to spend most of her life on the move. But no, she
was born in the northern Italian town of Vigevano. (A later international
icon, Rudolf Nureyev, actually *was* born in a train—and his life was as
nomadic, contradictory, and highly charged as hers.) In fact, there was
nothing romantic about Eleonora's childhood; it was hard in every way.

The Duse family had come down in the world from the days when her
grandfather had been a famous interpreter of Venetian comedy. Her father was a mediocre performer; her uncle, who now led the Duse family
troupe, was not much better. And her mother, Angelica, with no theatrical
background, ambition, or talent, had been forced by circumstance onto
the stage. Eleonora grew up in an impoverished and often desperate touring company, performing in ramshackle theaters, in barns, in town
squares. She made her debut at the age of four (as Cosette in a dramatization of *Les Misérables*; "Now scream—make the tears come, big tears!"
her mother coached her), and when Angelica died of tuberculosis, the
fourteen-year-old Eleonora found herself taking the company's leading
female roles. There was no one else.

She had almost no formal education—the company was never in one
place for very long—and she had no friends; there was no time to make
any. There was also, frequently, no fixed lodging, and often very little
food. ("I know what hunger is," she was to tell her daughter, "and what it
means to see night approaching when shelter is uncertain.") Perhaps worst
of all for a sensitive child, there was the stigma of the theater. *"Figlia di
commedianti!"* local children shouted after her—"Daughter of actors!"

Helen Sheehy begins her biography, *Eleonora Duse*, with a colorized

Eleonora Duse in *La città morta*

account of what many have seen as the turning point in Eleonora's early career: the occasion when she played Juliet "in Verona's ancient arena." According to Duse herself, reminiscing many years later, she was fired by the idea of playing this girl her own age—she was fourteen—in Juliet's own city. Every word she spoke seemed "to go right through the heat of my blood. There was not a fibre in me that did not contribute to the harmony. Oh, grace, it was a state of grace!" Among Duse's biographers, only William Weaver, in his highly informed *Duse* (1980), is dog-in-the-mangerish enough to suggest that the *Giulietta e Romeo* in which Eleonora found grace that day may not have been Shakespeare's but a version by a Veronese "printer and autodidact, whose drama was a local favorite."

The young Duse graduated from one touring repertory company to the next, always making a powerful impression—though not always a good one; there were those who found her unconventional looks off-putting, and her insistence on pursuing her unconventionally realistic acting style offended certain managers. Others found her strange but thrilling. When she was twenty and playing leading roles in a first-rate company, she allowed herself to be seduced by an influential newspaper editor/man-about-town in Naples, and to become pregnant by him. He abandoned her and the baby died. Soon after, she married an undistinguished actor in her company, Tebaldo Checchi, more for protection and counsel, as she acknowledged, than out of love. Her second child, Enrichetta, born in 1882, was the product of this union. Less than two months later, Sarah Bernhardt, at the height of her glory, came to Turin and enjoyed her usual triumph—exciting Duse, who was to say, "Only she was spoken of in the city, the salons, the theatre. One woman had done that! And, as a reaction, I felt liberated, I felt I had the right to do what I wanted, something other than what was imposed on me. . . ."

What she wanted to do was to challenge Bernhardt's position as the world's leading actress, and she was already well on her way to succeeding; by her mid-twenties, she was a major force in the Italian theater. And she had done it by imposing a new manner of acting that was diametrically opposite Bernhardt's—she was "natural" rather than stylized, simple rather than declamatory, life-sized rather than larger than life. Her repertory, however, under which she was already chafing, was mostly conventional and Bernhardtian—*La Dame aux Camélias, Fédora, Frou-Frou*. One breakthrough came with Giovanni Verga's verismo *Cavalleria rusticana*; another with *Thérèse Raquin*, adapted from Zola; another with one of her few comedies, Goldoni's *La locandiera*, in which she went on charming the world for decades.

Throughout her career she was on the lookout for more serious roles. She succeeded in Sudermann's famous *Magda*—a mix of Ibsen and the typical Bernhardt melodrama—and in Pinero's *The Second Mrs. Tanqueray*. Her sometime lover and lifelong friend Arrigo Boito translated *Antony and Cleopatra* for her—eliminating most of the historical elements and therefore most of Antony. She tried Goethe's *Egmont* in Berlin, acting in Italian while the rest of the cast spoke German. She thought she found greatness in the plays of her lover Gabriele D'Annunzio. She did find it in Ibsen: *A*

Doll's House, Hedda Gabler, Rosmersholm, Ghosts, The Lady from the Sea—plays, particularly the last, which were her mainstays in the later years of her career. Alas, she never played Chekhov, and although the young Pirandello admired her, she never appeared in his work.

In order to impose her methods, she formed her own company and was soon touring everywhere—triumphant in Vienna, Berlin, St. Petersburg. In the spring of 1885—she was twenty-six—she sailed for South America, opening in Rio (as Camille). At her benefit performance she was presented with diamonds, emeralds, pearls, and—from the emperor—a heavy gold bracelet. By this time she had acquired a lover (her leading man) and shed her husband; Tebaldo Checchi was no longer an asset. As for Enrichetta, she was carefully left behind in Europe and was never to be part of Duse's daily life—that is, the life of the theater. "Enrichetta an actress? Ah! No, no! Not while I live!"

The central attachment in this period of her life was to Boito, the composer of *Mefistofele* and librettist of Verdi's *Otello* and *Falstaff*. He was considerably older than she was, an eminant, sympathetic, but private and fastidious intellectual, who, Sheehy tells us, eventually "began to reveal impatience with Duse's suffocating neediness and her volatile emotions. . . ." Not surprisingly, the romantic relationship cooled and died, but he remained a faithful mentor until his death.

When she was in her late twenties, a friend saw her as an "excitable, morbid creature . . . an egoist who loves suffering." By the time she was thirty-five and celebrated throughout the Western world, she was, according to an early biographer, yearning for "an art in which her epoch would discover its greatness." She was ready, in other words, for Gabriele D'Annunzio, who both promised greatness and would all too readily satisfy her love of suffering.

Duse's relationship with D'Annunzio was the turning point of her life. He was five years her junior and already Italy's most famous writer—famous not only for his searing lyric poetry and impassioned literary and political manifestos but for his scandalous love affairs, which he publicized in overheated novels. When he and Duse began their affair, there were an aristocratic wife and three children stashed out of sight, to say nothing of a glamorous and highly vocal mistress. His attraction was not physical—it was his voice, his mesmeric life force, his "genius"—yet it was he who released her sexually. As for him, he had the satisfaction of more or less owning Italy's most exalted actress, who would carry his plays around the world—plays that were generally considered lacking in dramatic validity. No doubt he had felt genuine passion for her early on, but it faded; after all, by the time she reached forty she was *old*. She seems to have concurred, frequently referring to him as "my son."

Duse had always been in fragile health, and she was indeed aging prematurely, whereas D'Annunzio's appetite for younger and prettier women was insatiable. As he explained to her in a letter dated 1904, when their relationship finally ended, "My imperious need of the violent life—carnal life, the life of pleasure, physical danger, gaiety—has taken me far away . . . can you hold this need against me?" Apparently, she couldn't. Five years earlier, she had staged *La Gloria*, possibly his worst play. "The opening night audience in Naples," Helen Sheehy tells us,

> tried to stop the play and threatened to turn into a mob. A large claque whistled and booed and called out for d'Annunzio's death. Not even Duse's fame and reputation could stop the uproar. . . . Where was d'Annunzio while she was defending his play? "Me?" d'Annunzio told his friend Scarfoglio, "I was busy raping a nun!" In fact, while Duse was onstage, he had a "quick fuck" in the dressing room of a young actress who played a sister of charity in the play. Duse heard about the remark and the fornication, and she was furious.

But not furious enough to leave him. That same year he wrote to a friend,

> She is in the grip of a kind of evil demon that gives her no peace. The most profound tenderness, the purest devotion, are of no avail! She sees, on all sides, falsehood and intrigue around her.
>
> The sweet creature becomes unjust and cruel towards herself and towards me, irreparably.

What exactly did he expect?

If he had betrayed her only sexually, it would have been painful enough, but he also betrayed her professionally. Behind her back he gave a new play to her great rival, Bernhardt. Even more traumatic: Illness forced her to postpone another new play, at which point he handed it over to a much younger actress who had once been her protégée, and then demanded that Duse surrender the costumes she had already had made for herself. Duse accommodated him, and suffered the further humiliation of seeing the play and its young actress score a great success. Nevertheless, she went on producing his plays—at tremendous cost to herself. His leaden *Francesca da Rimini* almost bankrupted her, and when she insisted on touring America with an all-D'Annunzio repertory, it was a near disaster; she was forced to add *Magda* to the repertory. No wonder that one of her managers "reacted to every d'Annunzio play as if he had been offered the stinging end of a scorpion."

Finally, there was D'Annunzio's novel *Il Fuoco*—"The Flame"—which appeared in 1900 and became an immediate sensation in Italy and abroad. It was a rhapsodic, semipornographic account of his relationship with Duse in which she is portrayed as an aging woman desperate for sex, consumed by jealousy and a Phaedra-like passion for a younger man. ("They had fought together as though in combat, breath against breath, heart against heart; they had joined together as though in combat, they had tasted blood in their saliva. . . .") The book, set in Venice, is a delirium, and almost unreadable. Duse—"La Foscarina" in the book—is the quintessential fin de siècle all-consuming woman:

> Poisoned by art, weighed down by voluptuous knowledge, with the taste of ripeness and corruption in her eloquent lips, with the dryness of her vain feverish hands that had crushed the juice from deceitful fruits, with the traces of a hundred masks on her face that had imitated the wildness of all mortal passions. . . . Why was she joining her despairing vision to the magnificent purity of youth?

Wilde's *Salomé* lurks in the background.

D'Annunzio's pathology manifests itself throughout. "The woman's whole body had suddenly become a huge absorbing mouth that sucked him in entirely," he writes. And her embrace is compared to "the arms of a corpse that stiffen around a living man." But the dominant image is of "poison"—a word that runs through the book: "The poison burned through every fibre of her being. With him at the furthest point of pleasure, she had experienced a spasm that was not quite death but yet was beyond life."

Does this passage offer us literature's first female orgasm? (Henry James fails to comment on it in his guarded appreciation of *Il Fuoco*.) D'Annunzio could have offered the intensely private Duse no greater humiliation than to parade her sexual behavior before the world. Yet it seems that she read pages of *Il Fuoco* as D'Annunzio was writing it. She wrote to her manager, who was anxious about its possible effect on her career, "I know the book and I have authorized its publication. Because my suffering, whatever it may be, does not count, when it is a question of giving another masterpiece to Italian literature.... And besides, I am forty years old ... and I am in love!"

The relationship between Duse and D'Annunzio lingered on, Duse abandoning herself to a mania of jealousy, making violent public scenes. In one three-month period in 1899 she bombarded him with 162 telegrams as well as dozens of letters. Not until 1904 could she write to him, "Today I say to you: farewell—we are two—But I dead." Although she loyally went on presenting his work, they didn't meet for eighteen years. The drama had finally played itself out for her.

After D'Annunzio, it was at first business as usual—Scandinavia, the Balkans, South America. Duse entered into a collaboration with the renowned young French director/manager Lugné-Poe. She encountered and befriended Isadora Duncan, and employed Isadora's beloved Gordon Craig to design new sets for *Rosmersholm*—an episode that ended in disaster when his megalomania came up against her professionalism. And then her health began to give out and her will faltered; clearly, she was suffering from a serious depression. In January 1909 she stopped acting. She spent the war years, 1914 to 1918, in Italy, quietly assisting soldiers and their families, her only professional activity the making of her one film, *Cenere* (Ashes), a mother-son drama that gives us glimpses of her luminous presence. The immediate post-war years she spent in aimless drifting. Only in 1921, driven in part by financial necessity, did she go back to the theater, opening to tumultuous acclaim in Turin, in *The Lady from the Sea*. The audience, Sheehy recounts, "all stood and cheered. 'Viva Duse! Viva Italy!'" She had been off the stage for twelve years.

By now, she had gone beyond celebrity. The scandal of *Il Fuoco* behind her, she was perceived as a spiritual force; her rare performances— sometimes no more than two a week—were greeted as near-religious occasions. On her final American tour, early in 1924, her body collapsed; the weak lungs she had inherited from her mother betrayed her—she needed oxygen tanks in the wings to keep her going. It was in Pittsburgh, a city she hated, that she was stricken with pneumonia. She struggled through her last performance and was carried back to her hotel. "I do not want to die here," she said, but she did die there.

Her body was taken first to New York, where thousands lined the streets outside the funeral parlor. Among the tributes was a bouquet from Mussolini, the Duce, with the inscription "To Italy's First Daughter." She had recently rejected his offer of a state pension, but D'Annunzio, hearing the news of her death, sent a telegram to his onetime political rival: "The tragic destiny of Eleonora Duse could not be accomplished more tragically. Far from Italy the most Italian of hearts has died. I ask that the adored body be returned to Italy at the Government's expense. I am certain that my pain is the pain of all Italians. Listen to my prayer, and answer."

Mussolini listened, and complied.

The testimony to Duse's greatness as an actress is almost universal. The most famous assessment came from George Bernard Shaw in several reviews that convincingly propose that Duse was far superior to Sarah Bernhardt. Shaw speaks of the "extraordinary richness of her art," "this rare consummation," her "magical skill." Perceptive observers everywhere were overwhelmed by her powers. The young Hugo von Hofmannsthal, Sheehy tells us, "compared her Vienna debut to the ancient Great Dionysia in Athens." To the most respected American theater critic, Stark Young, she not only understood *Ghosts* and *The Lady from the Sea* better than Ibsen did but she "does not exemplify the art of acting so much as she illustrates the fundamentals of all art." To Eva Le Gallienne, in her hagiographic book on Duse, she was "the incarnation of everything that the theatre, in its very highest form, could be." Chekhov, seeing her in Moscow, wrote to his sister, "I don't understand Italian, but she played so beautifully that I had the feeling that I understood every word. . . . I've never seen anything like it." Nazimova: "She is art. She is inspiration itself." Chaplin: "Eleonora Duse is the greatest artiste I have ever seen."

It's almost a relief to turn to Max Beerbohm, Shaw's successor on *The Saturday Review*. "I am willing to take Duse's technique on trust," he writes, "but I cannot rave about it: I can but consume myself with envy of my colleagues, and wish I had made a better use of my opportunities for learning Italian." On a less impish note, he writes:

> I cannot surrender myself, and see in her the "incarnate woman-hood" and "the very spirit of the world's tears" and all those other things which other critics see in her. My prevailing impression is of a great egoistic force; of a woman overriding, with an air of sombre unconcern, plays, mimes, critics and public. . . . I dislike it. I resent it. In the name of art, I protest against it.

In the twenties, the great English actress Sybil Thorndike said, "Duse had the universal spirit. She was humankind; that is why, to me, she is greater than all others." But Beerbohm wanted her to play specific characters, not humankind; no one was more allergic than he to the ineffable.

Many aspects of Duse's nature and history are open to reconsideration, and Sheehy's book is in certain respects a refreshingly corrective one. But sometimes the evidence she presents is slim. She gives us Duse as a mother repelled by her child. "Who can you tell, for example," Duse wrote to Boito, "about the sadness, the physical, yes physical repulsion, alas, of a hand that touches you? The heart goes back and forth all day between the desire to help, and the instinct that revolts, because of a word, some minor thing, some character trait that reminds you, implacably, of its origin—the father's like that—in her, and you see him. No—it's horrible!"

It *is* horrible, but it is counterbalanced by a stream of testimony from others of Duse's concern and affection for Enrichetta. Her strongest impulse toward her daughter was to keep her away from the theater, to raise her as a proper, upper-class girl in convents and German or Swiss boarding schools. No one was going to run after *her* child shouting *"Figlia di commedianti!"* And she succeeded: Enrichetta married a sober, God-fearing Englishman, and raised two children who eventually entered the church. Mother and daughter met and spent time together, but no one could call their relationship an intimate one. Duse chose not to attend her daughter's wedding, in 1908, writing to a friend, "I'm happy to have her married far away, where my name isn't profaned by legend." (She's Stella Dallas!) She had always been her daughter's sole support, however; as Sheehy wittily points out, she "may have been a bad mother, but she had been, by the standards of the day, an exemplary father." It's telling, though, that whereas Duse saved Enrichetta's letters, Enrichetta burned hers.

Sheehy's treatment of Tebaldo Checchi is also one-sided. She has nothing good to say about this sad sack, for whom even Duse had kind words in later years, and who is warmly praised as a decent and devoted man by biographers who knew her. Sheehy prefers to believe, on the basis of what she acknowledges to be "circumstantial evidence," that on that first South American tour, Tebaldo took sexual advantage of a thirteen-year-old girl in the company. To Duse's friend and early biographer E. A. Rheinhardt, however, Tebaldo's nature "was great and magnanimous." Perhaps more significant is the testimony of Matilde Serao, a famous writer who had been the closest of friends to Duse since the early Naples days. She wrote to Rheinhardt that in later years the image of Tebaldo "became ever more beautiful to Eleonora."

More than her numerous predecessors—there are at least seven biographies in English—Sheehy makes much of Duse's extraordinary capacity for flattery, her relentless pursuit of those who could help her. It was Matilde Serao who "taught Duse practical techniques of ingratiating herself with prominent families, and the art of utilitarian flattery and self-promotion, which Duse would use on society leaders and critics for the rest of her life." Indeed, Sheehy is the only biographer who sees Duse less as the victim of her first seducer than as an ambitious, attractive actress happy to be taken up by an influential and sophisticated but physically unattractive man. (D'Annunzio, as we have seen, was no beauty, either.)

Wherever she went, Duse made friends who did their best to help her—rich ladies or ardent young women in particular, who would leave their homes to travel with her when she demanded companionship. What she could offer them was affection and the apparently enviable opportunity to serve her. On her first American tour she was befriended by the highly respected and well-situated Gilder family, whose New York home became a refuge for her. "I bankrupt myself to tell you that I love you," she cabled Helena Gilder on her return to London. The Gilders reciprocated by commissioning a cast of her right hand. Recently, there was an auction on eBay for a note from Duse to a Portuguese duchesa: *"Tendres amitiés!"* "Thinking of you always! Love from your Leonore!"

But that she flattered her adoring fans and accepted both gifts and service from them doesn't mean that Duse was hypocritical. She was clearly swift in her affections, and sincere—in the short run. Generous to young actresses, quick to pity, her own sufferings made her sensitive to the suffering of others. Her friend Jeanne Bordeux, whose biography appeared in 1925, only a year after Duse's death, sums her up convincingly:

> She had a dual personality in the fullest meaning of the phrase. She was a superb intellect, capable of doing the most absurd things; she was grand in thought and action, and she was petty. She was the personification of refinement, and in anger violent almost to the point of vulgarity. Sincere, but changeable as the wind; stubborn, yet easily influenced; strong to defend, easy to offend; a woman of intense desires, passionate friendships, that in a second might change to ardent dislikes. Hopelessly extravagant, mean to the point of stinginess with herself, generous to the extreme with those who had her sympathy. . . . A divine, difficult mistress, a tender, loving companion—until someone or something changed her. . . . Adorable, impossible.

Even more than Duse craved social respectability, she aspired to the intellectual and the cultured. Like so many autodidacts, she was a fanatical reader, carting trunkloads of books around with her on her endless tours: Emerson, William James's *The Varieties of Religious Experience*, Wilde's *De Profundis*, Dante's *La Vita Nuova*, Shelley, Byron, Goethe, Sophocles, Shakespeare. Her friendships were not only with rich people who could be of practical use to her; if anything, she was more interested in cultivating men she could revere, like Rilke—who admired her but, Sheehy tells us, saw the humor in her overwrought responses, suspecting that "because of her temperament she needed to dramatize the most ordinary moments"—and Romain Rolland, who records her quoting Plotinus. Her lack of formal education, in one biographer's words, "made her the eternal disciple."

With her colleagues—that is, with the actors she hired for her various companies—she was demanding and inspiring, veering from aloofness to generosity, but never matey. By far the most convincing account we have

of her as a professional comes from a young, obscure actor, Guido Noccioli, who played tiny roles on Duse's South American tour of 1906–1907
and kept a journal. (It was published in English in 1982 as *Duse on Tour*,
with a superb introduction by its translator, Giovanni Pontiero.) Here we
see her close-up, under pressure, and at times out of control. "'I am the one
who pays here. And I demand and fully intend to have things done my
way.'" "'After all, I am the Eleonora Duse who has done more than anyone else to enhance the reputation of Italian drama throughout the world.'"
At one rehearsal, "A stream of recriminations came pouring out from her
lips like lava from a volcano. . . . It is impossible to capture in words the
bitterness, anger, and spite that consume the Signora at such moments.
The rest of the cast looks on in terror—that is the only word to express
our dismay."

In extenuation, consider what Eva Le Gallienne has to say about the
"restless, feverish climate of theatre life," with all the "entanglements . . .
laid before the actor-manager—the 'star'—who is expected to untangle
them and solve them. Such a climate is not conducive to the attainment of
spiritual serenity."

Noccioli's journal has the ring of truth—and none of the narcissism
you might expect from a young actor in the presence of a great star. (No
wonder he vanished from the theater world.) Observing Duse closely, he
sees that she is uneven in performance. "The Signora muddles line after
line! The actors who have to converse with her do not know where to
turn. The prompter shouts himself hoarse but to no avail." He believes
another actor "to be correct when he claims that La Duse of today is no
longer the artist of former years." And yet he can say, in summation,

> To question anything with Eleonora Duse is quite impossible. For
> she possesses the most extraordinary powers of persuasion. . . . Her
> voice is so heavenly! Her teeth so perfect, her smile so winning!
> That is how La Duse strikes one: for, despite everything, despite
> the fact that she is about to celebrate her fiftieth birthday, despite
> the lines on her face and her grey hairs, La Duse is *beautiful*!

This was Duse in extremity, after D'Annunzio and before her volun-
tary exile from the theater. On her return to acting in 1921, only three
years before her death, she apparently had reached a transcendent purity

of expression that conveyed to the audience an aura of spiritual exalta-tion. She was, in fact, being seen in semireligious terms—perhaps the only stage performer in history whom audiences literally worshipped. William Weaver comments, "For her cult she was more than an artist: she was virtually a saint." Rheinhardt assures us, "She went on and on like St. Catherine of Siena." Saint Teresa of Avila is evoked as well. But Jeanne Bordeux trumps the saint ace, assuring us that "in the last ten years of her life Eleonora Duse walked very close to the Divine Son, bearing nobly her Cross, as in fact she had borne it from birth, fulfilling to the best of her ability the mission for which she was sent into the world."

The discrepancy between the late sanctification and the early notori-ety Duse had earned for her revolutionary sensuality onstage is startling. As her career got under way, reviewers everywhere, Sheehy points out, "remarked on her wild passion. Critics lingered over descriptions of her sensuous mouth, languid eyelids, nostrils that flared in anger, caressing fingers, and supple body." "In *La Dame aux camélias*, instead of kissing Armand Duval chastely and traditionally on the forehead, her Margue-rite kissed him on the lips, as if she were drinking him in one last time." Forty years later, she is Saint Catherine of Siena, if not Our Lord Himself.

One trajectory that can be compared to Duse's is that of Greta Garbo, who began as the steamiest actress ever to have appeared on the screen, her love scenes with her real-life lover John Gilbert shocking the world, and who ended as a hypnotic enigma of whom the world was in awe. Garbo's childhood was as unhappy and sordid as Duse's; her looks, at first, as questionable. She, too, was whimsical, perverse, aloof, completely de-termined on having her own way. Like Duse, she had a circle of adoring friends whom she counted on and used, but she was even more emotion-ally withholding than Duse (who did give herself completely once, though disastrously, to D'Annunzio). Both women were at heart outsiders, al-though Duse, as an international stage actress, had to be out in the world, whereas Garbo, insulated by MGM, could and did seal herself off from her surroundings. Garbo's famous resistance to the intrusions of the press was foreshadowed by Duse, who hated being interviewed, proclaiming that artists "belong to the public and to the critics only in that moment in which we appear on stage." Once, turning to a reporter in New York (who presumably spoke Italian), she insisted, "I wish to be left alone."

Helen Sheehy points out how her "convincing portrayal of an artist without ambition who cared only for art and nothing for publicity" only added to Duse's legend, and this of course was true of Garbo as well. But Duse's impulse toward privacy, even on occasion toward anonymity, also reflected a deep shyness and insecurity; she escaped her childhood but never overcame it. For all her proclaimed suffering, she lived most fully when she was inhabiting other women. She said it herself: "We actors bear a curse: being separated from life, not understanding human beings beyond those we pretend to be on stage, acting what other men live." Can it be this ultimate loneliness that gave these two women their mystery and allure? Were they worshipped because they were unreachable—and remain, despite all the biographies, unknowable?

December 18, 2003

The Silent Superstar

With the possible exception of his great friend Charlie Chaplin, the biggest male star of silent films, and the most loved, was Douglas Fairbanks, the idol of millions of young boys—and a large number of grown-up boys, too. He was number one at the box office in 1919, before he began swashbuckling, and he stayed number one through the 1920s, his eight major productions bringing in even more money than the movies released in the same period by his wife, Mary Pickford—America's (and the world's) sweetheart.

Fairbanks was born in 1883, and to coincide with his 125th birthday, an ambitious book—*Douglas Fairbanks*, by Jeffrey Vance with Tony Maietta—has just been published. At times it approaches hagiography, but it tells you a lot about its hero, and it's generously illustrated—essential for a performer whose impact was so overwhelmingly physical.

Douglas Fairbanks stood for pluck, vigor, decency, the healthy mind in the healthy body, good old American ingenuity, up-by-your-bootstraps optimism, respect amounting to shyness for the weaker sex, and—most important—success. ("Whenever he doodled with pencil and pad," wrote Pickford, ". . . he would write those two magic syllables over and over again, in strong printed letters.") Failure was not an acceptable option. Why was he disappointed in the Grand Canyon? "I couldn't jump it."

So whether he was playing the Lamb or the Matrimaniac or the Mollycoddle or Mr. Fix-It or the Nut, whenever Doug attempted something, he inevitably succeeded. His weapons before he took to the sword—and equally effective—were his astounding athleticism, his insouciant charm, his patent goodwill, and a huge, irresistible smile. He wasn't tall, he wasn't particularly good-looking, he didn't radiate sexuality—he was the anti-Valentino. Yet he left Valentino in the dust. His effective career, like

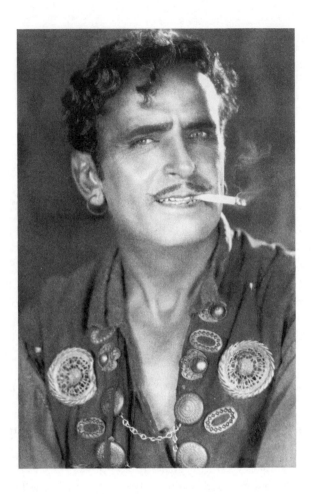

all silent-screen careers, was short, yet between 1915 and 1929 he made thirty-eight silent movies, every one of them a success and, once he got going, all of them conceived and produced by himself.

It was a career divided in two—the early romantic comedy-adventures followed by the swashbucklers—with a sad coda in the early days of sound. But Fairbanks didn't begin in film: By the time he took the plunge he was a highly successful young romantic lead on Broadway. That's why the movies wanted him, rounding him up for the camera along with a clutch of other "legitimate" actors, including Sarah Bernhardt and Sir Herbert Beerbohm-Tree. It was money that lured him into the decidedly déclassé world of the "flickers"—a guaranteed $2,000 a week, far more than he could hope to earn on the stage. Why not give it a try? Besides, part of the deal was that his films would be supervised by D. W. Griffith, whose *Birth of a Nation* had fired his imagination early in 1915. But Doug's first movie, *The Lamb*, was hardly supervised by Griffith, who wrote him off as "that jumping-jack, that grinning monkey" with a face like a cantaloupe, and suggested that he go work for Mack Sennett, along with the Keystone Kops and the custard pies.

As it turned out, film proved to be the perfect medium for Douglas Fairbanks. We get a sense of his stage persona from the amused theater critic Percy Hammond, writing about him in the 1913 play *Hawthorne of the U.S.A.*:

> Bounding, sprinting, diving, hurdling, he arrived in the last act in time to say "I love you" to the slim princess, as the curtain fell. Meantime Hawthorne, impersonated by Mr. Fairbanks, had also smashed the bank at Monte Carlo, arrested a regicide, escaped from jail, harangued a mob, acted as king for a few minutes, and had introduced slang and chewing gum into the Balkans. In one scene he punched the Secretary of War, upset much of the army, and kicked a seditious prince in the chest before jumping off a balcony for the second time in the act. It makes one breathless to write about it.

This all sounds far more like a movie than a play, and we can see in retrospect that the stage couldn't really contain Doug's almost manic energy and amazing physical prowess.

His screen character—the restless, eager, somewhat goofy young man who's flung into circumstances that allow him to morph into a hero (and win The Girl)—was fixed from the start. The story might have him playing an effete easterner converted into a "real" American by the Old West, or demonstrating manly American virtues in decadent Europe or corrupt Latin America, or good-humoredly asserting American common sense in response to vogues like health faddism or pacifism, but in all these plots he was the exact same wholesome, attractive fellow he had always been. And which, to a great extent, he was in real life.

That's why in his case the audience to a remarkable degree blurred the boundaries between actor and role. No one really believed that Lillian Gish was actually a fragile victim, or that Theda Bara (anagram: Arab Death) was an exotic man-killer, or that Valentino was a sheikh, but Doug's fans seemed to assume that all those Lambs and Mollycoddles up on the screen were simply projections of the actor himself, a man whom every mother could be proud of, every girl trust herself to, and every kid idolize.

You can't exaggerate the extent to which Fairbanks embodied what in the 1910s were accepted as the quintessential American virtues. He was a Horatio Alger paragon—cheerfully rising to the top through hard work and a happy disposition. He was, like his hero Teddy Roosevelt, a vigorous outdoorsman and an ardent patriot—not for nothing were three of his films called *The Americano, American Aristocracy,* and *His Majesty the American.* He was Billy Sunday, preaching sobriety (he didn't drink), clean living, and respect for God, Woman, and the work ethic. He was a Boy Scout—and, indeed, wrote regularly for *Boys' Life,* the official Boy Scout magazine. Yet he wasn't a goody-goody: He was a regular guy, enterprising but unaggressive—until roused to challenge (and, of course, trounce) bullies and mashers and crooks.

And he was an extraordinary athlete, totally at ease in the saddle and preternaturally agile; he was a master fencer, an archer, a swimmer, a boxer, a wrestler. Why enter a house through the front door and climb the stairs when you can bound up the side of the building and dive in through a window? Why not spring from a galloping horse into a speeding train, or outrun an automobile? Why not slide down the vast castle draperies or thrust your knife into the topmost sail of a pirate ship and slice your way down to the deck? Why not vault over anything in your path? Fairbanks never encountered a chair or a table he didn't hurtle over, not to show off but because his inexhaustible energy demanded it. And as the whole world knew, he did all these things himself—no stuntmen or doubles—except (very rarely) when he didn't. If Mary Pickford was America's sweetheart, he was the all-American boy.

That, however, was not the way he started out. Douglas Elton Ulman had two distinctly unusual parents. His mother, Ella, was self-proclaimed Southern gentry, who married a well-to-do planter named John Fairbanks. Their son, also John, was born in 1873, John Sr. dying of tuberculosis that same year. Ella then married Judge Edward Wilcox, by whom she had another son, Norris. When Wilcox turned out to be an abusive drunk, she procured a divorce with the help of a well-known New York lawyer, H. Charles Ulman, who in turn fell in love with her and married her.

In the many early accounts of Doug's life, we're told only that Ulman was an important figure in the New York legal community, but that the erratic marital career of Ella made it politic for them to get out of town—a move made simpler by her decision to take little Johnny Fairbanks with her but to leave behind with a paternal aunt even littler Norris Wilcox. (Many decades later, his half brothers would rescue the abandoned Norris from obscurity and bring him into the thriving Fairbanks enterprise.) In Denver, Ella and Ulman quickly had two more boys, Robert and Douglas.

Young Doug was a perplexing child. If you believe the official version, he was a glum, lethargic boy until one day he fell off the roof while clambering around and basked in all the attention he received, instantly and forever becoming the life of the party. He also was unusually dark-complexioned—for a while when Ella had him out in a baby carriage she would cover his face to ward off reactions from passersby. But that was merely an oddity of biology. There were secrets as well.

Number one: Ulman was Jewish.

Number two: Ulman was a drunk, whom Ella booted out when Doug was five. She also discarded his name and resumed that of her first husband, Fairbanks, bestowing it on Bob and Doug as well, baptizing them in the Catholic faith, and opening a rooming house. She now had three husbands and four sons under her belt, as it were.

Number three: Ulman hadn't been legally divorced from his first wife, back in Brooklyn—the real reason, clearly, why he and Ella had to hightail it out of town. (Only decades after Doug's death did this fact leak into print.)

In other words, Douglas Fairbanks was the son of a Jewish drunk and the product of a bigamous relationship—or to put it more directly, was illegitimate. Not exactly the all-American story.

Ella was the lodestone of Douglas's life—she adored him, pampered him, fought for him—yet Ulman, despite his transgressions, was also a strong influence on his famous son's life. He was passionately interested in the theater, claiming to have been a friend of Edwin Booth and worshipping (and often publicly declaiming) Shakespeare. Doug was infected by his father's love for the stage, and the far-seeing and businesslike Ella encouraged him, realizing that acting might be an escape route out of the genteel poverty in which they were living. When he was just short of sixteen, Doug managed to get himself expelled from high school so that he could jump-start his career.

The sequence of events that followed is obscure. Later he told stories of studying at the Colorado School of Mines (that was probably his brother Robert), of attending bullfights in Spain (where he had never been), of studying at Harvard (which had never heard of him), of a cattle-boat trip to Europe, of hiking across Cuba—or was it Yucatán?—on a bet. Fairbanks clearly was a serial fabulist—as Vance and Maietta put it, "neither a truthful or a comprehensive chronicler of his own life." (His most astute biographer, Booton Herndon, phrased it more delicately: "He would not permit objective reality to interfere.")

What's certain is that like a character in one of his own movies, by luck and pluck Doug insinuated himself early on into the good graces—and the repertory company—of a well-known actor-manager of the day. He liked to exaggerate the difficulties he had faced, but in reality he was a shoo-in almost from the start, his trajectory as an actor never wavering once he got going. By 1902, at nineteen, he was on Broadway; by 1908 he was a star.

He was also a husband. Beth Sully, daughter of "The Cotton King," was a pleasing, plumpish—and rich—young debutante who fell madly in love with him. Doug loved her enough to marry her, and things went well between them, since Beth dealt with him much as Ella had done—admired him, spoiled him, and deftly managed his career and his finances. The Cotton King eventually lost his money, but by then Doug himself was rich.

And he was a father. In 1909 a son was born, whom he named Douglas Jr., a decision he was to bitterly regret. He seems to have been utterly without paternal instincts or feelings, from the start ignoring the boy as much as he could. (Doug Jr.: "I always associated him with a pleasant, energetic, and agreeable 'atmosphere' about the house, to which I was somehow attached but which was not attached to me.")

Through the years after he and Beth separated, Senior barely acknowledged Junior's existence. With his frank and generous nature, Junior, in his memoir, *Salad Days*, tells us, "Mother minded his lack of interest in me dreadfully, but although I was sorry, I didn't brood about it. He remained my distantly related hero." When, however, at the age of fourteen Junior—needing to help support his mother and himself—got a start in the movies, his father was furious at the boy's presumption in using the famous name, and did his best to block his career. As he put it to Donald Crisp, who dared to cast the boy, "There's only *one* Fairbanks."

The great love of Doug's life was Mary Pickford, nine years his junior. They met almost casually and eased into an intense (and secret) relationship. Mary had been married to Owen Moore, a handsome but unreliable actor and drunk, who apart from everything else was loathed by the most important person in her life, her mother, another supremely capable businesswoman.

Mary had had a grim start, barnstorming the country from her earliest years in order to support her widowed mother and her two feckless younger siblings. She had no real childhood—no schooling, no friends— and was usually on the road, often alone. All this made her strong, anxious, serious, and gave her an almost compulsive interest in money and security. It did not assuage her anxieties that by the time she was in her earliest twenties she had browbeaten Adolph Zukor—the head of Paramount and no slouch when it came to negotiating contracts—into paying her more than half a million dollars a year.

The crucial moment in Mary and Doug's relationship came in 1916, just after Ella Fairbanks's sudden death. Doug was completely unmanned, and one day, riding with Mary in a car in Central Park, he broke down in a tempest of grief and sobbed in her arms. He had found yet another supportive, semi-maternal figure, only this time she was also a woman of unique beauty, riches, and prestige—indeed, the best-loved woman in the world. His agreeable, passionless marriage to Beth had no chance; he had fallen madly in love.

Divorces were taboo in those days, particularly for stars with the squeaky-clean reputations of Mary and Doug, but by 1920, with Beth's dignified acceptance and Owen Moore's bought complicity, they were finally able to marry. Terrified that they might fall out of public favor, they slipped away for a European honeymoon—and were astonished by the greeting they received, literally mobbed by fans wherever they went, even at times in danger from the uncontrollable crowds. After the madness of the major capitals, they fled incognito to Germany. But, confessed Mary, "it was in Wiesbaden that Douglas and I changed our minds about one thing: no matter how demanding and exhausting the crowds were, they were infinitely preferable to being either completely unknown, or, if known, completely ignored. . . . 'Let's go someplace where we are known. I've had enough obscurity for a lifetime.'"

This was also a time of rethinking their careers. In 1919, they had joined Griffith and Chaplin in forming United Artists, which allowed them to cut out the studios, financing and entirely controlling their movies and profiting even more greatly from them. Film lore gives most of the credit for this coup to the redoubtable Mary, backed by Ma Pickford, but Chaplin too was obsessed by money, and Doug was considerably shrewder than his devil-may-care image suggested.

The new arrangement gave Doug full license both to switch genres and to push the art of filmmaking in revolutionary ways. Not only were the spectacles that followed *The Mark of Zorro*, the first of them, on a scale that only Griffith had dared (and Fairbanks's *Robin Hood* cost twice as much as *Intolerance*), but Doug was free to hire distinguished (and expensive) artists and composers, often from Europe; first-rate action-directors like Allan Dwan and Raoul Walsh; and superb cameramen like Victor Fleming, the future director of *Gone with the Wind* and *The Wizard of Oz*.

And with the help of his engineer-brother Robert, he was able to dramatically expand the possibilities of set construction and special effects— slow-motion photography, double exposure, use of miniatures, even animation. It was not by accident that his *Black Pirate*, in 1926, was the first full-scale two-strip Technicolor film—a daring venture, since the costs of color were daunting, and there was real concern over possible eyestrain! (*The Black Pirate* turned out to be a terrific action picture, a huge hit, and the template for all those future pirates like Errol Flynn, Tyrone Power, Burt Lancaster, and Johnny Depp.)

Yet despite all the collaboration that Fairbanks solicited and appreciated, he was unquestionably the most active and authoritative figure in the creation of his films. He chose or invented his subjects, cast his fellow actors, co-wrote or polished his scripts, oversaw sets, costumes, props, music, editing. His directors, including Dwan and Walsh, were there to carry out his wishes—and were glad to do so. "You don't know—nobody can know, without working with him—how he is loved and admired by the people he gathers around him," said Al Parker, who directed *The Black Pirate*.

The Fairbanks heroes in the swashbucklers show more variety than those in the comedies. His performances in *Zorro* and *Don Q, Son of Zorro* (he plays both father and son) are sheer scintillating bravura. Although his *Robin Hood* movie drags at times, and is almost overwhelmed by its mammoth sets, his Robin conquers with his dazzling action sequences and dazzling smile. His young d'Artagnan in *The Three Musketeers* has the right swagger, although he's considerably less loutish than the Dumas original, and the aging d'Artagnan of *The Iron Mask*—the last of the spectacles—has a moving elegiac tone.

The most strikingly original of the eight extravaganzas is *The Thief of Bagdad*. There was no precedent for so artistically ambitious a fantasy-adventure. The Fairbanks crew created an elaborately stylized Baghdad, and Doug, at forty, depicted a charming young(ish) Thief who was focused less on thrilling audiences with his physical tricks and more on the ease and grace of his flowing and effortless movement. As he soars joyously around—and above—the streets of Baghdad, the obvious model is the Nijinsky of *Schéhérazade*. After seeing *The Thief of Bagdad* (ten times!) Vachel Lindsay wrote: "The history of the movies is now David Wark Griffith, Douglas Fairbanks, and whoever rises hereafter to dispute their title."

The most atypical and controversial of the spectacles is *The Gaucho* (1927). On the one hand, it projects a heavy-handed religiosity, featuring a cameo performance by Pickford as a vision of the Madonna—no one else was considered pure enough to assume the role. (Mary saw this as "a lovely compliment.") On the other hand, *The Gaucho* is the only one of all his movies in which Fairbanks is frankly sexual. He's a hot-blooded Latin lover, with the equally hot-blooded Lupe Velez (at nineteen) as his love object. When he wraps his bullwhip around the two of them, then tucks his cigarette inside his cheek and mashes her lips with his, he's a long way from *The Lamb*. But then it was generally assumed that he and Lupe were considerably more to each other than co-stars.

Doug and Mary were now not just the biggest of movie stars and the most famous of married couples, they were the closest America had come to royalty. As a perceptive journalist wrote in 1927, they were

> the King and Queen of Hollywood, providing the necessary air of dignity, sobriety, and aristocracy. Gravely they attend movie openings, cornerstone layings, gravely sit at the head of the table at the long dinners in honor of the cinema great, Douglas making graceful speeches, Mary conducting herself with the self-abnegation of Queen Mary of Britain. . . . They understand thoroughly their obligation to be present, in the best interests of the motion picture industry.

Their famous house, Pickfair, was second in fame only to the White House among America's residences, and there they graciously received Hollywood's most important visitors (the Duke and Duchess of Alba, Lord and Lady Mountbatten, the King and Queen of Siam) as well as the industry's A-list. The table was always set for fifteen, and after dinner and an evening with their guests spent watching movies in the living room, "at around eleven, Albert, 'the majordomo,' passed around fruit and cups of Ovaltine, the guests went home and Mary and Doug climbed the stairs to bed."

By the mid-twenties, though, the marriage had begun to erode, along with the world that had given birth to them both. Crucial was the coming of sound. Although Doug had a good, stage-trained voice, his world was visual, physical. Silent, he was unique; speaking, he was no more exciting than a lot of other capable actors. As for Mary, she had spent her childhood on the stage, even working for Belasco on Broadway, but her appeal, too, was lessened by sound. In 1929, they made their one and only film together, *The Taming of the Shrew*. Petruchio was well within Doug's range, though Mary is clearly pushing herself to achieve shrewdom. The film is respectable, but it proved a major commercial disappointment. Doug went on to several inconsequential sound films, while Mary had a few successes in sound, including the embarrassing *Coquette* (for which she bobbed her hair and won an Oscar). But both of them knew it was over.

For Doug this was an emotional and psychic disaster. Although he was totally invested in the challenges and solutions of filmmaking, his triumphs were those of a boy at play. On his sets he surrounded himself with pals and hangers-on. When the day's shooting was done, the guys plunged into the pool and sauna or played a free-for-all tennis-like game called "Doug," in which everyone—except Chaplin—knew better than to beat Fairbanks. There were constant practical jokes. For Doug, making movies meant having fun, and as he aged, and was constricted on the set by the demands of sound, he stopped having it. In 1928, gazing at one of the new soundstages, he turned to a friend and said, "The romance of motion picture making ends here."

He was overcome by restlessness—and aimlessness. Leaving Mary behind, he roamed the world with his entourage, filming what amounted to travelogues, which bombed at the box office. "Douglas always faced a situation the only way he knew how, by running away from it," said Mary. "I found I just couldn't keep up the pace with a man whose very being had become motion, no matter how purposeless." He was also increasingly and snobbishly engaged with Britain's aristocracy. And his indiscretions grew more and more indiscreet. Mary could no longer deal with them—or him. She withdrew into drink, the curse of her family. ("All the Pickfords were alcoholics! All of them!" said Anita Loos, who, by the way, wrote nine of the Fairbanks comedies.)

There were last-minute attempts at patching up the marriage, but they came to nothing. In 1936, Doug and Mary were divorced, Doug having backed himself into marrying a notorious lady-come-lately, Lady Sylvia Ashley. (She would later marry Clark Gable.) And by then Mary had entered into a warm and satisfying relationship with the young Buddy Rogers, who had once been her leading man and whom she would eventually marry. As their friend Hal Mohr put it, "We were all glad to see Miss Pickford find happiness with Buddy. Doug was just too much Doug."

The ultimate word on their relationship came from Chaplin, who knew them so well: "If you will read the story of Peter Pan and Wendy, you will know a great deal more about Mary and Doug than you do now."

The public knew only the happy, vigorous, outgoing Douglas Fairbanks, but those closest to him witnessed recurring bouts of depression and self-doubt. Writing years later about the travelogue expeditions, his sidekick Tom Geraghty reported "the mounting conflict that had begun to envelop Doug. He asked Tom to share his room with him; he didn't want to be left alone, even at night. Now, more than ever, he appeared to need companionship to ward off the depression and sense of futility that harassed him."

Everyone was aware of his lifelong, almost pathological jealousy—of Beth, later of Mary, even of his occasional girlfriends, now of Sylvia. He had always insisted, for instance, in being seated next to Mary at dinner parties—hostesses were warned in advance—and she was never to dance with another man, not even the Duke of York (later King George VI). The most virile and buoyant man of his time had in many ways stayed the unsure boy he had once been, depending on perpetual motion and constant acclaim to conceal—particularly from himself—the doubts and insecurities of his childhood. When the party ended, he was adrift, unable to deal with the collapse of his career and the encroachments of middle age. The one happy aspect of Doug's last years was the close relationship that, at last, he developed with his son, who, with Mary's support, had never ceased trying to win him over. Junior was with him at the end, attentive, loving, and—finally—loved in return.

Richard Schickel, in his book *His Picture in the Papers*, comments that in Fairbanks's retirement he seemed to the public

> little more than a faintly absurd roué and the newspaper photographs of him, heavy and balding, and very often glaring angrily at the camera, confirmed their direst suspicions. The contrast with his previous image—lithe and clean-spirited, perpetually youthful, cheery, decently romantic—was unbearable. They did not turn against him, but they did turn away from him.

His death, in 1939—he was only fifty-six—was worldwide news. Perhaps it came just in time. Not long before, he had remarked to Raoul Walsh, "There's nothing as humiliating as being a has-been."

Of all the great silent stars, Fairbanks may have given the vast movie audience the purest pleasure—pleasure untinged by the pathos of Chaplin or Keaton or Pickford. What he offered the world was the fun and vigor of healthy, joyous youth, but when his youth ran out, he had nowhere to go. The all-American boy never grew up into an all-American man.

February 26, 2009

The Art of Pleasing

The stories of most great ballerinas, however different their temperaments, are basically the same. They start preparing professionally as children; their lives are ruthlessly and narrowly concentrated on their work; they have a mother to nurture them, fight for them; they inspire a powerful creative personality, who then shapes them (Pavlova had Petipa; Karsavina had Fokine; a dozen or more, from Danilova and Toumanova to Farrell and McBride, had Balanchine); and they find themselves in their forties either finished or hanging on precariously— ballerinas don't age gracefully into character roles and grandmother roles, the way talented actresses can. And they share a quality that, late in life, Margot Fonteyn identified as the one that "has helped me most": tenacity.

The life of Fonteyn, the most celebrated ballerina of the twentieth century after Pavlova, fits all these circumstances almost to the point of exaggeration. She not only started studying at the usual early age, but she was thrust into tremendous responsibility, as the leading dancer of the young Sadler's Wells Ballet, when still in her mid-teens. She not only had a famously devoted and levelheaded biological mother, known to one and all as BQ, or the Black Queen (after a character in the chess ballet *Checkmate*), she had a second ballet mother in the formidable, all-powerful Ninette de Valois—"Madame"—founder and absolute ruler of Sadler's Wells, who never wavered from her conviction that little Peggy Hookham, quickly renamed Margot Fonteyn, was the Chosen One. She not only became the muse of one of the greatest of choreographers, Frederick Ashton, but late in her career she found in Rudolf Nureyev a second if very different artistic inspiration. And although she was preparing to retire

Margot Fonteyn in *Cinderella*

early in her forties, her connection with Nureyev revitalized her and kept her going past sixty, still in demand even if sadly diminished.

As for tenacity, she overcame what she herself called "no elevation, no extension, no instep and feeble pirouettes"; she blossomed under the draconian conditions of having to give nine performances a week in wartime

England; she gamely endured the humiliations her marriage provided, and heroically coped when an assassin's bullets left her husband a quadriplegic. And she faced a painful death with a fortitude that we can only marvel at.

But it was not only the extraordinary breadth of her career and the drama of her personal life that set her apart from her coevals, or the exceptional beauty and purity of her performances, her early technical weaknesses long forgotten or forgiven in light of her perfection of line, her exquisite proportions, her unerring musicality, and her profound identification with her roles. It was the charm she radiated, the lovability, that made her so cherished by audiences for more than four decades. As Lincoln Kirstein once remarked, "Of all the century's ballerinas, Margot Fonteyn most embodied the art of pleasing." Her hold on her audience was exceptionally personal, which should guarantee an eager response to the new biography *Margot Fonteyn: A Life*, at least ten years in the making, by the dancer-turned-novelist Meredith Daneman. There have been many books about Fonteyn, including her own appealing *Autobiography* (I was its American editor) and four sumptuous accounts by her photographer-friend Keith Money, but none of them can compare in comprehensiveness and frankness with Daneman's.

From the start, Daneman makes clear, nothing could move Peggy Hookham from her path once she had decided on it. One of the many virtues of her book is that she has been able to draw on an unpublished memoir by the Black Queen which adds considerably to our picture of Fonteyn's childhood. Little Peggy, her mother confirms, was well-behaved, self-controlled, hardworking. But when she made up her mind, nothing could change it. Many children, for instance, resist healthy diets, but not many are, as Daneman puts it, "capable of becoming ill for three foodless days" to get their way. (Meat, fish, eggs revolted her; her favorite meal was baked beans on toast.) It's fascinating to see how this quality of stubborn determination, for which Fonteyn became famous (or notorious) in later life, manifested itself from the beginning. "I learnt never to force an issue but to skirt round it," wrote her mother, herself hardly a shrinking violet. "Her will was stronger than mine if it came to a showdown."

Mrs. Hookham was the illegitimate daughter of a lower-middle-class English girl and a very rich Brazilian—his name was Fontes, which became

Fonteyn when the family made it clear that they didn't want their name associated with the stage. Mr. Hookham was a fairly successful engineer, whose work eventually took him (and his wife and children, Peggy and Felix) to China in the early 1930s. In Shanghai, Peggy continued with the dancing lessons she had begun in London, and eventually Mrs. Hookham decided to take her back to England to find out whether she had real talent. That, to all intents and purposes, was the end of the Hookham marriage; he stayed on in China, was interned by the Japanese during the war, and eventually remarried. The Black Queen never looked back.

Peggy was accepted at the Sadler's Wells school—"No money you can spend on the child will be wasted," pronounced de Valois. "Unless some disaster occurs, I know she has a great future ahead of her"—and despite her weaknesses her talent was so obvious that within a year she was appearing in the corps de ballet and then, quickly, in solo roles. And when the fledgling company's one genuine ballerina, Alicia Markova, left for greener pastures, Peggy-Margot was quickly propelled into many of her roles, including *Swan Lake*'s Odette (at first, Odile was beyond her technical capacities) and Giselle. But her reception in the company had by no means been unanimously enthusiastic. Her famous partner-to-be, Robert Helpmann, found her "rather uppity, tiresomely remote for one so young, and, in appearance, rather scraggy." Frederick Ashton himself was unimpressed. He found her "strangely lacking in warmth, charm, temperament and variety. . . . I sensed a streak of stubbornness." But Madame had spoken, and Margot was soon appearing in Ashton ballets.

There was a showdown: When she failed to meet the technical demands he made on her, he grew more and more incensed, until one day she broke down in tears, threw herself on him, and burst out, "I'm trying my best; I can't do any more." He was to say that this was the moment when she "conceded" to him, and that he knew he would be able to work with her. Daneman, however, sees it differently: "Men never know when they have been conquered. To the end of his life, Ashton believed that it was he who had won the battle"—a feminist touch that perhaps owes more to Daneman's background as a novelist (and to *The Taming of the Shrew*) than to the realities of Sadler's Wells.

Even so, the most telling sections of Daneman's book are those that explore Fonteyn's relationships with the powerful people who dominated her and/or succumbed to her charm and her talent. With her mother she was respectful and obedient—up to a point. With Madame, she was *always* respectful and obedient. (When in 1954 de Valois informed her that she was to be the new president of the Royal Academy of Dancing, Fonteyn replied: "The Academy is boring, and it is absolutely not the kind of thing I am good at." "Never mind," said Madame. "It's all arranged." And that was that.) But the crucial early influence was that of the brilliant and self-destructive composer/conductor Constant Lambert, who despite his tempestuous marriage and his alcoholism was her mentor and her lover through her formative years. (In her memoirs, she mentions him only in passing—which is more than she does for several of her other lovers, with one of whom she had an ongoing relationship for ten years.)

The great emotional adventure of her life was with the man she eventually married—Roberto "Tito" Arias, the scion of one of Panama's great families, whom she first met, glancingly, in 1937, when she was eighteen. When they met again many years later, he was married, plump, the father of three children, and a diplomat. Suddenly, in 1951, there was a phone call from New York to Atlanta, where she was performing. ("I couldn't believe it was Tito. He was talking as if we had seen each other last week, when it was twelve years since I had heard a word.") It was another two years before he turned up again, this time backstage at the Met, and the next day he announced that they were to be married; his wife, he insisted, would be pleased to divorce him. He persisted, he cajoled, he wooed, and, Reader, she married him. "I so much wanted to love," she was to write, "and it seemed so difficult for me to love." It was Tito who "rescued this human heart trapped inside the ballerina." She had already recognized that "my need to love far outweighed my need to be loved."

She certainly had found a man whom she could love more than he loved her. Tito's philanderings went beyond those apparently to be expected from a Latin aristo husband, and his cavalier disregard for her needs and comfort only pushed her to more extreme measures of self-abnegation. He was rarely there when she needed him, while she always managed to be there when he needed her. She participated without hesitation in his half-baked revolutionary activities in Panama, involving herself in adventures that were as farcical as they were dangerous—and that made headlines around the world. (Visiting Fonteyn in a New York hotel, Daneman tells us, her close friend the dancer Nora Kaye "was astounded to find her... in the basement, engaged in a spot of gun-practice.")

She doted on Tito, embraced his family, forgave him, and never indicated to the world that she was suffering. His word was law: Her friend Colette Clark told Daneman, "She always did what Tito said. That's what you have to realize. It's nothing to do with what she thought; she wouldn't consult her own thoughts." It was Tito who brought her into the orbit of Aristotle Onassis and Winston Churchill, Panama's Noriega, Chile's Pinochet, and the Philippines' Marcos—and to the shameful episode of Margot's choosing to dedicate her book *The Magic of Dance* to "The magic of Imelda." (Daneman reports that I, as her American publisher, was horrified, and I was.) She had, by the way, previously accepted from Imelda a bracelet composed of seven bands of jewels—emeralds, rubies, diamonds, pearls. "What can I *do?*" she said. "I can't give it back."

The Fonteyn of the Tito years was in many ways a different person from the unaffected and collegial girl whose loyalties and affections had been so closely committed to the company. (By this time, Sadler's Wells had become the Royal Ballet.) Now she was the wife of Panama's ambassador to Britain; she was a favorite of the royal family; she was dressed by Dior, then Saint Laurent. Daneman's view of "this one and only woman who was also a great dancer" comes perilously close to idolatrous at times, but it turns distinctly caustic when Tito comes into her life: "Times had changed, and so had the company she kept. Her highly principled, sensitive nature was now diverted away from its ruling sense of duty to the public, and directed solely towards her husband."

One suspects that Daneman would not have thoroughly approved of *any* man who exercised authority over her heroine. She is clearly uneasy about Rudolf Nureyev's effect on Fonteyn, although she credits his role in reshaping and extending her career. The book quotes approvingly the testimony of the dancer Annette Page, who was with the Royal Ballet on its extended tours of 1962 (the "happy" tour) and 1963 (the "unhappy" tour); that is, pre- and post-Nureyev. On the "unhappy tour," says Page, Margot

> behaved badly for the first time, like a sort of temperamental ageing ballerina. . . . She was the head of the company, the perfect model—up to a certain point. And that point was the arrival of

Nureyev. I think she was infected by his narcissism. With his advent, the company became background—a montage. We no longer felt her support.

The Fonteyn-Nureyev partnership was to a large extent the creation of de Valois, who was fascinated by "Rudi" and understood both his value at the box office and the value of the example of his Kirov classicism to her other dancers. And of course she understood what he could do for Margot: "He brought her out, and she brought him up." But when at first Margot demurred at entering into a partnership with a dancer nearly nineteen years her junior, it was Tito who made the decisive remark: "Get on the bandwagon, or get out." "So onto the bandwagon," as Daneman recites, "at the age of forty-two, she gamely jumped." In her account of what Nureyev meant to Fonteyn, Daneman soars into the higher altitudes of prose. To his charm and bad-boyishness,

> Margot's maternal nature, so long suppressed, now rose and sprang to flower like a bloom raising its face to precious rain. . . . Even in the short time that she had known Rudolf, the earthly limitations of their bond—her marriage, his homosexuality, their disparate ages—had taught her about transcendence, and now she could base her interpretation [of Giselle] on her own spiritual resources, drawn not from the nebulous air, but from the vast, unfathomable sea of maternal passion.

Well, maybe. But all that maternal bonding doesn't deter Daneman from exploring at great length "the question which, despite its implicit prurience, none of us can, in the end, quite refrain from asking: Did Fonteyn and Nureyev sleep together?" Nor can she quite refrain from answering that question:

> When I admit that . . . yes, I *do* believe that Margot and Rudolf were lovers, you must understand that I, like the rest [of the implicitly prurient?], am telling you more about my personal prejudices and predilections than ever I could about what really went on between these two people who, as if sharing some complicit laugh, took their secret, undivulged, to their separate graves.

Having addressed the question, Daneman backs up onto higher moral ground:

> For great practitioners of the arts, whose lives are at the mercy of a vocation, the discovery . . . of a fellow aspirant both willing and worthy to give and take support along the way, is a blessing of almost mystical proportions. . . . Perhaps the most intimate union that an artist can ever forge will be with someone who shares, not his bed, but his dreams.

In other words, the question she couldn't quite refrain from asking turns out to be irrelevant. But we should never underestimate the appetite of the English for sexual gossip. Ashton and Lambert and Helpmann were particularly adept at it, and so Daneman is able to quote Ashton on Lambert's virtues: "Very good balance, very reliable tempi, very large cock." And to quote Lambert to Ashton on Margot's vaginal muscles (only he employs the vernacular term), they "are so strong that she can activate me of her own accord." But did the world really need to hear such things about a woman who was famously reticent and fastidious, and whose family and friends will presumably be reading this book? I don't think it's prudery on my part that makes me recoil, on Margot's behalf, from this gratuitous invasion of her most private life.

Still, there is considerably more to appreciate than to deplore in Meredith Daneman's biography. We will have no fuller or more canny account of the arc of Fonteyn's amazing career, and the author's background as a dancer gives her special insight into Fonteyn's qualities as an artist. De Valois, the Black Queen, Ashton, Lambert, Tito, Nureyev are penetratingly observed. (The only major figure in Fonteyn's life who seems scanted is her brother, Felix, around whom Daneman tiptoes.) As for accuracy, I spotted very few errors—the surrealist artist Leonor Fini, who usually had her (male) lover and (male) ex-lover in tow, was far from being a lesbian; Maria Tallchief didn't dance *The Firebird* at the Met, where the New York City Ballet never performed; Lincoln Kirstein is bizarrely identified as "the American dance commentator"—and these aren't important. Best of all, Daneman is acute on what Fonteyn was really like—the complexities of a nature that presented itself as simple and direct.

When Fonteyn deserves censure—most important, when she "grabbed" (her own word) the premiere of Kenneth MacMillan's *Romeo and Juliet* from Lynn Seymour, on whom it had been created—Daneman is appropriately severe: "Where is the specific, passionate endorsement of a young artist by a mature one, the generous acknowledgement that genius, when it strikes, must have its day?" She grasps Fonteyn's extraordinary capacity for denial, and knows whom to quote about it. Keith Money: "Margot's way of getting through life was to have sort of steel bulkheads like a ship, and if she couldn't cope with something . . . a relationship, a problem, whatever, if she didn't solve it by dusk, it went into a box, the box went into the cupboard, the cupboard was locked and the key was thrown away."

And she quotes Fonteyn herself who, in her twenties, had told her teacher Vera Volkova: "I'm determined to be happy. If an unhappy thought comes into my head, I suppress it. I put it at the back of my head."

This talent for suppression was to see her through the stresses of her marriage, and free her to unleash the fierce—Daneman calls it "almost maniacal"—devotion with which she tended Tito after his near-assassination. Yet she was never grim. One friend remarks aptly that "she had this talent of laughing at misfortune—it was the secret of her happiness that she could laugh at the most incredible moments and make them disappear." Indeed, her laugh and her smile were among her most potent weapons. She herself noted that she may have conquered America with her smile.

The triumph of Sadler's Wells's opening night in New York, in October 1949—exactly fifty-five years ago—is probably unmatched in the history of ballet in America. Fonteyn danced Aurora in the full-length *Sleeping Beauty*, and ballerina, ballet, and company were wildly hailed. She had been unknown here—the famous one was Moira Shearer, star of the movie *The Red Shoes*—but overnight Fonteyn was accepted as a great artist and a beloved personality. She was on the cover of *Time*, the cover of *Newsweek*; her performances automatically sold out. And when she and Nureyev joined forces, her fame turned into real celebrity—"Margot and Rudi" became familiar to the general, nonballet public, like Callas, like the Beatles. They were pursued by the paparazzi. Audiences went berserk: Curtain calls for the *Corsaire* pas de deux sometimes lasted longer than the performance itself.

She went on and on. Once Tito was incapacitated, her earning power became essential to their lives, since he never moderated his extravagant way of life. By the time she finally retired and they had settled down on a small, isolated farm on a Panamanian beach, the money had run out. The conditions under which they lived were extraordinarily primitive—at one point, not even a telephone. Tito's nephew reports, "They lived in something akin to destitution. Her only consideration was his welfare." She was essentially a farmer now—breeding cattle. Buenaventura, the manservant who had tended Tito for years, says she had become "*una ranchera*. A Cow Lady." Yet she could say,

> If anyone questions my happiness, will you please reassure them. I'm the happiest woman in the world. I'm doing exactly what I want to do, which is to be with Tito, in Panama, on our farm, looking after the cattle, learning how to keep the stock records and everything else, and just thoroughly enjoying myself, wearing shirts and jeans and not having to fuss about anything.

Invited to tea by the Queen and Princess Margaret, she sent her regrets: There was a cattle sale coming up, and "I don't think the Queen liked it when I said, 'I can't come because I've got to buy semen.'"

She had only a few years of this happiness. Tito died in 1989, causing scandal to the end. A well-known society woman who had been close to him—who would come to him at the farm when Margot was away—committed suicide on the day of his death. Margot had already developed the painful cancer that was to kill her. She spent more and more time in a hospital in Houston, pretending to the world that her medical problems were not serious. One friend who visited her told Daneman that "there were moments when I would go to the end of the corridor and I would listen to those screams and start perspiring and think, 'Why doesn't she die? This is not a life.'" Yet she returned to the farm, telling an interviewer, "I want to stay here till the end . . . in the place I chose to live with my husband."

There was to be one last public moment—a gala at Covent Garden organized to raise money for her. Soon afterward she retreated to Houston and, Daneman movingly recounts, "finally gave up the fight," doing it in "her own calm but powerfully disciplined way." Her stepdaughter Querube was summoned, and Margot said to her, "I've decided not to have any more treatment. That means I'm going to die, so I want you to call Felix and tell him." When the answering machine picked up, she said, "Well, give me the phone," and left a message: "Felix, this is Margot.

Querube and I are here and I've decided that I'm going to die." She managed to get back to Panama, and when she died, Querube says, "She wasn't scared or anything. . . . She died like a fish, you know. A little fish. A fish receiving air."

That was in 1991. Her death was front-page news everywhere, and she remains vivid in the minds of those who saw her dance. For me, the great revelation was the radiance of that 1949 *Sleeping Beauty*; for others, it was her *Firebird* or *Giselle* or *Swan Lake* or *Marguerite and Armand*, the highly romantic vehicle Ashton created for her and Nureyev, which exploited the contrast between her contained pathos and lyricism and his febrile exoticism. For people who never saw her, there is a considerable amount of film, including television documentaries that are shown and reshown. Recently, a popular exhibition at the Performing Arts Library in Lincoln Center celebrated the impact on America of her art and her effortless projection of dignity, stylishness, and charm. She is taking her rightful high place in the history of her art, and Meredith Daneman has given us what, despite lapses of tone and judgment that are, perhaps, the inevitable price of so personal a labor of love, is certain to be the definitive Life.

December 2, 2004

Something Happened on the Way to Oz

S omewhere over the rainbow Judy Garland is plaintively asking the bluebirds why then, oh why yet another biography? Didn't the job get done in 1975, the year of Anne Edwards's less-than-accurate book, and Gerold Frank's exhaustive study, and *Young Judy* by David Dahl and Barry Kehoe, and Christopher Finch's excellent *Rainbow: The Stormy Life of Judy Garland*? Two years earlier there had been *Little Girl Lost*, a fan's tribute from Al DiOrio Jr., and three years before that, *The Other Side of the Rainbow*, Mel Tormé's unhappy account of Judy's doomed television series. And what about the paperback quickie, *Judy Garland*, by Brad Steiger, rushed out in 1969, the year of her death? (In his extended section on "Judy and the Occult," neatly divided into subsections on astrology, graphology, and numerology, Mr. Steiger reveals that when young Frances Gumm changed her name to Judy Garland, "she took on the vibration of the number nine.")

More recently there have been *The Complete Judy Garland: The Ultimate Guide to Her Career in Films, Records, Concerts, Radio, and Television, 1935–1969* (1990) and John Fricke's handsome, fact-filled *Judy Garland: World's Greatest Entertainer* (1992) and David Shipman's solid *Judy Garland: The Secret Life of an American Legend* (1993). John Meyer called his 1983 memoir *Heartbreaker* (the heart was Mr. Meyer's: In 315 pages he chronicles its breakage, day by excruciating day, through the two months during which he and Judy met, fell in love, got engaged, and split). There are also memoirs by her last husband, Mickey Deans, and her younger daughter, Lorna Luft, and her star turns in so many other autobiographies, from Mickey Rooney's to second husband Vincente Minnelli's. Just last year saw *Judy Garland: Beyond the Rainbow* by Sheridan Morley and Ruth Leon, and *Rainbow*, a collection of Judyana ranging from MGM press releases to "in-depth" journalism by

Shana Alexander and Barbara Grizzuti Harrison—and, in case you missed it back in 1975, a reissue of Gerold Frank.

When is enough enough? What is there left to say? And—more than thirty years after her death—who cares?

Well, I care—at least enough to read all of *Get Happy: The Life of Judy Garland*, by Gerald Clarke, biographer of Truman Capote. I'm not a Judy cultist—I didn't standingly ovate at the Palace or the Palladium or Carnegie Hall (I never saw her perform live); I wasn't one of the twenty thousand mourners who filed past her open coffin at Frank Campbell's funeral parlor in 1969; I didn't bid on her ruby slippers when they came up at auction. And I'm not drawn to sagas of self-destructing divas. I suppose I just still love the girl who was up there on the screen in the thirties and forties—not only the girl from Oz and St. Louis, the Babe in Arms, the Harvey Girl, but the pre-star girl in earlier and slighter movies like *Everybody Sing* and *Love Finds Andy Hardy*, the girl who cheers her underdog team on to victory in *Pigskin Parade* and sings "Dear Mr. Gable" to a photo of dear Mr. Gable in *Broadway Melody of 1938*.

And I love her singing. Not the over-the-top, desperate mess it became in the final years but the big, joyous love of putting a song over and trying to make you feel good that is the essence of her early and mature work. When she was a little girl in vaudeville she often blasted out inappropriate torch songs, but when she was given material like "Zing! Went the Strings of My Heart," nobody ever had more appeal. You can hear it all—the singles, the air checks, the movie numbers—on countless compilations. And just recently, a two-CD repackaging of her famous 1961 Carnegie Hall concert has been released. The sound is excellent, though not really superior to that of the bestselling LP version. The only difference is that on the CDs all of Judy's patter is included—a peculiar little anecdote about a collapsed hairdo in Paris; a loving nod to the composer Harold ("Over the Rainbow") Arlen, who's in the audience; a joke about her sweating. All of it's fun to hear—once.

The Carnegie Hall performance was a bravura display of talent and stamina—a whole lotta beltin' was goin' on. The complicated arrangements worked, mostly, and the voice was certainly strong—which was fortunate, since so many of the songs rise in key and swell in volume as they approach climax. She sang a passionate and moving "Alone Together" and an original and very effective "Stormy Weather." There were Al Jolson songs (of course) and—surprise!—"The Trolley Song" and, yes, she was over that rainbow again. Through twenty-six numbers she hardly faltered. At the age of thirty-eight, after thirty-six years of performing and some very unhappy headlines, she was telling the world, "Don't count me out! I'm back again—Judy Garland the legend, but also your little pal, dear audience, and I love you." And the audience loved her and loved her and loved her in return.

On-screen in the early years she was the ideal kid sister, daughter, girl next door. She was never phony, never "cute." She wasn't mechanical like Shirley Temple or frantic like her pal Mickey Rooney. Her early rival Deanna Durbin, who was talented and charming, didn't approach her in spirit or range. Like all great stars, Garland was unique: not worshipped, not lusted after, not someone to make you laugh or scare you or awe you but someone to believe in and to love. You'd have to go back to Mary Pickford to find another star whom America felt that way about. And because of the ubiquitous *Wizard of Oz*, there's no way to forget her.

The disparity between what Judy-Dorothy means to people and what became of Judy herself is what one reads these books to understand. Something terrible happened, but what was it? One moment she was dancing and singing away—with Fred Astaire in *Easter Parade*, with Van Johnson in *In the Good Old Summertime*—and then, suddenly, there were suicide attempts, ejection from MGM, broken marriages; rumors about addiction to pills, to alcohol. Those were things you expected of a Clara Bow, a Jean Harlow, a Marilyn Monroe—it made sense that sex goddesses were punished with breakdowns, even early death. Not Dorothy of Oz. (When Judy was finally allowed to grow up and suffer as Mrs. Norman Maine in *A Star Is Born*, it seemed as if her adulthood was just a phase—she'd get over it, the way other people get over adolescence.)

Gerald Clarke lays it all out: the driven and unnurturing mother, the charming but weak (and bisexual) father who dies when she's still a kid; the ogres of Metro who starve her (she's fat and she's hungry) and infantilize her both off and on screen, binding her very developed breasts in order to disguise her advanced age of sixteen while she's making *Oz*; her despair at not being beautiful in an MGM world of Lana Turners and Elizabeth Taylors (Louis B. Mayer is said to have referred to her as "my little hunchback"); the Benzedrine to keep her thin, to keep her energy going, and the sleeping pills to counteract the Benzedrine; the relentless schedule of picture after picture to cash in on her popularity; the search for a husband to replace the father (she succeeded all too well: At least two of her five husbands were gay); the collapses, the comebacks, the horrifying descent into illness, addiction, and degradation.

Clarke is particularly good on the mother, Ethel Gumm, who regarded Judy "as an asset to be exploited, rather than as a child to be cherished." He's also convincing about Frank Gumm, and very specific about Frank's homosexuality, which he believes is the reason the Gumms had to move from town to town while Judy was growing up. As the manager of the local movie house, Frank encountered lots of boys. (Clarke's most explicit account reads: "In the high school locker room, two of the school's top athletes . . . bragged about the pleasure Frank was giving them with oral sex, not neglecting a description of how they made him beg.") Sexual revelations punctuate the book: "What is certain is that Judy had lost her virginity by the age of 15." Buddy Pepper, "her senior by just seven weeks, who had several trysts with her in his apartment," is the source for this information (he kissed in the thirties and told in the nineties), and Garland isn't here to confirm or deny it. Again, do we care? Determining precisely when a dead movie star lost her virginity isn't high on everybody's list of scholarly priorities.

More disturbing are accounts of later sexual encounters, which Clarke supplies to demonstrate that "to give pleasure to a man ... was the proof she required, ever and always, that she was something more than Mr. Mayer's little hunchback." "One ugly-minded lover bragged that after she gave him oral sex, for example, he made her sing 'Over the Rainbow' so he could hear those famous words sung through a mouthful of semen." The "ugly-minded lover," we're told, "made that boast to a source who requested anonymity." No doubt. But where was the polygraph test? The kind of man who could tell such a story could just as easily have invented it.

As for MGM's responsibility for what happened to Judy, Clarke gives us a Louis B. Mayer who is sometimes the brutal overseer, sometimes the loving paterfamilias. This sounds fair: Mayer was running a huge business and Judy was a major asset, but he was also clearly fond of her, and indeed "loaned" her money of his own when she needed hospitalization. At times, Garland demonized Mayer as she demonized her mother and many others, yet Lorna Luft tells us in her honest and moving memoir that "Mom" always spoke with affection and regard for "Mr. Mayer." In Clarke's account, it's not necessarily Louis B. but "the dark-suited people in the Thalberg Building" who are the villains. And of course Mother Ethel, who, in this telling, started Judy on pills before she was ten, betrayed Frank with (and later married) a lover whom Judy detested, and dissipated Judy's fortune.

So perhaps there were villains in the piece. But to what extent was Garland complicit in her own destruction? We can't blame her for being an extroverted two-year-old who grinned and piped her way into the Gumm Sisters' vaudeville act—and immediately became its star; she couldn't help having her talent, and the need to express it. But although she repeatedly said that she longed for an ordinary small-town life, few people have stardom thrust upon them. And though she had many friends and mentors, and a number of men cared about her and tried to take care of her, she became one of those people, all vulnerability and pathos, whom others rush to help but who can't be helped. When she was in the grip of her demons, the passive aggression turned to active and fierce aggression. As her health deteriorated, her grasp of reality grew increasingly uncertain: Two years before her death she blithely stated, "Isn't it remarkable that with all the horror, with all that I've been through, I never drifted into booze or pills?" Garland loved to play games, and her humor was not always kind.

She was never pretentious, though, and that's more than you can say for Gerald Clarke. Tyrone Power's charm was "so exundant that few could withstand it"; Judy's voice "ripened into the rutilant maturity of midsummer." And how about this: As Judy's audience at the Palace left the theater, "they displayed not merely smiles of happiness" but "the ecstasy of deliverance. They had not attended a concert; they had participated in an incantation, a rite more ancient than the pyramids themselves. Her altar may have been a stage on Times Square, with the subway rumbling underneath and taxis honking outside, but Judy had more than a little in common with those shamans of old Nile, chanting their cures in the crouching shadow of the newborn sphinx." As the young Judy might have put it, "Golly!"

Despite the literary excesses and prurient flashes, there are reasons to read *Get Happy* if you care about Garland. Gerold Frank had access to all the prime sources (including Garland herself), but writers back in 1975 had to be discreet. Both Christopher Finch and David Shipman are more knowledgeable about Hollywood and about singing than Clarke, and Finch is particularly useful as a corrective to Garland's self-mythologizing— he's an admiring skeptic—but his treatment of the later years is thin. Shipman is judicious and frank without being salacious, though he's sometimes a little distanced. Clarke goes further than his predecessors in illuminating the darker corners of Garland's life, and if at times he accepts Garland's self-dramatizing testimony too uncritically, his account can be gripping. Most important, he makes us feel yet again the tragedy of this wonderfully gifted girl who brought happiness into so many lives while leading such an unhappy life herself.

April 9, 2000

Long-Distance Runner

Nothing is stranger in the history of popular culture than the fate of the silent film stars. Their day lasted fifteen years or so, and when the break came, it was sharp, quick, and total—Hollywood was hit by a cataclysm, and most of its stars were extinguished almost overnight. There were survivors, of course: relative newcomers like Joan Crawford, Myrna Loy, William Powell, Ronald Colman, Norma Shearer, and Janet Gaynor made the transition easily. Garbo, an exception to every rule, took her time (or MGM took it) and emerged triumphantly in 1930 with *Anna Christie*; Chaplin simply went on as he began.

Of the older stars, only a few have survived as figures meaningful to us. There are the great comics—Keaton and Lloyd, as well as Chaplin. Valentino has become a byword, partly for his exotic sexuality, partly for his untimely death—the James Dean of his day. Gloria Swanson would have been forgotten if not for her remarkable comeback in *Sunset Boulevard*. Mary Pickford and her husband Douglas Fairbanks still faintly register, she with her golden curls, he with his swashbuckle. Lon Chaney: the man of a thousand faces—the Hunchback, the Phantom—but who's seen his movies? The Talmadge sisters, John Gilbert, Blanche Sweet, Colleen Moore, Pola Negri (than whom no one was more legendary)—they're off our radar screen.

And then there is Lillian Gish, who not only survived the death of the silents, going on to a sixty-year career in sound film, theaters, and TV, but is considered by many the greatest of American actresses. How did this happen? She had been less popular by far—and less well paid, too—than her friend Pickford, than Swanson, than Norma Talmadge. She was reserved offscreen, cooperating with the usual puff journalism but pulling up her skirts at such gimmicks as allowing her image and autograph to appear on one of a set of silver-plated "Oneida Community" movie-star spoons. Her private life was so private that not even her close friends knew for certain whether she had been to bed with the great man of her life, D. W. Griffith, or with Charles Holland Duell Jr., a businessman who was at one time her manager (he sued her for breach of promise and a lot of other things—and lost—in a series of spectacular court cases), or with George Jean Nathan, the famously acerb critic, who for years was her "constant companion," but whom she steadfastly refused to marry. Marriage? She never "found a name which I would rather carry into eternity than Lillian Gish."

She was considered a great beauty, with her perfect oval face, pale complexion, and casque of blond hair that was highlighted and glorified by superb cinematographers as well as by photographers like Edward Steichen, but her beauty was childlike rather than glamorous. Although there was a sophisticate or two among her roles in Griffith two-reelers, and some lovely pastoral features like *True Heart Susie*, her image in the silents was remarkably consistent: Lillian Gish was virginal, true, and generally in peril—her near-rape by the mulatto villain of *The Birth of a Nation* is a characteristic Gish situation. (A journalist once said that "an optimist is a person who will go to the theater expecting to see a D. W. Griffith production in which Lillian Gish is not attacked by the villain in the fifth reel.") In fact, through most of her Griffith career—from 1912 to 1921—she was essentially a heroine of melodrama; only in the extraordinary *Broken Blossoms* does she inhabit what can be called a tragedy.

Yet even while she was playing these somewhat mawkish roles—the seduced and abandoned Anna of *Way Down East*, turned out into the blizzard, fleeing across the ice floes; the about-to-be-violated-and/or-guillotined Henriette of *Orphans of the Storm*—her reputation as a serious artist grew. Her major post-Griffith silents were important events: *The White Sister*, *Romola*, *La Bohème*, *The Scarlet Letter*, and *The Wind*, although it took decades for that film, her last silent, to be recognized as a masterpiece. By the time in the late twenties that she abandoned Hollywood, or it abandoned her, she had established herself as an extraordinary film tragedienne and a darling of New York intellectuals and writers.

Two things unrelated to her actual work helped to create and maintain her reputation. One was her longevity. It is now established that she was born in 1893—later dates were put forward throughout her life—and not only did she live until six months short of her hundredth birthday but she worked almost ceaselessly from 1902, when she was nine, crisscrossing the country in melodramas like *Her First False Step* and *East Lynne*, to *The Whales of August*, the feature film she starred in with Bette Davis in 1986, when she was ninety-three. She didn't need a comeback the way Swanson did because after *The Birth of a Nation*, made in 1915, she never went away.

What also helped secure her reputation was her association with Griffith. Famously, it was her slightly older friend "Little Mary" who made the introduction, in 1912. Pickford was far more ambitious for fame, money, and independence than was acceptable to Griffith, a benevolent dictator who distributed roles almost as favors among the crowd of eager young girls at his disposal, and she soon left him for greener pastures. Lillian and her sister, Dorothy, found themselves vying for plum Griffith roles (though not with each other: Dorothy was immediately typed as the comic, Lillian as serious). Almost from the start, Lillian devoted her heart and soul (and body?) to the Master but, more important, she devoted her mind to learning the business of making movies. Alone among the Griffith players, she watched rushes, learned about cameras and editing, made helpful suggestions about scripts; his trust in her was such that in 1920 he asked her to direct a film (starring Dorothy), an assignment she carried out with her customary thoroughness.

But what confirmed her connection with Griffith in the public mind was her lifelong proselytizing for his work. She called her 1969 autobiography *The Movies, Mr. Griffith and Me*, and it is heavily weighted toward her Griffith years, which even by then represented less than a sixth of her working life. She lectured everywhere on his importance in film history, struggled to defend him against the charges of racism that greeted *The Birth of a Nation*, left a large trust fund to preserve his films, lobbied (successfully) for a Griffith stamp. Griffith's movies stand on their own, but Gish's unending efforts to perpetuate his name and reputation certainly worked in his favor. And in hers.

That this was the result of deliberate policy on her part is the contention of a biography, *Lillian Gish: Her Legend, Her Life*, by Charles Affron. The

Lillian Gish in 1924

subtitle underlines a basic theme of his book. Although Affron scrupulously tracks the life—a welcome and valuable account, since previous Gish literature has been long on rapture and short on data—and pays sensitive homage to the art, it is attacking the legend that preoccupies him. His reading of Gish's motives in promoting both Griffith and silent film is typical. "The cult of Griffith was, after all, the path to her own artistic apotheosis. . . . If his legacy were forgotten, she would lose her place in movie history." (This is not only ungenerous but untrue—Gish's great performances, both for Griffith and after, are more than enough to ensure her place in movie history.) "The *Way Down East* episode, like so many others involving Lillian, came to embody the myth of the birth of the movies and to place her at its center. . . . Lillian Gish devoted her life, public and private, to promoting the centrality of that position."

Certainly, Lillian Gish, young and old, worked to establish a sympathetic public persona, and succeeded in doing so, along the way cooperating with some fairly stomach-turning publicity. One can share Affron's distaste for such nonsense as a nine-part *Liberty* magazine interview from 1927 titled "Lillian Gish, the Incomparable Being: The True Story of a Great Tragedienne." And perhaps she encouraged journalists to refer to her as "the Madonna of the screen," "the virgin queen of the screen," "ethereal, aloof, and very beautiful—but hardly human." On the other hand, it's always been the business of stars to create legends about themselves, however inaccurate. Pickford presented herself as Little Mary long after she had proved herself one of the most astute businesswomen Hollywood has ever seen; Valentino—the Sheik—was a sweet, rather passive fellow, happiest when at home making pasta for his friends; "vamp" Theda Bara—"Kiss me, my fool!"—was in reality Theodosia Goodman, a nice Jewish girl from Cincinnati.

Bara, though, was too bad to be true, and nobody took her legend seriously. Gish was too good to be true, and Affron, taking her legend all too seriously, has suffered the disappointment romantics tend to suffer when they realize that their idealized one is not, after all, incomparable. He's even critical of her for lying about her age ("As late as 1987, when she was ninety-four, she still indulged in the creative chronology that actors often think their prerogative"), as if all kinds of stars don't claim this prerogative almost automatically—and sensibly. Griffith, everyone knew, liked very young girls. When Lillian arrived at Biograph, in 1912, did her integrity require her to inform him that she was already an elderly nineteen?

Affron is equally censorious in his take on the relationship between the temperamentally opposite sisters. Dorothy was a madcap with an open, happy nature and a great sense of fun. As she matured, that turned into normal enjoyment of boys, parties, drinking—everyone at Biograph knew that she and the appealing young actor Bobby Harron were in love, and what they were up to when they went off together. Nobody knew anything about Lillian—if there was anything to know. Interviewed by Richard Schickel for his valuable biography of Griffith, *D. W. Griffith: An American Life*, Anita Loos recalled that in the early Biograph days she was speculating with Dorothy "as to what, exactly, her sister and Griffith did when they walked out together. One night the two youngsters followed them in hopes of finding out. But the director and his leading lady were models of propriety; they dined in a restaurant and Griffith escorted Gish home at a seemly hour."

Lillian was to say over and over that Dorothy "got the happy side that God left out of me," and "I never learned how to play." (In 1970, she even tells an audience, "I'm as funny as a barrel of dead babies!") In a pair of articles for *Stage Magazine*, written by the sisters in the twenties, she says, "I envy this dear darling Dorothy with all my heart. . . . When she goes to a party, the party becomes a party; when I go to one, I'm afraid it often stops being a party. And I don't like it. I want to be like she is." Dorothy on Lillian: "How I envy her the singleness of purpose, the indefatigability, the unabating seriousness which have taken her straight to the heights and will carry her on and on! I never cease to wonder at my luck in having for my sister the woman who, more than any other in America, possesses all the qualities of true greatness."

Even given the wholesale hyperbolic ghostwriting that obviously took place here, these remarks must to some degree reflect what these two young women felt about themselves and each other.

Dorothy Gish was a talented and charming actress and, indeed, became a real star—both Lillian and Griffith insisted that she was the more naturally talented of the two girls. When she was eighty, Lillian was still saying of Dorothy, "She was the talent in the family. I didn't have her gift for comedy." Affron's jaundiced view is that "from the start of their careers to the end of her life, Lillian remained steadfast in putting forth the image of sisterly devotion, selflessness, and generosity" and "the image of untroubled sibling relationship was one of the constants in Lillian's life story." Was it only "image," though? No doubt there were conflicts and abrasions between two such dissimilar sisters over seventy years of intense professional and personal relationship, but their interdependency and mutual affection are beyond question. Can one really discount Lillian's frequent assertions that "Heaven was to me a place where I could be with Mother and Dorothy all the time"? This is not the language of *What Ever Happened to Baby Jane?*

In almost bizarre contrast to Affron is *Lillian Gish: A Life on Stage and Screen* by Stuart Oderman. Oderman is the quintessential fan. In 1954, he was a stagestruck fourteen-year-old from Newark who cut school to attend Broadway matinees and found himself sitting next to Gish at a MoMA screening of *Broken Blossoms*. So began a friendship of thirty-nine years, the culminating moment of which takes place when he is the pianist at a MoMA screening of *The Wind*. Typical of his feeling for her—and his style: "My fantasy had come true—my hope that one evening, I would be playing, and Miss Gish would be in the audience. . . . 'Play well. I have always been proud of you.' . . . I quickly wiped away my tears with my tuxedoed right arm as I *tremoloed* with my left hand."

The value of Oderman's book lies in the many rich interviews and conversations he held with Gish throughout the almost four decades of their friendship, questioning her, hoarding her words, and as a result able to give us a sense of the living woman. Even more informative, perhaps, are the interviews he conducted through the years with Lillian's contemporaries and friends—with Constance Talmadge, Blanche Sweet, Colleen Moore, Anita Loos, Frank Capra, Louise Brooks, and many others. Their reminiscences may be distorted by the passage of time (or by affection, or malice), but they give us a strong sense of how Gish was perceived by her coevals.

On the bedeviled subject of Lillian's relationship with Griffith, for instance, Donald Crisp (who played her murderous father in *Broken Blossoms*) told Oderman: "He knew that the Gish girls would do anything he wanted. Especially Lillian. Lillian was in love with him." Thinking back to *The Birth of a Nation*, Dorothy Reid, widow of the handsome star Wallace Reid, laughingly remarked, "If Lillian would have kissed anyone on the set, it would have been Mr. Griffith! If she could get away from her mother. And if Mr. Griffith could get away from his wife!" Lillian herself: "I suppose people in those days made all kinds of jokes about Mr. Griffith and his harem, but we didn't pay attention to them. Mr. Griffith was the father we never had." We can decide for ourselves if these are accurate reflections; what matters is the sense they convey of what life at Griffith's Biograph felt like to these young people long before they had been canonized (or forgotten).

What was Lillian like? All the evidence points to the accuracy of her judgment of herself: that she was preternaturally serious, determined, single-minded. She had to be. When she refers to Griffith as the father she never had, she is touching lightly on what was the central fact of her youth. Her real father, James Leigh Gish, was an alcoholic who soon abandoned his wife and children. (The Pickfords and the Talmadges were fatherless, too.) It was then, in the 1890s, that through taking in theatrical boarders, the well-bred Mary Gish found herself—and later her little girls—on the stage; at first, the family back in Massillon, Ohio (President Zachary Taylor was an ancestor), had to be protected from this scandalous turn of events. When Lillian was six, Mr. Gish committed an unpardonable, and traumatic, act: His wife had entrusted him with the three dollars meant for the weekly installment payment on their shoddy furniture, and presumably he drank it away. The furniture was repossessed, and James Gish was more or less gone from their lives.

But Lillian thought of him with longing. And it was Lillian who at seventeen, doing her duty as always, traveled alone to Oklahoma, where he was gravely ill. She spent months there, attending school and visiting her father in his sanatorium. He was to die in 1912, cause of death: "Gen. paralysis of insane." (Not only does Affron crow that "in one of her early biographical pieces, Lillian reported him as having died in Baltimore of pneumonia"—as if a famous young woman of that period was under an obligation to reveal the ghastly truth of her father's death—but he assures us that "Lillian's stay in Shawnee was a relatively happy time.")

It was always their mother on whom Lillian and Dorothy counted —the rock of strength, the dispenser of all wisdom. And the wisdom Mrs. Gish dispensed, and that Lillian adhered to all her life, can be (and frequently was) expressed in two sentences. About her work when she was barnstorming as a child: "Speak loud and clear, or they'll get another girl." About men: "Your father destroyed me. Another man would destroy us." Anita Loos put it clearly: "Lillian had two great fears: being abandoned the way her mother was, and being out of work." Her entire life can be seen as a response to these two fears: Apparently, she never gave herself fully to a man, and for eighty years she made sure that she was never out of work for very long.

As she quickly became first a leading Griffith player, then a star, Gish's discipline, her self-control, and her emotional distancing grew. She had assumed these qualities early. In her autobiography she relates that during a performance of her first play, *In Convict Stripes*—she was nine—a gun was accidentally discharged and she was hurt. The show, of course, went on, and after the curtain came down, a doctor "used long needles to pry out the buckshot. It hurt badly, for he used no anesthesia. But I had already been trained to conceal my private feelings in public." There are the famous stories of the physical hardships she ignored, such as those endured during the climactic blizzard scene in *Way Down East*: "At one time my face was caked with a crust of ice and snow, and icicles like little spikes formed on my eyelashes, making it difficult to keep my eyes open."

Just as hardships were to be ignored, emotions were to be suppressed—the only strong feelings she acknowledges relate to her mother and sister. ("Our greatest fear was being taken away from mother.") She may, early on, have been in love with Griffith, but her description of him in her autobiography has a Dreiserian clarity: "He always looked uncomfortable in a house—out of place, caged in. The only surroundings in which he seemed comfortable were the studio, a hotel dining room, a lobby."

There had been adoring boyfriends back in Massillon, but Lillian showed little compunction about dropping them. Griffith she worshipped at first, but he was primarily mentor, father, boss. Charles Duell was a failed attempt at security: Though born rich, he was not only incompetent but dishonest. And there was George Jean Nathan, who represented the world of intellect and culture. For years she was with him at opening nights, at parties, on trips to Europe. His circle—H. L. Mencken, the novelists Joseph Hergesheimer and James Branch Cabell (both of whom wrote novels about her), Eugene O'Neill (who said of her, "There's a girl who has one of the smartest beans"), Condé Nast—was one she aspired to. But it turned out that Nathan, who claimed to have a Philadelphia Main Line, Episcopal background, had misrepresented himself. (Nathan's political views were "slightly to the right of Marie Antoinette's," as indeed were Lillian's—for years she was a highly vociferous and prominent America Firster.) One day in 1937 he let slip the fact that his mother was in a hospital in Philadelphia—apparently this was the first time Nathan had ever mentioned that his mother was alive. Lillian went to the hospital and "before the drama critic's mother could complete her first sentence, Lillian immediately knew that George could never have been the son of Main Line Philadelphia Episcopalians." Responding to a direct question, George's sister-in-law said, "If George's brother is Jewish, I suppose George would be, too!" Lillian broke with Nathan—not, Ruth Gordon testifies, because he proved to be Jewish but because he had lied.

When the break occurred, Lillian was forty-four, and as far as is known, there was never another man in her life. Which would not have come as a surprise to the flapper star Colleen Moore, who remarked to Oderman, "How could Lillian play a love scene convincingly when she never had one in real life? . . . Her sister liked the men, but Lillian had all of that repressed emotion. . . . Suffering is easy. Loving is harder." What she played with consummate genius was frigidity. The scene in *The Wind* when her new husband attempts to caress her is so disturbingly convincing in the revulsion she manifests that it's very hard not to make the leap from actress to woman.

In an uncharacteristic moment of self-analysis about her later Griffith years, Lillian wrote, in an unpublished memoir, "At the time, I hadn't enough insight to know that I was using hard work as a smoke screen to cover my almost complete retreat from life. . . . There was a curious gap between emotional conflicts I portrayed in motion pictures and those presumably suffered by the men and women whom I knew. Or my own life problems, for that matter." True to form, Affron dismisses the authenticity of these feelings.

Where Affron is on firm ground is in his appreciation of Gish's artistry. He had already, in 1977, anatomized her work, film by film, in a book called *Star Acting: Gish, Garbo, Davis*: "Melodrama is by definition excessive. Gish nourishes it with something that approaches religious fervor, and an ability to arrange her features in configurations so extreme, so lucid, so open that authenticity is extracted from the patently bathetic." He has identified the quality that sets her apart from almost every other screen actor: her refusal—or inability—at crucial moments to hold anything in reserve.

This quality illuminates the most famous scenes of her silent-film career. There is the terrifying climax of *Broken Blossoms*, when she is battered to death by her father. ("When we filmed it," she wrote, "I played the scene with complete lack of restraint, turning around and around like a tortured animal. When I finished there was a hush in the studio. Mr. Griffith finally whispered, 'My God, why didn't you warn me you were going to do that?'") There is the emotional climax of *Orphans of the Storm*, when she hears the voice of her long-lost, blind sister (played by Dorothy) and cannot reach her. There is the harrowing sequence in *The Wind*, when, maddened by the relentless wind itself and terrified by the man who has attacked her, she shoots and kills him. In such moments, as Affron suggests, melodrama is transcended by feeling heightened to unbearable limits without any loss of emotional truth.

Her contemporaries knew how special she was. Eva Le Gallienne,

Lillian Gish in 1978

hardly a sentimentalist, wrote to her after seeing *Romola*, "The joy that you give me is a poignant and throbbing thing that makes me want to go down on my knees and pray." But the praise that must have meant the most came from America's most admired actor, John Barrymore, in a letter to Griffith about *Way Down East*: "Her performance seems to me to be the most superlatively exquisite and poignantly enchaining thing I have ever seen in my life. I remember seeing Duse in this country many years ago . . . —also Madame Bernhardt—and . . . it is great fun and a great stimulant to see an American artist equal if not surpass, the finest traditions of the theater."

Affron's generous response to Gish's art is, of necessity, more focused on her film work than on her work in the theater, of which he can have seen relatively little. But theater was where she was to place most of her energies from the early thirties on. Unlike the other silent stars, Gish had a beachhead in New York, and quickly she was triumphing in *Uncle Vanya*.

From there it was a succession of triumphs (most notably, Ophelia—she was forty-three—to John Gielgud's Hamlet) and failures. She played *Camille* in Central City, Colorado ("Even the ushers wept"). She played *Life with Father* in Chicago for more than a year. She was a fixture on radio. She did *Arsenic and Old Lace* on television with Helen Hayes. In 1947, she played opposite Gielgud in *Crime and Punishment*. (It was the first time I saw her onstage—I barely knew who she was—and I was transfixed by her emotional power.) And she was back in the movies, playing character parts and old women. Her death scene in *Duel in the Sun* has the old power. Her unshakable resolve in holding off Robert Mitchum with a rifle in *The Night of the Hunter* is justly famous. (Mitchum said of her, "One of the toughest women I ever met. Why do you think she lasted so long?")

In 1965, she played the Nurse in *Romeo and Juliet* at the American Shakespeare Festival in Stratford, Connecticut. The Juliet was my not-yet wife, Maria Tucci. Gish's performance was sly and loving, not bawdy—bawdy was certainly not her métier. Her behavior was impeccably professional—always on time, no demands, no star turn; her only quiet complaint was that she couldn't understand rehearsing on Sunday mornings: "When do the actors go to church?" She was also extraordinarily generous. In rehearsal she gently adjusted one of their embraces so that it was Maria who was facing the audience: "They're here to see Juliet, dear, not the Nurse." She loved to repeat what her pal Gielgud said when he came to see her in the show: "You were wonderful, darling—as Mary Poppins, not as the Nurse, but wonderful." And she absolutely insisted that Maria procure a Pierce's Slanting Board; from 1940 on, Affron tells us, Gish lay on one of these upside down every morning, starting at seven. "Time is your friend; you get wiser," she was to say. "But gravity is your enemy. It sucks you into your grave."

In the early eighties, I had the opportunity to discuss with Gish the knotty theories Louise Brooks had put forward about her, Garbo, and MGM. Lillian had no more and no less to say than she had said in dozens of public statements. Fair enough, but there was something steely (a word often applied to her) in her guardedness: She had decided on her version of the past, and no other version was discussable. This stubbornness, which she frequently deployed in the face of the evidence, is a quality of hers that particularly offends Affron. Yet most of her inaccuracies are too small to matter, or are obviously the result of lapsed memory. On one major issue, though, she definitely distorted the truth: her contention that after *The Wind* was completed, MGM forced her to tack on a happy ending. By examining the various dated scripts, Affron demonstrates that the ending we know—Lillian and Lars Hanson standing in the doorway of their shack, facing the wind and the future together—was always intended. Clearly, Gish felt that if she had to retreat from Hollywood, it would look better if she could lay the blame on the crassness of studio moguls rather than on her diminishing box-office appeal.

Much as Affron disapproves of what he sees as Gish's mendacity and self-glorification, he is positively worshipful compared to a disgusting 1978 novel called *Vanessa*, written by Ann Pinchot, who had been Gish's collaborator on the autobiography. *Vanessa* begins with the barely disguised Griffith character, Joshua Fodor, deflowering the even-less-disguised Lillian character, Vanessa, in a hotel bedroom. And here she is seducing her sister Cassie's (Dorothy's) young boyfriend, Richie: "My most intimate parts were moist with excitement and desire. . . . I responded as Mr. Fodor had taught me so ingeniously, with my mouth, my lips, my tongue on his strong handsome penis, playing, teasing, kissing it until it gushed with a magnificent spurt into my mouth." Richie promptly blows his brains out.

This would be merely ludicrous if "Richie" wasn't modeled on the much-loved Bobby Harron, the young actor whom Dorothy had cared for and who in 1920 died of a gunshot wound, possibly a suicide. His death devastated the entire Biograph family, and in particular the Gishes—it was Lillian who had to break the news to Bobby's mother. For Pinchot even to suggest that Lillian might have been responsible for Harron's death seems an astounding piece of cruelty to a woman in her eighties. But *Vanessa* is so filled with resentment that it leads one to speculate what Gish can possibly have done to her collaborator to so alienate her. (Of course, we've been asking ourselves that question about Othello and Iago for four hundred years.)

Perhaps it was Gish's unassailable reserve that provoked Pinchot—all that rigor and independence doesn't leave much room for an acolyte. Oderman tells us that in 1975—Gish was eighty-two—he was watching her in her dressing room "raising and lowering her heavy Russian costume and concentrating on a hook on the wall." "I can hang that up for you," he says. Lillian shakes her head and whispers, "Ssh!" After three more attempts she lunges forward and gets the costume on the hook. "You're not here every night," she tells him, "and if you were, I would become dependent on you. That's not good, to be dependent on anybody. . . . If I became dependent on other people, I'd lose my will to live."

Besides, who was there to depend on? Her father had abandoned her, Griffith had been unreliable, her mother and sister had died. Men? Colleen Moore explained that the reason every man in Hollywood was after Gish rather than the latest sex bomb was that she was unobtainable. Children? Hardly. Her life was her work. As she said to Stuart Oderman in 1954, the year they met, "It isn't easy being a Lillian Gish."

November 1, 2001

Him + *Her* = Them

You don't have to be a member of the New York Psychoanalytic Institute to figure out that when you title a memoir of your parents *Them*, you're performing an act of distancing. And that if you dedicate that book "To Them with love and longing," you're revealing a powerful ambivalence. How many of us at Francine du Plessix Gray's age (almost seventy-five) are still "longing" for our parents, however much we may have loved them? How many of us, for that matter, think of them as Them?

But then how many of us have had a Tatiana Yakovleva du Plessix Liberman for a mother and an Alexander Liberman for a (step)father? With luck, none of us.

Them: A Memoir of Parents is a riveting, passionate, and deeply confused book. Almost thirty years have gone by since the publication of *Lovers and Tyrants*, the author's bestselling novel that covered much of the same emotional territory, yet nothing has been resolved. Here again we are being told the story of a girl with a supremely narcissistic mother whom the child yearns to be loved by. The chief difference between the two books is that in the treatment of their heroine's early years, the father—mostly offstage in the novel—is now front and center. The author's anger at him appears to be a relatively late development.

Ms. du Plessix Gray is at her narrative best when evoking Tatiana's and Alex's pre-Francine years. Ladies first:

HER: Tatiana came from a highly cultured, high-achieving family (even apart from her insistence that she was a direct descendant of Genghis Khan). Her maternal grandfather, for instance, had a considerable career as a dancer and administrator at the Maryinsky ballet. As Francine wryly remarks, "one of our best-documented progenitors, he character-

Arriving in New York, 1941

izes many of our family traits, most particularly in his affinity for striking poses." On her paternal side there were her elegant gambler father, an aunt with a significant career as a contralto, and an uncle—Alexandre, or "Sasha"—who was a "legendary" explorer and an eminent artist and man-about-town in émigré Paris (he had a three-year affair with Anna Pavlova). When Tatiana was nineteen, suffering from tuberculosis, she succeeded in getting to Paris, the dream of all cultivated Russians. Her outstanding beauty helped her become a model, and soon she was taken in hand by Uncle Sasha, who educated her, smoothed out her (very) rough edges, and led her to her eventual career in fashion as an upscale hat designer.

There were various men interested in Tatiana, but no one struck a chord until, in 1928, the great Russian poet Vladimir Mayakovsky turned up in Paris, and history was made. Or almost made. Yes, they adored each other (although apparently they never slept together); yes, he wrote several of his most famous poems to her; yes, when he had to return to Russia he swore he was coming back to marry her and sent her outpourings of love. ("My lovely , beloved Tanik don't forget me. I love you so much, and

I'm so longing to see you. I kiss all of you, your Vol.") Instead of coming back, he killed himself. Meanwhile, Tatiana had been covering her bets. Within months of Mayakovsky's departure, she had agreed to marry Vicomte Bertrand du Plessix, Francine's father. (There was gossip suggesting that Mayakovsky was her real father, but the dates make that impossible; besides, as Tatiana often said, he was an "absolute gentleman.") Du Plessix was intelligent, attractive, and he had a title—very important to her. She was later to acknowledge: "No, I didn't love him."

HIM: Alex Liberman wasn't descended from Genghis Khan, unless Genghis Khan was Jewish, but his mother had Gypsy as well as Romanian-Jewish blood and a good deal of the famously anarchic Gypsy spirit. She became a student revolutionary in Odessa, eventually moving on to a career as actress, successful creator of a children's theater under the Bolsheviks, and sexual adventuress. "Anyone not acquainted with Henriette Pascar's background," writes Francine, "might classify her erotic behavior— the one-night stands and numerous affairs indulged in every year with dozens of lovers—as a case of simple nymphomania." But no: "Like all gypsies, Henriette had her own codes, her own prerogatives, and above all her own sexual ethos."

In 1912, she married Semyon (later Simon) Lieberman (later Liberman), who was also a dedicated revolutionary, and produced (three months after the marriage) their one child, Alex. The ultra-capable Semyon became Russia's leading expert on timber, not only carrying out commissions for the czar but managing the estates of the czar's brother, uncle, and other immensely wealthy aristocrats—one of them owned 2.7 million acres. Alex's lifelong "penchant for luxury," Francine suggests, began when, as a little boy, he accompanied his father on extended tours of these estates in opulent private trains.

Semyon Lieberman was so important to his country's economy that after the revolution, despite his affiliation with the late, despised czar, he effortlessly became essential to the Soviets—a close associate, even a friend, of Lenin (he had direct access to Lenin's private phone line at the Kremlin). Indeed, in 1921, when Alex was nine and in physical and psychological difficulties, it was Lenin, according to the minutes of the five-man Politburo then controlling the state, who okayed his leaving the country for treatment abroad. Francine speculates that "the fact that it had taken the Politburo to decide his fate may well have helped to give

Alex that sense of self-importance, and the accompanying delusions of grandeur, which were to mark his character."

Alex was taken first to England and deposited in a series of schools there, separated from his parents and—according to the 1993 biography *Alex,* by Dodie Kazanjian and Calvin Tomkins—writing them "heartbroken letters, which often went unanswered. 'I cried very much yesterday, thinking of you. My darlings, why is it that you don't write me?'" Once he had internalized English comportment, however, his natural snobbery asserted itself: Henriette took him to a hotel in London for a weekend, "and he found her so garishly dressed that he told her point-blank: 'I can't have dinner with you looking like that.'"

By the mid-twenties, the Libermans were living apart. Semyon was in Russia and Henriette took Alex to Paris, succeeding through connections in placing him in the most exclusive school in France. Although when filling out the application form she had carefully specified Alex's religion as "Protestant," he was actually the first Jew ever to be admitted to Les Roches.

Alex's Jewishness was a vexed issue. Francine tells us, "Without ever denying or belittling his Jewish identity, Alex always emphasized that his intellectual heritage, his entire culture, 'was exclusively based on a Protestant, Calvinist ethic.'" Yet a hundred or so pages later, she's reporting a scene in a French railroad carriage during which Alex is rude to a man who is clearly Jewish and Tatiana turns on him, shouting, "I've always known you were anti-Semitic! And you suffer from the worst kind of anti-Semitism, Jewish anti-Semitism! . . . There's nothing worse than Jewish anti-Semitism, especially at this time of history!" (It's 1940.) On the other hand, years later when Alex asked a friend to approach Tatiana about having a baby (he found it impossible to broach the matter to her directly), Tatiana—never considered an anti-Semite—replied, "And why should I have another child? To bring another Jew into the world?" To complicate the Jewish issue still further, Francine's biological father, the vicomte, was rabidly anti-Semitic, as was his entire royalist-Catholic family—"Jews are intelligent but detestable"—whereas the man Francine married, Cleve Gray, was Jewish.

Alex was a great success at Les Roches. Then, encouraged by his mother and one of her lovers, who happened to be Tatiana's Uncle Sasha, he took up the life of an artist, while earning his living in the world of commercial art. By the time he was nineteen, he was assistant art editor for France's most prestigious illustrated magazine, *Vu*, whose editor, Lucien Vogel, happened to be yet another of Henriette's lovers. Alex was launched in his career and, through Uncle Sasha, would eventually discover Tatiana, the woman who was to be his destiny.

THEM: Before there could be a Them, there were two half-Thems— Tatiana's and Alex's first brief sorties into marriage. Alex, who was conspicuously backward sexually, fell in love with and married an older girl, a fashion model and star skier, who tried to "make a man out of him," stripping their bed every night and turning it into "a sports arena." It didn't work. Already suffering from ulcers, he now had a breakdown and spent three months in a sanatorium. He and Hilda tried to patch up the marriage—he kept her well supplied with jigsaw puzzles—but, as he liked to tell it, Hilda disappeared for good "the morning after she had finished the largest puzzle in France." The decks were cleared for Tatiana.

She, meanwhile, had married du Plessix in 1929 and accompanied him to Warsaw, where he held a minor diplomatic post. Tatiana was, to put it mildly, the opposite of diplomatic, and she was a spendthrift as well. What Francine calls her mother's "proclivity for high living" led Bertrand to partake in some shady dealings, nor did it help that she announced loudly at an official dinner, *"Je déteste les Polonais."* Bertrand was dismissed from his post, and he and Tatiana were shortly back in Paris, where her hat-making business helped support them.

By the mid-thirties, the marriage had gone permanently bad, although appearances were maintained. Little Francine adored her father and happily recounts various of her adventures with him: He'd become a first-rate pilot, and he took her up stunt-flying; he'd become a serious adulterer, and he took her to call on his current mistress. (Oh, those French!) At the collapse of France in June 1940, Bertrand joined the Free French Air Force and in July was shot down over the Mediterranean. But by that time, Tatiana's relationship with Alex had sparked and flamed. They had been thrown together in the summer of 1938, and by November he was writing to her: "You know how to love me as no woman has ever loved me, and thanks to you a man was born.... To love you has become a prayer, a benediction sent by heaven.... I only know life through our glances, our bodies, our thoughts, I have loved you I love you and shall continue to love you until the day when death will part us." And he did.

When the Germans arrived in Paris, the Jewish Alex was already on the run, and Tatiana, Francine in tow, became part of the dramatic exodus to the south, eventually meeting up with him in the unoccupied zone. There were dangers, there were deprivations, yet, Francine tells us, "I recall those tragic summer months as some of the most blissful ones of my life." One reason for this was clearly the presence of Alex, whom she adored from the start. (About her father, she was only told that he was away on "a secret mission.") Alex's ingenuity—his nonpareil émigré talent for surviving—plus help from their connections in America (both of his parents were already there) made their escape possible. They found their way to Madrid, where Alex secured tickets for a desperately crowded train to Lisbon from the concierge at the Ritz, and at last boarded a "pleasure yacht" making its maiden voyage to New York. On hand to meet them at the dock, on January 8, 1941, were Alex's father, Simon, and—amazingly—Tatiana's father, Alexei Iacovleff, now known as Al Jackson, whom she hadn't seen in twenty-six years.

FRANCINE: She's now ten years old. What do They do with her? They pack her off with Grandpa Al. "Some eight hours after arriving in the United States I found myself in the third-class carriage of a night train bound for Rochester, New York, being taken by a total stranger, my grandfather, to a city I'd never heard of until that very afternoon." It's more convenient that way—for Them.

Today, sixty-four years later, Francine has it both ways. On the one hand, "I was again being looked on as a lost parcel of sorts . . . SOS, burdensome child here, needs to be forwarded somewhere, who'll take care of her?" On the other, "Looking at it in retrospect, from Mother and Alex's point of view it all seems perfectly lucid . . . to consider my psychic needs might still have seemed like an extravagance." But the attempt to rationalize their behavior is unconvincing; abandoned children have every right to be angry.

Rochester turns out to be pervasively gloomy but bearable. Grandpa, a defeated man, does nothing after coming home from his dull factory job but listen to his radio. (The high point of his week is *Major Bowes' Original Amateur Hour.*) Francine doesn't object to her daily domestic chores or to sleeping on the living-room sofa. Besides, she has English to learn—she hadn't known a word of it—and learns it by listening to the soaps: *Our Gal Sunday, Life Can Be Beautiful, Young Doctor Malone.* ("What will Nancy do? Will she tell Dr. Malone about her suspicions?") All very well, but "As soon as I put my head on the pillow, a flood of tears overcame me. Why, why had they sent me away?" And, of course, there was her building anxiety about her father. Where was he? Why didn't he write? "The possibility of my father's survival, over the months, was growing increasingly tenuous and more improbable and was demanding an increasingly arduous act of faith."

After a couple of months Francine is summoned back to New York, "labeled and tagged, like a package, with the help of the Travelers Aid Society." But Tatiana and Alex still can't absorb her into their lives—they park her with some friends in Greenwich Village, who arrange a scholarship for her at the Spence School and who can "help me with my homework, do all kinds of things for me that she, Mother, was incapable of doing." And how was Mother faring in their first months of exile? "Without me she and Alex were prospering."

Francine is finally allowed to move in with her mother, but no one has yet told her that her father is dead. Tatiana and Alex know it has to be done, but they just . . . can't. Various friends refuse to do it for them, and eventually the job falls to the remarkable Gitta Sereny, an eighteen-year-old Hungarian girl who's been helping out with Francine (and who was to become one of Europe's best-known and fiercest journalists). More than a year after Bertrand du Plessix's death, Gitta gently but firmly tells Francine the truth, and she accepts it relatively calmly. But "I recollect as if it had occurred yesterday the storm of tears that overcame me and that also overwhelmed Mother as she ran to me the following morning and wrapped me in her arms. 'Why didn't you tell me?' I remember sobbing, repeating the word 'you,' 'why didn't you, you, you tell me?'" Tatiana, weeping: "'I'm sorry, I'm sorry, I didn't know how.' . . . We sobbed like equals that morning, like the two lost children we both were."

Sorry, Francine, but you weren't two lost children: You were one lost child and she was a pathetic excuse for a mother. Yet even as Francine is finding a way to condone her mother's behavior, she's letting you in on how she really felt: "The terrifying thing is that from then on Mother was seldom able to recapture my trust. And we spent the rest of our lives—she lived on for another half century—not ever having any kind of a true emotional encounter again."

Sometime later, Francine comes home from school and learns from a pile of opened telegrams of congratulation that Tatiana and Alex had got married that day. "I was stunned, hurt, enraged . . . once more they'd excluded me . . . but in my habitually diplomatic way I concealed my feelings." When she writes about "Mother's and Alex's cowardice" and "those years when I still remained, emotionally, their slave," we feel we're overhearing the work she did in analysis with "Dr. Norvell Lamarr, of blessed memory." *Them* is only the latest of her struggles to resolve her fury at her mother, and she still can't bring herself to express it full-out.

HER: Tatiana quickly found her place as a fashionable hat designer at Saks Fifth Avenue. She was "Tatiana of Saks," whose clients included stars like Claudette Colbert, Marlene Dietrich, Irene Dunne, and Edith Piaf, and rich women like Mrs. E. F. Hutton, Mrs. Pierre du Pont, Mrs. Walter Annenberg, and Estée Lauder. And even before the Libermans had any real money, she was establishing herself as a unique kind of hostess—generous and gregarious in that all-embracing Russian way; superb in her clusters of huge costume jewelry; and most of all, tactless and almost perversely outspoken. Among her many pronouncements: "Fireplace without logs is like man without erection." "Meeecnk is for football." "Diamonds are for suburbs." To one astonished guest, "I can tell by the way your wife walk whether she has clitoral or vaginal orgasm." To Francine's Bryn Mawr roommate, who was wearing a plastic raincoat: "Take off raincoat! Eet look like contraceptive!"

As for her snobbery, it was unmediated and forthrightly declared—"Snobs are always right"—and was always about success: "One does not argue with winners." In the mid-seventies, by which time Francine, The Child, had morphed into Francine du Plessix Gray, The Bestselling Writer, the family's beloved cook could say to her, "Thank God you've become a writer.... The Madam, she never even looked at you before you wrote that book."

Tatiana made no effort to modify her Russian accent, rarely read anything in English, specialized in making lavish gifts. Everyone came to her parties, from Dietrich to Dalí to Dior. (In the fashion world, only Balenciaga spurned her. Francine seems to enjoy noting that he "thought the Libermans were arriviste rabble and was seen solely in the company of Alex's archrival, Diana Vreeland.")

Here's what Tatiana didn't do. Until Francine's graduation day, she never set foot at Spence. In fifty years, she never once bothered to visit Alex's office at Condé Nast. ("Why go, I know just what ees like. Ees like one beeg ice cube.") She demanded—and received—adoration and subservience from both husband and daughter. Francine recalls how, from her earliest childhood, she would enter her mother's bathroom "for my almost daily crouch (arms about my legs, head on my knees to make myself as unobtrusive as possible), every few minutes she blows me a kiss with her fingers and then returns full attention to the image in the mirror, to the buffing and polishing of that marvelous face." Yes, Francine understands her mother's narcissism—"Mirrors were the central metaphor of her life." Yet she can't help being hypnotized by her glamour.

And she can't help mythologizing her. In the introduction, she presents Tatiana as "my flamboyant Russian-born mother—who was one of the foremost fashion icons of her generation, whose life had to do with the art of putting on a spectacular show and of casting her spell on as many people as possible." She deplores the mythology and at the same time clings to it. "She strode into a room, shawls spectacularly draped about her shoulders, like a tribal war goddess and moved through life with a speed and fierceness that recalled the howling wind of the steppes. Tatiana was one of the most dazzling self-inventions of her time, a force of nature all right, and those of us who loved her may well remain under her spell until the day we die." Sadly, it looks as if that will indeed be Francine's fate.

HIM: If Francine's take on her mother is complicated, her view of her stepfather is straightforward. She's properly grateful to him for the unending care and affection he gave her. And she's shocked and repelled by what she's learned about him as a fair-weather friend and a Machiavellian corporate player.

To begin with the good: "Over the years [Alex] listened with intense interest to any issue I brought up. . . . I increasingly looked on him as a confidant as well as a role model and offered him a kind of blind trust." He's the only emotional lifeline she has. And he's the one who provides practical support. "From our first months together in the 1940s, it is Alex who had assumed paternal and maternal roles, who with unfailing patience and tenderness dealt with my teachers and braces and report cards, heard out my heartaches, and imposed curfew hours and taboos on teen behavior." It was even he who, when she was nineteen or so, had the job of advising her ("with a tinge of embarrassment in his voice") about contraception. "There are condoms, certain rubber objects, which men can put on their . . . dum-dums, you know . . ."; "There are diaphragms, which women can use and which I believe are quite comfortable. There is the possibility of the man withdrawing before orgasm . . . a time-honored tactic!" Best of all, "There is abstinence!" "I already have a diaphragm," Francine shoots back.

Her dependency on him continues into her twenties, when she's leading a troubled life in Paris. She writes to him (the letters are quoted in *Alex*): "Each word from you clarifies my life and calms my spirit," and "One page a month from you packs in more affection than ten letters a month from any other father," and "I have come to some kind of breaking point which is very hard to live through sanely, and I need your voice." Alex's serious, intelligent, unremitting concern for Francine is his great redeeming virtue.

As for the rest, the picture she paints is almost unrelievedly damning, except for her appreciation of his large talents, both as an impresario of magazines and, eventually, as an artist in his own right. If you've read the generally apologetic *Alex*, you already know how he dealt with his old benefactor from Paris, Lucien Vogel, another refugee now at Condé Nast. Vogel just didn't fit in at *Vogue*. Alex, the authors tell us, "would never have said or done anything to undercut his friend, but the time was coming when he would be obliged, as he later described it, to 'cast him off.' For a refugee and a survivor, such divestitures were sometimes unavoidable."

Some opinions of Alex, as collated by Francine:

The former travel editor Despina Messinesi: "He had a great gift for jumping into the lap of power." (Rosamond Bernier: "Alex instantly jumped into the lap of anyone who enabled him to increase his power.")

His friend and protégé Irving Penn: "He wasn't a person of true relationships. . . . People were useful to him or they were not. . . . I was useful."

Lord Snowdon: "He was as arduous a self-promoter as you can meet, very slippery, like an eel, always wheeling and dealing for himself."

Pierre Bergé: "He was a totally false, utterly unoriginal man. . . . He never had an idea of his own. He swiped ideas from everyone else."

The former Condé Nast chief financial officer David Salem: "He rarely displayed any true conviction or loyalty of any kind."

Tina Brown: "Just as Salieri was jealous of Mozart, Alex was often envious of people of true talent. . . . When he sensed that someone had risen too high in the esteem of Si Newhouse, for instance, he'd say to me, 'So-and-so is second-rate, I must go and plant the poison.'"

Anna Wintour: "Alex was very much Si's courtier."

He engineered countless firings, with predictable results. I myself can testify to Diana Vreeland's loathing of him. Leo Lerman, fired from *Vanity Fair*, was deeply hurt, referring to him as "that housemaid's delight." Grace Mirabella, fired from *Vogue*: "I was stunned, Alex was my closest friend."

It would be too painful to recount all the stories of friends he turned on or abandoned. One will suffice. The man who made his career at Condé Nast, Iva (Pat) Patcèvitch, was as close a family friend as an outsider can be—you can tell how Francine adored him—and his wife, Nada, was more than a friend to Tatiana; they were "like sisters." The moment Pat left Nada for Marlene Dietrich, Marlene became Tatiana's closest friend. "I noticed that from the time Nada was officially separated from Pat, my parents never once returned her calls." Francine stays loyal to her, however, and reports her saying, "How are they? I often think of them, of my so-called sister." Then, as Pat's star waned at Condé Nast and Alex's rose, the inevitable happened. One night in 1967, Sam Newhouse, Si's father, asked Alex whether Pat was doing a good job. "I couldn't lie," Alex explained. Almost twenty-five years later, on his way to dying, Pat whispers to Francine, "How is my brother Alex?"

Among Alex's most perceptive critics was his mother, Henriette, who in one of her passionate and tactless letters, quoted in *Alex*, pronounced sentence on the life the Libermans lived: "You have become a slave to a certain 'milieu.' In my view, there is nothing live, original, or human in it. . . . I have not seen at your house one single live person. For me you are a living human being who 'mummifies' himself among the dead."

My sole encounter with Alex, which took place while I was at *The New Yorker*—the meeting, as I remember it, was suggested by Si—left me feeling that I was being measured for a shroud.

THEM: Their marriage went on as it had begun, with Alex worshipping and Tatiana happy to be worshipped. She was capricious, outrageous, and infinitely demanding. Soon after they arrived in America, Alex—"clearly terrified, his mustache trembling"—offers her a little black jewelry box. Opening it, she cries *"Mais c'est minable!"* ("It's pathetic!"). According to Francine, it was a very pretty if conventional aquamarine brooch set in gold filigree. Tatiana snapped the box shut and hurled it across the room at Alex. "How could you not know that this is just the kind of object I detest?" "I thought it was beautiful," he says. "You can't possibly think it's beautiful," she cries. "It looks, it looks . . . Indian, that's what it looks like!" and she rushes upstairs. When Francine (age eleven) tries to comfort him, he whispers, "These moods don't last long with her."

Another snapshot: When Alex is advising Francine about contraception, he volunteers that "Your mother has often refused herself, made herself unavailable, and this is an absolutely central part of her great magic."

During the long period of Tatiana's final illness, Alex is on hand to administer her Demerol shots night and day. She grew "more devious, more intractably selfish, more self-absorbed. . . . Both his prostate cancer and his heart attack had seemed to fill her with jealousy and anger." (Tatiana: "He's not at all as sick as I. I'm the one who's really sick.") She used the blackmail of starving herself to hold his attention. "In the space of eighteen months, Alex hired and fired thirty-four cooks in a vain attempt to get her to eat."

The end was protracted and ugly, Alex finally fleeing from her hospital room. After more than fifty years, it was over. Who knows what Alex was really feeling? One clue: A day or so after the funeral, Francine tells us, Alex decides to go out to dinner. "But is that wise, darling?" she asks. "Are you well enough?" And then, "In a burst of fury, with a kind of meanness I'd never yet witnessed in him—Dr. Jekyll suddenly turned into Mr. Hyde"—Alex snaps, "I'm going out tonight, and from now on don't ever delve into my affairs. . . . And please clear out Mother's closet as fast as possible. I want everything out in the next three days!"

FRANCINE: Long before Tatiana's death, each of them had pronounced an epitaph on the marriage. Alex: "Your mother's always right." Tatiana: "Didn't we have the luck of the devil finding him." Their daughter's take is more equivocal: "Like the gang in the Kremlin, the Libermans exuded an absolute assurance that in every possible area of their life . . . they had made the most perfect choices, had created the greatest achievable harmony." Francine is aware of the discrepancy between the fantasy and the reality. At Tatiana's parties, she tells us, Alex "hovered at the edge of the room like a high-class maître d', looking affable and yet utterly detached." In fact, Francine realized that he'd always "loathed" Tatiana's parties, "[t]hat he considered himself to be a man with no friends. That most other humans bored him to death. . . . That he looked on hospitality as merely serviceable, as another boring expedient that humored Mother and helped him to climb the power ladder." A few hours after Mother's death, Alex barks at Francine, "No more inviting people to my house, ever again!" The worm had turned, but only after the bird had flown.

Before the bird had flown, however, no husband could have been more ostentatiously uxorious: "Flirtatious but utterly chaste, he became noted for brandishing his adoration of my mother and his unswerving fidelity to her." Was he ever tempted? That question leads to what is perhaps the oddest passage in Francine's book, on the nature of Alex's sexuality. She goes out of her way to emphasize his "curious lack of sexual presence," quoting people who knew him well on his "aura of a flirtatious eunuch," on his "terribly limited libido." (Asked whether he could have been homosexual, a very old friend, Nicolas de Guinzbourg, commented, "He wouldn't dare.") To Francine herself, "He was the most sexually neutral man I have ever known." She realizes that as a teenager she might have been "disembodying him as a way of positing a barrier, of avoiding any possible attraction between us," yet her interest in his sex life and his focus on "personal cosmetic concerns"—his obsession, for instance, with "controlling facial hair"—seems excessive. Strangest of all is her description of his "cool, impersonal, ascetic" bathroom, "in which I never observed any object in the least associated with sexuality or sexual enticement—except just once, when I was in my late teens and saw, pathetically curled up in a neat heap, a little yellowish condom, clearly unused." What can it mean that she has felt it incumbent on herself to share that little condom with the world?

Emotional truths start breaking through in the final pages of *Them*, those dealing with the period after Tatiana's death. Alex leaves the house that the family lived in for fifty years and moves into an apartment in the building where Si Newhouse lives. ("I couldn't repress a smile.") Although in her will Tatiana had left Francine her precious letters from Mayakovsky, Alex doesn't turn them over to her for eight years, at which point she just takes them: "Only then . . . did I understand why my possessive, jealous stepfather, who had worked hard to create the legend that he was the center of Tatiana's universe, was determined to deny the poet's letters to their rightful heir, the adopted daughter he had supposedly cherished." Alex also "failed to offer me so much as one memento from Seventieth Street . . . only later did I feel rage at this omission."

One suspects that the real blow came a year and a half after Tatiana's death, when Alex married his Filipina nurse of many years, Melinda, about whom Francine says all the right things: "Melinda's devotion to Alex was heroic"; "Melinda did her own act with admirable dignity and dedication and tenderness." Yet her tone suggests something different: "Alex was now totally under Melinda's sway . . . constantly adjusting his opinions to hers, and the two were now holding hands and calling each other 'Babycakes.'"

Francine and her family—Cleve, the beloved grandsons—are not wanted at the wedding. Alex: "I have no family." (Eventually, they're permitted to come.) But Alex does have a family now, a new one: "Melinda placed a baby carriage in the entrance hall of her New York apartment, a permanent reminder to Alex that it was all those little nieces and nephews of hers who were now his family, his babies." And—its significance disguised by its being tucked away in a parenthesis—"They were to be well remembered in his will."

At the end, Francine claims resolution. When she sees Alex just before his death, "We offered each other the sweetest gift any parent and child can exchange—that of total conciliation." The writing gets fancy here, and the sentiments noble. I have my doubts, though. This is not a book born of resolution and "conciliation." But it's not a simple act of assassination, either. The author is too intelligent and decent a person to perpetrate a *Parents, Dearest*; her revenge, if it is revenge, is more subtle than that. When her mother died, something akin to a sense of gratitude emerged: "Dear God, I've survived her." With both of them gone, she can say, "Now that you are in my custody, fierce parents, you have become my own docile little children." Having the last word is the best revenge.

Nonetheless, at almost seventy-five, Francine du Plessix Gray is still suffering from the pain of her upbringing. The dedication says more, perhaps, than she meant it to. Yes, she looks back on Tatiana and Alex with love, because however monstrous they may have been, she can't help loving them; and, yes, she looks back with longing, because—despite all the evidence, despite the lateness of the hour, despite her self-exorcisms through fiction and analysis and a fruitful life honorably led—she's still longing for Them to turn into parents.

May 5, 2005

Bringing Up Biographer

W hat is one to make of this odd and unsettling book? It's a complicated question for me, since I had professional relationships with both its author and its subject, and was very close to a third powerful presence in the book, Irene Mayer Selznick. And yet, reading *Kate Remembered*, I felt I was in uncharted waters, despite an occasional familiar landmark. Oh, yes, that sounds like Irene. . . . There's the Scott Berg we like to admire. . . . Typical Hepburn chutzpah or charm.

The problem is that two different stories are being told here. One is Katharine Hepburn's. The other is A. Scott Berg's. "She more than merits a full-scale biography," Berg says at the start of his author's note (as if she hadn't already been the subject of a dozen or so). "Alas, I am not the one to write such a book." And he hasn't. Instead, he has made himself the vehicle for her posthumous version of her life story. He is the ghost to her ghost. They had been talking for twenty years or so, he tells us, with the understanding that one day a book like this would emerge, though only after her death—only twelve days after, as it turned out: *Kate Remembered* had been buried, like a land mine, in its publisher's vault, waiting for the moment of opportunity.

In 1991 Hepburn pieced together and published *Me*, her "stories of my life." It was a mess of a book—strident, evasive, patchy, willful—but it had its virtues: It was direct, unfiltered; clearly in its subject's own voice. Whereas *Kate Remembered* is a peculiar mix of her voice as mediated by Berg—for whatever reason, he didn't tape their conversations—and the voice of his own narrative. You see the difference between the two books when you compare stories that turn up in both of them. Take the account of how Hepburn snatched the lead in *Morning Glory* from Constance Bennett, for whom it had been written. One day, she just happened to see the

script on the desk of the producer Pandro Berman and made off with it. Berg: "'I usually don't look through people's desks,' Hepburn told me one afternoon—somewhat disingenuously, I thought. . . . She spent the next several days meeting everybody connected to this production, talking up this 'thrilling' screenplay . . . until she convinced them that she was 'born to play this part.'" Here's how Hepburn put it in *Me*: "Went to Pandro and said I must do it. He said no. It was for Connie Bennett. I said No—ME. I won." There's the difference between Kate alive and Kate remembered.

The new book contains few revelations. In *Me*, Hepburn refers to her selfishness in regard to her complaisant husband, "Luddy," as "piggishness." When Berg asks her "why she had bothered to marry Luddy . . . she looked me right in the eye and, without thinking twice, said, 'Because I was a pig.'" Give her A-plus for consistency, but barely a passing grade for further illumination. Not that we should be surprised at her telling the old stories in more or less the same way. We all do it; our memories become set pieces in the retelling, and this is particularly understandable in people used to the spotlight, who have to repeat things over and over. As Berg takes us through Hepburn's life, we encounter all the central events we've encountered in her own book and in other accounts of her life: the tragic death (presumably by suicide, in a family that seemed to have had a genetic disposition to suicide) of her beloved sixteen-year-old brother, Tom, whom she found hanged in his bedroom; the lucky break of George Cukor casting her, practically a nobody, opposite the great John Barrymore in her first movie, *A Bill of Divorcement*; her rapid ascent to stardom; her relationships with Leland Hayward, Howard Hughes, and several of her famous directors; her fall from grace as "box-office poison"; her comeback through her canny acquisition of the film rights to her hit play *The Philadelphia Story*; the adventure of *The African Queen*—she wrote an entire book about it (I was its editor); and of course the twenty-seven-year relationship with Spencer Tracy, which was the cornerstone of her emotional life and has become the cornerstone of her myth.

She is slightly more open about Tracy here than she has been elsewhere, though nowhere near so prodigal with insights as Berg, who gives her (and us) the benefit of his psychological diagnosis of why Tracy behaved so badly to her: "And then you came along, and you were the best and most beautiful creature he had ever seen. You got high on life. And he couldn't quite believe that somebody like you could be interested in somebody like him; and he figured he could never keep up with the likes of you. And so he often tried to tear you down, squash your good nature." And on and on in this vein, I'm afraid. Her response? "You should write all that down."

Katharine Hepburn was many things—accomplished, driven, high-handed, hardworking, stylish, demanding, generous—but she could hardly be called reflective. She didn't believe in it. She believed in never looking back, not wasting emotion, getting on with things. She also needed to exert control, and never more so than in the calculated way she presented herself to the world—classy, even haughty, a touch hard, but never dangerous. Bette Davis was dangerous—she went all the way, and imploded. Joan Crawford was an artifact that lasted until it wore out. Barbara Stanwyck was too much an actress to be a Personality. Garbo was ... Garbo, whatever and whoever that was. Because we thought we understood Hepburn's "aristocratic" background; because she gamely kept working on the stage, in Shakespeare and Shaw as well as in shows like *Coco*; because she ostentatiously shunned Hollywood and publicity; because she was so vital and independent and apparently straight-shooting, she became a Figure as well as a star, closer in our minds to a Mrs. Roosevelt than to a Davis or a Crawford. And she never stopped working on her image. Of course, that's what people in her position do or they don't hold on to that position, but few have done it with her relish. She always knew what she wanted—fame—and she demanded, and obtained, it from the world.

Unfortunately, as she grew old and her film career wound down, she couldn't let go—she trivialized her reputation by appearing in worthless films and TV dramas, and she began exposing her private life to the public in books and interviews, grabbing whatever attention she could command. Berg cannily observes: "She opened the door and followed me to the little black iron gate at the sidewalk, looking up and down 49th Street. I wondered if she wanted to be seen or not. 'Let us know when you're coming back,' she yelled, when I was a few doors away; and I turned back to see that several passersby, recognizing the voice, had, in fact, stopped and stared at her. She was smiling." And now, with his collaboration, she has made a final, successful grab for attention from beyond the grave, and a final stab at telling her story the way she wants it told.

Yet *Kate Remembered* turns out to be less Hepburn's story than Scott Berg's. We're with her whenever he quotes or describes her, but we're with him all the way, from the first starstruck moment—"I've never felt so intimidated ringing a doorbell"—to the recurrent daydream he describes in his last paragraph. He's in a white dinner jacket at a Main Line country club when "suddenly a striking young woman appears—fresh from Bryn Mawr—with big, luminous eyes and high cheekbones. A gentle breeze blows through her auburn hair. We notice each other; and with her long legs, she is striding right toward me." Apart from astonishment that if someone actually had this daydream, he wouldn't be too mortified to share it, what registers most sharply is that the first word of Berg's book is "I've" and the last is "me."

In between is the story of their relationship. He comes to her house to interview her, and from her first words we know who's in charge: "Did you use the bathroom?" Soon he's a treasured guest, with his own key to the house and a standing invitation to stay there whenever he's in from the West Coast. He's also spending weekends at the family house, Fenwick, in

Connecticut, and one of the most valuable aspects of his book is the detailed view he gives us of her life there—important to understanding her, since Fenwick was Kate Hepburn's Tara (and yes, she wanted to play Scarlett). The house in Turtle Bay where she lived for more than sixty years always seemed to me a setting she had constructed for herself; Fenwick, Berg demonstrates, was her natural shell.

From the start, his book is a paean of praise and love, beginning with his declaration that he believes—"unabashedly and without qualification"— that Hepburn "established the greatest acting career of the twentieth century, perhaps ever." Cautiously, he doesn't suggest that she was the greatest actor of our—or all—time, but even his hedged claim is ludicrously off the mark. Forget Bernhardt or Duse; in the movies, stars from Pickford, Chaplin, Valentino, and Garbo to Monroe and John Wayne had greater impact and were more cherished than she was. As for Hepburn's acting, in at least half her movies she's anything from miscast to an embarrassment. She's superb, everyone agrees, in *Alice Adams*, in which she triumphantly capitalizes on her most annoying qualities. I'm one of those who enjoy her swanky impersonations—*Holiday, Bringing Up Baby, The Philadelphia Story*—though others find them grating. I'm not one of the many who love her films with Tracy: They're so self-reflecting, so full of studied banter, and so compromised in the working out of the male-female relationship—Hepburn, the famously liberated icon, winking at us as she goes down for the count. It's in *The African Queen* that she stops being Hepburn and starts playing a character. How come? It may have been John Huston, it may have been Africa, it may have been a good script with a real story, but I suspect it was Bogart. Hepburn and Tracy are two cocky characters who spar their way into love. Hepburn and Bogart are two hardened souls who gradually melt into it. That's a lot more difficult to pull off, and a lot more appealing.

Reading between the lines of *Kate Remembered*, you start to realize that not all was sunshine and light between star and scribe. She pushes an ice-cream cone into his face. He finds her in his room at Fenwick rifling through his overnight bag (she smiles sheepishly, but no apologies). When he tries to talk to her of a new relationship in his life, "she almost never wanted to hear about it. 'I don't like to think of your living anywhere,' Kate had said to me shortly after giving me the key to her house. 'I like to think that this is your home.'" It's the old story: When you're in thrall to royalty, your life isn't your own. No matter how gratifying it was to Berg to be adopted by this star of stars, it can't always have been easy.

Apart from Berg, Hepburn herself, and Tracy, the most powerful presence in *Kate Remembered* is Irene Mayer Selznick, daughter of Louis B., wife of David O., and producer of several important Broadway plays, most famously *A Streetcar Named Desire*. Berg calls her "easily the most challenging" person he has ever met, and he is exactly right in saying that "emotional, volatile and analytical, she took nothing at face value, probing layers beneath layers in even the simplest matters." He's wrong, though, in his interpretation of why, during her last years, she backed away from Hepburn after half a century of close friendship. It wasn't that she felt increasingly excluded from Hepburn's new life; it's that she wanted no part of it. The turning point was a TV documentary in which Hepburn not only went public in depth about her relationship with Tracy but described in detail his dying as she crouched by his bed.

Irene's word for this abandonment of privacy and flaunting of intimate matters was "disgusting," and she felt betrayed—as if, through the years, she had been deliberately misled about Kate's character. (It's not by accident that Irene's memoirs were called *A Private View*.) She determined to withdraw, assuring me that she would do it so gradually that Kate would have no grounds for demanding explanations. Berg, in a wonderful comic set piece, describes the night that Michael Jackson came to dinner, and mentions that, according to Kate, Irene was uninvited. But I vividly remember the morning Irene called me, exploding with fury: "Can you believe what she's done now? She *dared* to invite me to dinner with Michael Jackson! Is she insane?" To her, Michael Jackson was just another symptom of Kate's vulgar and pathetic desperation to stay up to date and in the limelight.

Some months before she died, Irene gave me a hundred-odd letters she had received from Kate over a period of thirty years. ("I don't want the wrong people to get hold of them, particularly her.") They're chatty, affectionate, appreciative, occasionally incisive; very much the letters of one sister to another—and indeed they're almost all signed "Sister Kate." But the happy comradeship of the letters had faded away and been replaced by rancor and disillusionment. It's a sad story, and Kate got the message. Berg tells us that it was only under pressure that she attended Irene's memorial service; she had already refused to speak at it.

It's fascinating to watch Berg pick his uncomfortable and delicate way between "my friend Irene" and "my friend Kate." In the telling, he emerges with his image of himself intact. Indeed, his book's chief fault is not that it's relatively unrevealing and unsurprising—it's fun, after all, to canter through the basic Hepburn story once again—but that a strain of self-aggrandizement runs through it, as well as the feeling one gets of an author using his book to pay off old scores. Why refer so sneeringly to an unnamed Knopf editor who worked on his *Goldwyn*—what does this have to do with Katharine Hepburn? (I, by the way, am given inflated credit for what modest help I gave Berg on that book.) And why the tone of resentment that permeates his account of how he helped Warren Beatty get Hepburn to appear in Beatty's (dreadful) version of *Love Affair*? It reads as though Berg were a disappointed suitor—not for Beatty's hand but for his favor.

Other questions arise. Why the speculations about Cynthia McFadden's marriage? McFadden was a young woman who became close to Hepburn—in fact, frequently usurping Berg's bedroom on Forty-ninth Street—but surely the world doesn't need to know what Hepburn felt about her friend's personal life. And—far more serious—was it a favor to his beloved Hepburn to expose to the world Irene's late conclusions regarding "Sister Kate's" sexual nature?

Also disturbing is the frequent sloppiness of the writing, particularly jarring from someone whose previous biographies—of Maxwell Perkins, Samuel Goldwyn, and Charles Lindbergh—justify large expectations. Solecism follows solecism. "The Hepburn boys were equally disparate from one another." "She was, instead, trodding the boards." "Unlike herself, Hepburn felt that [Elizabeth] Taylor 'preferred being a movie star to being an actress.'" While the manuscript was ticking away in Putnam's vaults, couldn't some copy editor have cast an eye over it to protect Berg from himself?

No. It was apparently more important for the book to be kept Top Secret and rushed out pell-mell after the death than to be professionally vetted. No doubt a clever commercial decision, but it adds to one's general unease about the entire project—a sense of exploitation, though who was exploiting whom would be hard to pin down. All biographers to some extent exploit their subjects by reinventing them, and Hepburn exploited everyone. The only conclusion I can draw is that Katharine Hepburn and Scott Berg loved each other, needed each other, and used each other. Which may not be the worst definition of friendship.

August 17, 2003

The Escape Artist

Almost the first thing you see after entering the Houdini exhibition at the Jewish Museum is a large-screen film of Harry Houdini hanging by his ankles upside-down from a tall building, high over a sea of men in fedoras, and thrashing his way out of a straitjacket. It's terrifying, just the way this exploit—which he repeated again and again—was meant to be. This is not a stage magician pulling rabbits out of hats or cards out of sleeves; it's a death-defying demonstration of courage, showmanship, and psychopathology—three of the King of Handcuffs' most conspicuous and enduring qualities.

No one ever doubted his courage, although many of his stage effects were far from hazardous—the Metamorphosis, for instance, the trick that made him famous, in which he and his partner changed their clothes and replaced each other in a locked trunk within three seconds. Other tricks, though, took not only ingenious preparation and years of practice but nerves of steel, culminating in the Chinese Water Torture act in which Houdini's feet were locked into stocks and he was lowered by his ankles into a cell filled with water (there was a glass door through which the audience could see him, his head touching the floor, his hair swirling, his feet exposed through an opening at the top). A cabinet was drawn around the cell, and while the orchestra played "Asleep in the Deep," his assistant standing by with an ax in case of an emergency (and to heighten the drama), he would effect his escape in a couple of minutes or even less. He had been perfecting his breath control for years. "Imagine yourself jammed head foremost in a Cell and your shoulders tightly lodged in this imprisonment," he wrote. "I believe it is the climax of all my studies and labors. Never will I be able to construct anything that will be more dangerous or difficult for me to do."

Kenneth Silverman, the best of Houdini's biographers, describes him flinging himself, handcuffed or straitjacketed or nailed into a packing case from countless bridges; escaping, chained and spread-eagled, from the chassis of a speeding car; extricating himself from being roped to a girder on the roof of the under-construction Heidelberg Tower in New York, overlooking a three-hundred-foot drop to Forty-second Street. Again and again he devised perilous situations for himself to survive and his audience to gasp and shudder at. He understood the risks: "I'll get in the water some day, my trick will fail, and then good night!"

Nor did he get away scot-free. In their fascinating *The Secret Life of*

Houdini, William Kalush and Larry Sloman tell us that "In 1909 alone Houdini had serious difficulties escaping from a wet sheet challenge, injured his wrists severely when he was hung from chains, and 'all but choked to death' from the pressure of a leather collar when his bed slipped from position during a challenge to escape from a 'crazy crib' restraint used on lunatics." Even in his fifties he was raising the danger bar.

As for his showmanship, it was supreme. From the start he had realized that how he presented his feats was as important—maybe *more* important—than the feats themselves. His stage presence was soft-spoken, affable, attuned to the expectations and gratifications of his audiences. (Not everyone accepted him at face value, though: A reporter in Sydney, Australia, wrote, "I find it hard to give him my unreserved sympathy. He is too aggressive to pose as a mild genial character.") His looks were appealing, with his tightly curled dark hair, bright blue eyes, and boyish smile; Tony Curtis was the perfect choice to play him in the far-from-accurate 1953 biopic. Although he was very short, he was definitely masculine. He went about his routines in an almost matter-of-fact manner, but he very deliberately timed them for maximum effect: "If I go out too quickly, the audience would reason that the escape was easy. Every second that ticks by during my struggle builds up to the climax. When they are sure I am licked, that the box will have to be smashed open to give me air, then—and only then— do I appear . . . The pent-up mass emotion explodes into an ovation."

Offstage, he was a relentless self-promoter. (He was once described as "a Barnum with only one side-show—himself.") When he arrived in a new city, he would present himself at police headquarters and challenge the chief to handcuff him, straitjacket him, lock him up in an escape-proof cell, whereupon—to the excitement of alerted journalists and, through them, the public—he would free himself in moments. The leaps into rivers and canals, the danglings from tall buildings, were also consummate coups of free publicity. A New York reporter wrote that one of these stunts was "the biggest free show ever seen in New York or anywhere else": As many as a hundred thousand spectators lined the docks and gaped from windows.

His ego was notorious. He abhorred and ruthlessly attacked and undermined real or potential rivals. And he was close to paranoid about secrecy and loyalty. All his assistants had to sign an oath: "I the undersigned do solemnly swear on my sacred honor as a man that as long as I live I shall never divulge the secret or secrets of Harry Houdini . . . I further swear never to betray Houdini . . . So help me God almighty and may he keep me steadfast." This obsession with loyalty was not new. His wife, Bess, reports that almost immediately after their marriage, Harry took her and one of his brothers out onto a bridge at midnight, clasped their hands, and cried: "Beatrice, Dash, raise your hands to heaven and swear that you will both be true to me. Never betray me in any way, so help you God." Houdini never bothered to mask or qualify his highly theatrical approach to himself and to life; even in such highly personal matters, he was first and foremost a showman. The astute Ruth Brandon, another of his biographers (they are legion), remarks that through self-dramatizing scenes like this one, "Houdini reassured himself that his interests would always come first, not only in his own mind but in the minds of all those who might be close to him."

The pathological aspects of Houdini's emotional landscape have frequently been recognized. Silverman, for instance, writes that, with their bondage and writhing, "many of Houdini's . . . escapes smacked of torture and sadomasochistic display," and notes the many grisly articles and photographs he pasted in his diary, among them "a photo of pirates decapitated by Chinese officials, the cutoff heads strewn on the ground like cabbages." In the same spirit, "in an envelope labeled 'Chinese Tortures' he kept a set of revolting snuff snapshots that showed chunks of flesh being hacked from a woman tied to a stake, her gouged-out breasts and thighs pouring blood."

In 1976, Bernard Meyer, a respected psychoanalyst and author of a "Psychoanalytic Biography" of Joseph Conrad, published *Houdini: A Mind in Chains*. He too focuses on the theme of bondage, given that being roped, shackled, handcuffed, straitjacketed, and trapped in claustrophobic devices made up so large a proportion of Houdini's repertoire. Yes, engaging with such practices would be a sine qua non for any escape artist, but that does not preclude the psychic importance that Meyer imputes to them.

What, moreover, are we to make of the insistent, almost obsessive allusions to nudity in the self-presentations of this privately prudish Central European Jew? Not only is he endlessly photographed semi-naked in chains, but in city after city he would strip himself "buck naked" to be examined and probed by the police from whose jail cells he was preparing to escape. What's odd isn't the fact of such incidents but the relish with which he recounts them. On one of his first business cards he boasts of being STRIPPED STARK NAKED before performing. In a Philadelphia police station he performed his famous Needle Swallowing trick in what a reporter called "charming and total dishabille." In Berlin he's stripped naked in front of a crowd of three hundred antagonistic policemen. In Russia, where he had to deal with the virulently anti-Semitic police, "four burly policemen spread-eagled him on an examining table . . . 'What a searching,' he later told a friend. 'Three secret police, or what we would call spies, searched me one after the other, and talk about getting the finger, well I received it three times, but Mr. Russian Spy found nothing.'"

Perhaps even more peculiar, because so matter-of-fact, is this incident recounted by the magician Milbourne Christopher. In 1908 Houdini was to perform his famous Water Can trick at the Harvard Union. "As he stripped to a pair of blue trunks there was a roar of disapproval. Yale blue at Cambridge! 'Wear Harvard crimson,' came the shouts. Harry, the showman, calmly stripped off his shorts and amazed his all-male audience by escaping from the water-filled canister in the raw." This is exhibitionism beyond the call of duty.

Ehrich Weiss— Harry Houdini to-be—was not born in Appleton, Wisconsin, as he originally claimed; he was born in Budapest. His father, Mayer Samuel Weiss, was probably never ordained as a rabbi as he claimed to have been; he had worked as a soap-maker in Budapest, had taken some law courses, and had some experience as a solicitor. In 1876 he immigrated to America, and two years later, when Ehrich was four, was followed by the rest of the family—the mother, Cecilia, and their five boys. Mayer Weiss did set up as a rabbi in Appleton, but his small congregation soon shriveled away—apart from anything else, although he lived until 1892, he never learned English. Things were so bad that the family had to move, but in Milwaukee their circumstances grew even worse. By 1887, Mayer and Ehrich were in New York, living together in acute poverty, working at whatever jobs they could find—Ehrich, for instance, as a necktie cutter. (By now, Cecilia had produced another son and her only daughter.)

No one at this point could possibly have predicted what Ehrich Weiss would become, yet he had blundered into the perfect apprenticeship. By the time he was seven, while still in Appleton, he was already fascinated by traveling circuses and acrobats and contortionists—and by the local store that sold locks and keys. When he was nine, in Milwaukee, he was recruiting pals into a neighborhood circus, billing himself as "Ehrich, the Prince of the Air." He was athletic from the start, a superb gymnast and eventually a star boxer and long-distance runner. (At eighteen he set the record for the run around Central Park.) He also avidly pursued a childhood interest in coin- and card tricks, performing them at such venues as the Young Man's Hebrew Association, where he billed himself as either Ehrich Weiss or Eric the Great.

The turning point was a crucial encounter with a book—the *Memoirs of Robert-Houdin*, the most famous magician of the nineteenth century and the source of the Houdini stage name. ("Harry" was an Anglicization of his nickname, Ehrie.) It was this book that inflamed his love of magic and set him on his lifelong path. In 1891, now seventeen, he formed a magic act called the Brothers Houdini, first with a friend, later with his brother Dash, eventually with his wife, Bess, and began a half-dozen years of exhausting, uncertain, meagerly paid work in dime museums and traveling circus sideshows.

But he was watching everything and learning from everyone. He befriended the circus freaks, one of whom, Kalush and Sloman tell us, was an armless man who "so impressed him with his ability to use his toes as fingers that Houdini practiced and practiced until his own toes developed prehensile abilities, which would be invaluable to him in later escape work. He learned the techniques of circus strongmen, fire-resisters, and sword-swallowers." And from a member of a Japanese balancing act, he learned how "to seemingly swallow objects and then regurgitate them at will by hiding them in his gullet."

Eventually the hard work—plus the never-fail Metamorphosis act— paid off, when in 1899 a leading vaudeville impresario, the manager of the Orpheum circuit, spotted the Houdinis and booked them around the country. They were in (comparative) clover. Vaudeville was the big time, and by the next year they were performing in England, and Harry was the King of Handcuffs.

Presumably to help erase in his own mind the humiliation of his father's failed life, Harry Houdini would repeatedly insist that he came from a long line of scholarly, writerly ancestors ("We have records for five generations that my direct fore-fathers were students and teachers of the

Bible"), yet he himself had almost no schooling, and although he was to write a great deal—biography, autobiography, short stories, screenplays, articles and books on both magic and Spiritualism, plus thousands of letters—he never mastered spelling or punctuation, or editorial restraint.

Mayer Weiss was not, however, the central figure in Houdini's psychic development, unless we conclude that his utter failure to establish a solid life in America was the prime goad to his son's relentless drive to succeed. The person for whom Houdini lived—whose happiness meant everything to him and whose approbation he desperately sought—was his mother, Cecilia. There are few recorded mother-son relationships as intense, as overwhelming, as theirs. One of the family legends is that on Ehrich's twelfth birthday his father said to him, "Promise me, my boy, that after I am gone your dear Mother will never want for anything," and he never stopped keeping his promise.

There were exaggerated gestures—pouring gold pieces into her apron; buying her a dress supposedly designed for Queen Victoria and taking her to Budapest to flaunt it; dedicating a book to her:

IN WORSHIPFUL HOMAGE
I
DEDICATE THIS BOOK
TO THE MEMORY OF MY SAINTED MOTHER
IF GOD
IN HIS INFINITE WISDOM
EVER SENT AN ANGEL UPON EARTH IN HUMAN FORM
IT WAS MY
MOTHER

Until she died, his first thought was always of her (he claimed to believe that his wife, Bess, never resented this). When in 1907, in Rochester, he performed his first manacled jump into a canal, "he wanted his mother to see it . . . because 'I thought something might happen.'" Dr. Meyer remarks on "the habit this grown man had of laying his head on his mother's breast—in order to hear her heart beat. It was just one of those 'little peculiarities,' Houdini noted, 'that mean so much to a mother and son when they love each other as we did.'"

He was working in Germany in 1913 (he was close to forty) when Cecilia died suddenly. When he heard the news, he fell in a faint, then canceled his tour and rushed back to New York, having wired the family to postpone the funeral until he could get home—contrary, of course, to Jewish custom. Utterly devastated, he took months before he was able to get back to work, and then, as he reported to brother Dash (now himself a well-known magician called "Hardeen"), "I . . . am hoping that eventually I will have my burning tears run dry, but know my Heart will ALWAYS ACHE FOR OUR DARLING MOTHER."

Again and again he returned to her grave—a midnight pilgrimage on the anniversary of her death; on his birthday; on *her* birthday, which, Silverman tells us, "he honored by having the body of her mother disinterred and reburied near her, to 'make her a birthday present.'" And in 1915 he wrote (and several times later confirmed): "It is my wish that all of my Darling Beloved Mother's letters . . . shall be placed in a sort of black bag, and used as a pillow for my head in my coffin, and all to be buried with me." And so it was done.

The only other important relationship of Houdini's life was with Bess, whom he met on a blind date when she was eighteen and he was twenty, and whom he married three weeks later—to the anger and distress of her German Catholic mother. (He didn't have the money to woo her properly; she later cracked that she had "sold her virginity . . . for an orange" and that she had to put up the two dollars for the marriage license.) Bess had been part of a singing act, but now she became his onstage assistant, her tiny, piquant look a happy balance to his somewhat chunky manliness.

What were they to each other? He was the official boss, she the caregiver, yet although this arrangement was carried to extremes, it contained its own ambivalences. She took care of his grooming (he was hardly fastidious): According to her account, through the thirty-three years of their married life she had to wash his ears every day (he didn't know how) and steal his underwear every night to make certain he wore fresh linen in the morning. In other words, she infantilized him. He once noted that his idea of comfort was to be sitting in an armchair in his library "Hearing Mrs. Houdini call up 'Young man your lunch is ready.'" But as Silverman tells us, peculiar clippings about marriage that Houdini had culled from various sources and then filed suggest a different dynamic: HUBBY'S RIGHT

TO SPANK WIFE IS UPHELD BY COURT; POLYGAMY AFTER THE WAR; and HITCHED WIFE TO PLOW; GETS 3-DAY SENTENCE.

The Houdinis never had children, and Ruth Brandon proposes in *The Life and Many Deaths of Harry Houdini* that Houdini may have been impotent. That seems unlikely, though, given that many of the notes with which he showered Bess throughout the day imply physical intimacy. From his diaries: "Bess has been very sweet lately; hope she keeps it up." Then, two weeks later, "When I get home, she is sore, and is sore for the night." Which certainly sounds like sexual withholding. After his death, Bess let it be known that "Houdini created a dream child, a son named after his own father, Mayer Samuel," and for years went on keeping her posted on Mayer Samuel's progress, the letters stopping "only when this 'son' became president of the United States."

She herself was apparently the victim of severe mood swings, and he is always pacifying her, complimenting her, declaring his eternal love. "Why," asks Brandon, "all those protestations? . . . Why this constant need to reassure both Bess and himself?" Why, indeed, was she so exigent and reprimanding? It would appear that their relationship was to a large degree a reflection of his bond with Cecilia—Bess the mother to be doted on and pacified, Harry the loving, occasionally naughty boy. At a 1924 Senate hearing about fortune-tellers and mediums, after his character has been attacked by hostile witnesses he called Bess to the stand:

Houdini: "One of the witnesses said I was a brute and that I was vile and I was crazy . . . Outside my great mother, Mrs. Houdini has been my greatest friend. Have I shown traces of being crazy, unless it was about you?"
Mrs. Houdini: "No."
Houdini: "Am I brutal to you, or vile?"
Mrs. Houdini: "No."
Houdini: "Am I a good boy?"
Mrs. Houdini: "Yes."
Houdini: "Thank you, Mrs. Houdini."

For the five years following his first success in England, Houdini performed more in Europe, particularly Germany, than at home. The pattern was almost exactly that of Isadora Duncan who, manifesting the same level of ambition and self-confidence, made her way to Europe just a year before he did and like him became a great international star there, rather than at home. His fame escalated—in fact, it never diminished. Famous trick followed famous trick, the most impressive, possibly, his making an elephant disappear from the floor of the huge Hippodrome theater in New York. (To this day, no one understands how he did it, though we have hints about his less phenomenal tricks: tiny picks for opening locks embedded in the thick calluses of his soles; weakened panels in the wooden containers in which he was habitually confined.) He now saw himself less as a "magician" than as a "mystifier," but whatever he was called, he was world-famous and triumphant.

And his fame came not only from his stage performances. In 1910 he became fascinated by the recent invention of the airplane, bought a plane, learned how to pilot it, and took it to Australia, determined to become the first person to fly there. ("I want to be first. I vehemently want to be first.") He succeeded—to immense publicity.

Then, in 1919, he embarked on a movie career with a fifteen-episode serial called *The Master Mystery* (it features an evil robot). Another serial was followed by three feature films: *Terror Island, The Man from Beyond*, and *Haldane of the Secret Service*. (Their heroes all sported his own initials: Harry Harper, Howard Hillary, Heath Haldane.) It would be hard to exaggerate how dreadful an actor Houdini was—blank, rigid, dull, and not very photogenic. He's a complete stiff, in fact, and things aren't improved by the fact that he wrote or collaborated on his screenplays, all of them conventional melodramas of the period. Even most of the stunts are dull. *The Man from Beyond* has a touch of originality, though: The hero has been frozen in the ice for a hundred years. But the melodrama that follows his thaw is standard stuff, and *Haldane* is considerably worse. The critics caught on, the public caught on, and the company Houdini had founded to make and distribute his films quickly tanked. His movie career had lasted four years.

He'd had fun in California, however, hobnobbing with stars like Charlie Chaplin and Gloria Swanson, who gave him an autographed photograph: "To Mr. Houdini, Please show me some of your tricks." California also produced a friendship between the Houdinis and Jack London and his wife, Charmian, with whom, after Jack died, Houdini did or didn't have the one serious fling of his life. Charmian's diary tracks the affair: one visit "stirred me to the deeps," and according to her, Houdini told her, "Now I know how kings have given kingdoms for a woman. You are gorgeous—you are wonderful. I love you." Whatever happened between them, it didn't last long, but Bess is recorded as saying that after Houdini's death, she found a cache of letters to him from several women, "one a widow whom she considered a very dear friend."

Whereas his movies do Houdini a disservice (not that anyone watches them), the poster art that he commissioned and displayed throughout his career is startling and vital. These posters are among the highlights of the Jewish Museum exhibition, along with an imposing straitjacket that looks like a sculpture of medieval armor and a convincing replica of the Chinese Water Torture cell. The photographs, too, are arresting. But the curators are especially invested in showing how a number of contemporary artists have riffed on Houdini's iconic persona, and these works are far less interesting than the posters are, or than the curators seem to believe they are. (I was, I have to admit, engaged by the installation of half a dozen bewildered live pigeons in an enclosed glass room, complete with pigeon droppings.)

The last several years of Houdini's life were dominated by his increasingly fierce assault on the mediums who were rampant in post-war America, fastening on naïve widows and mothers hoping to be in touch with their lost husbands and sons. In his early days on the circus circuit he had indulged in some lighthearted involvement with this kind of thing, but had quickly decided it was distasteful and pernicious.

Now he became a crusader, and the harder the mediums fought back, the harder he harassed them, pursuing them in the press, in the courts, and from the stage. He attended scores of séances incognito, and by 1925, had put together a band of investigators ("my own secret service department"), made up primarily of women posing as widows, the chief of whom was, according to Kalush and Sloman, "ordained six separate times as a full-fledged spiritualistic reverend with the right to perform marriages, baptize infants, and bury the dead. It took her as little as twenty minutes and five dollars to obtain her certification."

What made this travesty possible was the confusion between what the mediums were up to and a vague "religion" known as Spiritualism that was accorded some of the privileges religions receive in America. Houdini was always careful to make the distinction, assuring the public that he was respectful of the true Spiritualists and only interested in denouncing those he saw as phony magicians whose tricks he could readily expose. Yet he would write in *The New York Sun*: "I have never seen or heard anything that could convince me that there is a possibility of communication with the loved ones who have gone beyond." And as the crusade intensified, he crowed: "I drove out the fakes in California, and I intend to drive them out of Massachusetts."

This last reference was to Houdini's most sensational and longest-lasting investigation of a medium—a cause célèbre. Mina Crandon, spirit name "Margery," was pretty, clever (she was reportedly an excellent cellist), highly seductive, and married to a prominent Boston surgeon who taught at Harvard Medical School (the Crandons lived on Beacon Hill), and she did not take money to conduct her séances. When *Scientific American* offered a prize to someone who could prove real psychic powers, she was the preferred candidate, and for two years the battle between believers and skeptics raged, consuming much of Houdini's time and emotional energy, to say nothing of endless yards of newspaper coverage. (A crucial aspect of her act was ectoplasm presumably issuing from her vagina. Dr. Meyer commented: "Margery seemed to relish holding sittings in the nude—for which she can hardly be blamed—for it is not every day that a girl from Boston has a chance to display her ectoplasmic phallus and to have it photographed, too.") Eventually she was proved to be a fraud.

It was this experience that turned Houdini into a full-time anti-Spiritualist, not only writing almost obsessively on the subject but signing on for cross-country lecture tours denouncing the fakery of the mediums—becoming, in other words, an educator, a role psychologically important to him. Having had no education, he was a passionate autodidact, and indeed more and more of his life at this time was devoted to his immense library of books, journals, art, and memorabilia relating to magic; he had been collecting compulsively for decades, and a number of rooms in his house were crammed with his booty. (Bess was not amused.) He also employed a full-time librarian. After Houdini's death, the collection went to the Library of Congress.

Even more curious than the Margery story was the tragicomic arc of Houdini's friendship with Sir Arthur Conan Doyle, which began on a high note of mutual respect and affection. Doyle was perhaps the world's most famous supporter of Spiritualism—not only a man almost dementedly convinced of communication between the dead and the living but the willfully gullible victim of such obvious hoaxes as a photograph purportedly of four little fairies floating around a garden. It turned out that two teenage girls had taken some snaps of a nine-year-old niece and perpetrated this fraud as a joke. Doyle became a pubic laughingstock—headlines ran from POOR SHERLOCK HOLMES to HOPELESSLY CRAZY?—but he maintained his belief in the fairies until his death.

There have been two books devoted entirely to the relationship between these two men, and they tell the same story. A genial correspondence sprang up between them in 1920, followed by happy social contact between the Houdinis and the Doyles. The first rift came when they were all staying at a hotel in Atlantic City and Lady Doyle held a séance to bring Houdini messages from his mother. This did not go down well, particularly since the messages were transmitted in perfect English, a language Cecilia barely spoke. No one ever really got over this debacle; the Doyles were furious, the Houdinis distressed. There followed a storm of vehement public disputes, insults, reproaches, and recriminations, although the two men continued to insist on their friendly personal relations. Only after Houdini's death was there a proper reconciliation, with Doyle, as serenely confident as ever, writing to Bess, "I am sure that, with his strength of character (and possibly his desire to make reparation), he will come back. I shall be very glad, if you get a message, if you will tell me."

Houdini died in 1926, at the age of fifty-two. Always proud of his cast-iron stomach muscles, he had allowed a young college student to punch him repeatedly in the abdomen, soon after which he was in terrible pain and within days, dead. The official cause, it turned out, was peritonitis, and medical experts insist that the kind of blows he had received could not have contributed to the terrible result—which didn't prevent speculation that "the spiritualists" had murdered him. He himself told the journalist Fulton Oursler: "They are going to kill me . . . Every night they are holding séances and praying for my death."

What did not die was his name. "Houdini," as the Jewish Museum show demonstrates, is still very much a part of the culture. E. L. Doctorow, for instance, presented him in *Ragtime* as one of the quintessential figures of his era.

But what was he really like?

In 1928, Edmund Wilson, an admirer, reviewing an early biography, concluded: "To follow his early life among the East Side cabaret and the dime museums is to be stirred as one can always be stirred by the struggle of a superior man to emerge from the commonplaces, the ignominies and the pains of the common life, to make for himself a position and a livelihood among his less able fellows at the same time that he learns to perfect himself in the pursuit of his chosen work."

Will Rogers, no mean expert on such matters, proclaimed, "Houdini was the greatest showman of our time by far. . . . He had that something that no one can define that is generally just passed off under the heading of showmanship. But it was in reality, Sense, Shrewdness, Judgment, unmatched ability, Intuition, Personality, and an uncanny knowledge of people."

Ruth Brandon notes how Doyle, with his typical generosity, dwelt after Houdini's death on his immense physical courage, his cheery companionability, his devotion to his family, his impulsive charity. "In a long life . . . Houdini is far and away the most curious and intriguing character whom I have ever encountered."

Yet despite these and many other attempts to pin him down, he remains a mystery. His naïveté and his shrewdness, his shyness and his exhibitionism, his kindness and his unforgiving antagonisms proclaim a complicated and unknowable man. Bess put it this way: "It was Houdini who was the secret."

He went on mystifying his contemporaries until the end. At his funeral, in Manhattan's huge Elks Lodge Ballroom, the honorary pallbearers included the most powerful of establishment show-business figures, among them Lee Shubert, Adolph Zukor, Adolph S. Ochs, Marcus Loew. As the coffin was lowered into the grave, one of them whispered to Florenz Ziegfeld, "Suppose he isn't in it!"

February 10, 2011

The Man Who Was Rip Van Winkle

D
id you ever see Jefferson?" George Hurstwood asks Sister Carrie as he leans toward her in the Chicago theater to which he's invited her and her "husband," Charlie Drouet; "He's delightful, delightful." And when, later, Hurstwood reports to his wife that the play was very good, "only it's the same old thing, 'Rip Van Winkle,'" every contemporary reader of *Sister Carrie* would have known exactly what he was talking about. Long before 1900, when Dreiser's novel was published, Joe Jefferson was the most famous actor in America, and the richest. He was also the most beloved, his unparalleled genius for blending humor and pathos having endeared him to the entire national audience.

Yet it's hardly surprising that today he's completely forgotten: Who can remember the names of *any* American actors of the nineteenth century, except perhaps Edwin Booth and his notorious brother, John Wilkes? What's surprising is that within the current decade, two scholarly yet engaging full-length biographies of Jefferson have appeared. In retrospect, though, you can see why two respected academics—Arthur Bloom (*Joseph Jefferson: Dean of the American Theatre*) and Benjamin McArthur (*The Man Who Was Rip Van Winkle*)—would choose to write about him. Joe Jefferson is not only a fascinating figure but the perfect vehicle for tracking the history of nineteenth-century theater in America. In a sense, his history is *its* history.

To begin with, acting was the family trade: He was the fourth generation of Jefferson actors. His great-grandfather, named Thomas Jefferson, was an English lawyer-turned-performer who was a protégé of the great David Garrick. His grandfather, the first Joseph Jefferson, immigrated to America and became the leading comedian in Philadelphia's Chestnut Street Theatre, the nation's most highly regarded playhouse. His father, the second Joseph, although a less resourceful actor, was a talented scenic artist. His mother, Cornelia, had been a very successful singer whose son by a first marriage, Charles Burke, was to become a great stage favorite. And there were sisters, cousins, and aunts in the business, as well as brothers and uncles—it was a clan, a tribe, a dynasty.

It's natural, then, that Joe the Third, born in 1829, could confidently report sixty years later that "whenever a baby was wanted on the stage, either for the purpose of being murdered or saved, I did duty on those occasions." At three, having fun backstage, he so charmingly and accurately mimicked the famous T. D. Rice, who had more or less invented the minstrel show, that Rice secretly got him up in blackface and dumped him out of a sack onto the stage while singing, "O Ladies and Gentlemen, I'd have you for to know / That I've got a little darky here that jumps Jim Crow." Laughter, applause, and a rain of coins were his rewards—and these were the rewards Joe would go on assiduously pursuing for the next seventy-odd years. At six he received his first mention in a review: He was little Alexis in a melodrama called *The Snow Storm* in which he cried out "Mother, Mother" to the offstage heroine, "Lowina of Tobolskow," before freezing to death in a savage Siberian blizzard.

The fortunes of the Jefferson tribe began to erode when Joe's grandfather lost his popularity, quit Philadelphia, and died, disheartened, not long afterward. The family troupe, lacking its star, tried New York, Washington, Baltimore, but by 1838 was forced to head west to the new boomtown of Chicago (population four thousand) where family connections were waiting to welcome them. Through the next few years, the Jeffersons ranged the Midwest, reduced to a group of itinerant players, and eventually proceeded down the Mississippi. Within days of arriving in Mobile, Joe's father died of yellow fever. Joe, at thirteen, and his younger sister were now the chief breadwinners, acting, singing, dancing in almost every performance, while Cornelia opened a boardinghouse to help make ends meet. But soon the Jefferson company ceased to exist, and the mother and two youngsters joined another itinerant company, which, having "constructed a barge, using scenery as a sail," floated down a series of rivers back to the Mississippi. Things got so bad that at one point the family and all its trappings were abandoned on a lonely road because they couldn't pay the wagoner.

In 1846 they were in Texas, wary of Comanche raids, until during the Mexican War they followed Zachary Taylor's army to the filthy, lice-ridden, dangerous town of Matamoros, where loud, drunken soldiers were demanding to be amused. (Some of them were pressed into service as players: Lieutenant Ulysses S. Grant was rehearsing Desdemona until a real actress turned up to relieve him.) When the army moved on, the Jeffersons were stranded, Joe and an actor friend running a cigar stand until they managed to get back to New Orleans on a government boat.

In his memoirs, *The Autobiography of Joseph Jefferson*, Joe drapes a veil of nostalgia, even romance, over this turbulent decade, but there was nothing romantic about his father's death, the family's desperate attempts to establish a new footing in the theater, and the anxieties of an impoverished, itinerant life. What saved them was the web of family connections and loyalties that yet again came to the rescue.

It was Joe's beloved half-brother, Charles Burke, who proved to be the lifeline, summoning them all to join him in Philadelphia where he was already a successful young actor installed in a first-rate company. Joe had grown up as a precocious all-purpose entertainer; now, at seventeen, he began his serious apprenticeship to his art, slowly moving up the pecking order of the traditional stock company. He was already conspicuous for his ambition: From the first he saw himself as a potential star, just as from the first it was obvious that he had talent—as well as that essential quality for an actor, the ability to please. Yet it would take another decade of persistent hard work, false starts, and, eventually, good luck before he became a name to be reckoned with—a star attraction if not quite a star.

By the late 1850s, Joe was an established leading comedian—and a married man. At the age of twenty-one, he had married a young actress with whom he quickly had six children, two of whom died as babies. In his autobiography, he never gives her name (Margaret Lockyer): "If I dwell lightly upon domestic matters, I do so, not from any want of reverence for them, but from the conviction that the details of one's family affairs are tiresome and uninteresting."

He was far more forthcoming about the blow that had struck him in 1854 when Charles Burke died (of tuberculosis) in his arms, murmuring, "I am going to our mother." Joe's love and admiration for Charles never wavered—although "only a half brother, he seemed like a father to me"— and he always maintained that if "my brother Charley had only lived, the world would never have heard of me." Typical Jefferson self-deprecation, yet obviously heartfelt. It was hardly surprising that Joe's oldest son was named after Charles.

By this time, Joe had begun evolving his near-revolutionary approach to character acting: Again and again he would invest a one-dimensional farcical character with a simple and appealing humanity. It was a new brand of realism that critics as well as audiences came quickly to embrace and cherish. You laughed at Joe Jefferson, but it was a laughter of appreciation, not mockery.

His breakthrough came when he joined a prestigious New York company and in 1858 was instrumental in launching a new comedy—Tom Taylor's *Our American Cousin*. Joe played Asa Trenchard, the cousin from Vermont who turns up in England and sorts out all the family problems as well as finding true love with a milkmaid who happens to be an heiress. The stage Yankee was traditionally a stock comic character with uncouth manners and mannerisms, good for a derisory laugh. Contemporary reviews underline that Joe played Asa with rough dignity and warmth, demonstrating Yankee common sense rather than Yankee eccentricity. The heart of gold—a Joe Jefferson specialty—shone through, and *Our American Cousin* achieved an almost unprecedented run of 139 consecutive performances (only *Uncle Tom's Cabin* and *The Drunkard* had run longer).

A streak of other hits followed: Dion Boucicault's *Dot*, an adaptation of Dickens's *The Cricket on the Hearth*, in which he played Caleb Plummer, the lovable but forlorn old toymaker; a version of *Nicholas Nickleby* in which his Newman Noggs, Ralph Nickleby's clerk, became the central character; Boucicault's sensational abolitionist melodrama, *The Octoroon*, whose final line (at least in the version Jefferson preferred to play) he delivered as the heroine expired: "Poor child—she is free."

Finally, and fatefully, in 1860 Joe happened to reread Washington Irving's famous tale of Rip Van Winkle and realized that the character of Rip was tailor-made for him. There had been at least ten previous stage versions, but none of them had really succeeded in dramatizing Irving's narrative effectively. Tinkering with the text, Joe took the crucial step of making the encounter between Rip and the ghosts of Hendrik Hudson and his crew the heart of the play. "I arranged that no voice but *Rip's* should be heard. This is the only act on the stage in which but one person speaks while all the others merely gesticulate." Convinced that he had a career-changing hit, he toured *Rip* through the Northeast, but the expected triumph didn't materialize. Perhaps only he himself could imagine at this point that he had in his grasp what would become the most popular male role of the century.

In the spring of 1861, a concatenation of events led to a decisive moment in Joe's life. Twenty-eight-year-old Margaret died in March, leaving him with four children to raise; his own health was a concern, since like his mother and half-brother he had weak lungs and a predisposition to tuberculosis; *Rip* hadn't prevailed—his route to official stardom was blocked. But most important, the Civil War was breaking out, and he intended to play no part in it. After his death, a friend wrote: "Early in 1861 Jefferson came to me and said: 'There is going to be a great war of sections. I am not a warrior. I am neither a Northerner nor a Southerner. I cannot bring myself to engage in bloodshed or to take sides. I have near and dear ones North and South. I am going away and I shall stay away until the storm blows over.'"

It certainly rings true that Joe would not take sides if he could avoid it—his entire life was spent attempting to please everyone and offend no one. No surprise, then, that on June 1, 1861, seven weeks after the Confederates fired on Fort Sumter, he left New York for California, taking with him ten-year-old Charley and leaving behind, with his late wife's parents, the other three children, whom he would not see again for five years.

He was to recall the California experience (disappointing reviews, disappointing box office) as "an unmistakable failure," and after four months, he made the decision to move on to Australia, where from the first he enjoyed a sensational success. During his initial stay in Melbourne, for instance, he played for 164 nights, and as Charley was to write, "We just simply coined it. It was like a mint." *Our American Cousin, The Octoroon, Newman Noggs, Rip,* Bob Acres in *The Rivals*—it was the old repertory, plus a few novelties, including a stab at Bottom. Season by season he was achieving greater mastery of his craft, while piling success on success.

A critic in Australia who came to know Joe well left us in his journals an appealing portrait of him that helps explain his lifelong popularity:

Joseph Jefferson about 36; slight & consumptive, with a small, sharp, eager face; forehead very prominent above eyes, soft brown hair, Napoleonic chin, & a quick bright eye, full of expression. One of the most unassuming men, charming companions and most finished comedians I ever met with. . . . Nothing of the actor about him off the stage; none of the professional envy & jealousy; fond of hunting, fishing and sketching.

Young Rip

When father and son finally left Australia, in April 1865, they headed for England, not America (and the other children). When their ship stopped along the way in Callao, Peru, they heard the latest news: "Oh! The war—that's all over; the South caved in and Richmond's took." They also learned that President Lincoln had been assassinated by John Wilkes Booth in Ford's Theatre in Washington. "Father tottered," Charley would write, "and I believe he would have fallen had not the captain and I caught him. He was as white as a sheet, and for a minute trembled like an aspen. He and Wilkes Booth had been friends. . . . I can't recall the time I ever saw father so moved as that information moved him."

No wonder. Not only was Wilkes a friend but his brother, the great tragedian Edwin, had been Joe's closest friend since early manhood and Ford was yet another old friend and colleague. The play being performed was, of course, *Our American Cousin.*

Old Rip

Yet in Joe's memoirs there is no mention of the assassination. As Arthur Bloom puts it: "Once again, he was covering his tracks. In 1888, twenty-three years after the war's end, Jefferson was not going to allow himself to be associated with the man who had shot Lincoln. It was bad for business."

Joe came away from Australia a rich man. He came away from England a great star—at last, at the age of thirty-seven, he had received the validation he had always longed for. It was *Rip* that did it for him. Arriving in London, he hired the hit-maker Boucicault to doctor the play, and Boucicault convinced him to make a critical change: to present Rip in the first act as a young, merry, energetic fellow, not a cranky and disappointed man approaching middle age. The resulting contrast between the young

Rip and the old Rip gave Joe an irresistible dramatic line for the role. It was pointed out that the transformation after only twenty years of this young happy-go-lucky idler into a Lear-like old man with a flowing white beard made no sense, but Joe's art and lovability conquered disbelief.

London took Rip, and Joseph Jefferson, to its heart, a typical review (from the *Times* of London) calling him "one of the most original . . . and finished actors ever seen upon any stage." He and the play were so established there that he was able at last to send for his other children, and he was as popular in person as onstage. (Among the guests at a celebratory dinner after the final London performance of *Rip* were Dickens, Thackeray, and Wilkie Collins.) When he returned to America after a year in London, his English reputation preceding him, it was as an established star, and *Rip* quickly grew into a national institution. The eternal touring—and the eternal gush of money—had begun: His fees were unequaled in the business, because his box-office results were unequaled. The role, Bloom remarks, had become an American icon, the editor of *Harper's New Monthly Magazine* likening Joe's Rip "to shrines at which worship is imperative like the Pieta in St. Peter's." Just as the heart-stopping melodrama of *Uncle Tom's Cabin* had galvanized pre-war America, the heartwarming nostalgia of *Rip* now had a healing effect. By 1869, only three years after his return from England, Joe was said to be worth half a million dollars.

He was also remarried. Sarah Isabel Warren was a second cousin, the well-bred daughter of a thriving Chicago family connected to the theater, though never an actress. He was thirty-eight, she was seventeen (a little younger than Charley), and their apparently happy marriage lasted until Joe's death, giving him four more children. His personal reputation had always been spotless—he was by nature clean-living—but he also was responding to Victorian America's expectations for a family entertainer, never, for instance, allowing himself to be seen drinking in public. (In private it was a different story.)

The one aberrational episode in his life remained hidden from everyone except Sarah. In 1889 he received a letter postmarked Melbourne, in which a twenty-six-year-old named Joseph Sefton wrote that he had just learned from his dying grandmother that he had been born of a liaison back in the 1860s between the new widower, Joe, and a young soubrette employed in Joe's Australian company. The facts were irrefutable, and the letter was modest, deferential, and undemanding: "If I am misinformed in this matter pray dismiss from your mind any thought of me. . . . Whatever your reply is, Yea or Nay, it will be accepted by me as a final disposition of the matter."

It was five months before Joe replied (could he have been consulting private detectives in Australia?), but when he did, his response was forthright and welcoming: "My Dear Son, all that your grandmother has told you is true. . . . If the world connects any shame with such matters, and it usually does, the blot should fall upon me rather than on you."

As to whether the young man should reveal the relationship, Joe replied: "You are a man and have a right to act as you please. . . . I place the matter unreservedly in your own hands. . . . When we meet . . . you will find that neither me or mine will receive you with anything but affection."

They never did meet, and young Joseph chose to keep the facts of his paternity to himself, but father and son corresponded until Joe's death, Joe sending his son money through the years and remembering him in his will. He did, however, instruct Joseph to write to him at the Players Club, not at home.

Joe's nontheatrical pursuits were lifelong, passionate, and respectable. Most important to him, from childhood, was painting. Wherever he was, whenever he had a moment, he was at his easel, turning out scores of unpopulated landscapes derivative of Corot and the other Barbizon artists, but well above the level of the average amateur. (When his great friend William Winter—who happened to be America's most influential theater critic—was preparing to write Joe's biography, he asked, "What *would* you do if you couldn't paint?" Joe replied in all seriousness, "Die, I think.")

His passion for fishing was almost as strong, alone or with a carefully chosen companion—one of his sons, or a close friend like Grover Cleveland. His homes were bought or built in relation to their proximity to water. And in fact, his third almost compulsive private occupation was acquiring real estate—not as an investment, although he was extremely shrewd about anything involving money, but as if to reassure himself of his prosperity. He first bought estates in Yonkers, New York, and Ho-Ho-Kus, New Jersey; then an extensive plantation in the bayous of Louisiana (which he turned into a paying proposition); then a substantial house in Buzzards Bay, Massachusetts (along with 156 acres), which when it burned down he replaced with an even grander one; and eventually a large spread in Palm Beach. Careful to maintain his homespun image, he lived, as Bloom puts it, "in the midst of romantic rusticity, but he lived in baronial splendor."

Everything was for the family—they were never going to suffer as he had suffered. He dotted the various properties he owned with houses for the children and their own families, with happy get-togethers of food, games, and family theatricals. His homes, Benjamin McArthur remarks, "were essentially great, sprawling playhouses." Charley, and then others of his sons, managed his affairs. And, it was noticed, his generosity to his family was exclusive: Joe Jefferson gave no money to causes.

He was, however, central to a famous moment in theater history. In 1870, a much-loved old actor named George Holland died in New York, and Joe accompanied one of his sons to the church where Holland had worshipped and where his family wanted the funeral held. The Reverend Lorenzo Sabine, however, would not countenance burying an actor from his church. Joe, far from being a churchgoing religious man, was indignant, but he restrained himself and asked: "Well, sir . . . is there no other church to which you can direct me, from which my friend can be buried?" and was told that "there was a little church around the corner" where he might get it done. "Then," Joe replied, "if this be so, God bless 'the little church around the corner.'" The ensuing public outrage (Mark Twain called Sabine "a crawling, slimy, sanctimonious, self-righteous reptile") turned the Little Church into a shrine for the profession, helped promote the respectability of actors, and further burnished Joe's reputation.

The most obvious result of Joe's anxiety about money was his refusal, or inability, to stop performing; he was still touring in his seventies and still raking in immense fees. Critics complained about the rickety quality of his productions—this was another area in which he chose not to spend money—as well as the staleness of his repertory, but audiences kept coming, even when, as we can see from Hurstwood's remarks in 1890, they acknowledged the staleness.

His repertory, however, was not as totally restricted as people assumed it was: He always kept his early successes in readiness, and eventually he parlayed one of his oldest characterizations, Bob Acres, into a triumphant alternative to Rip, radically reshaping *The Rivals* to center on Bob, and as usual humanizing an essentially farcical character by making him more sympathetic. Critics complained at this distortion of the text, but as he well knew, the audience came to see Joseph Jefferson, not Richard Sheridan; he toured his Bob for more than three years. It was only in the year before his death—having performed *Rip* well over five thousand times and, it was estimated, being worth more than five million dollars—that he retired from the stage to the benign climate (and boom real-estate market) of Palm Beach.

Of the two recent biographers, Bloom takes the more skeptical view—admiring and even fond, but insistent that Joe's eye was steadily fixed on the main chance and that his constant self-deprecation and aw-shucks homeyness were partly a construct that masked his great ambition and his determination to charm everyone: "As both child and adult, Jefferson really was lovable, but he also learned to be lovable, how to play lovable, and how being and playing lovable produced substantial rewards." Bloom's account places Joe in the direct line of American go-getter success stories, which stretches from Benjamin Franklin through Horatio Alger to Bing Crosby. He was accomplished, he was genial, he was industrious, but most of all he was compulsively upwardly mobile.

Bloom also sharply questions certain of the legends that Jefferson encouraged—the story, for instance, of how when his family was struggling to get a foothold in Springfield, Illinois, in the 1830s, it was a young lawyer named Abraham Lincoln who procured for them the necessary license to perform. Perhaps; but whatever Lincoln did or didn't do was done for the advance guard of the larger Jefferson tribe, before Joe and his parents arrived in the Midwest. Benjamin McArthur, given to special pleading for his hero, has to acknowledge that here at least Joe fudged or forgot the facts. (His word is "embellished.")

McArthur's greatest strength lies in his knowledge of the way the American theater developed during Joe's lifetime. When he was growing up, for instance, a great star moved around the country with his famous roles, dropping in to perform with established stock companies everywhere, all of which knew and could mount the basic repertory and, with a single rehearsal, put on *Macbeth* with Edwin Forrest or *Richard III* with Junius Brutus Booth, father of Edwin and John Wilkes. The touring star was the jewel, the local company was the setting— much the way international opera works today.

What changed things irrevocably was the expansion of the railroad system during and after the Civil War. Now entire companies could form in New York and road-show their wares with cast, costumes, and scenery intact. Between 1873 and 1880, the number of local stock companies plummeted from more than fifty to fewer than eight, centralizing the American theater and, incidentally, altering the way young actors learned their trade.

The conditions under which actors performed changed even more drastically. Joe's memoirs paint a grim if somewhat romanticized picture of the roughness of the venues—barns, barrooms, even a pork house (in Pekin, Illinois)—and the audiences that actors had to contend with during the earlier decades of the century. McArthur gives as an example the story of an intoxicated South Carolina congressman who took offense at an actor's lines, "pulled out his pistol and fired at the stage." (The stage manager, in what McArthur refers to as "a classic of understatement," warned the audience that "if there is to be shooting at the actors on the stage, it will be impossible for the performance to go on.") This is a far cry from the proprieties and pretensions of late-Victorian theatergoers—Hurstwood and Carrie in their box at a resplendent Chicago theater.

McArthur's work is occasionally blemished by sociological overthink and eruptions of overwriting. (About the friendship between Joe and Edwin Booth: "Raised in the theatre and now hitched to Thespis's cart, the two forged a bond. Their simpatico may also have been rooted in a complementarity of temperaments.") These defects, however, don't negate his achievement in helping reveal to us our forgotten, and fascinating, theatrical past.

Joe had no faith in his being remembered: "There is nothing so useless as a dead actor." Despite his acknowledgment of, and gratitude for, his spectacular good fortune, there was a strain of melancholy in him. "I am not an optimist," he said, "I too often let things sadden me." And, "The saddest thing in old age is the absence of expectation." At the age of seventy-six—his health having given way completely, and the touring finally at an end—there was nothing left for him to do but die.

And as he had predicted, he soon slipped out of the national consciousness. The homespun America that *Rip* (and he) represented was now beyond nostalgia; it was forgotten, except perhaps in the pastoral romances of D. W. Griffith, and they too were quickly outdated by World War I and its aftermath. Loving memoirs of him appeared after his death, and then an occasional appreciation in a magazine. The last public sighting of him that I've come across is a 1941 *Saturday Evening Post* ad for Maxwell House coffee. WHEN THE GREAT JOSEPH JEFFERSON WAS FETED AT

THE FAMOUS MAXWELL HOUSE runs the headline, above an insipid watercolor of Nashville society feting him.

> From the handsomely garbed men and women sipping their coffee
> in the Maxwell House, to the very gamins in the street, the talk is
> of nothing but the distinguished Mr. Jefferson and his play.

It would be nice to think that this ad sold some coffee.

Today, all that is left of him, apart from a few scraps of film and a couple of faint recordings, all from the 1890s, are a Joe Jefferson Playhouse in Mobile and Chicago's annual theater awards called the Jeffersons, or Jeffs—though it's unlikely that anyone either presenting them or receiving them knows much about the renowned actor for whom they were named. Even so—unexpectedly and unpredictably—a century after his death we have these two excellent new accounts of his life and achievement. No one would have been more surprised than Joe.

October 22, 2009

Anger Saves

Elia Kazan was a man of large talents, large ambitions, and large appetites, and he deserves a book that reflects both his achievements and his complicated passage through life. Luckily, he has one—his extraordinary autobiography. *A Life*, published in 1988, is a relentless attempt to make you understand him, and to help him understand himself. It's proud, self-lacerating, provocative, and—even when you feel you're being manipulated—convincing. It's also very long. (I was his editor, so you can blame me.)

Now there's a book about Kazan by the film critic Richard Schickel, who's also written about Cary Grant (*A Celebration*), James Cagney (another *Celebration*), Marlon Brando, Clint Eastwood, Woody Allen, and D. W. Griffith (his best work)—a score of books in all. Schickel is industrious and well-intentioned, but he has two strikes against him: He's an undistinguished writer, and he's up against Kazan himself. In his author's note, he forthrightly acknowledges that his book "offers no more insight into Elia Kazan's personal life than he himself offered in his own autobiography, on which I have relied for many details of his day-to-day existence. It is a wonderful work—one of the truly great theatrical autobiographies." And, indeed, those parts of his book that attempt to re-create Kazan's harrowing life (who could resist?) read like a pale reduction of Kazan's own blistering account. Still, readers who don't want to commit themselves to the almost 850 pages of *A Life* will find the basic story in these mere 500-plus pages.

The main focus on Kazan in recent years has been on his film work—most of his movies are easily available, and film studies have become a basic part of higher education. Not many young people, however, are studying theater history, not only because once plays close there's nothing

left of them except scripts, memories, and reviews, but also because, in the last half century, theater has ceded its preeminence in our culture. A lot of us can readily identify Kazan as the director of *Gentleman's Agreement* or *A Tree Grows in Brooklyn* or *America, America*, to say nothing of *On the Waterfront* and the movie version of *A Streetcar Named Desire*, but who remembers that he directed a Helen Hayes Broadway hit, *Harriet*, about Harriet Beecher Stowe? Or the smash Kurt Weill musical *One Touch of Venus*? Or the charming *Jacobowsky and the Colonel*, adapted by Sam Behrman from Franz Werfel? (It ran for a year.) Or even his most important early success, Thornton Wilder's *The Skin of Our Teeth*, which was the occasion for Kazan's titanic clashes during rehearsals with Tallulah Bankhead? ("I could see from the glint in the bitch's eye that she smelled blood.")

A virtue of Schickel's book is that he takes us through the theater career, first writing at length, if not with much new insight, about Kazan's association with the Group Theatre in the thirties—from his early years as actor/stage manager/general dogsbody for the Gods of the Group (Harold Clurman, Lee Strasberg, Cheryl Crawford) to his eventual emergence as a successful Broadway director. It's useful to be instructed about Kazan's early efforts, although much of this material reads like nose-to-the-grindstone homework. We learn, for instance, that Helen Hayes, set in her unrelenting adorable ways, couldn't perform with the spontaneity Kazan demanded of his actors, although she tried, and that Agnes de Mille, who provided the famous choreography for *One Touch of Venus*, found that Kazan "had no visual sense . . . no eyes at all. He had a wonderful ear, though, not for music, but for speech." (Kazan on de Mille: "The most strong-minded stage artist I've known.") And it came as a surprise, at least to me, that during the war he directed something called *It's Up to You*, sponsored by the Department of Agriculture. (Kazan devotes only a short paragraph to it in *A Life*, without bothering to name it.) This unlikely venture (it featured Woody Guthrie) "was designed to enhance public support of rationing and to rally it against black marketeering," and for our amusement Schickel quotes from it this stirring bit of agitprop:

The man behind the plow is the man behind the gun
Farmer, save democracy.
Farmer, save civilization.
Farmer, save the world
DIG, FARMER, DIG

All these productions took place before the first play for which Kazan is still more or less remembered, Arthur Miller's *All My Sons*, almost a decade into his directing career. I remember how impressed I was with it as a kid back in 1946, although today the play reads like (badly) watered-down Ibsen, in particular *An Enemy of the People*. What actually happened onstage, though—as Joe Keller, guilty of shipping defective equipment to the air force resulting in the death of his pilot son, is exposed to the world and to his grieving family—was excitingly confrontational and alive; Kazan got more out of the play than was in it. His earlier successes had relied on the charisma of established stars—Bankhead, Hayes, Mary Martin; in *All My Sons* he elicited gripping performances from non-star actors like Ed Begley, Karl Malden, and Arthur Kennedy. Other directors could stage star vehicles effectively, but Miller's play *wasn't* a star vehicle, and it alerted everyone to Kazan's extraordinary ability to prod or hypnotize actors into surpassing their previous work.

It was, however, the stage version of *Streetcar*, in 1947, that conclusively set him apart from other directors. Naturally, Schickel deals with it at length, quoting liberally from Kazan's incisive and instructive notes. The biggest problem he faced while the play was in production stemmed from the electrifying performance the almost unknown Marlon Brando was giving as Stanley Kowalski, totally overshadowing that of the first Blanche Dubois, Jessica Tandy. She was an accomplished actress—careful, hard-working, honest—but she was up against the most thrilling new actor Broadway had seen since . . . since whom? John Barrymore? Brando was incandescent. "What would I say to Brando?" asked Kazan in his book: "Be less good? Or to Jessie? Get better?"

Ironically, when *Streetcar* opened in New York, most of the reviews concentrated on Tandy, who was the official star. But it was Brando who made the overwhelming impact on both the audience and the theater world. Overnight, he became a byword. When I saw the production, soon after it opened, Brando was mesmerizing, shattering. No one doubted that he would have the greatest of careers—here, at last, was the American theater's answer to Olivier and Gielgud. Who could have imagined that *Streetcar* would be his last performance on the stage? In retrospect, one can see that Brando's abandonment of the theater was a foreshadowing of what would become Hollywood's conclusive ascendancy over Broadway.

It seems to me, trying to reconstruct a performance I saw fifty-odd years ago, that Kazan's direction of *Streetcar* was exquisitely evocative of its time and place as well as being perfectly balanced—not only in winning sympathy for both Blanche, even at her most maddening, and Stanley, even at his most brutal, but in harmonizing the play's impulses toward both realism and poetry. (Kazan knew he had to do this: "This is a poetic tragedy," he wrote in his notebook, "not a realistic or a naturalistic one.") Certainly he sympathized with Blanche's fragility and desperation, but he could also identify with Stanley's inarticulate force and assertive sexuality, which is what made it possible for us to do so, too. Post-Kazan, *Streetcar* has become a vehicle for divas, with Stanley reduced to the boorish instrument of Blanche's destruction. The change began immediately, when Harold Clurman was given the job of directing the road company and, wrote Kazan, turned the play into a "moral fable"—"a play of the thirties, when we in the Group blamed everything on the System and never on anything in ourselves. We would bemoan our alienation rather than accept what Williams accepted, that there was a tragic element in life itself."

Kazan had moved on; Clurman (and Strasberg) never did.

The production that sealed Kazan's reputation as well as Arthur Miller's was *Death of a Salesman* in 1949. It ran on and on, won all the prizes, and was even a bestseller when the text was published. It was considered Important. (The other bestselling play of the period was T. S. Eliot's *The Cocktail Party*.) But even back then there were those who thought it inflated and unspecific. Mary McCarthy, that acerb and rigorous theater critic, found Willy Loman to be "a capitalized Human Being, without being anyone . . . demanding a statistical attention and generalized, impersonal condolence, like that of the editorial page." Louis Kronenberger wrote in *Time*, "The idea of the play is everywhere more moving than the play itself." That, as it happens, was my own view, too, but again—as with *All My Sons*—the intensity of Kazan's staging and his uncanny ability to extract extraordinary performances from his actors almost succeeded in masking the thinness of Miller's thinking and the pretentiousness of his writing.

Having in fairness acknowledged the negative voices, Schickel goes on to defend the play against straw men (that is, intellectuals and academics):

> When an artful, emotionally sound work reaches out beyond its ruling conventions, reaches out across the years, across all kinds of geographical divisions (and *Salesman* has been successfully performed everywhere from Communist China to beleaguered Israel), niggling questions about form tend to be obviated. Why should we care about the maintenance of, say, the classical unities or about the nobility of the protagonist or the nature of his fall from grace? Why, indeed, should we care if the vehicle taking up these matters is, technically, a tragedy at all—if we are moved by it to silence, tears or long, long thoughts? The thing simply is.

If this kind of inflated writing and specious argument appears to you to be serious and effective criticism, then Schickel's book is the book for you.

And while we're on the subject of his prose: Countless sentences and phrases are maddeningly off-key or badly clichéd. "There were, of course, love affairs that caused teapot tempests." "He invoked no high, wide or handsome principles." People strut their stuff, snivel in reply, are modest to a fault, beam approval, are awash with talent. The text is peppered with irritating authorial hiccups: "It must be said," "Be that as it may," "It is not too much to say," "If you will," and, most insistently, "Frankly" and "Of course." ("Of course," of course, is the lazy writer's crutch; I stopped counting after registering twenty-five of them.) But the book's strangest and most damaging technical failing is the frustrating—the disastrous— lack of a formal filmography and list of stage productions. What can Schickel and his publisher have been thinking?

This lack makes it particularly difficult to track the career, given that during the years of Kazan's greatest success, he was practically alter- nating hit movies and hit plays—unlike Brando, he never abandoned Broadway for Hollywood. The films *A Tree Grows in Brooklyn, Boomerang!, Gentleman's Agreement* all precede Broadway's *Streetcar* and *Salesman*, and his work in the theater continued on through his later years as a top film di- rector, with Tennessee Williams's *Camino Real, Cat on a Hot Tin Roof*, and *Sweet Bird of Youth*; Robert Anderson's sentimental *Tea and Sympathy*; William Inge's *The Dark at the Top of the Stairs*; and Archibald MacLeish's ponderous *J.B.* There were also three productions for the ill-conceived Lincoln Center repertory company: Miller's *After the Fall*, Sam Behrman's *But for Whom Charlie*, and Kazan's one (disastrous) stab at classic theater, the Jacobean melodrama *The Changeling*. All this theater work was going on while he was directing the movie of *Streetcar, Viva Zapata!, On the Wa- terfront, Splendor in the Grass*, and the rest. There has never been a career like it. (Mike Nichols's comes closest.)

Schickel is clearly more at ease discussing movies than plays, going through them one by one, plots and all, the text leavened with revealing remarks from Kazan's notebooks and punctuated by amusing stories, al- though Kazan's own versions are almost inevitably more vivid than Schickel's. One example. Schickel's Kazan on Katharine Hepburn in *Sea of Grass*: "Every time she went to the bathroom to take a piss in that picture, she came out with a different dress." Kazan's Kazan: "It looks to me that every time she goes in to take a piss, she'll come bouncing out of the can in a snazzy new outfit!"

The movie Schickel focuses on most closely is *On the Waterfront*, with which Kazan was so powerfully and personally engaged. He provides us with a highly detailed and interesting account of the long struggle to get the film made, involving an early approach to the story by Arthur Miller called *The Hook*, Kazan's eventual collaboration with Budd Schulberg, and the last-minute rescue of the project by the independent producer Sam Spiegel after all the big studios, obsessed with large-screen extravaganzas, had rejected it. Schickel is perceptive and sensitive on Brando—on the strain of tenderness that informs the movie and differentiates his Terry from his Stanley Kowalski. (In his notes, Kazan—without denying that *Waterfront* partially reflects his and Schulberg's politics—stresses that "this motion picture is about one thing only: a young man who has let his dignity slip away, regains it.") And it's fun, too, to be reminded of Brando's inflexible rule about abandoning the set (in Hoboken) late in the afternoon in order to get to his psychiatrist (in Manhattan) on time, or to learn that "there exists an early poster for the film, on which this line, the desperate concoction of an anonymous ad man, trying to warm the public to a harsh subject, appears: 'A story as warm and moving as *Going My Way* . . . but with brass knuckles!'"

In sum, despite his efforts at interpreting the film itself, Schickel's approach is for the most part anecdotal—and the anecdotes are too often warmed-over. To get the flavor of what it was really like making *Waterfront* you have to go back to *A Life*:

God, it was cold that night, and the snow didn't help, and the crew was awfully tired after a long, tough schedule.

That was the night our producer decided to come out about one in the morning and give the crew a boost—not by praising them but by scolding and threatening them. It was freezing cold, and the snow was half sleet but thickening, and the tarpaulin over the alley was filling up with the stuff and threatening to collapse. The crew had just put the canvas cover up and one of their number had fallen off a ladder and broken his leg and been driven to the hospital. The crew had taken a break, ducking out of the arctic wind into a little factory off the alley to get warm again. And up comes Sam [Spiegel], fresh from the Stork Club, and he had on his camel's-hair coat and those one-hundred-and-twenty-five-dollar alligator shoes—so Charlie Maguire [Kazan's first assistant] remembers it—and everybody was getting ready to go outside again and finish the job, when Sam orders Charlie to get the crew together, and as soon as they were there, staring at him resentfully— again according to Charlie, because I wasn't allowed in—Sam launches into his speech of complaint and outrage. "You're killing me," he said, "you're absolutely killing me with your incompetence and your laziness." Mind you, they'd been out all night in ten degrees of temperature (no one measured wind chill in those days), and they'd had enough. But Sam didn't sense it. "Apologize later" was his motto.

There was a little prop man on that crew, Eddie Barr was his name, and he's been around working props for a million years, and he stood up and he said, "You Jew cocksucker!" Barr was a Jewish guy, and he could get away with that. "You Jew cocksucker, if it weren't for Charlie Maguire and that little guy outside"—me— "we'd all be home. Nobody wants to be out here tonight. This is blood money tonight. We don't need this kind of money. Now you better get your ass out of here if you want us to make this picture." So Sam left; you couldn't blame him for that, only for not having the humanity to thank the men for the work they were doing on that very hard night. The only discomfort Sam could ever appreciate was that of the wealthy and of the established snobs whose friendship he valued.

Kazan's writing is always so alive—and his take on his work always so stimulating—that reading him makes reading Schickel even more of a chore than it already is. You can agree with Schickel's judgments—he appreciates the early *A Tree Grows in Brooklyn* and the underrated *Baby Doll*; admires the autobiographical *America, America* while registering its faults; demonstrates Kazan's ruthless encouragement of the conflict between James Dean and Raymond Massey during the filming of *East of Eden*; and sees a great deal in *A Face in the Crowd* (perhaps more than others see)—but reading him on these movies, and the others, is more like taking a basic course (Kazan 101) than encountering any compelling vision of them.

How, for instance, did Kazan's talent for creating heightened emotion on the stage, together with his talent for liberating actors from staginess, carry over to his movies? Was his impulse to make such films as *Panic in the Streets* and *Boomerang!* on location and with non-stars a deliberate attempt to create a new film style or a reflection of his powerful impulse to be on his own, far from the constrictions of the System? Can we say that his movies add up to a consistent if uneven body of work, like those, for instance, of John Ford, Ernst Lubitsch, and King Vidor (or for that matter, Renoir, Ozu, and Murnau)? If so, what is their common denominator?

David Thomson, in fewer than three columns in his *Biographical Dictionary of Film* (another book with which I've been associated), provides fresher insights into Kazan's directorial career than are to be found in Schickel's hundreds of pages. One quick moment in Thomson: "*Splendor in the Grass* . . . is intense to the point of hysteria, the most extreme instance of Kazan's emotional involvement with his characters, the source of all that is vital and most alarming in his work." Arguable, perhaps, but certainly something to think about.

And, finally, Schickel doesn't address the likelihood that if Kazan had never made his movies, we would be missing a number of superior individual works but the history of Hollywood would remain relatively unaffected, whereas if he hadn't invented the Actors Studio and revolutionized stage direction by keeping his plays so emotionally true while making them appear larger than life, the American theater and American acting would have been radically different. Although the films remain on hand to be studied and enjoyed and the stage work has disappeared, it was in the latter that Kazan made his most lasting mark.

For all the work Schickel has put into anatomizing Kazan's career, he seems to me more deeply invested in parsing and justifying Kazan's political history. As time passes, certain complicated lives become reduced to a single pivotal event that defines the way the world considers them. Bruno Bettelheim is a case in point—remembered first and foremost by many today as the psychiatrist who hit children under his care. In the same reductive spirit, as Schickel points out, Kazan has become first and foremost the man who named names to HUAC—as if his identifying Communists he had known in the thirties was the only defining act of his life. Yet Schickel (who insists, "This book is a *critical* biography"—it's his opening line) lends credence to this view by starting off with an account of the dismaying controversy that surrounded the honorary Oscar presented to Kazan at the 1999 Academy Awards. (He had already won two Oscars back in his directing days, for *Gentleman's Agreement* and *On the Waterfront.*) A number of people indulging in overheated rhetoric tried to shame Academy members into remaining seated and silent during the award presentation, but their attempts fizzled, partly in response to Warren Beatty's defense of the man who had given him his first break, in *Splendor in the Grass.*

Schickel is cutting about those who attacked Kazan inaccurately or unfairly during the Oscar incident. Rod Steiger—referring to *Waterfront*—was quoted by *Time* magazine as saying,

> If a person's a good director, he's almost the father of a family and must know how to handle his children. . . . He was my father and he double-crossed my family [by naming names to HUAC]. We were shattered. One person died of a heart attack. There were suicides. Time does not forgive a crime. The crime still exists. There is no forgiveness. He was our father and he fucked us.

But as Schickel reminds us,

> The person who died of a heart attack, J. Edward Bromberg, was named by Kazan, but posthumously. The suicide, Philip Loeb, was not mentioned by Kazan . . . [and] if Steiger and the rest of the cast had been "fucked" by Kazan, the deed had occurred almost a year and a half before they went to work on the picture—plenty of time to make a principled decision not to do so if one so chose.

He goes on to cite "victims" who claimed they had been named by Kazan but hadn't been—"it seemed that it was not enough to have been called a Communist by some virtually anonymous informant. If you were going to be named, it was apparently better to have been named by the most famous of the friendly witnesses."

Perhaps Schickel's emphasis on the Oscar storm stems from the role he himself played in it, having volunteered to produce the film tribute that preceded the award presentation. Whatever his reasons, the book he's given us is essentially a defense plea. He acknowledges, "To testify as Kazan was obliged to do in 1952 is not a pleasant matter; it sticks in one's craw." But *was* Kazan obliged to testify? And doesn't that use of the impersonal "one's" suggest that he can't bring himself to say "my"? His defense of Kazan faithfully reflects the position Kazan took in *A Life*. By 1952, he tells us, he hated communism: He was, he insists, an émigré who owed everything to America, and he believed that the Communists were seeking to destroy it. Certainly he felt he owed nothing to unrepentant Stalinists. Yet when he addresses the issue it's with his usual streak of self-inquisition:

I always saw two sides to every issue and every judgment. And so, in the body of my conviction, there appeared the worm of doubt. I still believed that what I'd done was correct, but no matter that my reasons had been sincerely founded and carefully thought out, there was something indecent—that's how I felt it, as shame—in what I'd done and something murky in my motivations. What I'd done was correct, but was it right? What self-concerns were hidden in the fine talk, how powerful a role had my love of film-making, which I'd been discounting, played in what I'd done?

You may feel that all this is merely self-serving, that the committee was illegitimately forcing people to name names that were already known to the government and that presented no threat, and that Kazan deserves all the opprobrium he reaped; my point is that his defense of himself is considerably more nuanced than Schickel's defense of him.

At the time of the hearings, Kazan made his situation worse than it already was by running a defiant ad in *The New York Times* explaining his decision to testify. (Actually, "A Statement" was written by his wife, Molly, who was, as Schickel says, "more fiercely ideological—and intellectual—than her husband was.") I think Schickel is right in suggesting that to a large extent it was this misconceived, provocative ad accusing the Group Theatre of "dictatorship and thought control" that turned Kazan into the "celebrity informer": It was one thing to do something morally repugnant; it was another to defend it. (Others who did the deed kept their mouths shut and quietly lived down the blot on their reputations.)

But pugnacity and defiance were deep strains in Kazan's nature, carefully hidden by him since childhood under what he calls his "Anatolian smile." When people attacked him, he might have had self-doubts but he would spit in their faces. As he wrote,

> When Brando, at the end [of *On the Waterfront*], yells at Lee Cobb, the mob boss, "I'm glad what I done—you hear me?—glad what I done!" that was me saying, with identical heat, that I was glad I'd testified as I had. . . . Every day I worked on that film, I was telling the world where I stood and my critics to go and fuck themselves.

His consistent and aggressive refusal to recant surely is the main reason why Kazan, alone of all those who named names, has gone on being excoriated. By 1999, the year of the honorary Oscar and almost half a century after Kazan's "treachery," the ad was ancient, mostly forgotten history. Yet the eighty-nine-year-old Kazan, whose mind was slipping, remained a target, not only to those few of his "victims" who were still alive but to those for whom attacking him had become a defining—and comforting—gesture.

Schickel's greatest scorn in regard to this ugly, complicated history is reserved for Arthur Miller, who evokes his most loaded language. But then he isn't very generous to others close to Kazan. He's openly antagonistic to Lee Strasberg, faintly patronizing to Thornton Wilder and Clifford Odets. He appears to have no more than an ambivalent tolerance for Harold Clurman, to whom Kazan was strongly attached. He seems to judge Brando primarily by his behavior toward Kazan—and toward himself. (At first, Brando refused to grant Schickel permission to include film clips from his performances at the Oscar retrospective.) There's room for only one hero in Schickel's book, even if he's a flawed one. And, indeed, the book's most attractive element is the author's wholehearted embrace of his hero's qualities.

Yet Kazan is a larger figure than the man Schickel gives us. What he leaves out is what to me is the essential Kazan—his lifelong, unremitting attempt to eradicate his early feelings of ethnic, intellectual, and sexual inadequacy; and, equally important, his obsessive need to take charge of his life by defying outside authority of any kind. At the bottom of everything was his life-and-death struggle with his powerful, controlling father, whom he feared. Then he had to shed his mentors, Clurman and Strasberg, and go on to wrest for himself unique power as a Broadway director. (In his book he tells us that as early as 1946, with *All My Sons*, "it was becoming increasingly difficult for me to collaborate with anyone.") He was determined to escape from the constrictions that the Hollywood studios, even the benign ones, imposed on him, more or less becoming his own producer, until eventually he felt impelled to escape from the limits even independent filmmaking imposed on him. He did this by becoming a writer, at first with great success—*The Arrangement*, a raw, autobiographical account of a man struggling to redeem his life, was the bestselling novel of 1967. As a writer he could feel, at last, that he was in complete charge of himself.

But even this was not enough. He was still driven to transcend the person who—through luck, persistence, talent, and dissimulation—had escaped the constricted world of his unmoored émigré family and forced his way into the mainstream of American cultural life and on to unimaginable reward. "I wasn't the man I wanted to be," he says on page five of *A Life*; instead, in order to get ahead he had turned himself into the fellow nicknamed "Gadget"—the charmer, the manipulator, the wielder of the self-protecting Anatolian smile that hid the rage and resentment that motored him. The lesson he had yet to learn was "You have a right to anger. You don't have to earn it. Take it. Anger saves." His face as an old man, he tells us proudly, finally revealed the anger that had always been hidden behind that smile—but the anger itself was gone. I believe that for Kazan, achieving this—even more than his successes on Broadway and in Hollywood—was his greatest triumph. As for judging him today: Other men have had a tragic flaw or have committed a despicable act; not many of them have led lives as full, as productive, and as bewildering in their contradictions as Kazan's. He was both a force of nature and a canny operator, which may explain why so many people even today can neither get around him nor get to the heart of him.

April 6, 2006

Those Mitford Girls!

W hy another book about the Mitfords? Think how many there already are. Nancy's semiautobiographical novels, Jessica's two volumes of memoirs, Diana's autobiography, Deborah's memoirs and books about Chatsworth, Harold Acton's memoir of Nancy, Selina Hastings's book about Nancy, Jan Dalley's book about Diana, David Pryce-Jones's book about Unity, Jonathan Guinness's *House of Mitford* (he's one of Diana's sons), Sophia Murphy's *Mitford Family Album*, two volumes of Nancy's letters (Jessica's are in the works), plus books by or about Diana's second husband, Sir Oswald Mosley, and Jessica's first, Esmond Romilly. It's an epidemic. And yet the latest entry in the Mitford sweepstakes, *The Sisters: The Saga of the Mitford Family*, by Mary S. Lovell, is fascinating the way all great family stories are fascinating. Is there a dull book about the Brontës? And the Brontës, let's face it, were only the kids of a poor Irish parson stuck somewhere up in provincial Yorkshire. The Mitfords were aristocrats: gorgeous, eccentric, talented. The Brontës had to write *Jane Eyre* and *Wuthering Heights* to make an impression; the Mitfords, living in an age of an avid press, only had to behave like their very odd selves.

The parents of this bizarre brood—Lord and Lady Redesdale, David and Sydney—became notorious in their own right when Nancy, their eldest, barely bothered to disguise them as Uncle Matthew and Aunt Sadie in her bestselling novel *The Pursuit of Love*, and later when Jessica, known first, last, and always as Decca, anatomized them in a memoir, *Daughters and Rebels*. One of the virtues of *The Sisters* is that Lovell goes to sources to demonstrate that these versions of the Redesdales—or Farve and Muv, as they were known in the family—were exaggerated for comic effect or

Set of portraits in pen and ink done in 1937 by William Acton:

from resentment. Yet the Redesdales were not exactly common coin. Farve was famous for his erratic temper—"he barred Gladys, Duchess of Marlborough, from Swinbrook because on her first visit she had left a paper handkerchief on a hedge"—and for blasting the children's friends. One male guest was turned out of the house for wearing a comb in his breast pocket ("a man carrying a comb!"). And Muv, though loyal and profoundly responsible, was not exactly warm; Nancy was to say, "I had the greatest possible respect for her; I liked her company; but I never loved her, for the evident reason that she never loved me." Decca and Diana felt this way about her, too. In later years, the politics of the older Redesdales were so violently opposed—Farve turning on the Nazis when the war began, Muv honoring her personal recollections of Hitler ("he is very 'easy' to be with and no feeling of shyness would be possible, and such very good manners")—that they could not live in the same house together.

Well, what was a mother to do? Her children lined up this way: Pam and Deborah (Debo) relatively unpolitical. Nancy, furious at Muv's support of Hitler. ("She is impossible. Hopes we shall lose the war and makes no bones about it.") Tom—the one son—before the war had been sympathetic to Nazi Germany. The incomparably beautiful Diana divorced Bryan Guinness, the Guinness brewing heir, to marry Sir Oswald Mosley, the leader of the British Union of Fascists, and spent years during the war imprisoned with him as a danger to the state. (There was no specific charge and they were never put on trial.) Unity, whom everyone loved despite eccentricities that stood out even by Mitford standards, grew ob-

from left to right: Nancy, Pamela, Diana, Unity, Decca, and Debo

sessed with Hitler and became his friend and confidante (she made him giggle!) before attempting suicide when the war broke out. Hitler paid her hospital bills and got her out to Switzerland in a private railway car, but she eventually died in Scotland as a result of the bullet wound to her head.

Decca, ardently left-wing (eventually a card-carrying Communist in America), at nineteen ran away to the Spanish Civil War with her cousin Esmond Romilly, Churchill's nephew. (The papers blared MIXED UP MITFORD GIRLS STILL CONFUSING EUROPE, but Nanny could only worry, "Good gracious, she didn't take any clothes to fight in.") In the bedroom they had shared, Unity had scratched swastikas on the window-panes, Decca countering with hammer and sickles. No wonder Sydney one day complained to Nancy, "Oh, why do all my daughters fall for dictators?" Actually, that was unfair: Pam married a prominant scientist and Debo's husband, Andrew, was to become Duke of Devonshire.

It was politics and the war that destroyed the Mitford family. Tom was killed in Burma in the last days of the fighting. Esmond Romilly's plane had disappeared over the Atlantic much earlier, leaving Decca a widow alone with a baby in Washington. Unity was permanently incapacitated. Diana was disgraced; Nancy had actually informed on "Mrs. Quisling," and Decca never forgave her favorite sister for her pro-Nazism and anti-Semitism. In a letter to her mother, explaining why she hadn't been writing: "I was so disgusted when they were released . . . that it actually made me feel like a traitor to write to anyone who had anything to do with them." Perhaps she was remembering that the Mosleys had been married in Goebbels's apartment in Berlin. (Debo reacted to sister Diana's disgrace in a somewhat different fashion: "I do so wish you weren't in prison, it will be vile not having you to go shopping with.")

Despite all the eccentricities of their childhood and the disruptions to come, the family had been in many respects a happy one. They were all high-spirited, and all exceptionally humorous. Everyone had nicknames for everyone else. Deborah was not only (and still is) Debo but also Dana, Dina, Bodley, Nardy, Cord, and Hen. Pam was Woman (because she was so womanly), sometimes reduced to Woo. Debo called Decca Honks, and Sydney called her Little D.; Tom was Tuddemy. Unity was usually Bobo, but she was Boud to Decca, and the two girls developed a secret language called Boudledidge. Muv was often TPOF (the poor old female), and Farve, of course, was TPOM, as well as "the poor old subhuman." Farve might blow up at any moment, but you can tell from some spoof newspaper articles the teenage Decca wrote for him how much she appreciated him, and how open he was to being teased:

> Lord Redesdale is to be tried in the House of Lords for the unnecessary murder of Miss Belle Bathe, a bathing Belle of Totland Bay. Lord Redesdale was interviewed today by our special correspondent. "I was imagining myself in a skating rink," he said, "when this damn girl came up and tried to hire out a towel. So I unfortunately trampled her underfoot with my skates." . . . Miss Jessica Mitford was also interviewed by our correspondent. "I always expected something of the sort," she said. "You see he really is a subhuman and a pathetic old throwback, so what was one to expect?"

There's more than a whiff here of Jane Austen's juvenilia, with its relish for the ludicrous and joy in sending up beloved members of the family.

Everything was a tease, a joke, a game, roars of laughter. And though there were serious disputes and deep hurts—Decca never forgave her parents for denying her a proper education (it "burned into my soul")—there were no punishments, and the children were generally allowed to carry on as they pleased. Decca could have her favorite sheep, Miranda, in bed with her. Unity, when a debutante, wasn't stopped from taking her pet white rat, Ratular, to dances and, Lovell tells us, even to a Palace garden party. Nancy's tongue was barbed, but the others admired her as much as they feared her. Diana was wonderfully patient and big-sisterish, helping the unhorsey Decca to trot around the paddock on her pony: "Do try to hang on this time, darling. You know how cross Muv will be if you break your arm again." It's heartbreaking to read of these semi-halcyon days and think ahead, say, to the undying hatred Decca came to feel for this big sister; after the war there was no communication between them until the 1970s, when Nancy was dying of cancer in Paris and they were forced for a while to share the responsibility of looking after her. Think of the sadness of Decca's break with her father; she never saw him after her flight to Spain with Esmond. And contemplate the lonely end Muv came to on the tiny, barren island off Scotland where she chose to spend her last years. As Nancy put it, "Alas one's life."

In her tapestry of the sisters' lives, Lovell has handled some of the big things very well. It's not easy to keep six narratives going at once, particularly when the lives of your subjects start to diverge. Yet *The Sisters* keeps track of everyone with a minimum of confusion; things are revealed in a straightforward and sensible order, so that we always know where we are. Even more important, she has managed to present everyone both clearly and with sympathy. No sides are taken. Yes, the Mosleys' politics are vile, but Lovell makes them understandable—too understandable, you could say—and acknowledges Oswald's brilliance and Diana's charm and good nature. (Her former wardress at Holloway Prison told a journalist, "We've never had such laughs since Lady Mosley left.") Yes, Nancy is acerbic and wounding, but we come to feel the pathos of her increasingly empty life. Decca's life in America is scrupulously followed: her happy second marriage, the loss of two of her children, her radical politics, her extraordinary career as "Queen of the Muckrakers," her glee at demolishing idiots and frauds, her generosity, her implacable enmity when earned, and most of all, her courage. (It's a portrait I can verify: I knew her for thirty-five years, first as the editor of *The American Way of Death* and other books, but more as part of her very extended family. And yes, she had nicknames for us: She was Bites, I was the Biter—a calumny, since my view, of course, was that *she* was the biter.)

Pam's life was the least dramatic of the sisters', but Lovell shows her to have more substance than previous accounts have credited her with. Debo, the youngest and the one most bruised by her older sisters' notoriety, is seen as inheriting her mother's role as mediator, keeper of the Mitford peace and flame, and of course as the chatelaine of the great

Derbyshire house, Chatsworth, which she and her husband rescued from the rigors of taxation and dilapidation by turning it into a highly paying proposition. Diana, serene and still beautiful in her old age, is unapologetic in her well-written memoirs. (Her sycophantic biography of her friend the Duchess of Windsor is another matter.) Unity emerges as foolish, willful, lovable (even Decca never turned against her), and very sad. But the one who surfaces as the most complicated and the most moving member of the family, though not born a Mitford, is Sydney. She was undemonstrative with her children, she was politically unspeakable, yet her unyielding efforts to hold them all together, to absorb the pain of Tom's death, to tend the damaged and incontinent Unity, to maintain relations with the prickly Decca and the equally prickly Nancy, to reach out to her American grandchildren, to tread cautiously among her constantly feuding girls, reveal a formidable and selfless character. Lovell has no favorites among the sisters—she appears to admire or be fond of them all—but it is their rigid, difficult mother who emerges as the pivot of this tragic family drama.

Mary Lovell has written several well-received biographies, in particular her lives of Beryl Markham (*Straight on Till Morning*) and of Amelia Earhart (*The Sound of Wings*). How odd that someone who can deal with large matters so capably is so sloppy with her grammar. (Is this the famous English love of amateurism, or simply a comment on the absence of copy editors in London? The American publishers have done only a cursory job of cleaning things up.) She confuses "who" and "whom," "between" and "among," and sprinkles her pages with clichés and danglers: "On arrival at their hotel in Vienna in early January the manager came out to meet them." What can she possibly mean by "But back in England matters merely candesced?" And try this for style: "That a young American aviatrix had shown that a woman could perform feats previously regarded as a wholly male preserve cut no ice with David and Sydney." There are also odd errors: *The Herald Tribune* was the rival of *The New York Times*, not of *The Washington Post*; Lord Berners couldn't have been writing the score of a ballet for Diaghilev in 1933, four years after Diaghilev's death; it's Katharine, not Katherine, Graham. These are petty complaints, yet such mistakes undermine a reader's confidence.

No matter. This is a book that will educate those who hope to understand the Mitfords' hold on the imagination of an entire era and entertain those who enjoy an upper-class family saga. It's Upstairs without the Downstairs. Lovell grasps an essential fact: that the Mitfords' eccentric home life, at least in the early years, was not so very different from that of many other aristocratic families. "What lifted the Mitfords from the ranks of the ordinary among their peers was not their lifestyles but their exceptional personalities." This perception rescues them from the brilliant exaggerations of Nancy's and Decca's versions of their past and restores them to their humanity. As for their sisterhood, let the two famous writers have the last word. When in the mid-1960s a journalist asked Decca to comment on Nancy's statement "Sisters are a shield against life's cruel adversity," Decca replied, "But sisters *are* life's cruel adversity!" Except when they weren't.

February 17, 2002

SCOTT PETERSON

American Zero

The Scott Peterson literature begins in 1925, with the publication of Theodore Dreiser's great novel *An American Tragedy*. If you know it only from the famous film version called *A Place in the Sun,* you have a false impression: Shelley Winters as the pregnant girl who's drowned is so whiny and charmless that you want to murder her yourself. In the novel, Roberta's death is unbearable—as we sense it approaching, we shudder. She's a decent, generous, loving girl, and, yes, her death is a tragedy. Yet it's not the tragedy of Dreiser's title. *His* American tragedy is the tragedy of Clyde Griffiths, the murderer himself, who is morally unanchored, unable to resist the lure of a more wealthy, more worldly, more beautiful girl, yet who also, in his own way, is decent, generous, and loving. So that our anguish as the fatal moment draws near is as much for him as it is for Roberta. We like this boy, we understand his longing for the good life, we even respect his struggle with himself as the idea of the murder takes hold.

> Murder! The murder of Roberta! . . . But he must not think of that! The death of that unborn child, too! . . . He was not that kind of a person, whatever else he was. He was not. He was not. He was not. The mere thought now caused a damp perspiration to form on his hands and face. He was not that kind of a person. Decent, sane people did not think of such things. And so he would not either—from this hour on. . . . He must never think of it again! He must never think of it again! He must never, never, never think of it—never.

He does, of course, think of it again—and again and again. At the final moment on the lake he wavers, and as the boat tips over he can convince himself that he hasn't actually killed Roberta, he's only failed to save her. The jury, condemning him to death, does not agree.

At first glance, this story—the young man, the murdered pregnant girl, the death penalty—could almost be a template for the killing of Laci Peterson; even the possibility that Laci, too, was drowned (in the back-yard pool) is raised by Scott's half-sister Anne Bird. But the current Scott Peterson literature—three books, with another, by Laci's mother, Sharon Rocha, on the way—lacks a Dreiser, which is a polite way of saying that it's mostly plodding and unperceptive, however well-intentioned.

At first my interest in the case was professional; I had never read a word about it or seen anything about it on the news, but was intrigued by the fact that a single publisher had issued all three books within weeks of one another, and that all of them had rushed to the top of the bestseller list. The publisher is Judith Regan, who has achieved tremendous success as a purveyor of books that, to put it charitably, are not directed at the highest common denominator. But why should they be? They're merely canny extensions of today's tabloid/Fox News mentality, and she's pub-lished them with enviable confidence and panache.

It's not just clever publishing, though, that makes bestsellers. These books have succeeded because something about this particular murder galvanized the country's attention. Perhaps it was Laci Peterson's famously radiant smile. Perhaps it was Scott Peterson's publicized "golden boy" good looks and the fact that everyone who met him seemed to think he was so great. ("My God," thought his girlfriend, Amber Frey, soon after meeting him. "This guy is perfect.") Perhaps it was the sense among their families and friends that Scott and Laci had "an ideal marriage." Perhaps it was the mounting tension of the search for a missing young woman in the last stages of pregnancy. Perhaps it was the slow, inexorable revelation of the gap between Scott's golden-boy image and his endless lies and increas-ingly erratic actions. (One of the saddest aspects of the story is the way those who most believed in him—not only his own family but Laci's fam-ily, the Rochas, as well as Amber—had to face the growing likelihood, then the certainty, that he was a murderer.) Finally, as in a classic detective story, this was a planned murder, not a sudden outburst of violent rage; it was a crime that needed solving: Scott Peterson secretly bought a boat and made anchor weights out of concrete, and only then killed his wife at home, using his new boat to dump her body in San Francisco Bay.

If you know nothing about the case and want to grasp what happened, your only choice is to begin, as I did, with *A Deadly Game: The Untold Story of the Scott Peterson Investigation*, by "*Court TV* Host" Catherine Crier (with the help of Cole Thompson). Ms. Crier, who was the youngest state judge ever elected in Texas before becoming a star of broadcast journalism, starts her book with the "Why this case?" question, but she doesn't really answer it. Instead, she begins at once to present her *own* case—that of an investigative reporter and analyst who from the beginning had her doubts. "I began to raise questions on the air about whether he was showing signs of a behavior disorder. Scott seemed to display many of the textbook qualities of a sociopath." In other words, if I understand the sequence here, she was publicly judging the suspect's pathology well before he was arrested—not only trial on television but trial *by* television. Is this standard procedure for TV courts? Isn't there a confusion here between the roles of reporter, analyst, and semi-judicial authority?

About one thing there's no confusion: the author's repeated insistence on the "unparalleled access" she had to the "inner workings" of the case. One of many examples: "It is rare to obtain the kind of access that gives rise to such an in-depth look at an investigation and trial." (Her access at work: "According to records I obtained in my investigation, Laci's pregnancy was normal.")

The "I was there" mode of the prologue's opening sentences immediately erodes one's trust in the narrative: "His look was California chic—jeans, a dark T-shirt, dress shoes. He turned to go, then paused. Removing his wedding ring, he slid the band into his pocket. Now he was ready." Nor is this the only time the writer bears witness to what no one can have witnessed; we're told that when Scott got home after disposing of Laci's body, he "entered the backyard through the gate and patted McKenzie, the couple's beloved golden retriever, as the dog bounded out to meet him." Who can have reported this? McKenzie? (*That* would certainly constitute unparalleled access.)

Throughout her book, the quondam judge judges. She is convincing about the nature and extent of Scott's psychopathology—what she identifies as his flat emotional affect and his "discordant and disturbing" behavior. And she follows the chain of events carefully and closely. (Too closely at times, one feels, as she crams in every conceivable detail.) Her tone is too often prosecutorial. An egregious example: In the midst of recording the pathetic pleas of Scott's family to spare him the death penalty, she quotes his father as saying, "Losing someone you loved and now having your son in this kind of jeopardy . . . I just can't imagine anything worse." Her comment: "Of course, the Rochas could."

Crier is at her most condemning in regard to the Petersons. Scott's mother, Jackie, is a frequent (and easy) target as she savagely defends her son and attacks his accusers. Scott's father? "He is certainly showing the protective instincts of a parent. Yet his denial seems so strong that I'm not sure he knew exactly what he was protecting. Did Lee Peterson ever really know his son?" Scott's half-sister Susan? Yes, she defended her brother, but "reportedly" didn't contribute to his defense fund. Instead, she constructed an "infinity pool" in her backyard: "Like Scott himself, she had failed to give to others while quietly arranging to sink her money into a lavish swimming pool." More than once she suggests that the way the Petersons spoiled their golden son contributed to his murderous narcissism. "Once again, Scott's parents were reinforcing the kind of anything-goes behavior that Scott showed throughout his adult life. Go ahead, hang out at the country club while your wife is missing. You had an affair? Don't worry about it. You can do no wrong. And, by the way, we'll take care of your bills." And yet, Your Ex-Honor, not all spoiled boys grow up to murder their pregnant wives. I speak from experience.

In their very dissimilar books, two women who were close to Scott tell essentially the same story: Both Amber Frey, the girlfriend, and Anne Bird, the half-sister, fell hard for him, then backed away as the truth emerged. Amber's book, *Witness*, is the more immediately appealing, since in it she comes across as a wholesome if astonishingly naïve person. Living alone with her baby daughter, Ayiana, beginning her dream career as a massage therapist in Fresno, she is longing for a permanent relationship. When a friend produces Scott Peterson, she's bowled over—to the extent of sleeping with him on their first date. He was romantic, he was sexy, he was sensitive: "a tender, caring person." He was also married, but she had no way of knowing that. When he finally acknowledges (through his tears) that he had been married, he lets her believe that Laci is dead. "Can I trust you with my heart?" Amber asks him. There's no direct answer, but he does tell her, "You know, I live a certain lifestyle, and I can see you living that lifestyle, too. When I get back from Europe, I need to make some decisions. Can you say yes to me without question?" (He's pretending that he'll soon be off to Europe on business, though it's not clear why his work as a fertilizer salesman in Modesto would take him to Paris and Brussels.)

All this is happening in December 2002, during the weeks leading up to Laci's death. On Christmas Day, the day after her disappearance, Scott is on the phone to Amber, supposedly calling from Maine, and Amber is singing to him one of Ayiana's favorite songs, "Five Little Ducks Went Out to Play." "I love it," he says when she finishes. "The next time I see you, I want that song to be the first thing I hear." It's details like these that bring Scott's duplicity and cruelty to life more tellingly than Catherine Crier's accusing commentary. Scott picks Ayiana up at school. He goes with Amber and Ayiana to the zoo. He comes over to Amber's house, where he makes lasagna and they down a bottle of wine he's brought. (Amber writes their names and the date on the cork. "There are plenty of corks to come," Scott tells her.)

Food, in fact, is peculiarly important to all the principal actors in the Scott Peterson story. Laci was a perfectionist as a housewife and hostess, with Martha Stewart as role model; whether she and Scott, on the morning she disappeared, were watching Martha on television doing something with meringue turned out to be a crucial question at the trial. Amber stops to tell us that when she and Scott had lunch at Whole Foods, "I had the tortilla soup, which was great." Scott not only makes lasagna, he makes a Pink Lady caramel apple for Amber. ("It's my first attempt," he says. "I hope you like it.") Most bizarrely, the following April he calls some friends to tell them, "I made you some lavender cookies . . . but I got arrested a couple of hours ago so I have to go." Wine is practically the currency of all their lives.

As the world knows, Amber took her story to the police—not the press—and helped them by holding long phone conversations with Scott, which were taped. (About sixty-five people were secretly wiretapped during the course of the investigation, including members of the media like Diane Sawyer, Larry King, and Greta Van Susteren.) Thanks to her well-publicized honesty and ingenuousness, Amber went from being the Other Woman to being a heroine, embraced even by Laci's family. Late in the game, she's still concerned for Scott, sending him a copy of Rick Warren's *The Purpose-Driven Life* (twenty-two million copies sold). "I want Scott to know God and to have hope through God and to try to learn something about being a good person."

A doubter might at first find Amber's religious dedication exaggerated or insincere, but one's doubts are gradually dispelled. She talks to God, she hears from God, she does a "prayer request." A what? "This is where you take a slip of paper and write down exactly what it is you want, and you leave the paper in a box at the church." At the suggestion of her "youth minister," she goes to a meeting of the Chosen Women: "It was an astonishing experience. Thousands of women attended, filling an entire football stadium, praying, singing and giving witness. . . . I closed my eyes and listened to the sea of sobbing women around me, and I was completely overwhelmed." When she's about to be cross-examined at Scott's trial, she's ready: "[M]y attorneys had prepared me"; besides, "I also had God on my side." And she's ready for the future, too, because, as she says, "I felt that God had big things in store for me." It's impossible not to hope that God will come through for her. Yet it's also impossible not to be amazed by the glimpse she gives us of this (to me) exotic born-again world. Think what a novel Dreiser could have written about *her* life: *Sister Amber.*

Anne Bird was one of the two babies (fathers unknown) whom Jackie Peterson gave away at birth; she was persuaded to keep a third—all this before she married Lee Peterson and had Scott. Anne was lucky in her supportive and loving adoptive parents, and sounds considerably more sophisticated and better educated than Amber or anyone in her birth family, even though Scott liked to use words like *agape* (Greek for love) and to quote from Boris Pasternak.

When Anne is thirty-two, as she recalls in her book, *Blood Brother*, she meets her birth mother for the first time. It goes well, though Jackie seems more interested in talking about Scott—"her baby, her golden boy"—than about her newly rediscovered daughter. They keep in touch, and a few months later—this is in 1997—Anne meets Scott and Laci. "He was a real charmer, the kind of guy who lights up a room. I had always considered myself a good judge of character, and I thought Scott was about as solid and genuine as they came."

Their relationship takes root, and Anne grows close to Laci, too—"so warm, so full of life, and such a kick in the pants." But there are moments when she finds "something distant" about Scott, "moments when I felt he wasn't there at all." In 2002, when Anne is a mother of two little boys and Laci is very pregnant, they're all together in a fourth-floor hotel suite complete with terrace when Anne's older boy, a toddler, disappears: "For thirty seconds everyone in that room had been thrown into a panic by my screams. . . . Only Scott was oblivious." He just went on talking on his cell phone, which "struck me as very odd indeed."

During the months between Laci's disappearance and Scott's arrest, he spends a good deal of time in Anne's house in Berkeley. Despite her own passionate belief in her brother's innocence, Anne's husband is increasingly suspicious of him, so much so that their marriage is being undermined. Then, as her own suspicions set in, she draws up a list that becomes the subtitle of her book: *33 Reasons My Brother Scott Peterson Is Guilty.* "I had gone from doubting his guilt to suspecting him of premeditated murder."

Her account of all this is straightforward, but her account of her birth mother is not. *Blood Brother* is punctuated with anecdotes that show Jackie in an unfavorable light. Not long after their first meeting, Jackie takes Anne to the antique shop she runs, where Anne sees a little piece of beaded embroidery that Jackie sells her at "a nice discount." (There's mother love for you!) Again: Jackie calls Anne to criticize a thank-you card she's received from Laci: "I'm going to send her a book on how to write thank you notes." These snapshots—and there are many others—are trivial in themselves, but they add up to an unsettling portrait.

After the murder, Jackie's behavior grows more and more out of control. "That Sharon Rocha," she says of Laci's mother, who comes across in everyone's account as a dignified, grieving parent, "there's a word to describe that woman. She is evil. That's what she is, evil. She and her friends and family are destroying my son. How dare they stand there and point the finger at Scott?! . . . As for that Amber Frey, what's the big deal? So Scott slept with a bimbo? So what?" During the time when Scott, still pretending that Laci is alive, is hiding out at Anne's, Jackie calls and gets the babysitter. "Oh, Lorraine," she says, "this is Scott's mom. . . . I wish Scott could meet someone like you." (Anne: "It sounded like Jackie was becoming unhinged.") When Amber testifies at the trial about Scott's lies, Jackie shrugs: "What does that prove? . . . There's no evidence against Scott. They have nothing." "Wow," thinks Anne. "She was in complete denial." (Denial runs in the family. Here are Scott's last words to Anne when she visits him in prison: "Don't worry about a thing. Everything is going to be all right.")

Anne Bird is also in denial—about her feelings for Jackie. She doesn't seem aware that in writing this book, she's strengthening the argument against reversing the death penalty that's hanging over Scott, Jackie's favorite child. Why would she do this? Inadvertently, she provides us with an explanation. When the police were first questioning Scott's alibi, Anne tells us, Jackie began to panic and lash out. "I honestly can't say I blamed her," Anne writes. "This was her son they were talking about, her little boy. This was one of the children she had kept."

What lesson can we take from all this? That it was Anne's good fortune that Jackie didn't keep her? That Scott's criminal behavior in some way stems from the way he was raised? Despite the microscopic examination he's undergone—at the trial, in the press, in these three books—Scott remains a mystery, and one, perhaps, that not even a Dreiser could unravel.

The surface resemblance of *An American Tragedy* to the Scott Peterson story only underlines the crucial difference between them: the nature of the murderer. Clyde Griffiths is a weak, well-meaning young man who struggles against, and eventually succumbs to, a fearsome temptation. Scott Peterson would seem to be an empty man—empty, apparently, of everything but the conviction that he has the right to indulge himself in any gratification, at no matter whose expense. There's no indication that he struggled against temptation, and he seems to have no need to justify himself: It was apparently enough that he wanted Laci dead for him to feel justified in killing her.

There's nothing, then, to be learned from his actions; nothing to sympathize with in his nature. He isn't even malign, like Iago; in fact, he's more or less a man without qualities, apart from his unrelieved self-absorption. Which means that while what he did grips our imagination, he himself is utterly uninteresting—he's a cipher at the center of the havoc he wrought. Today's language describes him as a sociopath, a psychopath, and the only moral to stories about psychopaths is that we should try to avoid them.

There is no consolation for anyone in the Scott Peterson story, and no final illumination. Dreiser's driven characters reflect the optimistic strains of post–Horatio Alger America: Carrie floats upward, unmoored, unaware of the damage she causes along the way; Frank Cowperwood—*The Financier*, *The Titan*—is simply living the capitalist dream; Clyde Griffiths is a disadvantaged boy dazzled by undreamed-of opportunity. If we accept the testimony of the current books about Scott Peterson, he reflects a very different world: one of unmediated consumerism, narcissism, and license. Are we to conclude that today's American tragedy is America itself?

May 1, 2005

Di, the Queen, and I

What are we to make of England's royal family? Can they possibly be as ridiculous, as childish, as irrelevant as they seem? Forget the past—the rakish Prince Regent putting his wife, Caroline of Brunswick, on trial for adultery (she was acquitted); the rakish Edward VII with his good-natured and highly public adulteries; Edward VIII, abandoning his throne for "the woman I love" and dwindling into the useless Duke of Windsor. In our own day, we've had the shenanigans of Fergie, Duchess of York; Prince Charles's humiliating tampon tapes; and, needless to say, the disastrous marriage of Charles and Diana. But then there are the "good" royals, too: Queen Victoria, trailing clouds of rectitude; George VI, sticking to London while the Luftwaffe did its worst; and his daughter, the current queen, whom some of us have been contemplating since she was "Lilibet," one of the darling "little princesses" who charmed the world in the thirties—the perfect antidote to the bad odor of the abdication. Since her early ascension to the throne, she's led an apparently blameless life, even if she was a somewhat chilly mother. And she's always done her duty.

In *The Queen*, as impersonated by Helen Mirren in an award-hungry performance, she's in extremis—her back to the wall at Balmoral Castle, where the royals spend two months every summer, stalking stags. But this isn't every summer—it's the one when her ex-daughter-in-law Diana is killed in the Paris car crash. Since there's no precedent for dealing with the sudden death of a divorced, immensely popular Princess of Wales, the royals flounder, for days showing themselves at their worst. Yes, Prince Charles flies to Paris to bring home the mother of his two sons, but the Queen stays immured and silent at the castle while London turns into a scene of mass mourning—or you could call it mass hysteria.

Tony Blair, no favorite of the royals despite his eagerness to please, is pushing her to do something before the people's anti-monarchist sentiment gets out of hand. But the Queen Mother and the Duke of Edinburgh are vehemently opposed: Diana is no longer a royal, no longer a daughter-in-law—"this is a private matter"—so it makes no sense (to them) that the Queen should disturb her routine. The crux of the matter, if you can believe it, is whether or not the royal standard should be flown at half-mast over Buckingham Palace to honor the tragically dead mother of a future king. You see, the palace only flies a flag when the monarch is in residence.

As the days pass and the situation in London (and the press) grows trickier and the prime minister more exigent, the Queen is forced to re-think. The big moment—the Oscar Moment—comes when she's out alone in the hills and sees a magnificent stag that her men are stalking. It's too beautiful to die! Shoo, shoo—and it's gone. A tear, a tender smile, and we get the point: The beautiful Diana, too, was at bay, and the Queen . . . cares. (In case you *don't* get it, the stag reappears later on, now a slaughtered carcass.)

This movie has it both ways: The Queen is uptight, cocooned, trapped in protocol, but the reason she's so stern and uncompromising is that she was brought up to the mantra "Duty first, self second," and to maintain that stiff upper lip. At last, she realizes that she must adapt: However repugnant she finds it, however much she deplores the touchy-feely Blair, from now on emotions must be publicly expressed, hearts worn on sleeves. Meanwhile, we see the Blairs in their kitchen with the kids, she dishing out the fish fingers, he doing the washing up. Mrs. B. loathes the monarchy—"a bunch of freeloading, emotionally retarded nutters"—but Tony has come to respect both the institution and the woman who represents it.

The message: The royals may have screwed up temporarily, but it's okay to love Her Majesty.

What gives the film its energy is the clever crosscutting between the fictional scenes and the documentary footage of Diana flashing her provocative smile; of Londoners mourning—crease-worn old ladies and solemn children placing flowers at the palace gates, burly young guys weeping and being consoled. There's something a touch ghoulish—*Day of the Locust*-ish—about all this, but then to an unreconstructed American republican like me, there's something ghoulish about the whole royal business: the kowtowing, the slavish obsession, the *fuss*.

Yet *The Queen* keeps us interested in the Queen. Helen Mirren's impersonation of Her Royal Highness owes as much to her steel-colored, tightly curled wig as Nicole Kidman's Virginia Woolf owed to her extended nose, but beneath the wig and the accent and the county clothes, she seems to catch Elizabeth II—controlled, controlling, and just maybe a human being. It's an admirable effort, though I have to confess I'd rather be seeing Mirren as Jane Tennison in the terrific TV series *Prime Suspect* (come to think of it, another take-charge role).

Meanwhile, three new books about the royals have turned up, all of them featuring Diana. Why more books about her? After all, we already have a bunch of biographies, to say nothing of the countless tell-alls by former lovers, friends, staff, and journalists: *Diana: The Secret Years, Diana: Closely Guarded Secret, Diana in Private: The Princess Nobody Knows, Diana: In Pursuit of Love, Diana: Her Last Love, Little Girl Lost: The Troubled Childhood of Princess Diana by the Woman Who Raised Her,* etc., etc. The obvious reason is that these books make money for writers and publishers. But as you read, you begin to respond to something compelling about Diana. Conflicted, endearing, gallant, trouble-making, aspiring, out of her depth, dying so young—she's a combination of Marilyn Monroe and Marie Antoinette, two other tragic stars whom biographers won't let alone.

The most formal of these new books is *Diana*, a full-fledged biography by the prolific Sarah Bradford, who stresses the fact that Diana Spencer had been "a very sad little girl," as her nanny put it, with an irresolute if loving father and a strong-willed mother who "bolted" from her marriage for another man when Diana was six, and never came back. No wonder Diana had a lifelong fear of abandonment and a craving for love and approval.

She was educated, if that's the word, at a traditional school for upper-class girls, where she hardly shone. ("She never carried off any academic prizes but she did win a prize with Peanuts for 'Best Kept Guinea Pig' and the Leggatt Cup 'for helpfulness.'") Then came London and various odd jobs appropriate for aristocratic girls, including the famous stint working in a nursery school. The Spencers knew the Windsors well—indeed, older sister Sarah had dated Prince Charles for a while. In fact, everyone in this world knew everyone else: One of the cozy specifics of their situation was that Camilla Parker Bowles's husband, Andrew, had once been involved with Charles's sister, Princess Anne.

By the late seventies, the Charles-Camilla situation needed to be resolved. Charles was in his thirties and had to marry. What better choice than a pretty, naïve nineteen-year-old of impeccable lineage and a romantic temperament? Diana believed it all, and perhaps Charles did too, at first. But soon it was clear that Camilla wasn't a thing of the past. It wasn't sex so much—according to Sarah Spencer, Charles's libido was low (indeed, the chronically indiscreet Diana confirmed that years later to her voice coach). It was that Charles *needed* Camilla—the slightly older, experienced woman who would take charge of him and take care of him. On the Waleses' honeymoon on the royal yacht *Britannia*, Charles might, Ms. Bradford comments, "have been an indulgent father observing the antics of a newly acquired puppy." And every day, apparently, he was on the phone with Camilla.

To what extent was Diana manipulated and deceived by older, more worldly people, as Isabel Archer was by Madame Merle and Gilbert Osmond in *The Portrait of a Lady*? Ms. Bradford quotes one "seasoned royal observer" who suggested that Camilla was the prime mover: "Mrs P-B reckons that Lady Diana is sufficiently moronic that we can have our Princess of Wales and she can go on having our Prince." Camilla as Madame Merle?

Later, Diana would say that she had been sold to the royal family to produce one "heir and a spare," but the royals don't come across as particularly cunning, and Charles in the various accounts seems less a sophisticated villain than a confused, weak, and not especially bright man. According to Diana, when years later she asked the Queen what to do to salvage her marriage, the Queen replied, "I don't know what you should do. Charles is hopeless." But not heartless. In 1986, he writes to a friend: "It's agony to know that someone is hating it all so much.... It is like being trapped in a rather desperate cul-de-sac with no apparent means of exit.... It seems so unfair on her."

As the world knows, the marriage was unsalvageable, with Charles returning to Camilla and Diana taking lovers—both in revenge and to make Charles jealous. The situation became public, as both husband and wife aired their stories, egged on by their supporters and the ravenous press. They did their best for their sons—everyone agrees that Diana was a marvelous mother—but even so the boys were "aware of the fierce rows that took place."

The situation was beyond repair, and the Queen (not Charles and Diana) decided that divorce was the only answer. Diana accepted a £17 million settlement, refused to move out of Kensington Palace, and eventually gave way on the critical (to the royals) issue of whether she would retain her title. The compromise: She would no longer be "Her Royal Highness" but would remain the Princess of Wales. It was a weird recapitulation of the refusal by George VI to grant "HRH" status to the Duchess of Windsor—a slight the Duke never forgave. Have these people nothing better to worry about? (Prince William comforted his mother by promising, "Don't worry, Mummy, I will give it back to you one day, when I am king.")

Bradford sums up the marriage: "[T]he couple were basically incompatible. Both were psychologically needy, each seeking comfort, devotion and reassurance which the other could not provide." Or to put it another way, they were both trapped in their dysfunctional childhoods. "In the master bedroom, the 7-foot 6-inch oak bed from his apartment at Buckingham Palace presented the poignant, even somewhat pathetic spectacle of the couple's toy animals ranged upon it: Charles's worn teddy, which he took everywhere with him and was tucked up in the bed at night by his valet, and Diana's 'family' . . . overflowing from the bed to shelves." *Somewhat* pathetic?

But Diana's marriage and divorce aren't the most interesting thing about her—stripped of their royal regalia, they're all too similar to a million other marriages and divorces. What's extraordinary is her determined attempt to grow and change—to leave behind the bulimic, tormented, insecure girl and become a worthwhile and useful human being. Her methods may seem ludicrous to us, but remember—this was a muddle-headed, uneducated young woman under terrible pressure. She tried everything: crystals, reflexology, colonic irrigation, acupuncture, aromatherapy, psychics, healers, astrologers. She read and reread Dr. M. Scott Peck's *The Road Less Traveled*. She treasured the rosary that Mother Teresa gave her. And are we surprised to learn that Oprah was one of her favorite luncheon guests?

With whatever reinforcements she could muster, she swung out on her own, turning herself into a major player on the world stage, with her highly publicized campaigns to help AIDS victims and to clear the world of land mines. Was she sincere? Was she merely seeking to validate her sense of herself? Was she seeking publicity? Maybe all three—certainly she'd learned the hard way how to manipulate the press. But undoubtedly she felt genuine compassion on a person-to-person level: There are countless stories of private, generous interventions. She cuddled maimed children, returned again and again to the hospital beds of the dying, comforted the survivors.

She was also ruthless when it came to cutting off people she felt were disloyal (her mother, for instance); she was prey to violent mood swings and prone to self-destructive decisions. Her judgment was, to put it mildly, patchy. But she had charm, beauty, and style. Against my will, I was impressed the one time I met her—at the entrance to Katharine Graham's house on the occasion of Kay's eightieth birthday. Kay introduced us, Diana smiled her smile and offered her (gloved) hand, and I covered myself with glory by coming up with the following Wildean remark: "It's a pleasure to meet you."

Ms. Bradford is just about as dazzling: Her book is thorough but perfunctory. There's nothing perfunctory, though, about the other two Diana books at hand. If you want up-close, no-holds-barred accounts of the rich and famous, go to their most ardent advocates and adversaries: their servants. And as it happens, we have newly before us a "His" and a "Hers."

"His" is by Sarah Goodall, the "lady clerk" who is the central figure in *The Palace Diaries: A Story Inspired by Twelve Years of Life Behind Palace Gates.* A clerk, in royals-speak, is a kind of secretary, and the young Sarah Goodall, on the loose in London in need of a good job, is taken on as the lowliest of a crew that sorts Prince Charles's mail. She's with him for a dozen years, climbing the ladder to jobs of more importance and greater proximity to His Royal Highness, and she's clearly besotted with her boss. And just as clearly un-besotted with Diana. "I do not for a second doubt Diana's great qualities. . . . But I also saw the other side and feel it can be honestly said the sainted Princess could be deceitful, manipulative and pitiless towards those who stood in her way or those she chose to discard. . . . To be frank, she was a passionate woman. If you think that Captain Hewitt was the only stallion in her stable, then you're in for a surprise." And, she goes on, "For the ordinary person like myself, therefore, the question is: was she a fruitcake, or was she at times just a spoilt bitch determined to get her own way?"

(Ms. Goodall's exquisite taste extends to her account of her own romantic life—with "darling Andy, so charming and oh so eligible, the younger son, if you please, of a belted earl, no less. Cripes. Had I played it differently, I might now be the daughter-in-law of a peer of the realm!" She tries to play it right, going to a more sophisticated clerk for the crucial data: "Geraldine, how do you give a blow job?" Here's Geraldine's recipe: "The top is the most sensitive. Think of it like an ice cream that you wish to lick from the side. When you go further down, be careful with your teeth: never touch him with your teeth. Remember, he is very sensitive. Otherwise it will be like serrating a sausage. He won't like it." Obviously good advice, and I'm going to take it to heart the next time I'm romancing the son of a belted earl.)

Sarah has no complaints at all about Charles. They meet at a staff party. "Take a deep breath. Treasure this moment, Sarah. You are sitting next to the future King, here, right now. Look around. Remember this scene. You will be telling your grandchildren about it one day." (Actually, she won't have to; they'll be reading this book.) "You are touching the face of God . . . well, not quite, but close enough."

As she rises through the ranks, Ms. Goodall is even invited to take meals with her royals and their guests. But after twelve years of service, she's dismissed, having, as she admits, gotten above herself: "By the end of my Royal employment, I had succumbed to a bad case of red-carpet fever." Finally, she gets things in perspective: "[W]e shouldn't take the Royal Family too seriously, even if some of them take themselves seriously. . . . The Royals serve a purpose, but reverence is for gods, not people. Unless, like me, you can't help yourself worshipping Prince Charles."

A more serious case of royals-worship is that of the famous butler, Paul Burrell, for Diana. (His second book, *The Way We Were: Remembering Diana*, is already a bestseller.) As a young man, after studying at a catering school where his prize was "for sculpting Chesterfield's famous crooked spire entirely out of margarine," Paul had gone to work in Buckingham Palace and quickly became one of the Queen's two pages. (His most onerous job was walking the nine corgis.) His admiration for Her Majesty is boundless: "She is a remarkable, kind, Christian lady. . . . The Queen is one of the easiest people to converse with, and is not at all grand or pompous. . . . Her Majesty is like a gracious country lady who just happens to be the monarch." He also insists that the Queen and Diana got along well and never quarreled. At summer barbecues at the log cabin on the Balmoral estate, in fact, Diana "was known to find a pair of rubber gloves and muck in with someone else not averse to washing-up—Her Majesty the Queen."

After eleven years at the palace, Paul was snatched away by Prince Charles to be his butler, and although he's respectful of the Prince, he's somewhat less idolatrous than the lady clerk. From his first book, *A Royal Duty*, we learn, for instance, that—preferring to communicate by memo— Charles once wrote to Paul: "A letter from the Queen must have fallen by accident into the wastepaper basket beside the table in the library. Please look for it." Another micromanagerial memo: "Would you please inform guests staying at Highgrove NOT to dispose of tampons or condoms down the toilet as they strangle the [environmentally friendly] reed beds." On the other hand, Paul acknowledges that, at least in the early years, "Prince Charles did his best to understand his wife and be patient with the mood swings brought on by the eating disorder bulimia, which she later admitted to suffering."

When the Waleses separated, Paul went to work for Diana at Kensington Palace and stayed with her for the rest of her life. His duties grew as her staff shrank, and eventually he became her closest support, and her friend. It's obvious that she trusted him completely, telling him all her news, showing him her letters from the Queen and from her husband, sending him on secret missions to collect lovers and sneak them into the palace. (He was her "emotional washing machine," she told him; "I can come home, tell you everything and tip it all out.") His two little boys were in and out of Diana's apartments, romping with William and Harry. It was he who went to Paris to oversee arrangements after her death and help Prince Charles bring her home. And it was he who kept vigil beside her coffin through the night before the funeral.

It was also he who supervised the dismantling of her apartments, and who decided to remove certain papers of hers for safekeeping—the action that eventually led to his trial for theft. His account of all this, in *A Royal Duty*, is harrowing and convincing; reading it, one is relieved to witness the Crown's case collapse when the Queen herself confirms that after Diana's death, Paul told her in a private audience that lasted almost three hours about his taking the papers, and why.

But why a whole new book from Paul Burrell, apart from the money and attention involved? He seems to have had three motives:

1. To protect and burnish Diana's reputation. He admired her, he devoted himself to her, and he loved her, though he doesn't allow himself to say so. Although he was a happy husband and father, Diana took over his life: Just as Camilla was the third person in the Waleses' marriage, Diana was the third person in the Burrells' marriage. His obsession with her only grew after her death. In the middle of one night, he wrote in *A Royal Duty*, he woke up from a nightmare, left his home, and went to Diana's now-empty rooms. "Having just dreamed about the princess, I needed to sense her presence. . . . I went into the L-shaped wardrobe room, pulled back the curtains where her dresses hung, and crawled into the gap between the floor and the clothes. I could smell her scent. In that position, I fell asleep for the night."

2. To underline the specialness of their relationship. (Memoirs are always self-serving—how could it be otherwise?) After his rejection by the Spencer family, about whom he has nothing good to say, and the horror of the trial, he needs to remind the world again that he was closest to her, most trusted by her.

3. To bury once and for all the idea that Diana was planning to marry Dodi al-Fayed. "The cold truth about Dodi is that, to the princess, he was an intense, short-lived fling. He only spent ten minutes at KP [Kensington Palace], and the boss had spent just 26 days in his company." "I want another marriage like I want a bad rash," she said to Paul and others. Besides, she was still in love with Hasnat Khan, the Pakistani surgeon she'd been having an affair with and who, she told Paul, was her "soulmate." ("The princess could disappear from KP to spend whole days in his one-bedroom flat, and the joy she derived from those occasions was immeasurable." She would come home to the palace and tell Paul "how she had spent the day in a poky, sparsely decorated flat, vacuuming, polishing, dusting, doing the dishes, ironing piles of laundry, stripping and re-making his bed. . . . 'I don't mind ironing shirts,' she said. 'It reminds me of when I used to look after an American family and washed and ironed all of theirs.'") Paul liked and admired the doctor, while on the subject of al-Fayed, he's relentless: "The world must stop believing that Diana and Dodi were due to get married, because that is not the truth."

On the subject of whether the fatal car crash was less innocent than it appeared, he—like Sarah Bradford, like Sarah Goodall—is cautious. But he certainly feels, as Diana did, that there were secret forces in the palace and in the intelligence services that threatened her. Mysteriously, he quotes the Queen as saying, during their long private conversation, "Be careful, Paul. No one has been as close to a member of my family as you have. There are powers at work in this country about which we have no knowledge." Did she say it? Can it be true? Or is paranoia an occupational hazard of being royal?

Paul Burrell is the ultimate royal servant/courtier—devoted beyond reason to his "boss," convinced of his special place in her life, certain that he would never have suffered the fate of so many of the other "special" friends whom she eventually cut off at the knees.

Maybe he was right; I'd like to think so. And, given the amount of attention paid to the royal family, I'd also like to believe that there's more to them than meets the tabloid eye: that Helen Mirren's decent and sincere Queen reflects the real one; that Prince Charles is worthy of Sarah Goodall's worship; and that Diana, Princess of Wales, was the woman Paul Burrell took her to be.

October 8, 2006

Man of Pleasure

A nd let us now praise famous men, with particular attention to those who were famous only for being famous. They were heroes, too—they kept tongues wagging and gossip columnists gossiping and rumors flying, until they didn't any longer and slipped into oblivion. But occasionally one of these figures rouses the interest of a journalist or biographer or social historian, and then he's back among us—interesting as an artifact of a vanished zeitgeist if not interesting in himself.

Which brings us to the latest disinterred hero of this species: Porfirio Rubirosa, or *The Last Playboy*, as his biographer, Shawn Levy, calls him. Raise your hands, boys and girls, if any of you under the age of fifty remember him. It doesn't count if you're from the Dominican Republic, have specialized in the history of polo, or have been studying the memoirs of Zsa Zsa Gabor. Zsa Zsa and "Rubi" specialized in each other when they weren't marrying everyone else; in fact, they would seem to have been each other's nearest equivalent, their lives lived in headlines and nightclubs and between the sheets, although she was sometimes to be found in front of a camera, while he could be found on a horse or behind the wheel of a racing car.

Rubi was born in 1909, the last child of a fierce, dominating father and a pious mother. The father, Don Pedro, was macho to the max, what Mr. Levy calls a *tíguere*, or tiger, the "essential defining characteristic of the Dominican alpha male." A *tíguere* "bore the savor of low origins and high aspirations, as well as a certain ruthless ambition that barred no means of achieving his ends: violence, treachery, lies, shamelessness, daring, and, especially, the use of women as tools of social mobility. A *tíguere* always married to advantage." *Tígueres* were also "handsome, graceful, strong, and well-presented, possessed of a deep-seated vanity." Don Pedro quali-

Zsa Zsa and Rubi

fied on all counts, but he was to mellow through the years, becoming a diplomat whose career took him to Paris when Rubi was six—Paris, which was to remain Rubi's lifelong spiritual home, if "spiritual" is a word that can usefully be applied to him.

To call Rubi's formal education checkered is to flatter it, but he effortlessly mastered the things that counted—clothes, sports, sexual charisma; the things that were essential to becoming what he recognized himself to be: "I am, and will always be, a man of pleasure."

By the time he reached manhood, his country was firmly under the rule of the notorious strongman Rafael Trujillo, who had a string of puppets "elected" president while he chose to reign as the Generalissimo, "adding an unprecedented fifth star to his epaulets and another title to the encomia by which he demanded to be addressed." (That unprecedented use of "encomia" is echt Levy, a *tíguere* of English prose. Stand by for further examples of his original way with words.)

From the start, entwined with Rubi's life as a man of pleasure was a sometimes official, sometimes hidden, sometimes antagonistic relationship with Trujillo, his leader, his occasional boss, and—oh, yes—his first father-in-law. Trujillo's daughter, Flor de Oro, had been sent off to Paris as a young girl to acquire some French polish. Summoned home by the Generalissimo at the age of seventeen, she was soon swept off her feet by her country's most polished young man. He seems to have loved her in return, but under the strains of Rubi's womanizing and Flor's divided loyalties, the marriage collapsed, leaving Rubi dangerously out of favor with her father and Flor on her way to husband number two . . . and eventually on to husbands numbers three through nine. Rubi managed only five marriages, but made up for it with countless affairs, flings, and quickies.

His post-Flor wives included France's most highly paid movie star, Danielle Darrieux, and the two most famously rich women in the world, Doris Duke and Barbara ("Babs") Hutton. Doris, whose fortune amounted to more than $3 billion in today's money, demonstrated her love for Rubi with gifts ranging from a plantation back in the Dominican Republic to a "B-25 bomber fitted out as a private airplane." The wedding was huge news everywhere ("Doris Duke Weds Smoking Latin"). The divorce, which took place fourteen months later, was quieter, with Rubi netting their elegant house on the rue de Bellechasse and alimony of $25,000 a year (more than $200,000 today). There were attempts at a reconciliation, despite her almost catching him in bed with Christina Onassis, but they didn't pan out. Even so, Doris, according to Rubi's brother, Cesar, was "by far the nicest of any of Porfirio's wives."

Among the many other women he was linked to on his detour from Doris to Babs were "actresses such as Gene Tierney, Dolores del Rio, and Veronica Lake; the great Portuguese fado singer Amália Rodrigues; no-name showgirls in London and Paris; the wives and girlfriends of his polo and race-car-driving peers; women from noble circles such as the Contessa Nicola-Gambi of Italy, Countess Marita of Spain, and Queen Alexandra of Yugoslavia. ('Rubi,' an old friend joked, 'has become a baron by a process of bedroom osmosis.')" All of this highly publicized activity got him back into the good graces of the Dominican regime, which viewed his notoriety as the best public relations it could muster. "The only way Rubi can fall from favor in the Dominican Republic is if he loses his sex appeal," is how one official put it. The Generalissimo (now known as "The Benefactor") put it this way: "He's good at his job because women like him and he's a wonderful liar." An unbeatable reference.

It was during the lull between billionaire wives that Zsa Zsa came into the picture, "in the throes of fame and stardom." They met in a hotel elevator in New York, and Rubi "found himself agog." Instantly, he installed himself in the suite next to hers and, wouldn't you know it, she couldn't zip up the dress she was wearing to the premiere of her movie *Moulin Rouge*. A quick phone call and "He was over in a flash, zipped her up, helped her on with her coat: a complete gentleman. But the air between them was as thick and electric as before a thunderstorm. She extricated herself from the pregnant pause and made off for her premiere." You won't be surprised to hear that the storm soon broke. Within months she was telling her mother, "Rubi is a disease of the blood. I cannot be without him."

Many dramas would be acted out before she *was* without him, the most notorious involving a jab in the eye when Zsa Zsa provoked him by asserting that, despite all, she still loved her ex-husband, the movie star George Sanders. I SAID NO, SO PORFY POKED ME, headlined the New York *Daily News*. And on page one the very next day: BABS WEDS RUBI— KEEPS MONEY / SAYS "SÍ" AS DOMINICAN CITIZEN. The *Post*? RADIANT BABS YEARNS FOR A BABY; COUPLE PLANNING TO LIVE IN PARIS. The following day in the *News*? RUBI MOVES IN HIS WARDROBE; HE IS STAY-ING. Barbara Hutton had acquired her man (among her previous acqui-sitions had been Cary Grant) for the modest lump-sum payment of $2.5 million. Within months, the marriage was essentially over—you could say Babs had rented him for the season—and Zsa Zsa was back on the scene. But not permanently. "I could not marry Rubi. He wants me to give up my career and live with him in Paris. I could never give up acting. It is my life."

However heartbroken he may have been, Rubi managed to console himself. "By the time he and his Hungarian soulmate ended their mad intercontinental caravan of sensations, he had dallied among the likes of Eartha Kitt and Ava Gardner and Rita Hayworth and Empress Soraya of Iran." Or, in the case of Hayworth, he hadn't dallied. "The rumor was that Rubi didn't go through with it because Aly [Khan, Rita's ex] said he'd consider it a favor if he didn't." Anything for a friend. As for Ava, "She denied the whole thing up and down."

Does it really matter whether they did or they didn't? The only im-portant question is what exactly he had that drew all these ladies to him. A hit Cuban song of the fifties put it this way: "¿Qué Es Lo Tuyo, Rubi-rosa?" ("What Have You Got, Rubirosa?") And if you know only one thing about "Porfy," you already know the answer, though it takes Mr. Levy 125 pages to get to it: "There is no way around saying it out loud: The man was well-hung, hung, indeed, legendarily, his superhuman endowment a calling card that recommended him to circles into which he might otherwise never have gained admittance. Women heard about it, wondered about it, whispered about it, had to see it, hold it, have it—and who was he to deny them?"

And who are we to doubt? The evidence is ironclad. Society photographer Jerome Zerbe "on a dare, followed Rubi into the men's room. He skittered out gleefully, the story went, with the intelligence, 'It looks like Yul Brynner in a black turtleneck!'" Even more persuasive: Doris Duke reported to her godson, "It was the most magnificent penis that I had ever seen . . . six inches in circumference . . . much like the last foot of a Louisville Slugger baseball bat with the consistency of a not completely inflated volleyball." I can't quite picture it, but I'm impressed.

Sexual adventures and sports weren't the only elements of Rubi's life, however. He spent a good deal of his time on tawdry moneymaking schemes that never paid off—he wasn't, he ruefully acknowledged, much of a businessman. And he continued to make himself useful to Trujillo, who "had come to rely, curiously, on Rubi's contacts, renown, and blend of palaver and charm as tools of diplomacy. . . . Who could believe that such a superficial fellow was actually an important cog of Trujillo's machinery of power?" He was named ambassador to Cuba, then inspector of embassies, a gig happily located in Paris. And when the Benefactor was assassinated, Rubi performed the same kind of services for his semi-psychotic son, Ramfis. He did extensive lobbying for Dominican interests, trying to persuade Washington that the Trujillo regime was an essential bulwark against communism in the Caribbean, and impressing the Kennedys, with whom he had become friendly—cruises off Hyannisport, partying with the president and Sinatra and the Lawfords . . .

When the Trujillo dynasty was finally dismantled and replaced by a frail democracy, Rubi's career ended. As a result, his diplomatic immunity was gone, and he was finally vulnerable to investigation by the New York district attorney for his presumed involvement, decades earlier, with the murders of various anti-Trujillo exiles. He got away unscathed, but his effective life was over.

He cared for his fifth and final wife, Odile Rodin, an actress twenty-eight years his junior, but she was growing restive with their increasingly circumscribed existence in Paris. He was fifty-six, and his body was slowing down. At eight in the morning of July 5, 1965, after a night spent celebrating a successful polo tournament, he crashed his silver Ferrari in the Bois de Boulogne. He had been going eighty miles an hour, and he was alone.

A year later, Harold (*The Carpetbaggers*) Robbins published a bestselling novel centered on Rubi's life. (The word "loins" is in constant play.) It was called *The Adventurers*, its hero was named Dax, and the cast of characters included barely concealed "adventurers" like the Kennedys, Doris Duke, Oleg Cassini, Maria Callas, Elsa Maxwell, Zsa Zsa Gabor, Danielle Darrieux, the Trujillos—you get the picture. All of them were instantly identifiable, and not one of them was remotely believable. Dax was nobler than Rubi—a true patriot at heart—but, I'm afraid, considerably less amusing. A few years later, this 781-page epic (I'm putting in for combat pay) was translated into a risible three-hour schlock-fest of a movie, featuring as Dax a young Yugoslavian actor named Bekim Fehmiu who, as Mr. Levy puts it, looked like "a degenerate cross of Ringo Starr and Jean-Paul Belmondo." What a sad comedown for the elegant, charming, worldly Rubi.

On the other hand, there is this biography, which makes what may be a lasting contribution—not with its content but with its insidious use of a kind of alternative English. Again and again, Mr. Levy gets words and phrases almost right; you start to wonder whether it's he or you who's crazy. Just a few examples: "It seemed the destiny of the country always to roil"; "the kidskin coat he wore as a redoubt to the astonishing cold"; "a caravan of trucks . . . wended from the capital"; "It helped to have an equanimous sense of humor about yourself"; "He gadded for a while"; "Then Barbara arrived, and that inkling of joy quickly vanished"; "she shed herself of Alexis"; "his presence was decidedly vestigial"; "leaving behind a note that read, in its gist, 'I am bored'"; "He steered Ramfis with a ginger hand"; "By eleven-thirty everyone had filtered away."

Did the editors at Fourth Estate filter away before *The Last Playboy* went to press? No. In his acknowledgments, the author credits Rachel Safko, who "served the office of traffic cop genially," and David Falk, who "was equally genteel in his copyedit." Mr. Levy is also "in the perennial debt" of his agents Richard Pine and Lori Anderman, "my longtime partners in genteel crime." Which reminds me to acknowledge here my perennial debt to Adam Begley, my own longtime genteel editor.

Uh-oh—can this kind of thing be catching?

September 25, 2005

The Fabulous D.V.

A ll right, children, you have only one guess. Who said, "Peanut butter is the greatest invention since Christianity"? No fair—you peeked at the headline and the pictures. But did you know that she practiced what she preached? Diana Vreeland's lunch every day at her desk was a glass of Scotch and a peanut-butter-and-marmalade sandwich on whole wheat bread. (White bread? "How common, you know, flour and water. That's what white bread's made of and that's what we use to make library paste out of.")

And do you know who said, "The Civil War was nothing compared to the smell of a San Diego orange"?

And do you know (and do you believe) that when President Kennedy was shot, her first reaction was: "My God, Lady Bird in the White House. We can't use her in the magazine!"?

But then Mrs. Vreeland—D.V.—wouldn't have objected to an invented, or exaggerated, story about herself: She had made it clear from the start that a good story was more important to her than a good fact. Fantasy, imagination, glamour were her stock in trade; why bother saying you were born in Paris when it was so much more amusing to have been born in Vladivostok, as she insisted one day to her grandson that she had been. Or in the Atlas Mountains—"in a nomad community, accompanied by Berber ululations." To the famous model Veruschka she insisted, "If somebody asks you about where you are from or where you were born, never say what is true. It's too boring! You have to always be dramatic."

Lies, or exaggerations, or tall tales, or self-mythologizing are essential to anyone who completely invents herself, as Diana Dalziel Vreeland did. Even at fourteen she wanted to be a Chinese princess, and though she didn't quite make it, she did turn herself into some kind of Kabuki figure,

surrounded in her red apartment by swags and sconces and torchères and fur throws and blackamoors. In the diary she kept when she was about fifteen, she wrote, "I am Diana, a goddess, therefore ought to be wonderful, pure, marvelous, as only I alone can make myself.... Dalziel—I dare, therefore I dare, I dare change today, & make myself exactly how I want to be." The D.V. she invented was a triumph of personality and will, but why should she have to invent herself in the first place? As usual, the roots go back to childhood, and in particular to her mother's rejection of her. In the biography *Diana Vreeland* by Eleanor Dwight we get the whole picture, but D.V. has already told the story, chillingly, in her memoirs: "There was the most terrible scene between my mother and me. One day she said to me, 'It's too bad that you have such a beautiful sister and that you are so extremely ugly and so terribly jealous of her. This, of course, is why you are so impossible to deal with.'"

Her mother was a spoiled American beauty, who became embroiled in a scandal just as Diana was getting married. Her father ignored it: "Worse things happen at sea." He was an Edwardian gent—Frederick Dalziel (pronounced "Dee-el," Diana tells us). In her memoirs, she hardly comments on her mother's antipathy to her beyond saying, "My mother and I were not really sympathetic," but her being judged extremely ugly by her beautiful mother was obviously the central trauma of her life; all she knew as a child, she tells us, was that "my mother wasn't proud of me. I was always her ugly little monster." Not only did this view of herself focus her attention on surface beauty as a crucial element of life, but it led to her choice of husband: "I never felt comfortable about my looks until I married Reed Vreeland. He was the most beautiful man I've ever seen." And she went on worshipping Reed until his death. "Isn't it curious," she wrote, "that even after more than forty years of marriage, I was always slightly shy of him? I can remember his coming home in the evening—the way the door would close and the sound of his step. . . . If I was in my bath or in my bedroom making up, I can remember always pulling myself up, thinking, 'I must be at my very best.' There was never a time when I didn't have that reaction—ever."

The marriage flourished, first in Albany, where Reed was training to be a banker and the Vreelands had a little house and a little baby and a totally domestic life, and where Diana was in bliss. ("I loved our life there. I was totally happy. I didn't care what any other place was like. I'd still be there now if Reed hadn't wanted to move to London.") It flourished in London, where the Vreelands slipped effortlessly into high society (and where Diana first met her great-friend-to-be Wallis Simpson, well before she became the Duchess of Windsor). It flourished back in New York, when—transformed by financial necessity into a working woman—Diana went to work first at *Harper's Bazaar*, then *Vogue*. During the war—for seven years—Reed was working in Canada and Diana lived alone; her two boys were mostly off at school. The marriage survived the separation, as well as Reed's apparent infidelities (with, among others, Edwina Mountbatten), about which Diana never spoke. She took him as he was—good-natured, easygoing, and, above all, elegant. But he accepted her quirks, too. In 1940, as the phony war was drawing to an end, he sailed for America, leaving her behind in Paris. "Look," he said, "there's no point taking Diana away from Chanel and her shoes. If she hasn't got her shoes and her clothes, there's no point in bringing her home. That's how it's always been and that's how it has to be."

D.V. is direct on why she left *Bazaar* for *Vogue*: money. In twenty-eight years, she says, she never got a raise until finally they came through—with a thousand dollars. ("I was the most economical thing that ever happened to the Hearst Corporation.") "We're offering you the moon and sixpence," *Vogue* said, and so in 1962 she switched. It was the perfect moment, because she got not only the moon and the sixpence but the sixties, her favorite decade except for the twenties. You can see why—everything suddenly topsy-turvy and exciting, just waiting to be harnessed to her aesthetic ambitions. And with all that Condé Nast money to back her up! Imagine Hearst sitting still for those elaborate photo shoots around the world. Just check out the pictures in Dwight's book of the model Antonia perched between some giant crumbling stone heads at the summit of Nemrud Dagh (that's in Turkey's Göreme valley, in case you didn't know) and of Lauren Hutton in the midst of a male initiation rite in Bali. These were the great days of Avedon and Penn and David Bailey, of Twiggy and Penelope Tree and Marisa Berenson and Veruschka. No expense spared.

In these years, her invention never flagged. Dwight quotes Kenneth Jay Lane: "She made me realize the importance of positive thinking. She would say, 'Don't look back. Just go ahead. Give ideas away. Under every idea there's a new idea waiting to be born.'"

And these were the years when D.V., rapidly turning into an official legend, was able to indulge her passion for others of her kind. She adored Nureyev, Callas, Plisetskaya. And of course the Windsors—cozy little evenings at Les Moulins. ("Did I tell you about the Duke of Windsor's bathroom...? Oh, I'm sure he took showers. There was nothing unwashed about the Duke.") Chanel was never off her list: "Peasants and geniuses are the only people who count, and she was both," and "Coco was never a kind woman ... she was a *monstre sacré*. But she was the most interesting person *I've* ever met." Andy Warhol. And of course Jackie O., whom she advised on fashion, who edited her book *Allure*, and who, Dwight tells us, was the last person to call the apartment on the day Diana died. There's something a little fawning in her behavior to Jackie, and to Katharine Graham as well—I've seen some of the letters she wrote to Graham, whom she also advised on clothes, and who occasionally helped her out financially. But D.V. had always known how to please.

Her enthusiasms ranged from peanut butter, as we've seen, to boiled chicken "the way Queen Victoria used to like it," to certain colors ("All my life I've pursued the perfect red"), to blacks ("almost the only people I can stand to look at nowadays"), to Clark Gable's eyelashes ("the most beautiful eyelashes I've ever seen on a man—on a human being"). "How I miss fringe!" she cries. "Where is fringe today?"

The extravagance, the luxe, the bizarrerie—their time passed, and in 1971 she was abruptly ousted from *Vogue* by Alex Liberman, who both believed she had outlived her usefulness and resented her high-and-mighty ways. The new *Vogue*, under Grace Mirabella, shot up in circulation even as it came down to earth. D.V. felt betrayed and bereft—the superb impersonation of her by Mary Louise Wilson in the play *Full Gallop* caught her at this low point of her life.

But rescue was at hand, and soon she'd moved on to what some people, including Eleanor Dwight, clearly feel to be the apogee of her career: curating the fashion shows at the Metropolitan Museum of Art. Dolly was definitely back in town! By now she knew everyone as well as everything, and there was no one she couldn't call on to make these shows exactly what she wanted them to be. The first one—on the career of Balenciaga— set the tone. If you need proof of how central Balenciaga was to the world D.V. had made her own, here's a passage from her memoirs that I take to be more or less literally true:

> I was staying with Mona Bismarck in Capri when the news came. I was downstairs, dressed for dinner, having a drink. Consuelo Crespi telephoned me from Rome, saying it had just come over the radio that Balenciaga had closed his doors forever that afternoon, and that he'd never open them again. Mona didn't come out of her room for three days. I mean, she went into a complete . . . I mean, it was the end of a certain part of her life!

And if you look at the color photos of some of the Balenciaga gowns that Dwight displays in her book, you can hardly blame poor Mona— they're as close to great art, I would think, as clothes can get. But if Mona mourned, Diana eventually did something about it when she got her chance at the Met. This is a hallmark of her life: She may have looked like a Kabuki puppet, spent hours putting on her maquillage, palled around with the Windsors and their like, but at heart she was a worker. From her stint at *Bazaar* when, as fashion editor, she spent days clambering up flights of stairs to vet what was going on in Seventh Avenue ateliers, to her manic observations and commands to her staff at *Vogue*, to her determination to acquire for her Met shows everything from Peter the Great's boots to the dresses Vivien Leigh wore in *Gone with the Wind*, she pursued her goals with unflagging energy and cunning. In other words, she earned her success.

Dwight's book is strongest when dealing with the Met years—she's comfortable in that world, and knowledgeable. A lot of the earlier material is déjà vu all over again; anecdotes already recycled from *Allure* to *D.V.*, and a lot of secondary sources. The early diaries are fascinating, but where are the wonderful *Vogue* memos that have recently surfaced and been published in both *The New Yorker* and *Visionaire*? ("For goodness sakes, beware of curls." "I am extremely disappointed that no one has taken the slightest interest in freckles on the models." "I repeat again the importance of knee socks." "Is there anybody in the Village or slightly out of work or a poor old Arab who would make us some passementerie ornamental belts? . . . Let's give the Arabs a boost.") And why no quotes from George Trow, who anatomized Vreeland lovingly through the years in *The New Yorker*? Why not even a hint of certain darker matters that troubled some of Diana's intimates: her drinking, her possible anti-Semitism? The Dwight book is a celebration, almost a hagiography, and as such it's fun to read, despite some odd carelessness (no, JFK was not shot on November 21). It's also an appropriately handsome artifact, beginning with its gleaming red cover and binding and endpapers and, inside, its lavish illustrations.

But then, Diana Vreeland was herself a superb artifact. I had never met her before I began editing her memoirs and I was wary. As it turned out, I found in her an irresistible charm (no surprise), and an enviable energy and grasp (again, no surprise), and a warmth that was surprising because it really did seem genuine. I don't believe it was personal; I think it sprang from her insatiable curiosity, her passionate interest in whatever came into her line of vision. It could be you, it could be Peter the Great's boots, it could be Gable's eyelashes.

Not that she was equally interested in everything. Nothing takes precedence over shoes ("Unshined shoes are the end of civilization"), certainly not feminism: "I stand with the French line—women and children last." Everyone knows that she polished the soles of her shoes, but equally important is never putting scent on immediately after your bath: "That's the biggest mistake going—there's nothing for it to cling to." Yes, this is all superficial, but as she said, "I am entirely superficial and I mean to stay that way." She also said, "What's wrong with pleasure? What are we here for but for pleasure?" Yet she could stand on the outside and judge: "I was always fascinated by the absurdities and the luxuries and the snobbism of the world that the fashion magazines showed."

And then there was her core of resolute privacy. She may have made a spectacle of herself, but no one ever knew what she was feeling. Just as she never spoke of the painful seven years when she and Reed were living apart, she was silent while he was dying. Years later, she told George Plimpton, when he was collaborating with her on *D.V.*, that she didn't want Reed to be told that he had cancer. "This Godforsaken doctor said, 'Mrs. Vreeland, you're not at all modern. You're very old-fashioned. We always tell our patients.' But I said, 'What do you take my husband for, an idiot? Don't you suppose he knows he has cancer?'" The doctor asked if she had discussed it with him, and she answered, "Of course not, why would he and I discuss cancer?" When the doctor ignored her wishes and informed his patient, Reed turned his face to the wall. "Well," he said to her that night, "they've told you and they told me and now it's on the table and now there's nothing to do about it." They were two of a kind. Maybe it was this quality in her that Pierre Bergé was thinking of when he spoke of "the elegance of her soul and the elegance of her heart."

Her last words, which she cried out as she lay dying in 1989, were, "Don't stop the music or I'll tell my father!" Until then, for her, the music had never stopped.

November 24, 2002

Come Up and Signify Me

Poor Mae West! First, struggling up the hard way—the not-quite-savory background, burlesque, vaudeville; notoriety (well, she enjoyed that); sneered at by the classy side of Broadway and later of Hollywood (Miriam Hopkins huffed of her own films and West's: "They don't belong in the same conversation or category"); slow artistic and box-office death at the hands of the Hays Office; desperate attempts to reassert her appeal; the ghastly *Myra Breckinridge* (when she thought they were offering her Myra, she turned it down: "I like my sexes stable") and the even-more-ghastly *Sextette* (she was eighty-four; said *The New York Times*, "Granny should have her mouth washed out with soap, along with her teeth"), and, ultimately, retreat into fantasy in her all-white-and-gold, all-mirrored apartment—the preferred decor of America's infamous Diamond Lil.

But lucky Mae West, too—the slow but sure progress until she had hootchy-kootchied and shimmied her way up the showbiz ladder and was starring in her own plays on Broadway; overnight stardom in Hollywood in 1932, when she was thirty-nine; tremendous box office, huge salary, almost unparalleled control over her movies—writing her own dialogue, overseeing casting, slipping and sliding around the dread production code until even she couldn't get away with her innuendoes and provocations; enjoying as many comebacks as Judy Garland (though unlike Garland, she remained in strict control of her work, her image, and her money). She may have been a laughingstock to some, but to others she was a magnificent original—a woman of large talents, if not education, who triumphantly asserted the right to her rampant sexuality and created a type as unique as Chaplin, Garbo, or the Marx Brothers. Colette put it with her customary acuity: "She alone, out of an enormous and dull catalogue of heroines, does

not get married at the end of the film, does not die, does not take the road to exile, does not gaze sadly at her declining youth in a silver-framed mirror. . . . She alone has no parents, no children, no husband. This impudent woman is, in her style, as solitary as Chaplin used to be."

Celebrate Mae West or mock her, you have to feel sympathy for this game (and gamy) woman now that she's been discovered by academia. First, she was taken up by the genderists—wasn't she "empowered"? Didn't she fight for her rights as Independent Woman and prevail? She battled the censors, she battled the moguls, she defied the police (she and the whole cast of her play *SEX* were thrown in jail, where she seems to have had a good time). Like Catherine the Great—whom she impersonated on Broadway—she chewed men up and spat them out. And most important of all, she never allowed anyone—whether in a professional or personal relationship—to compromise her great creation, "Mae West." As much as any woman of the twentieth century, she took control of her life and kept it: an essential feminist heroine, and rightly so. Except that what gets lost in all the feminist-speak is the vastly amusing and canny entertainer, whose trajectory is part of a great American theatrical tradition of self-invented women stars. Think back to Isadora Duncan, think ahead to Madonna.

And now, as if the feminist approach weren't enough, along comes Jill Watts's *Mae West: An Icon in Black and White*, the book that tells us that it may just be possible, though there's no evidence whatsoever to prove it, that Mae was—are you ready?—one-quarter African American! Her paternal grandfather's early life is undocumented, although it seems he worked on whaling ships, and "50 percent of those serving on whaling vessels were black." On the one hand, Mae "proudly displayed a genealogy of a West family—purported to have descended from Alfred the Great"; on the other, John Edwin West was "the only grandparent for whom she volunteered no information on background or origins." As for his "passing": "While no documents substantiate that John Edwin did, similarly none prove that he did not." This cunning argument takes us to page four, and is providentially dropped.

What follows doesn't provide much new information and certainly lacks the scope, depth, and wit of Emily Wortis Leider's 1997 *Becoming Mae West*, or the zest of West's own (ghostwritten) story of her life, *Goodness Had Nothing to Do with It*. But Watts's book could serve as a plausible account of the life and career if it weren't skewed in two directions. First, by the insistence throughout on West's affinity for black music, black culture, black humor, and black men. Yes, she was influenced by the great black vaudeville (and Ziegfeld) star Bert Williams; yes, she performed in blackface; yes, her fame was secured by her adaptation of the shimmy; yes, she sang her version of the blues; yes, black maids in her plays and movies have more-than-usual prominence; yes, she wrote a novel and play about miscegenation (she approved of it); yes, she apparently enjoyed the company—and more—of a series of black studs (and an even-longer-running series of white ones). If Watts had written a monograph on the African American influences on Mae West, she would have provided us with a useful complement to the standard ways of looking at this very complicated performer. Instead, she has so overemphasized this aspect of West's life and art that her book tilts into obsessive argument: She sees black influence everywhere, until her agenda sinks both story and subject.

And then there's her modish language. The most valuable lesson West learned from Bert Williams? "The performative was the political." Or try this: "The ragtime-singing, bones-playing 'Parisienne' cooch dancer was just beginning to project an indeterminacy that challenged the whole idea of racial fixity so critical to the ideology of white racism." Or this: "On stage West had internalized oppositional and conflicting identities, eventually rejecting hegemonic societal forces by embracing African-American culture."

The author's favorite concepts involve West's supposed "signifying" and her identity as a "trickster." These two words are scrawled like graffiti across the text of the book. The movie censors, for instance, "were attempting to rein in West's signifying." (Translation: They were trying to clean up her act.) "For the public," we learn, "Mae West was no longer just a star. She had evolved into a signifier, both an agent and a symbol that communicated its own meanings." On her death, journalism's appreciation of her wordplay "indicated the pervasiveness of Mae's deployment of the African-American tradition of signification. The trickster's voice lived on to continue to challenge and upset society's conventions." And in a summing-up, Watts calls upon West's "links to the topsy-turvy world of African-American tricksterism and signification" to support her central thesis: "Mae West was and is a cultural agent that celebrates and perpetuates the African presence within American society."

The problem isn't that all of Watts's ideas are foolish; on the contrary, she is shrewd in her discussions of much of West's writing, and she performs a service in drawing attention to West's debt to African American culture. But the author undercuts her fresh ideas with sterile language and overstatement. It's a gross mismatch: West's own language was so direct, so witty, and so steeped in the vernacular. This is the woman who told Ernst Lubitsch, "Shakespeare had his style and I have mine." And who remarked, in the wake of the gigantic success of Disney's *Snow White and the Seven Dwarfs*, "I used to be Snow White but I drifted." Signifying? Tricksterism? As usual, cutting through the crap, Mae West put it best: "All my life I've been a put-on."

November 4, 2001

The Duke, the Duchess, and Their Jimmy

L et's have a frank exchange about the Duke and Duchess of Windsor and his/her/their gay lover, Jimmy Donahue. My answers to your questions may not be definitive—experts disagree and off-the-record sources can't be counted on. Still, our knowledge is growing, thanks in part to the latest addition to the Windsor literature, *Dancing with the Devil*, by Christopher Wilson (whose "authoritative account of the secret relationship between Prince Charles and Camilla Parker Bowles was made into a major TV movie"). Mr. Wilson forthrightly declares, "Some may consider it prurient to delve into the mysteries of the bedroom, but in the case of Jimmy and the Duchess there is a vital need." I second that emotion and I'm sure you do, too, so let's delve right in after him.

Question: What, actually, was the Duchess's gender?
Answer: Wilson quotes the Windsor insider Michael Bloch, who in turn quotes Dr. John Randall, "consultant psychiatrist at the Charing Cross Hospital in London and an expert in the differences between men and women." Randall to Bloch: "The Duchess was a man. There's no doubt of it, for I've heard the details from a colleague who examined her. She was a man." You may question this fourth-hand opinion, but Mr. Wilson explains that the Duchess might have been suffering from androgen insensitivity syndrome, which not only leaves "women" unable to bear children but "often" unable to experience sexual intercourse. On the other hand, Charles Higham, in *The Duchess of Windsor: The Secret Life*, the fullest biography to date, is convincing on the subject of the many men (including her first two husbands) with whom she clearly did experience intercourse, to say nothing of the odd abortion. Which may be why Wilson, having raised the issue, manfully acknowledges, "There is of course no direct evidence

The Duke and Duchess of Windsor with Jimmy Donahue

of this syndrome in the Duchess." Well, we'll never know, but my hunch is that the Duchess was in fact a woman. It would explain so much.

Question: Was the Prince of Wales/King Edward VIII/Duke of Windsor hetero-, homo-, or bisexual?
Answer: Further confusion. Various accounts, including Higham's, remind us that at Oxford the Prince was linked romantically with his tutor, Henry Peter Hansell (they were known around campus as "Hansel and Gretel"). Again according to Higham, gossip also linked the Prince romantically with his cousin Lord Louis Mountbatten, although "such gossip cannot be substantiated today." Lord Louis's diaries, Higham tells us, reveal that "on one occasion, [the Prince] sat on the head of the handsome

Lord Claud Hamilton of the Grenadier Guards and stripped him naked," but couldn't that just have been royal high jinks? Higham also suggests that it was the Duke, not the Duchess, with whom Jimmy Donahue had his royal fling, although "it is impossible to corroborate this story." Which is fortunate, since if Higham was right, we would not now be enjoying *Dancing with the Devil*, with its scholarly documentation of the oral sex enjoyed by Jimmy and Her Grace.

Far more to the point than the Duke's possible homo- or bisexuality is the likelihood that his sexuality was infantile and self-abasing. His last pre-Wallis mistress, Lady Thelma Furness, shared with friends tales of their childish games, their teddy bears, their embroidery, and their pet names for each other, "Poppa" and "Momma" ("Momma" for the Prince). To do justice to Christopher Wilson's devotion to historical minutiae, I feel it necessary to add that Thelma also complained of the Prince's "very small endowment"—the reason he was known in certain circles as "the Little Man."

Question: Just what were those arcane Chinese techniques the Duchess allegedly employed to give her men such exquisite satisfaction?
Answer: Well, we weren't there, but according to Charles Higham, she learned certain "perverse practices" in the "singing houses" of Hong Kong, where she was posted with husband number one, Earl Winfield Spencer, of the Navy Air Force. The art of Fang Chung, "practiced for centuries," involves "prolonged and carefully modulated" massage, particularly of the area between the urethra and the anus, and is of special benefit to men who suffer from premature ejaculation. Commander Spencer wasn't an immediate beneficiary—he was off living with a handsome young painter—but Fang Chung, as practiced by the dexterous Duchess, no doubt did a lot for the sadly dysfunctional Duke.

Question: Were the Windsors really Nazis, or neo-Nazis, or Fascists, or were they mere dupes?
Answer: Hard to say. But there was that trip to Berchtesgaden in 1937 (in one photo, the Duchess is smiling lovingly at the Führer as he bends over her hand). And the close friendship with the British Fascists Sir Oswald and Lady Diana (Mitford) Mosley. (Lady Diana actually wrote a fawning biography of her almost-royal friend, whereas her novelist sister, Nancy, ungraciously remarked, "I do hate that Duchess.") There was the friendship with Pierre Laval, whom the French executed for treason after the

war, and there was the affair in China with Count Ciano (which led to an abortion), but that, of course, was before Ciano married Mussolini's daughter and became his foreign minister. Then there's the 1941 American intelligence report that begins: "During conference in German legation [in Havana] Duke of Windsor was labeled as no enemy of Germany. [He was] considered to be the only Englishman with whom Hitler would negotiate any peace terms, the logical director of England's destiny after the war." What to believe?

Question: Who exactly was Jimmy Donahue?
Answer: The grandson of Frank Woolworth, founder of the five-and-dime chain. Jimmy's mother, Jessie, inherited a vast fortune that she spent on building Cielito Lindo, the second-largest spread in Palm Beach, gambling away millions and millions, and controlling her two sons by doling out money to them if they obeyed her. Jimmy's father, James Paul Donahue, was a bisexual from a less prominent family than Jessie's (his father ran the Retail Butchers' Fat Rendering Company), and who, among other things, stole some of her jewels, also gambled away millions (Jessie had thoughtfully given him $5,000,000 as a wedding present) and, one day in 1931, killed himself with poison while his two sons were in the house; Jimmy was thirteen. And then there was first cousin and best friend Barbara Hutton—when Jimmy was strapped for cash, Babs would just give him a million or so, and when they weren't on shopping sprees together ("retail therapy," Wilson calls it), he was accompanying her on her honeymoons. His education had been a disaster—Momma kept hauling him out of school and down to Palm Beach in her private railroad car—and he never made it to college. He wanted to be in the theater, but Momma disapproved, so despite a few abortive projects and friendships with such as Bill (Bojangles) Robinson, Libby Holman, Lupe Velez, and Ethel Merman, he gave it up, just as he gave up piloting after a notoriously undistinguished war.

Question: Was Jimmy really a very naughty boy?
Answer: That depends on your definition of "naughty." Yes, he was campy, promiscuous, exhibitionistic, even vicious, but lots of people were charmed by his "pranks." For instance, the time he buzzed an aircraft carrier ("The admiral got very mad"). And the time he dressed up as a nun,

pulled up his habit, and squatted in the middle of the road, defecating ("several cars collided with each other"). And the time he stood on a hotel balcony in Rome and, after loudly imitating Mussolini, urinated on the crowd below (he was expelled from Italy). And the time he rigged up a microphone in a lavatory when the Windsors were dining so that he could "regale guests afterwards with the sound of the 'Royal wee.'" And all those times at grand dinner parties when, according to Aileen Plunket, the Guinness heiress, he'd liven things up by unbuttoning his trousers and laying his private parts on his plate among the potatoes and gravy and sauces, "looking like some pink sausage." Surely all these japes can be ascribed to boyish high spirits?

Somewhat less jape-ish was the time Jimmy and some pals picked up a serviceman, brought him home to a party, and, when he passed out, took off his pants and started to shave off his pubic hair. Then, according to Truman Capote, "He came to in the middle of it and someone accidentally cut off his prick." They put him in Jimmy's car, the story goes, and dumped him near the Fifty-ninth Street Bridge, where the police found him and managed to save his life. All typical Capote exaggeration, Wilson reassures us: The victim was a salesman, not a serviceman, and it was part of his ear that got bitten off, nothing farther down, and he wasn't dumped at the bridge but in Long Island City ("at the junction of 43rd Avenue and 23rd Street"). Yes, it was freezing out, and he was found semiconscious and concussed, but the story had a happy ending: Momma paid him off with $200,000. And, says an anonymous source, "he didn't at all mind the fact that people thought he'd been castrated. That, and the money everyone knew he'd been paid by Jessie, gave him a certain cachet. Without it, he was a nobody." You could say that Jimmy had done him a favor! So let's not get too prissy about the waiter at the Waldorf whom Jimmy and a friend tried to rape and who either was or wasn't castrated, depending on whom you believe. Or about the male prostitute who "was made to eat an excrement sandwich." Not exactly pranks, perhaps, but nobody died.

Question: What actually happened between Jimmy and the Duchess?
Answer: They fell in love, Wilson is certain. Or at least she did. Jimmy was amusing, attractive, sexually adept, and she was starved for sex after so many years with the dysfunctional Duke (all those ridiculous nanny-

child scenes, he wearing diapers, she the master). Wallis was fifty-four, Jimmy was thirty-four. For four years they hung out together—in Paris, in New York, in Palm Beach, on cruises—often with the humiliated and grieving Duke in tow. Some people said they didn't have sex, but the most distinguished sources make it clear that they did: "The staff in Barbara Hutton's suite [at the Ritz in Paris], observing with fascination the state of the bed linen, took note of what was described as 'activity' in Jimmy's room." There's also Jimmy's own delicate testimony: "On one occasion an English aristocrat, lunching with Jimmy at Le Pavillon, noticed the Duchess sitting at a table on the other side of the room. 'Towards the end of luncheon she was making her face up, with a particularly ugly way of putting lipstick on her lips, moving her mouth around the whole time,' he recalled. 'Jimmy turned to look at her, then turned back and in a stage-whisper said, "Look at her, she's doing her exercises. I'm seeing her after lunch."'" And for conclusive proof: Leaving El Morocco one night, Jimmy declared loudly, "I am now going to have the best blowjob in all America." The defense rests.

But even more than sex, what held the Windsors and the Donahues together was money. To capture the world's most famous couple socially was Jessie Donahue's dream, and she spent millions to achieve it—the jewels, the furs, the accoutrements, the furnishings, the dinners, the travel expenses she paid for to acquire their "friendship" were accepted by the avaricious Windsors without hesitation, compunction, or gratitude. She was also happy to pay the Duchess with her son, and he was happy to be the coin of the realm. The Windsors made appearances in her various homes for years, until finally Jimmy's behavior grew too louche even for them, and they dismissed him peremptorily and permanently—the Duchess doesn't even mention him in her memoir, *The Heart Has Its Reasons*. Jimmy died at the age of fifty-one, leaving no book behind, but at the time of his death he had thirteen framed photographs of the Duchess in his bedroom. The heart has its reasons.

Question: Does Christopher Wilson do justice to these three ghastly and pathetic people, the weak and none-too-bright ex-king, the steely adventuress/consort, and the poor little rich prankster?
Answer: You might say that they've met their perfect chronicler in him. He's imaginative: The Duchess "followed the young man into the apartment and together they walked to the window. In the dawn light the grey

River Seine beneath them was touched with the first rays of summer sun.... As Paris began to waken, the couple took off their evening clothes and went to bed." (But maybe this wasn't imagined? Maybe Wilson was there with them?) He's hyperbolic: "In the history of love, it was possibly the greatest betrayal of all time." He's sensitive: "St. Patrick's Cathedral was a great cruising ground, particularly late Mass on a Sunday, and the cardinal [Spellman] was rumoured to have deflowered many young men." He's an original stylist, coining words like "rudery" and phrases like "occluded the fact" and "ineffably rich." He's fair-minded: one moment sympathetic to his characters, the next happily quoting their detractors. And if he's more interested in and convincing about money than romance, that's only appropriate—the Duchess of Windsor was, too.

March 4, 2001

Orientally Yours

Ah, the mysterious East. Oh, the lure of the Orient. Uh-oh, the Yellow Peril. Early Hollywood, in its pre-politically-correct days, which is most of its days, loved to drop in on the festering humanity of China (where life is cheap) and the inscrutability of Japan. But not many of the actors involved were even remotely Asian. Certainly not Myrna Loy, as the fiendishly sadistic daughter in *The Mask of Fu Manchu* (or Fu himself, in this case played by Boris Karloff). Not the Scandinavian Nils Asther, as the tragic Chinese warlord fascinated by (and fascinating) Barbara Stanwyck in *The Bitter Tea of General Yen*. Not Sidney Toler as the clever detective Charlie Chan. Not Peter Lorre as the clever detective Mr. Moto. Not Sylvia Sidney, that intelligent New York Jewish girl, as Madame Butterfly. Not—try to imagine it—Helen Hayes as "Star Blossom" in *The Son-Daughter*, surrounded by such fellow Asians as Ramon Novarro, Lewis Stone, and the brutish (and Swedish) Warner Oland, whom she strangles with her pigtail. Certainly not Katharine Hepburn, at her most risible as the heroine of Pearl Buck's *Dragon Seed*, or Luise Rainer as the heroine of Pearl Buck's *The Good Earth*. In the hundred years or so of pre–Jackie Chan Hollywood, there were only two genuine Asian stars: Sessue Hayakawa, who thrilled Western ladies in the silent period in much the same way Valentino did, and Anna May Wong, born to Chinese American parents in Los Angeles in 1905 and recently the subject of two biographies and a full filmography.

The two biographies are different in tone and approach, but they carry the same message: Anna May Wong was a major film artist whose career was fatally diminished by the fact of her being "Oriental." (That's a politically incorrect appellation these days, but Wong didn't know it back then;

she liked to sign her publicity photos "Orientally yours.") Of the two books, Graham Russell Gao Hodges's *Anna May Wong: From Laundryman's Daughter to Hollywood Legend* is the more hagiographic. It's persuasive on Anna May's background, but the introduction spells out the message: She was "a star of the first rank." Pickford? Chaplin? Fairbanks? Garbo? "Anna May was of their stature." When it comes to her most important role, in the Dietrich–von Sternberg *Shanghai Express*, Dietrich "could not afford to let Anna May distinguish herself in her extraordinary Asian outfits."

The rival biography, *Perpetually Cool: The Many Lives of Anna May Wong*, by Anthony B. Chan, is more an attempt to place Wong historically. It's at its most interesting when instructing us on how early Chinese immigrants made their way and on the legal and social restraints under which they lived. (The Page Law of 1875, for example, assumed that Chinese women entering the United States were prostitutes; the Scott Act of 1888 denied Chinese American residents the right of re-entry if they left the country.) But Chan's book, alas, is "informed by the theories of Edward Said, Michael Omi, Howard Winant, Antonio Gramsci, Stuart Hall, and David

Wellman," and makes much of Wong's journey toward "empowerment" and "agency": "By discovering her own empowerment," it explains, "she created her own inner hipness. It was the ultimate existential coolness."

Anna May Wong was third-generation American—that is, her grandparents on both sides had immigrated to California during the gold rush years, and her parents were born here. By the time she herself was born—the second of eight children—her father owned a successful laundry (the family lived behind it) in which the children helped out. The Wongs lived in a mixed neighborhood on the outskirts of Chinatown, and Anna and her older sister, Lulu, first attended a school in which they constituted half the Chinese student population. There they encountered overt racism; Anna May was to recall bitterly the afternoon when, walking home from school, she received

> the knife stab which, even today, has left a scar on my heart. A group of little boys, our schoolmates, started following us. They came nearer and nearer, singing some sort of a chant. . . .
> "Chink, Chink, Chinaman," they were shouting. "Chink, Chink, Chinaman."
> They surrounded us. Some of them pulled our hair, which we wore in long braids down our backs. They shoved us off the sidewalks, pushing us this way and that, and all the time keeping up their chant: "Chink, Chink, Chinaman. Chink, Chinaman."

The girls were moved to a Presbyterian Chinese mission school, where they studied English as well as Cantonese (and where Anna May excelled at baseball and marbles). They were also sent to a Chinese-language school, and Anna May went on to two years of high school. But the real preparation for her future life was taking place elsewhere: in the run-down movie houses of Chinatown and in the streets, watching movies get made during the film industry's earliest years in Los Angeles. And in her bedroom, where she practiced emoting in front of her mirror and dreamed of being a star. She was determined that "the everyday drudgery of laundry work" was not going to be her fate. Luckily, she was also becoming exceptionally beautiful.

In 1919, she was one of three hundred or so extras in *The Red Lantern*, an important feature film of the period starring the redoubtable Alla Nazimova in a double role: She's both blond Blanche Sackville and her illegitimate Eurasian half-sister, Mahlee, who falls in love with a white man and therefore must die, swallowing poison while sitting on a peacock throne and proclaiming "East is East and West is West." When the movie opened, Anna May couldn't even spot herself on the screen, but her striking looks and her eagerness were soon noticed by an important director, the hard-drinking ladies' man Marshall (Mickey) Neilan, who in 1921 not only gave Anna May her first billing—as Toy Sing, wife to Lon Chaney's Chin Gow, in *Bits of Life*—but seduced her, becoming, as Hodges puts it, "the prototype of Anna May's male lovers: white, older, and hierarchically more powerful in the business." (Her eventual female lovers, about whom neither Hodges nor Chan has much to say, may have included both Dietrich and Dolores del Rio.)

In her ninth film appearance, in 1922, she finally had the leading role, and gave an affecting performance as Lotus Flower in *The Toll of the Sea*. Again, East fails to meet West on any permanent basis—hardly surprising in this direct rip-off of *Madame Butterfly*. The famous screenwriter Frances Marion perpetrated the script (in which Lotus Flower flings herself into the sea after nobly handing over her baby to her ex-lover and his new wife to raise in America), and it was through Marion that Anna May came to the attention of Douglas Fairbanks, who cast her in the small but telling role of the erotic Mongol slave girl in his spectacular *Thief of Bagdad*. In the same year, 1924, she appeared in another important film, Herbert Brenon's *Peter Pan*, sixth-cast as Tiger Lily. In all, between 1924 and 1929 she appeared in about twenty movies, almost all of no consequence, in many of which her character doesn't even have a name: She's a "Harem Girl," a "Chinese Girl," a "Nautch Dancer." In the 1928 *Across to Singapore*, starring Ramon Novarro and Joan Crawford, she's a barroom prostitute.

Her career was going nowhere: There just weren't many good roles for a pretty Chinese girl at a time when interracial romance was taboo and/or doomed. Asians could be fiends, but they couldn't be lovers. Even so, Anna May was achieving some kind of visibility. Fan magazines found her story fascinating, partly because of the discrepancy between her screen image (mysterious, wicked, erotic) and her offscreen presence as a normal American girl—in fact, a flapper. In 1922 a journalist named Myrtle Gebhart interviewed Anna May for *Screenland*, having dropped in on her at the family laundry. As Hodges tells us,

> Anna emerged from the store dressed in a sport suit, her facial complexion resembling mellowed ivory flushed with rose. Her lips, gushed Gebhart, seemed to be a "Yuan Chen poem stepping from the embossed covers of a book of old lyrics." When Anna opened her mouth, however, her modernity spilled out: "My, that's a nifty car. It's the kitty's eyebrows, what?" Now that each understood the other to be a modern flapper, the two set out "to worry traffic cops."

As the twenties progressed, Wong became more and more of a presence in Hollywood, no doubt helped by her second affair with an older, alcoholic director—Tod Browning, best known today for *Freaks*. She was on hand early in 1926 to help turn the first spadeful of earth (with a gold shovel) for Grauman's Chinese Theatre. She was photographed by Clarence Sinclair Bull, by E. O. Hoppé; for *Theatre Magazine*, for *Vanity Fair*. She caught the attention of Carl van Vechten (they were to become lifelong friends), of Edward Steichen, of Cecil Beaton, who took a portrait of her "in a grotto of gypsophilia and cellophane suspended from billiard cues." At parties, Hodges tells us, she would sing a ballad written for her: "I'm Anna May Wong / I come from Old Hong Kong / But now I'm a Hollywood Star. . . . I look oriental / I am kind to other players / I make them smile. . . ." One witness reports that when she sang this she broke people's hearts.

She was making valuable contacts with such prominent figures as the famous German actors Emil Jannings and Conrad Veidt, while her looks, both on-screen and in still photographs, were winning her admirers internationally. Her friends recommended her to a leading director in Berlin, Richard Eichberg, and with her career stalled in America, she decided to go abroad to improve her chances. In 1928, at the age of twenty-three, she set out for Europe with her sister Lulu. "I think I left America because I died so often," she explained. At least, she reasoned, given the more relaxed racial attitudes in Europe, she might be allowed to live in some of her films.

Anna May Wong was, of course, not the only American performer who went to Europe in search of bigger opportunities or for reasons of color. Louise Brooks had walked out on Hollywood for the chance to make Pabst's *Pandora's Box*, although, unlike Wong, she didn't think much of Hollywood to begin with. And numerous black jazz performers, most notably Josephine Baker, had established themselves in more or less color-blind France. For Wong, Europe was a career opportunity and an opportunity to improve herself—to learn languages, attract publicity, move in elevated circles. In America, for instance, she was not likely to spend an evening with Walter Benjamin, who reported in the pages of *Literarische Welt* that her name "was like specks in a bowl of tea that unfold into blossoms replete with moonlight and devoid of scent."

With Eichberg, Wong made three films, in the first of which, *Song*, she yet again dies, having inevitably fallen for a European man. (She's working with a knife-thrower in a cabaret act and, as Chan puts it, "falls spectacularly on one of her own upright knives during a lapse of concentration while performing her Orientalist sabre dance.") Her final Eichberg film and her first in sound, *The Flames of Love*, was a tour de force. It was made in three different languages—English, French, and German—with three different leading men and three different scripts, and she quickly learned enough French and German to get by.

The only movie she made at this time that has any staying power is *Piccadilly*, in which, as the go-getting Shosho, she dances and vamps her way into a successful nightclub career and actually goes to bed with the leading (white) man before being murdered. (Miscegenation never pays.) This was a "quality" production: gorgeous costumes; Gilda Gray, "the shimmy queen," in the lead; script by Arnold Bennett(!). Wong is convincing, especially in the big dramatic moments—as a dancer she's heavy and dull—but finally *Piccadilly* is just a somewhat better movie than those she was used to.

It did lead, though, to a major London stage role, in a piece of chinoiserie called *The Circle of Chalk*, with Laurence Olivier not a success as the young male lead. Wong apparently did a creditable job, although she was criticized for the "squeaky American voice [that] shattered any attempt at illusion." And she was a social success in London—named "one of the best-dressed women in Mayfair," meeting the Prince of Wales, receiving "a standing ovation" when she ventured into the visitors' gallery at Parliament. She was a hit in Paris, too, and in Vienna, where an interviewer described her eyebrows as *O-mei* (tender moth caterpillars) and her eyes as *Hsing-Yen* (kernels of an apricot). But by October 1930 she was back in

Hollywood, hoping that her new European prestige would advance her career there.

She had a modest success in *Daughter of the Dragon*—she's Princess Ling Moy, seeking vengeance for the death of her father, Fu Manchu. At least she was playing the lead, and for a major studio, Paramount. Then came *Shanghai Express* and a strong performance as the dignified reformed prostitute Hui Fei, who kills the brutal warlord who has dishonored her. She made a powerful impression (but then she had Josef von Sternberg to direct her). After that, her career was essentially over. From 1932 on she appeared in about fifteen unimportant films, including some undistinguished B-melodramas for Paramount and a couple of wartime propaganda dramas (*Bombs over Burma, Lady from Chungking*) for cheapie studios. In 1960 she's Tawny, the housekeeper, in the Ross Hunter–Lana Turner movie *Portrait in Black*. She was going to play the aunt in Hunter's *Flower Drum Song*—a comeback of sorts—when in early 1961 she died of a liver disease. She had been a heavy drinker for years.

She hadn't been without occupation through the lean times, though. Or without romance. There was yet another older married man—the BBC producer and songwriter Eric Maschwitz ("These Foolish Things")—whom she was to call the love of her life. She toured Europe with a stage show in which she sang things like "Parlez-moi d'amour" and her specialty, Noël Coward's "Half-Caste Woman." ("Half-caste woman, / what are your eyes waiting and hoping to see?") She played summer stock in America. But the most important event of this period in her life was an extended trip to China in the mid-thirties—a combination celebrity tour and serious attempt to confront her roots; to learn how she could be both American and Chinese at the same time. She was, she said, traveling to "a strange country and yet, in a way, I am going home."

Wong was by no means universally welcomed in China: during the nationalistic twenties and thirties there had been considerable criticism of the exotic/erotic image of Chinese womanhood which she conveyed. (Or as Hodges puts it, "Even as the S.S. *President Hoover* sailed across the Pacific Ocean, waves of controversy about Anna May crashed hard along China's coast.") To a certain extent the trip was a round of fashionable dinners and parties, shopping, visits to movie studios. A pilgrimage to her family's remote village, according to Chan, evoked "an exhibition of exaltation fit for an Empress Dowager and awe reserved only for celestial beings." But even as she was swanning around being lionized, she was trying to grasp the nature of this bewildering world that in some way was also her world. She made an effort to master Mandarin, but found herself having problems even with the Chinese of her childhood. At a party in Shanghai, she met "one of the ladies (who) spoke my dialect and so I began to chatter away merrily in Cantonese. After a few minutes, she said, 'Miss Wong, do you mind going back to English? You speak Chinese charmingly, but you have such a marked American accent.'"

For Professor Chan, Wong's China trip is an opportunity for extended forays into Chinese history, politics, culture—Confucius, Mencius, the Long March, Shanghai's entertainment industry—that have very little relevance to her story. But his main point is that the trip was a kind of turning point in her life—"a spiritual reawakening." She herself told a journalist on her return to America that at last she was "in harmony with heaven and earth."

As her career rapidly petered out, she threw herself into working for the China War Relief Fund. After the war, she appeared sporadically on television—there was even a short-lived series, *The Gallery of Madame Liu Tsong*. She had made some modest real-estate investments and was secure financially. In 1953, she suffered a serious emotional and physical breakdown—cirrhosis had set in—but she recovered, partly, Hodges tells us, with the help of "Dale Carnegie's book, *The Power of Positive Thinking*." Actually, that's Norman Vincent Peale; Dale Carnegie's contribution to our well-being was *How to Win Friends and Influence People*. But neither Peale nor Carnegie could prevent cirrhosis from killing her eight years later, at the age of fifty-six.

It had taken determination, intelligence, and luck for Wong to reach the level of success she had achieved. The luck lay in her beauty and her ethnicity—and there is the issue on which both Hodges and Chan get it wrong. They believe that her skin color held her back, whereas it was clearly her skin color that made her unique in the Hollywood of her early years and gave her the place she occupied there.

Their greatest grievance lies in MGM's failure to give Wong the female lead in the 1937 epic film of *The Good Earth*, a novel that had topped bestseller lists for two years, won a Pulitzer Prize, and led to Pearl Buck's being awarded the Nobel Prize in Literature—a major embarrassment. The loss of this role had embittered Wong. But the heroine of *The Good*

Earth is a young peasant woman, leading a simple, arduous life: "Do not come into the room until I call," she says, as she prepares to give birth. "Only bring me a newly peeled reed and slit it, that I may cut the child's life from mine." What has this O-Lan to do with the exotic Daughter of the Dragon? In Hollywood, type is type, and stars are stars. For a major role in a major production, no studio would have cast a fading B-film actress, whatever her ethnicity; better to go with an admired European artiste, Luise Rainer, who had just won an Oscar (for *The Great Ziegfeld*). Although she won a second one for *The Good Earth*, Rainer is ludicrous as O-Lan. Indeed, the whole movie is ridiculous. But that doesn't mean that Anna May Wong, through some kind of premature affirmative action, had a right to the role.

Whatever the ugliness of bigotry in America in her time—pre–Gong Li, Maggie Cheung, Zhang Ziyi—and however her skin color may have limited her chances to become a real leading lady, Anna May Wong's far from negligible career came about *because* she was an Asian American woman. That's what made her interesting to Hollywood, and to canonize her as an underrated artist and a victim of racism is to do her a disservice. Today, ironically, Anna May memorabilia is commanding higher prices on eBay than that of her old colleague Dietrich. But then, no one has ever claimed that Dietrich was underrated, or a victim.

January 13, 2005

Who Was Charles Dickens?

There are a few writers whose lives and personalities are so large, so fascinating, that there's no such thing as a boring biography of them—you can read every new one that comes along, good or bad, and be caught up in the story all over again. I've never encountered a life of the Brontës, of Dr. Johnson, of Byron that didn't grip me.

Another such character is Charles Dickens. His history is less obviously dramatic than Byron's, but the turbulence of his emotional life, the violent contradictions in his nature, and the amazing story of his instant accession, before he was twenty-five, to the highest level of literary fame and popularity—where he remained for thirty-five years, and where he still resides—are endlessly recountable, and have indeed been endlessly recounted.

Dickens was born in 1812 and died in 1870, having produced fifteen novels, many of which can confidently be called great, as well as having accomplished outstanding work in activities into which his insatiable need to expend his vast energies—to achieve, to prevail—carried him: journalism, editing, acting, social reform.

He was almost certainly the best-known man in England in the middle of the nineteenth century, and certainly the most loved: His very personal hold on his readers extended from the most distinguished—Queen Victoria, say—to illiterate workers who clubbed together to buy the weekly or monthly parts in which his novels first appeared so that one marginally literate man could read them aloud to his fellows. And this popularity and influence carried to America, Germany, France, and Russia as well. There was universal sorrow when he died. "I never knew an author's death to cause such general mourning," wrote Longfellow. "It is no exaggeration to say that this whole country is stricken with grief."

Charles Dickens in the 1839 portrait by Daniel Maclise

Within months of Dickens's death the first biographies were appearing, and in 1871 the first volume of the cornerstone of the Dickens biographical industry was published: the long, personal, revelatory *Life of Charles Dickens* by John Forster, Dickens's most intimate and trusted friend since they met in their early twenties. Forster told the world much that it did not know, most startling the story of the twelve-year-old Charles's degrading (to him) employment in the blacking warehouse off the Strand to which his family's near-destitution had condemned him. He adapted this experience for *David Copperfield*, but no one—not even his children— had known that it was autobiographical.

Dickens never really recovered from the searing despair he felt at this plunge from respectable lower-middle-class family life and decent schooling into semi-abandonment, living on his own on sixpence a day in a shabby rented room, his father and family in debtors' prison: "It is wonderful to me how I could have been so easily cast away at such an age. . . . No advice, no counsel, no encouragement, no consolation, no support, from any one that I can call to mind, so help me God."

Apart from everything else—the lonely, hungry days and nights and his despair at being blocked from further education and checked in his ardent ambitions—it was a matter of class in this most class-conscious of societies. Again and again throughout his life the question would arise: Was Charles Dickens really a gentleman?

Forster also published in his book scores of private letters from Dickens that track his life and, to a certain extent—Dickens was always reserved—reveal his feelings. Despite Forster's inflation of his own importance, his occasional editorial meddling, and his understandable caution about how much to tell, his *Life*, with its unique eyewitness perspective and shrewd take on Dickens's nature, is a crucial document, essential to all the biographies that were to follow, including the latest: the large-scale, estimable *Charles Dickens* by Michael Slater, a leading and much-respected Dickens scholar.

The man Dickens whom the world at large thought it knew stood for all the Victorian virtues—probity, kindness, hard work, sympathy for the downtrodden, the sanctity of domestic life—even as his novels exposed the violence, hypocrisy, greed, and cruelty of the Victorian age. He was the defender of the poor and helpless, and the scourge of corrupt institutions—Parliament, the education establishment, the law. He was the unrivaled propagandist for Christmas. And he was before all else the greatest comic writer in the language—in any language. Perhaps the world's view of him was an unconscious reflection of his first immortal creation, the benign, universally beloved Samuel Pickwick, Esq.

Yet his clever, fond daughter Katey would write to George Bernard Shaw: "If you could make the public understand that my father was not a joyous, jocose gentleman walking about the world with a plum pudding and a bowl of punch, you would greatly oblige me."

In a sense, the history of Dickens biography has been an accelerating attempt to accomplish just that, although it's hard to believe that Katey would have been gratified by the relentless probings into her father's private history and inner life that have ensued.

First came a deluge of memoirs by those who knew him, including two slim hagiographic volumes by his other daughter, Mamie, and another by his one unquestionably successful son, Sir Henry (Harry) Fielding Dickens, an admired jurist. Biographies proliferated, including respectable if limited ones by André Maurois and Edward Wagenknecht. And there were many acute critical assessments by, among others, the singularly dissimilar George Gissing and G. K. Chesterton, plus a variety of public and private remarks by Shaw himself, who not only recognized that *David Copperfield* was a cheat as self-revelation—"Clennam [*Little Dorrit*] and Pip [*Great Expectations*] are the real autobiographies"—but in a letter to Katey pinned down the nature and scope of Dickens's genius: "All I can tell you is that your father was neither a storyteller like Scott, nor a tittle-tattler like Thackeray: he was really a perplexed and amused observer like Shakespear."

The immense Dickens literature of the sixty or seventy years following his death was, then, largely personal in approach and tone, the product not only of people who had known him or had lived in his immediate wake but of those like Gissing and Chesterton who wrote under the pressure—and anxiety—of his towering influence. A little later on, he might be out of favor with "modern" writers like Virginia Woolf and E. M. Forster, but there was no way they could ignore him. It was only by the close of the 1930s that serious critics and biographers were able to address his life and work disinterestedly. Edmund Wilson's "The Two Scrooges" and George Orwell's "Charles Dickens" are the two superb essays—both, oddly, published in 1940—that are the harbingers of the new Dickens criticism, to be followed by Lionel Trilling, V. S. Pritchett, Graham Greene, J. B. Priestley, and many other insightful commentators. And the scholarly work has never ceased. The journal *The Dickensian*, launched in 1905, is still flourishing.

As for post-war biography, it was in 1952 that Edgar Johnson published his two-volume *Charles Dickens: His Tragedy and Triumph*, which was not only received by critics as the first definitive life but had a remarkable popular success as an atypical full selection of the Book-of-the-Month Club. Johnson's book is still highly readable—capacious, sympathetic, fluent. Its one serious flaw—commented on by the otherwise admiring Slater and others of Johnson's successors—is his bias toward Dickens in the crucial matter of his relationship with his wife, Catherine.

Dickens's treatment of Catherine, we now have to acknowledge, is an inexcusable blot on his personal history and his character, as well as an indication of the powerful psychic derangement he was undergoing in mid-life. They had married young, after his anguished and fruitless courtship of the pretty, flirtatious Maria Beadnell, who led him on, then shooed him away, obviously not deeply smitten by this handsome, entertaining—and callow—boy who was making his way as a court reporter, but had no real prospects. It's easy to see in retrospect that his feelings for her were calf-love, but they were passionate, long-lasting, and led to intense humiliation. No doubt to salve his wounded feelings he quickly turned to Catherine Hogarth, from a family of some distinction—her father was the editor of *The Evening Chronicle*, a newspaper for which young Charles was now writing. Catherine was placid, admiring, and easily led, and his wooing of her was hardly fervent. What he was looking for, after the emotional upheavals of Maria, was a wife rather than a lover, a family of his own, and a settled establishment. His need to locate himself in middle-class domesticity was so strong that he simply allied himself with the first appropriate girl who came along.

In many ways, and for some years, it seems to have been a happy (and was certainly a comfortable) relationship. His letters to her are affectionate; she's a stalwart helpmate on the fraught American tour of 1842, despite her severe distress at leaving her four little ones behind in England; and she's liked by everyone, even if she doesn't make a highly vivid impression. But by the time she was well along in her childbearing years—seven boys and three girls, to say nothing of several miscarriages—she had grown overweight, nervous, and sickly. Can we be surprised?

As the family expanded, Dickens, although he was charmed by and cherished his children when they were little, grew more and more beleaguered and vexed. In his letters, it's always Catherine who's responsible for producing all these babies; apparently he had nothing to do with it. Yet he's in total charge of all decisions about them: Their mother is not even involved in choosing their names. What can Catherine have thought when he gave the name Dora to a newborn daughter just five days after having

written to her, "I have still Dora to kill—I mean the Copperfield Dora...."
What can *we* think?

The sad truth is that the modestly intelligent and not very worldly
Catherine couldn't really share either his working life or his inner life,
and as he became more and more of a world figure, he began to express
his dissatisfaction with her in letters to Forster. His deepest unhappiness
lay in his growing sense that he was missing out on the most important
thing in life: a fulfilling relationship with a woman. By his early forties
he had convinced himself that life with Catherine was unendurable, and
that he had to be free of her. Divorce was not a possibility for him in
mid-Victorian England, but as always he would not be thwarted, and he
gave orders that his dressing room, in which he would sleep, was to be
sealed off from his and Catherine's bedroom. He would, he informed
Catherine, occasionally turn up in London from their house in the country and stay with her to demonstrate to the world that they were still a
couple. But their life as man and wife was over.

Even passive Catherine could not accept this reprehensible arrangement, and with her angry family championing her, and infuriating
Charles, the situation escalated until Dickens published in his magazine
Household Words a self-serving and self-pitying statement about his dis-
solving marriage. (Thackeray, an admiring if wary friend, told his daughters that Dickens "is ½ mad about his domestic affairs, and tother ½ mad
with arrogance and vanity.")

Typically, as with all those with whom he quarreled—most fiercely,
his serially battered publishers—Catherine had to be demonized in order
for him to justify to himself his savage behavior toward her. He bombards
people with letters asserting that she was a neglectful mother and that her
children couldn't bear to be with her; he will have no personal dealings
with her ever again; she will have access to the children, yes, but they are
to live with him. Catherine is not permitted to attend the wedding either
of Charley, their eldest son, or of Katey. She has become a nonperson,
and anyone who takes her side is permanently banished from his life. As
always, and in every aspect of his life, Dickens must be in complete, dominating control, uncriticized and unquestioned, while consistently maintaining his keen sense of injured merit. What life was like in the Dickens
household at this time is summed up by Katey: "Nothing could surpass
the misery and unhappiness of our home."

Dickens's history with Catherine is only one of the relationships with women that define his private history and his emotional trajectory. And indeed, in an earlier book, *Dickens and Women* (1983), Michael Slater brilliantly anatomized these relationships, providing us with one of the most perceptive takes we have on Dickens's psychology and pathology—not too strong a word.

Unsurprisingly, the first dysfunctional connection is with his mother, toward whom he expressed a violent and lifelong resentment. Her crime was that when the family's improved circumstances led to the twelve- or thirteen-year-old Charles being rescued from the blacking factory, the practical Elizabeth wanted him to return there in order to help shore up the family's still-precarious finances. Charles never forgot and he never forgave. The central character of the clearly self-referential *The Haunted Man* (1848), the last of his wildly successful Christmas books, puts it succinctly: "I was easily an alien from my mother's heart."

And yet Elizabeth was not only an intelligent, lively, and appealing woman, but she was in various ways instrumental in Charles's development and success. Nor had she abandoned him as fully as he would have liked others (and himself) to believe. But she, too, had to be demonized, and Dickens allowed the world to believe that his Mrs. Nickleby, that ridiculously garrulous and foolish mother, was based on her.

Elizabeth Dickens, however, was neither ridiculous nor foolish—indeed, again and again she proved herself the realistic member of the Dickens household. Fred Kaplan in his *Dickens: A Biography*, the most psychologically penetrating of the biographies, convincingly suggests that Dickens's reduction of Elizabeth to the "vain, ineffectual, verbally comic Mrs. Nickleby" represents a "fictional neutralization of the pain in his relationship with his own mother." (Just as, we might add, the good-natured, generous, but irresponsible John Dickens, whose financial demands and irregularities would drive his grown son to fury, is neutralized in the character of Mr. Micawber.) All the abandoned or rejected children in Dickens's fiction—from Oliver Twist to Little Nell to Florence Dombey to David Copperfield to *Bleak House*'s Jo to *Great Expectations*'s Pip and Estella—are clearly central to his sense of himself. Their parents, either dead or destructively narcissistic, are unrelenting projections of his own emotional architecture.

On the other hand, the equally omnipresent innocent, loving daughters and sisters, and the barely distinguishable girls who are the love objects in, say, *Nicholas Nickleby* and *Barnaby Rudge*, are lifeless fantasies. Their chief prototype is easily identified. Soon after Charles and Catherine married and moved into their own establishment, Catherine's next-oldest sister, Mary, came to visit, and eventually to stay. She was a help in the house, a help with the babies, and—more important—an idealized figure of virginal young womanhood.

One night in 1837, coming home from the theater, Mary went up to bed in perfect health and high spirits, and two hours later was dying of an unsuspected heart condition. The following afternoon the seventeen-year-old girl died in Dickens's arms, her death the most severe trauma of his adult life. (It's both moving and disturbing to stand today in the bedroom in which Mary died, now part of the Charles Dickens Museum.) For the first and only time in his career he ceased writing—the serialization of both *The Pickwick Papers* and *Oliver Twist* came to a halt. He preserved Mary's clothes, wore her ring for the rest of his life, insisted that he be buried next to her. He dreamed of her night after night until—"interestingly," Slater comments—he mentioned these dreams to Catherine and they immediately stopped.

In his two books, Slater reveals Mary as especially bright and charming, but to Dickens she was far more than that. Her idealized figure is projected into much of his fiction, beginning with Rose Maylie in *Oliver Twist*, and her death prefigures the most famous of all of Dickens's death scenes, that of Little Nell. (When he was writing it, he told Forster, he summoned up Mary to maintain his heightened emotions.) What Peter Ackroyd in his *Dickens* calls "this strange concatenation of infatuation, obsession and disavowal of sexuality" was to haunt his entire life as well as his fictions.

After Charles and Catherine returned from their American tour in 1842, they brought into their household the next-youngest of the Hogarth girls, Georgina—she was fifteen—who would in time become the mainstay of the family, partially assuming, even before the breakdown of the marriage, Catherine's responsibilities as housekeeper, hostess, and mother. She was reliable, capable, selfless, and intelligent—in many ways a replacement not only for Catherine but for Mary. At last Dickens had found the ideal sister of his fantasies (neither of his own sisters fit the bill).

By the late 1850s, when rumors about him and a young actress were spreading, even nastier rumors were cropping up about his relationship with Georgina; he went so far as to have her examined by doctors who testified that she was virgo intacta. Georgina lived until 1917, a venerable and venerated figure in the Dickens world, presiding over and—in Claire Tomalin's words, in *The Invisible Woman*—controlling his image "with a quasi-religious zeal and tenacity." She remained close always to her two nieces, Katey and Mamie, as well as, perhaps surprisingly, being on excellent terms with Dickens's young actress, Ellen Ternan.

It is Ternan who was the most passionately loved, and remains the least known, of Dickens's women. She was eighteen when he first encountered her, the youngest of three sisters, all of whom, like their quite successful mother, were on the stage, and all of whom were raised as ladies. Ternan was beautiful, clever, interesting, and from 1857, when they met, she was his . . . what? The question of the nature of their relationship is the most disputed aspect of Dickens's personal history.

It wasn't until well into the twentieth century that the Ternan story fully surfaced, but it was soon accepted that for the thirteen years before his death, the relationship between them was intimate, that Dickens set Ellen up in a series of homes around London and probably in France, that he was her entire support (she quickly gave up the stage). There is still confusion and dispute, however, about whether and when the relationship became a sexual one. Edgar Johnson believed it did, but said so in an exaggeratedly guarded and qualified way. After a long siege of her virtue, Johnson writes, "it seems not unlikely that . . . Ellen's obduracy had at last given way," and goes on to say, "There is reason for believing that Dickens had won Ellen against her will, wearing down her resistance by sheer force of desperate determination, and that her conscience never ceased to reproach her."

In later years, apparently, she confided the story to a clergyman. "'I had it,' said Canon Benham, 'from her own lips, that she loathed the very thought of the intimacy.'" By then, though, she was an elderly and highly respectable widow.

Fred Kaplan argues cogently that

Having had sexual relations for much of his adult life, [Dickens] was not likely to renounce them voluntarily when he found himself deeply in love with an attractive young woman. He had no ascetic impulse. He detested prudishness. His concerns were of this world, and his long-held values and personality affirmed the naturalness of sexual union between lovers.

As for Ellen, "there is no reason to doubt that she loved him and committed herself to their relationship."

Yet Peter Ackroyd is insistent in his belief that the relationship never became sexual: "All the engagement of his nature, all the idealism and veneration, were elicited only by the innocent young girl or young woman; and, since this is the tone that Dickens always adopted towards Ellen Ternan, it seems almost inconceivable that theirs was in any sense a 'consummated' affair." The acute and persuasive Ackroyd may have intuited something that other biographers have missed, but this passage and others like it have the ring of a novelist's rather than a biographer's mind at work, and, in fact, he goes out of his way to remind us more than once that he is indeed a novelist.

Ackroyd has an extraordinary grasp of both the details and the context of Dickens's life, and his *Dickens* is a masterly performance that would appear to be definitive except for some of his truly odd methods—for one, his aggressive refusal to provide sources. The most egregious—in fact, bizarre—of these quirks is his interpolation into the narrative of at least half a dozen little sketches or dialogues of his own, in one of which, for example, a conversation takes place among Dickens, Thomas Chatterton, Oscar Wilde, and T. S. Eliot. (Dickens: "Have you considered the artist as the proclaimer of truths? Of truth? Let us take the *Four Quartets*—") You begin to feel sorry for Ackroyd, chained to the obligations of biography when he so badly wants to be the "creative" one.

Tomalin, in her widely praised biography of Ternan, is circumspect about Ellen's relationship with Dickens. She weighs the evidence—including the persistent rumors of a pregnancy that resulted in a baby who soon died—and arrives at no conclusive verdict, while sympathizing both with the torn and suffering Dickens, breaking down in tears during a performance in Paris of Gounod's new opera *Faust* at the scene in which Mephistopheles tempts Marguerite with jewels, and with sensitive and proud Ellen, hidden away for more than a dozen years except from her family circle and a few of Dickens's closest connections. It's *Back Street*, pre–Fanny Hurst.

Charles Dickens in 1864

On this subject Slater is as always judicious and disinterested. He doesn't consider the "did they, didn't they" issue mere gossip; obviously what happened with Ellen was central to Dickens's life. But it isn't central to his book.

To focus, as I have done, on Dickens and women, and on the turmoil of his inner life, is only one possible way of considering both him and his biographers. There are many other ways to approach this extraordinarily complex man and his astonishingly full life, which often seems to be a desperate struggle to find wholesome outlets for his limitless energy: the ten- or fifteen-mile walks he frequently undertook; the famous amateur theatricals that began with annual birthday parties for Charley and grew into elaborate stagings for private and public occasions (he organized and oversaw everything, as well as being the star performer—after all, he had almost become an actor instead of a writer); the countless speeches he made for countless causes; the restless travel around both Britain and the Continent; the almost obsessive way he rebuilt and redecorated his residences—a perfectionist in this as in everything else; the constant entertaining; the years of dedicated service to the charities he assisted his immensely wealthy friend Angela Burdett-Coutts in deploying—most conspicuously, the founding and micromanagement of her home for prostitutes hoping for a better life (in gratitude, she paid for Charley's education at Eton); the flood of correspondence; the devoted attention to his children when they were little and the mostly futile and frequently misguided efforts to prepare them for adulthood; the complicated, sometimes frantic maneuvers involved in sustaining Ellen Ternan and warding off scandal; the public reader-aloud of his own work, who literally drove himself to death with his compulsive and highly remunerative performances, climaxed by the wrenching, terrifying dramatization of the murder of Nancy by Bill Sikes.

And then there was his genius as the editor of his two hugely successful magazines, *Household Words* and *All the Year Round*. His editorship was not in name only: He was in charge of everything, corresponding furiously with his writers (trying to get Elizabeth Gaskell to make important changes, besieging George Eliot for serial rights to a novel), improving the prose of less accomplished writers (often rewriting it), planning every aspect of every issue, making every decision. Editing was for him a full-time second career. And then there was his own writing for the magazines—not only those novels that were serialized and a stream of novellas and stories but sketches, editorials, travel notes, reviews, reprinted speeches; at times, he came close to writing complete issues.

It is this last and least-understood aspect of his professional life to which Michael Slater makes the most original contribution: His command of Dickens's occasional writings and of his work as an editor seems complete. Which is not to imply that his overall narrative is ever less than large-minded and attractively composed. He is a scholar, but he has not written an academic book.

Does he bring to life the suffering child, the precocious young man who charmed everyone and vivified every occasion, the dandy, the disappointed husband and father, the warm friend, the bitter and implacable enemy, the ardent reformer who lacked a political philosophy and the true believer who had no personal religion, and all the other Dickenses? Does he grasp the genius of the work and convey it to us? To a large extent, yes. The most important issue, however, is whether he can be said to "understand" Dickens. But this question is also unrealistic and unfair. Who could?

During Dickens's second American tour, in 1867, Emerson remarked of him to Annie Fields, the wife of his American publisher, "You see him quite wrong, evidently, and would persuade me that he is a genial creature, full of sweetness and amenities and superior to his talents, but I fear he is harnessed to them. He is too consummate an artist to have a thread of nature left. He daunts me! I have not the key."

June 10, 2010

The Years with Thurber

Is the name of James Thurber, once a byword for humor, slowly slipping from the national consciousness? Only half a dozen years ago, the Library of America published a thousand-page volume of his work, edited by Garrison Keillor, and lately a massive collection of his letters has appeared. But despite this official appreciation, a doubt arises: Is Thurber still being widely read and enjoyed? The nod from the Library of America was meant as a coronation, but nobody can be funny for a thousand pages, and Thurber's writing—by definition, occasional—resists so exhaustive and formal an act of exhumation and canonization.

As for the new collection of his letters, your pleasure in it will probably depend on how much of the Thurber literature you've been exposed to—I mean the literature about him, not the literature by him. If this is your first dip, you're likely to be both fascinated and disturbed. But if you've been exposed to Harrison Kinney's twelve-hundred-page biography, or Burton Bernstein's five-hundred-page biography, or even Neil A. Grauer's derivative two-hundred-page biography, to say nothing of Brendan Gill's rancid portrait of Thurber in *Here at "The New Yorker"* and a previous collection of letters co-edited by Thurber's second wife, Helen, you're in familiar territory. Because the structure of the new book is chronological, it reads like a highly selective and unsatisfactory autobiography, and because the Kinney and Bernstein biographies made such heavy use of the letters, it can't help echoing them. Still, although *The Thurber Letters*—edited by Mr. Kinney "with Rosemary A. Thurber," Thurber's daughter—doesn't add much to the overall story, it does add to our understanding of this appealing and tormented man.

Thurber's letters aren't crafted, ornamented, polished. They're completely natural—as relaxed as conversation. They're the overflow of a professional writer to whom writing is so basic, so easy, and so necessary that he can't stop just because he's not being paid for it. Any experience or idea that comes to him is instantly down on paper and in the mail. One starts to get the impression that nothing was real for Thurber until he had written it out, and that the writing was more important to him than whatever it was he was writing about. Even when his sight was almost entirely gone, he was scrawling away, a few words to a page. "There is no substitute for the delight of writing," he wrote to a friend. And he told Harold Ross, "If I couldn't write, I couldn't breathe."

The letters don't stint; they rush forward headlong, especially when he's writing to people he cares about, like E. B. White, to whom, at least in the early years, he burbles on and on, throwing in anything and everything that's happened to him. In a letter written from Paris in 1937, for instance, he informs White that "what we need is writers who deal with the individual plight and who at the same time do not believe in [Walter] Lippmann"; that "David Garnett has come out with the quiet announcement that I am the most original writer living"; that his brother William is "losing one of his testicles at 43"; that he has figured out a way to bring Helen fresh orange juice every morning from the Café de Flore; that he hasn't had a common cold "since [Colonel] House and [Woodrow] Wilson were friends"; that he's arranged it so "that when the bombs start to fall Helen will lean out the window and say, 'Cut that out! My husband is trying to write a letter!'"; that H. G. Wells "has got the idea that he is three or four writers"; that "the sheep tick knows what he is doing"; that he's been told that Rosemary "looks like me now, poor child, but then it's possible for a girl to look like Ross or Joel Sayre and still be lovely. This is one of God's great dispensations." And he adds—as if we hadn't noticed—that "this letter has not held together in any way." Yet it does hold together, through its high spirits and sureness of touch. Even at top speed and at his most offhand, Thurber can hardly put a word wrong.

His need to communicate by letter revealed itself from the start. Through his early and mid-twenties, he was pouring out his heart to his closest friend, Elliott Nugent, who had rescued him from failure and oblivion at Ohio State University. Nugent—who went on to become a successful actor, director, and playwright (he and Thurber were to co-write the hit play *The Male Animal*)—was by far the more worldly of the two young men, and it's painful to imagine what he made of Thurber's endless callow effusions about his sadly ineffectual love life, torn between two women with neither of whom he had more than a fantasy relationship. "I once wrote this wonderful girl a letter, 7 years after we parted back in the grammar grades,—or three years ago. I was lifted aloft to places where cherubim twitters by a 12 page answer from Colorado Springs asking me to write again which I did in a way that set me back 8 cents for postage of the Rellum, addressed, as she requested, care of her sister 203 Underwood St., Zanesville, Ohio. No response. And, quite like the lackadaisical Thurber, I let it ride from thence to nownce." By the time he's twenty-four and working in Paris as a code clerk in the American embassy, his style has detumesced somewhat, he's grown marginally more sophisticated, and, around the time of his twenty-fifth birthday, he finally loses his virginity—to a girl from the Folies-Bergère. (Sex, for him, meant Bad Girls; Good Girls were for worship.)

We're not spared the embarrassment of reading his missives, poems and all, to one of his early flames, Eva Prout; it's unimaginable that a twenty-five-year-old man today could commit such sentimental stuff to paper. But then Thurber was a compulsive correspondent as well as a sentimental one, churning out streams of letters not only to Eva but to his family and his friends, even to comparative strangers. (The Kinney collection includes a four-thousand-word letter full of jokes and high jinks to three American Red Cross girls he knew casually in Paris who in 1919 were off traveling in "Roumania.") And by now it's evident that straightforward statement of fact is not what really interests him; anecdotes, impressions, feelings are amplified, dramatized—automatically turned into stories meant to amuse. Even the reporting he was doing for the *Paris Tribune* was often embellished when not totally invented.

But though Thurber may by temperament have been more fabulist than reporter, the years he put in as a journalist in both Europe and America had provided him with a reporter's skills, so that by 1927, the year he hooked up with the fledgling *New Yorker*—he was already in his thirties—he had everything he needed to succeed there: rampant humor, the power of close observation, and a limitless capacity to turn out copy. And as someone who had always depended on strong mentors—Nugent, teachers, newspaper editors—he was fortunate to find at the magazine two men who would help shape and direct his obvious talents: his young office mate,

E. B. White, already a fixture, and Harold Ross, the Editor, who would drive him nuts while demanding, and getting, the best he had to offer.

The New Yorker was the turning point, the crucial element, in Thurber's life, just as he was a crucial element in the magazine's development. But at the start no one knew quite what to do with him. Ross, as always, was in search of an administrative editor who could, through some arcane magic, make sense of the chaos that he thrived on, hiring a procession of young men ill-equipped to fill this slot—"Hell, I hire anybody"—then quickly dumping them. Given his anarchic spirit, Thurber was undoubtedly the least plausible of these luckless candidates. Besides, he knew that he was first, last, and always a writer. Ross persisted, though, and Thurber was kept busy rewriting and processing other writers' copy, being paid a small salary without extra compensation for any pieces of his own that found their way into the magazine.

From the beginning, his model as a writer—and Ross's—was White, for the clarity, precision, and intelligence of his prose. And Andy White went from being a colleague (who told him frostily "I always eat alone") to a pal to a friend to (almost) a soulmate. It was White who literally picked up Thurber's discarded drawings of men, women, and dogs (and the famous seal) from the floor and forced them down the collective throat of the art department. But though Thurber and White wrote a book together—the successful *Is Sex Necessary?*, in 1929—they were very unalike. Thurber was gregarious, a prankster (Ross invariably fell for his fake phone calls in peculiar accents), almost a rowdy; White was cautious, dispassionate. As one contemporary friend put it, "Andy was fearful of life. Jim was warm and involved with life." Nevertheless, they made a formidable, and happy, team. These early years of *The New Yorker*, when the course of the magazine was being set by the Founding Fathers (the two young men, together with Ross and Wolcott Gibbs and a few others) plus the Founding Mother (Katharine Angell, who was to marry White), became for Thurber, in retrospect, a golden age.

At first, he was writing Talk of the Town as well as humor—he wrote hundreds of Talk pieces in all, industriously making more out of less, and not infrequently something out of nothing. (Typical starts to his Talk pieces from the late twenties: "The new Reptile Hall was officially opened a few days ago in the Museum of Natural History and we visited it amidst a group of youngsters who kept crying 'Good night!' and their mothers who kept murmuring 'Mercy!'" And "Older residents around Gramercy Park were astonished to find one night in April no lights in Allaire's. A padlock hung on the hospitable doors of the famous old *bierhalle*.") He went on turning out this kind of thing until the mid-thirties, but by then the two main preoccupations of his writing career had emerged: the relations between men and women, and the remembrance of his past.

In 1922, Thurber had married Althea Adams, a strong-minded young woman he had met the year before, when she was still an undergraduate at Ohio State. Althea knew exactly how she wanted to live. It was at her persuasion that he abandoned his not very exciting journalism career in his hometown, Columbus, Ohio, and went back to Europe for a year or so, and it was at her urging that the couple eventually moved to Connecticut, so that she could raise dogs. "She always scared me," he confessed, and Helen Thurber, wife number two, said, "Jamie in that period needed somebody strong to steer him, and Althea was strong." (Not that Helen was a pussycat.) More and more, Jamie and Althea lived apart, perhaps not surprisingly in light of Althea's blurted-out confidence to Joel Sayre in 1926: "I've been married four years and I'm still a virgin." ("I worried about their marriage after that," Sayre remarked.) There was talk of permanent separation, but in 1931 Althea gave birth to Rosemary, providing Thurber with one of the great consolations of his life, and stitching the marriage back together for a while—they didn't divorce for another four years. Then he quickly married Helen Wismer, one of several girls he had been seeing for a while, but not THE girl. That was Ann Honeycutt, with whom he carried on a passionate but unconsummated love affair for years.

Honeycutt was a Southern firecracker, a pal to many of the *New Yorker* gang (for a short while, she was married to St. Clair McKelway, a prominent contributor), and she probably understood Thurber as well as anyone ever did. Their relationship was one of clashes and frustration, and he finally and in anguish grasped that it was never going to work out. Definitively breaking with her in May 1935, he wrote, "I suppose I should get married and that you should never get married. . . . I wouldn't try to conceal from you the fact that the final realization that you didn't want me was the hardest thing I have ever had to bear." A month later, he married Helen, and the marriage stuck.

To a great extent, Helen took over his life, particularly his financial life, becoming a dragon about fees, copyrights, contracts. But she also tended him, dealt gently with his family back in Columbus, was an unwicked stepmother to Rosemary, and, most important, shepherded him through the physical world when his eyesight finally gave out. When he was seven, his older brother, William, had accidentally shot him in the left eye with an arrow; he not only lost that eye but was left with only 40 percent of his normal vision in the other—until, despite a series of drastic operations, that was gone, too, and he was blind. "My seeing-eye wife," he called Helen.

The Thurber woman is generally thought of as bossy, angry, un-reasonable, whether encountered in his stories—most famously "The Secret Life of Walter Mitty" and "The Catbird Seat"—or in cartoons, like the one that shows a meek little husband approaching a house that is morphing into a huge, threatening wife. But his treatment of women is more nuanced than one might suppose. There's an early series of stories about a Mr. and Mrs. Monroe, clearly based on his life with Althea, which depict the husband as feckless and impossible, as often as not justifying his wife's impatience with him. And there's "The Case of Dimity Ann," in which a drunken writer husband, late at night, torments his wife with an account of having once tied up a cat in the cord of his dressing gown. "I hid in a closet," he tells her, grinning, "and then I came creeping out on all fours, calling, 'Kitty, kitty, kitty, kitty, kitty, kitty, kitty, kitty, kitty—'" "Scat!" his put-upon wife cries suddenly, "as much to her own surprise as to his." And then, realizing that for once she's had the last word, "she ran up the stairs as lightly and swiftly as a girl, restraining a new and unex-pected impulse to clasp her hands above her head and wave them, in tri-umphant greeting to the invisible wives of all the writers in the world." Thurber knew very well just how nasty he could be.

When it comes to his past, however—to his family, his childhood, his life in Columbus—he's never nasty. This is the material that seems closest to his heart, and he returns to it lovingly again and again. The pieces every-body knows—the most famous being "The Night the Bed Fell," "The Day the Dam Broke," "The Dog That Bit People," "The Night the Ghost Got In"—appeared in 1933 as *My Life and Hard Times*, and Thurber doesn't bother to disguise that he is exaggerating the humor of what really went on. And why not? This was comedy, not autobiography. His father got it exactly right when he remarked about these stories, "But pshaw! Jamie is a great hand to enlarge on those little things that used to happen when he was a kid."

Trouble arose, however, in the early fifties, when he returned to the family in the *New Yorker* material that became *The Thurber Album*. This time, the writing was straightforward, and his brother Robert, in particular, took violent exception to a lot of what was said, especially to the way their father was portrayed. The senior Thurber had been a good-natured, hardworking man who barely made a go of it in Ohio's political world; no one could have called him a ball of fire. The ball of fire was Mame, the mother, who had wanted to be an actress and remained a life-lover, a git-up-and-goer, and, like her celebrated son, a daring practical joker. The two brothers, William and Robert, inherited their father's lack of galvanic energy, and essentially did very little with their lives—Jamie helped support them, as well as his parents, until his death. His letters to them all are kind and attentive, and his visits to Columbus were fairly regular, if not frequent, but the family reaction to *The Thurber Album* suggests that a dynamic of anger and resentment had always underlain the amiable surface. Robert's criticisms may seem petty and pointless—Jamie hadn't, for instance, praised their father's beautiful penmanship!—but the rift was deep. To placate Robert and the others, Thurber modified certain aspects of the *New Yorker* pieces for the book, but it would be a long time before the family was reconciled.

Luckily, Mame Thurber, the member of the family who meant most to Jamie, quickly regained her composure. She had always enjoyed her son's celebrity, making happy visits to New York to see him, and she was always concerned about his well-being. In 1940, in an attempt to be useful, she wrote to his eye surgeon not only offering one of her own eyes in case a graft might be possible (she was seventy-four) but providing the "ideal" astrological moment for an upcoming operation—and enclosing a stamp for a return letter. Harold Ross, Thurber tells us in *The Years with Ross*, thought Mame was wonderful, while Mame worried about Ross's health: "You see, he's Scorpio, and with his moon where it is, his weak spot will always be his chest." Besides, the two of them shared a deep interest in the magazine *True Detective*.

Thurber's preoccupation with his past, and with *the* past, goes beyond mining his childhood for his work. His pieces about those closest to him radiate out into memories and reveries of *their* connections. In one of his most heartfelt and touching reconstructions, "Daguerreotype of a Lady," he restores to life "Aunt Margery" Albright, a warmhearted, fiercely protective woman who nurtured him throughout his childhood. Not only does he recall the objects that populated her house—"the card table, bought for a dollar or two before the Civil War," "the two brown plaster-of-Paris spaniels that stood on either end of the mantel," "the green tobacco tin that Aunt Margery used for a button box"—but he remembers "all the tenants of the front room upstairs, who came and went: Vernie, who clerked in a store; the fabulous Doc Marlowe, who made and sold Sioux Liniment and wore a ten-gallon hat with kitchen matches stuck in the band; the blonde and mysterious Mrs. Lane, of the strong perfume and the elegant dresses; Mr. Richardson, a guard at the penitentiary, who kept a gun in his room." He even memorializes visitors to Aunt Margery's house: "Mrs. Straub, who babbled of her children—her Clement and her Minna; Joe Chickalilli, a Mexican rope thrower . . . and the Gammadingers and their brood, who lived on a farm in the Hocking Valley." He's not just revisiting people from the past; he's rescuing them—rescuing Clement and Minna and Joe Chickalilli and the Gammadingers from oblivion.

But even as Thurber was engaged in this act of retrieval and homage, his daily life was rapidly deteriorating. By the early fifties, he could not see to draw or read or write; various ailments—Graves' disease, a burst appendix, pneumonia—were buffeting him (at one point, he estimated that Helen and he had endured fourteen operations since they were married); and 1951 brought the calamity of Ross's death. Even before that, though, he had felt that the magazine was changing, and for the worse. Since marrying Helen, he had been complaining about the inequities of the payment system; and in 1949 he had written to Ross that "the curse of our formula editing is that uniformity tends toward desiccation, coldness, and lack of vitality and blood. . . . We are afraid of warmth, as we are afraid of sex and human functions." The attacks on "the now crippled magazine" grew angrier and more intemperate. To William Shawn, Ross's successor, in 1954: "I realize as well as anyone our consternation at anything not monstrously clear to the fourteen-year-old girl for whom some dog said the magazine is written." To *Newsweek* in 1955: "It's a synthetic magazine today." To Katharine White in 1957: "You have made of the *New Yorker* editorial judgment a rigid thing and you have developed a certain sense of false infallibility." To Roger Angell in 1961: "The magazine has become more and more like a university English department, run by lecturers and instructors, rather than a publication conducted by editors."

In person, he was even more outspoken. The one time I met him (I had inherited responsibility for him at Simon and Schuster when, in 1957, my boss, Jack Goodman, one of the few publishers Thurber actually admitted liking, suddenly died), he was incoherent with rage against the magazine in general and Shawn in particular. Thurber and S. J. Perelman had been my heroes in my mid-teens, the highly successful anthology *The Thurber Carnival* practically my favorite book. Faced now at dinner with a drunken, abusive Thurber—and his somewhat less drunk but equally abusive wife—I was totally thrown; whatever I had expected, it wasn't King Lear in the Italian Pavilion spouting invective about a publication and an editor I so admired. (Perelman, I was to discover, had many of the same complaints about *The New Yorker*'s retreat from humor, though he expressed them more judiciously.)

What stung Thurber most was that so much of his writing was being rejected by the magazine, and by what he was determined to interpret as the dismissive attitude of the new regime. He certainly never established a warm or personal relationship with Shawn, who acknowledged to Harrison Kinney that "Thurber and I were never close. We had very few professional lunches together. . . . We made office space available for Thurber and the Whites whenever they wanted it. They're among the founders of the organization. That fact was never lost on me, whatever Thurber's charges. My response was to turn the other cheek."

The key word here, it seems to me, is "organization"—a word one can't imagine occurring to Harold Ross. What happened at *The New Yorker* is what inevitably happens when a highly personal mom-and-pop operation grows in size and importance until it changes its nature and—because it must—turns into an institution. I observed this same phenomenon at the New York City Ballet, at Simon and Schuster, at Random House. There are old-timers who not only ride out the transformation but approve of it and benefit from it; sadly for him, Thurber—like Wolcott Gibbs, like John O'Hara—couldn't bear it. The immensely successful post-Ross *New Yorker* was fortunate in having Shawn to provide the kind of leadership and management it needed to maintain itself at that level, but "management" wasn't a word you could apply to the locomotive that was Ross; he was simply the Boss. And Thurber didn't want organization or management; he wanted the magazine to be the place it had been in the twenties and thirties—his home.

An already ugly situation worsened when, in 1957, Thurber began publishing *The Years with Ross* in *The Atlantic Monthly*. He had written to his editor there that it was "now a great big valentine. . . . Let somebody else write 'The Tears with Ross,'" and to the Whites that it would emerge "*toujours gai*," with the magazine's weaknesses mostly "smoothed over, left out, but not prettified." Nevertheless, many people connected to the magazine felt that it diminished Ross by making him look foolish, and they resented the place Thurber assigned himself, front and center, in the magazine's formative years. He was especially distressed at the increasingly disapproving attitude of the Whites—particularly Katharine—as the *Atlantic* installments appeared. This disapproval was to cloud their relationship for the few remaining years of Thurber's life, eliciting, in a letter to a friend, almost the only negative remark about White I came upon in reading more than thirty years of correspondence: "I have just got a wintry letter from Andy White who, when he is in one of his self-bound phases, is the most selfful of men."

While it's true that *The Years with Ross* gets grumpy at times, and perhaps exaggerates Thurber's contribution to the magazine's early days, it is also a savvy, generous, funny, and loving tribute to his boss, the Gee Whiz Guy. "H. W. Ross," he sums up,

> had a world and wealth of warming and wonderful things to look
> back upon as he lay dying. He had been a great success, he had
> made hundreds of friends and thousands of admirers, he had con-
> tributed something that had not happened before in his country, or
> anywhere else, to literature, comedy, and journalism, and he was
> leaving behind him an imposing monument. He had got his frail
> weekly off the rocky shoals of 1925 and piloted it into safe harbor
> through Depression and Recession, World War II, and the even
> greater perils of the McCarthy era. His good ship stood up all the
> way. He sometimes threatened to quit, and he was at least twice
> threatened with being fired, but he kept on going like a bullet-torn

flag, and nobody captured his colors and nobody silenced his drums.

This may be a touch fancy, but it certainly isn't diminishing. Even so, Andy White saw in *The Years with Ross* "a sly exercise in denigration, beautifully concealed in words of sweetness and love."

By this period of Thurber's life, he had become a notoriously unbearable companion and colleague, given to alcoholic tirades, dominating and wrecking social situations. From the beginning, he had on occasion indulged himself in insults and violence, smashing up furniture and friendships. White had said about the younger Thurber, "Jim was good until his third drink and then sometimes he became a madman, tempestuous and foul-mouthed. . . . He was probably slightly insane. But there never was a kinder, nicer friend—when he was sober." Now that nicer friend was rarely in evidence. An English acquaintance found him to be, at least intermittently, "a storming, raging, vituperative madman." His most loyal friend, Jap Gude, acknowledged that "he was totally irrational and abusive." Helen Thurber told Burton Bernstein, "He was, I suppose, paranoid, feuding with the people he loved most. . . . It is very hard to understand somebody— even your own husband—when he's sick in the brain."

It emerged that he had, indeed, been sick in the brain. He suffered from a toxic thyroid, and immediately before his death, in 1961, it was discovered that he had a large hematoma; there had also been arteriosclerosis and strokes. But while his senescence may help explain his abnormal behavior, his rage also reflected a fundamentally despairing view of life that burst out of him at times. "I can't hide any more behind the mask of comedy that I've used all my life," he told Elliott Nugent. "People are not funny; they are vicious and horrible—and so is life."

Rereading Thurber, I find his mask of comedy less comic than I did a lifetime ago. A good deal of his output comes across as conventional *New Yorker* material, skillfully handled but dated; the comparison that people were always making to Mark Twain no longer seems justifiable. *My Life and Hard Times*, however, retains its charm, and there are a number of welcome surprises in the vast body of his work: several powerful stories revealing a state of depression that readers at the time seemed to ignore;

hilarious one-offs like "If Grant Had Been Drinking at Appomattox," "The Macbeth Murder Mystery," "File and Forget," "The Pet Department," and a score of others. The straight reporting—accounts of famous crimes, a five-part series, "Soapland," on radio soap opera—is oddly dry. *The Fables for Our Time* and the children's books—*The 13 Clocks*, *The Wonderful O*, et al.—tend to be too studied and moralistic. (Perversely, Andy White claimed that his favorite Thurber work was *The Last Flower*, a maudlin antiwar parable in words and pictures.) Even the parodies of Henry James, the writer to whom Thurber was most strongly drawn throughout his life, lack the easy perfection of Max Beerbohm's "The Mote in the Middle Distance."

The unquestionable achievement remains the amazing, outlandish cartoons and drawings, with their surreal captions: "I come from haunts of coot and hern," "With you I have known peace, Lida, and now you say you're going crazy," "That's my first wife up there, and this is the present Mrs. Harris," "She has the true Emily Dickinson spirit except that she gets fed up occasionally," "What have you done with Dr. Millmoss?," and, of course, "All right, have it your way—you heard a seal bark." These unique works of art still startle and amuse. And who would want to do without the goofy *Famous Poems Illustrated*, from "Excelsior" and "Barbara Frietchie" to "Curfew Must Not Ring Tonight"?

And then there is Thurber's best-known creation, Walter Mitty. For countless people who haven't read "The Secret Life . . ." or seen the execrable Goldwyn film starring Danny Kaye, the concept of Mitty, the henpecked fantasist of heroism, is standard cultural coin. He gives his name to an essential human type for which we didn't have a name before. Captain Ahab, Huck Finn, Sister Carrie, Babbitt, Gatsby, Scarlett O'Hara, Holden Caulfield are characters we recognize; Mitty is someone we are.

The character of Thurber himself remains elusive, which may be why the value of his letters lies less in their brilliance or their perceptions than in the way they reveal his contrasting qualities. He could be open and sincere, as in most of the letters to Andy White. He could be argumentative, rude, moving, witty. To one old friend he described a lunch, in 1946, at which someone "turned up with the Dowager Mrs. Cornelius Vanderbilt, who told me she had a funny mind, and proved it by urging us all to join hands and make the Russians like us. She then related how she had called, all alone, on the Gromykos to tell them about her dear friends, the late Czar and Czarina, and their nice charming circle. The ten days that shook Mrs. Vanderbilt." His letters to his daughter are tender and concerned. His letters to Ross are provocative, even taunting. He's at his nicest in his letters to his favorite younger couple, Ronnie and Janey Williams, with whom he and Helen spent many vacations in Bermuda. To his brother William, in 1927, he could erupt about marriage: "It's for life. All the tinsel and the glamour and the glory, and soon it all becomes one smelly substance." To his brother Robert, a year later, he could sympathize: "I live in the hopes that the adventure of death is something equal to the adventure of life which is pretty colorful and interesting even if hard. It would seem strange to me if God made such a complicated world and such complicated people and then had no more to offer than blankness at the end"—this in response to the death of Muggs, Robert's beloved dog. (All his letters of condolence, actually, are beautiful, unmannered, and must surely have given comfort.) It's for incidental fascinations like these that we read on and on through the seven hundred and sixty-two pages of *The Thurber Letters.*

Unfortunately, the book has not been helpfully edited. There's no apparent guiding principle as to what's been included and what's been left out. There's both too much and too little—many letters repeat one another or make no point, yet letters of considerable interest that appeared in the long-out-of-print Helen Thurber collection or are quoted in the biographies are pointedly omitted. Whole correspondences are ignored. Letters are edited differently from the way they were handled in the earlier books—at least one appears in four different versions, two in the biographies, two in the collections. The running editorial commentary is minimal and bland, with one odd exception: Twice, Thurber's feeling for Janey Williams is referred to as "infatuation." But the loving letters to the Williamses, as reprinted by Helen, are habitually addressed to "Dear Children," "Dearest Children," "Dearest Family"—to no one else does he write this way, and it is not the way of infatuation. What agenda, conscious or unconscious, on the part of the editors does this uncharacteristic barb imply? And why are so many of the letters to the Whites excluded, particularly those that reflect trouble in paradise? And why is Helen Thurber's collection barely acknowledged? None of this suggests editorial disinterestedness.

Thurber wasn't unaware of the possibility that his letters might be published. As early as 1920, when he was in his mid-twenties, he wrote to Nugent, "If anyone should ever want to compile my letters after I am famously dead . . . I fear you would have to censor and expurgate with a free wrist movement." And Helen Thurber prefaces her collection with a prophetic piece by her husband called "The Letters of James Thurber." "The effect of Thurber's letters on his generation," Thurber wrote with his customary rueful acuity, "was about the same as the effect of anybody's letters on any generation; that is to say, nil. It is only when a man's letters are published after his death that they have any effect and this effect is usually on literary critics. Nobody else ever reads a volume of letters and anybody who says he does is a liar."

September 8, 2003

The House That Gershwin Built

At different times and in different places there occur seemingly inexplicable explosions of new art forms: Greek drama; Elizabethan drama; the theater of Racine, Corneille, and Molière; the Victorian novel; the painting of the Italian Renaissance. But this phenomenon can also take place on less exalted levels. The first half of the twentieth century, for instance, saw in our country the apparently spontaneous eruption of three popular art forms that went on to conquer the world. Jazz is one, Hollywood movies are another, and they're both umbilically connected to the third: the large body of songs we now refer to as "standards."

Who created them? The great masters—Irving Berlin, Jerome Kern, George Gershwin, Richard Rodgers, Cole Porter—were all born within fifteen years of one another, four of them Jewish, growing up in New York. (Porter—from Peru, Indiana—boasted of how he painstakingly taught himself to "sound" Jewish.) They all got their real starts on Broadway. And they all cautiously admired one another—and sometimes not so cautiously. As Kern famously pronounced, Irving Berlin *is* American music.

How and why did it happen? The time was right, in post–World War I America, for a new music, and there were new, efficient ways of getting it to the public: radio, phonograph records, and, when sound came in during the late twenties, the movies. (No more standing around the piano singing "After the Ball.") And the genius? As Wilfrid Sheed puts it in the introduction to his entertaining new book, *The House That George Built*, "If someone will provide the stage and the cash, the genius will take care of itself."

And so the songs that are an indelible part of our national consciousness just kept coming, until suddenly, soon after World War II, they in turn were replaced. Time marches on, carrying the culture with it, but fortunately for us, the "standard" melodies lingered on, kept alive by jazz and cabaret artists and CDs.

If we accept Sheed's definition of "standards," we're talking about a large body of work that fits loosely into the quarter century between 1925 and 1950. George M. Cohan, a little earlier, doesn't make the cut—today's cabaret artists and jazz musicians aren't rushing to give us their take on "Forty-five Minutes from Broadway" or "Mary Is a Grand Old Name." No—in the beginning was Irving Berlin, and it's Berlin who's the subject of Sheed's first chapter centered on a specific songwriter, "The Little Pianist Who Couldn't"—a reference to Berlin's famous inability to read music or play the piano. ("Irving's pianism was so primitive," Sheed tells us, "that Hoagy Carmichael once said that it had given him the heart to go on, on the grounds that 'If the best in the business is that bad, there's hope for all of us.'")

It was in 1911 that Berlin wrote the song that catapulted him to worldwide fame, "Alexander's Ragtime Band," and his domination of the field lasted fifty years. He was the Champ—of Broadway, Hollywood, the Hit Parade. It was he who came up with our Christmas anthem, our Easter anthem, our showbiz anthem, and our unofficial national anthem—something he wrote in 1918 (oddly, Sheed has the date wrong) and pulled out of a trunk twenty years later for stately, plump Kate Smith, America's favorite radio songbird, who sang it (again and again) to inspire us into and through the war. Yes, it's corny, but as Sheed points out, "Right after the terrorists struck at the very heart of Irving's own city on the 9/11 that lives in infamy, nobody's words or tunes rang the bell more resonantly or accurately than good old 'God Bless America.'"

If that simplest of songs still rings true, it's because Berlin was a true believer. America had been astoundingly generous to the onetime singing waiter Izzy Baline, and he paid his adopted country back with a jubilant and unpompous patriotism—with "Oh, How I Hate to Get Up in the Morning" in the First World War and "This Is the Army, Mr. Jones" in the Second. (The closest parallel is Louis B. Mayer, another Russian-Jewish exile, just three years older than Irving, whose patriotism expressed itself most endearingly when he upgraded his birthday to July 4. Eventually, Louis and Irving would do a lot of business together.)

"As a small boy in England in the 1930s," Sheed writes, "I knew just two American songsmiths by name, Stephen Foster and Irving Berlin," the latter of whom he goes on to characterize as "a kind of finger-snapping Benjamin Franklin for immigrants." The comparison is apt. Berlin and Franklin both epitomized the sort of American success story that appears easy and inevitable but is actually based on hard work, practicality, and a somewhat suspect surface geniality.

Sheed's approach to Berlin is an irresistible combination of loving tribute to the composer's genius, cool-eyed perception of him as an emotionally withdrawn man, and a sharp personal response to the music. He contrasts the bland feel of "Always"—"a song of generalities, a kind of hymn to whatever you feel like today, almost a rental"—and "How Deep Is the Ocean," Berlin's "first full-throated love song. . . . It pulls out all the stops on the organ at once and plugs the air with genuine feeling." He's particularly incisive about the crucial partnership between Berlin and Fred Astaire (Irving wrote the songs for three of the great Astaire-Rogers films), and he's suggestive and touching on the lack of self-confidence that Berlin's lack of training condemned him to. Finally, he's provocative on the personal and musical relationship between Berlin and his junior (by ten years) rival and friend, George Gershwin.

Gershwin, needless to say, is the "George" of the title, and if you wonder why Sheed incorporates his name there rather than Berlin's (*The House That Irving Built*), the answer, I believe, lies in the message—almost the dogma—of his book: The best American popular music is all about swing. Even better, it's all about jazz. Yes, Irving could rag and Irving could swing (that's the crucial aspect of the Astaire connection), but that ten-year gap between him and George is the difference between jazz absorbed as a second language and jazz as the air one breathes. Gershwin's first big hit, "Swanee," is syncopated—his apprenticeship didn't involve things like Berlin's first published song, "Marie from Sunny Italy," or "Yiddisha Nightingale," or "Herman, Let's Dance That Beautiful Waltz."

George was not only jazzier, he was also more musically ambitious. Irving never strayed from Tin Pan Alley and Broadway except for lucrative raids on Hollywood; George had higher aspirations. "While all [Mrs.

Gershwin] basically wanted was for her gifted son to write a lot of hits like Mr. Berlin and make the family rich, some impulse (of snobbery? ancestral memory?) also told her to make sure that he got the best classical training that the Gershwin treasury could spring for." And so on to the *Rhapsody*, the *Concerto*, *Porgy and Bess*.

Sheed is caustic about the prissy music critics who pulled up their skirts at a mere songwriter storming Carnegie Hall, and points to the way Gershwin's classicism blurs into, and reinforces, his popular tunes; how they're part of the same musical impulse. But in his righteous reaction to those critics who "were guarding all the entrances to make sure Gershwin didn't smuggle any of his dirty Tin Pan Alley tricks into the classical shrine," he tends to overestimate the value of the classical ventures, even while nodding to Serge Diaghilev's barbed perception that the *Concerto* was "good jazz and bad Liszt."

Let's not complain, though. Sheed loves Gershwin for all the right reasons. He loves his amazing energy and irresistible charm, his movie-star charisma, his supreme self-confidence, and his remarkable generosity to his fellow composers, both famous and aspiring: There was no one he wouldn't lend a hand to. And, most important, Sheed has listened acutely and with feeling to the songs:

> The throwaway title song of the film *Shall We Dance*, for instance, now echoes across the years like music over water, conveying the jaunty, sad sound of a whole society that won't let the band go to bed, because tomorrow is going to be so awful: "The Long Week end" between the wars was almost over, Gershwin music and all. And the brothers' [George and Ira's] last song together, "Our Love Is Here to Stay," has since been rescued from the trackless waste of *The Goldwyn Follies* of 1938 to become an anthem to friendship—a final hand-clasp of the Gershwins as the ship goes down, an ode to immortality in four-quarter time.

As Sheed reminds us, everyone agrees that Berlin, Kern, Gershwin, Rodgers, and Porter are the Big Five, with the field open for a sixth favorite of your choice. (His is the ultimate Hollywood pro, Harry Warren: "42nd Street," "Chattanooga Choo Choo," "There Will Never Be Another You." For Alec Wilder—author of *American Popular Song*, the Bible in the field—it's Harold Arlen: "Stormy Weather," "Blues in the Night," "That Old Black Magic," "Over the Rainbow.") For Sheed, though, much as he reveres the talent of Kern and Rodgers, both of them are guilty of a cardinal sin: Sometimes they backslid into operetta.

Kern, with his formal classical education (he actually studied in Germany) and extraordinary facility, found it all too easy to turn from his snappy, lighthearted Princess Theatre shows, written with P. G. Wodehouse and Guy Bolton, to the Gay Nineties sentimentality of a *Sweet Adeline*. Yes, Sheed acknowledges, songs like "Smoke Gets in Your Eyes" and "All the Things You Are" ("this greatest of American songs") are incomparable, but except for the groundbreaking "They Didn't Believe Me" of 1914, Kern doesn't get around to swinging until he too (with the lyricist Dorothy Fields) is supplying Astaire. Sheed pointedly recounts the story of how Astaire, after finding Kern's first stab at the score for *Swing Time* hopelessly undanceable ("No syncopation at all"), successfully educates him on what swing is really about. The results: "Pick Yourself Up," "A Fine Romance," "Never Gonna Dance," and—swingiest (and least Kern-like) of all—"Bojangles of Harlem."

Yet the genius of Kern's score for *Show Boat*, the greatest of American musicals (or operettas, or musical plays), is tarred for Sheed by the show's lyricist and librettist, Oscar Hammerstein, toward whom he shows almost unrelenting hostility. What's the opposite of jazz? Corn! And that's what, in Oscar, was as high as an elephant's eye. Sheed just doesn't get it. Not only are the lyrics for *Show Boat* corny, but Hammerstein later commits the crime of replacing the witty, sophisticated Lorenz Hart as Richard Rodgers's collaborator. Sheed takes deadly aim at the new team: "You could move Rodgers and Hammerstein's *State Fair* from Iowa to Oklahoma, or the South Pacific or the Austrian Tirol, and it would still be the same old place: Broadway, in the Scarsdale years." All this in contrast to the unerring authenticity of the "great New York musical," Frank Loesser's *Guys and Dolls*.

Even so, Sheed celebrates Rodgers's preternatural talent as a collaborator: "Just say something like 'Bali Ha'i' or 'Oh, what a beautiful morning,' and out would pop the musical equivalent of these words, the perfect tune. But not the perfect jazz tune." And there's the rub. In his undeviating commitment to jazz, Sheed can't see that what he calls Oscar's "lush emotions and warm humor" can have a tremendous charm of their own. Since he's not only passionate but honest, he does acknowledge that the score of *Oklahoma!* is "a perfect specimen of show-tune writing." But even here he has to taketh away what he giveth: *Oklahoma!*, we're told, "was written under Hart's influence." Huh? Sorry, Wilfrid, but this time you've gone too far. It was *Hart* who was under the influence.

On the subject of Cole Porter, Sheed is dazzling. Porter "still sits up there high and dry on the ninetieth floor, untouched by time or fashion like a cast-iron statue of a basic joke. . . . His wit still clicks, his tunes lilt, and the mere mention of his name makes people smile in both anticipation and memory. . . . He had the formula down cold for alchemizing lust into romance." As for how Porter's homosexuality affected his work, we can only do Sheed justice by quoting him in extenso:

> Cole's gay lifestyle seems to have given him an awful lot of practice at falling in love, and he kept on doing it as assiduously as a research student and as ardently as a teenager long after most married men have finally conquered the habit. . . . And each new lover seems to have been an occasion of song, as he "concentrated" on this one, and kept "his eye on" that, and experienced yet again the torment of breaking up and the joy of starting over almost with the speed of a swinging door. In fact, it seems that Cole sometimes wrote his lyrics and love letters in the same giddy, boozy rush, which is why the love in the songs seems so real. And if his lyrics couldn't name who he loved or even precisely what, they certainly could show how much, and he doubled up on this part, expressing his passion with a gusto that simply blows away such pantywaist contemporaries as Ira Gershwin and Oscar Hammerstein. "Only make believe" coos Oscar, and "Come to papa, come to papa do" twitters Ira, and a couple of powerful tunes are slightly weakened, but "the look in your eyes when you surrender" writes Cole, and the tune picks up enough steam to drive home triumphantly.

Sheed recounts Cole Porter's triumphant and eventually tragic life with intense sympathy—*The House That George Built* is an exercise in biography as well as in criticism. Until the disastrous end, in uncontrollable agony and condemned to "mind-fogging painkillers," Cole had lived his entire life as fully and entertainingly as a life can be lived. This, after the myths have been enjoyed and put away for the night, may be the reason his songs still work. They have a pulse, as if someone is still in there, a real pining lover in the serious ones, eating out a real heart; and in the funny ones, a kid showing off as merrily as ever.

While he gives full measure to the Big Five (or Six, or Seven), Sheed is also seriously invested in the other major figures of the period, starting with Duke Ellington, for whom he has the deepest respect, but about whom he manifests a certain uneasy ambiguity. Just what *was* Ellington? A great band leader, a nonpareil orchestrator, a genius, an important composer—but did he write songs? Well, yes—"'I Got It Bad (and That Ain't Good)' is so songlike that it's even got a humpty-dumpty bridge that is manifestly just there to carry singers across." And "I'm Beginning to See the Light." And "Do Nothin' Till You Hear from Me." And a few others. But mostly, as Sheed sees it, the specific "song" aspect of Ellington's work is weak: "I can't think of a less inviting lyric to step up to than that of 'Sophisticated Lady.' . . . It sounds more like an army training film ('one minute with Venus can mean a lifetime with Mercury') than a great ballad." Or "In his own arrangements of numbers like 'Mood Indigo' and 'Prelude to a Kiss,' there don't seem to be any parts for singers at all that wouldn't sound better played on something else."

None of this is meant as criticism of Ellington; it's an attempt to place him as a musician. Clearly he was a unique figure—"an aristocrat in his own right"—and Sheed is interesting on his trajectory as a black American. His final word on the Duke is that he was "one of the two or three essential figures, the one who kept the music honest, and ensured that the proper jazz levels were maintained, even if he had to overdo it at times." Anything to protect the jazz baby, even if some songs get thrown out with the bathwater.

When Sheed isn't being defensive, he can always rely on his sense of humor. Writing about the complicated bond between Ellington and Gershwin, he says, "If jazz songs really were a Jewish meditation on black music, these two would be the prototypes, the best black musician and the most brilliant and thoroughly converted Jew. . . . But perhaps when George took the logical last step into *Porgy and Bess*, the Duke let out a yelp. 'What the hell are you doing *here?*' One man's homage is another man's encroachment." Sheed has already noted that "in a lawsuit over cultural rights, the Jews could always demand their Bible back."

It's when he gets past the universally accepted masters that he tends to hyperbole. Harold Arlen and his cantor father are "one of the most important father and son partnerships in music, at least since the Bach family." (So much for the Mozarts.) It's not enough that Hoagy Carmichael made hit records and was a charming presence in a number of movies (most memorably as "Cricket," pounding the piano with a cigarette stuck in his lips supporting Bogart and Bacall in *To Have and Have Not*) and wrote a raft of adored songs—first and foremost, "Stardust," then "Georgia on My Mind," "Skylark," "Baltimore Oriole," "How Little We Know," "In the Cool, Cool, Cool of the Evening," "Ole Buttermilk Sky"; he also had to "clinch" the "mythical title" of "the great American songwriter." What's more, "If Harold Arlen is the special favorite of jazz song connoisseurs, Hoagy Carmichael probably comes first with just about everyone else, regardless of time, place, or musical persuasion." I'm not convinced, and I'm not convinced that Sheed is convinced, either.

And then there is Johnny Mercer—"The All-American Voice"— whose "spirit was always pure pantheist and can still be found in woods and streams and blossom-covered lanes—not to mention railroad depots, late-night saloons, and any town in America that has a funny name." Mercer presents a problem for Sheed because although he composed a few good songs (the only ones mentioned are "I Wanna Be Around" and "Something's Gotta Give"), his achievement is as a lyricist—for many aficionados, the best of them all. In fact, his musical collaborators include a number of the central characters in Sheed's book, most prominently Arlen, but also Kern and Carmichael. So why is he included here, with a chapter of his own, in a book about composers? And why is this chapter so heavily—almost exclusively—biographical? Undoubtedly because, like everyone else, Sheed loves him. As Alec Wilder once put it to him, "You have to start with John," and though Sheed doesn't start with him, he can't bring himself to leave him out.

Besides, Mercer is a perfect bridge to one of Sheed's consuming interests: the songwriters of Hollywood. Not those who dropped in, like Berlin and Gershwin and Porter, but those slightly lesser talents who made their homes and fortunes there. He manfully (and to my mind, rightly) challenges "the unconditional contempt" that Alec Wilder felt for Hollywood—

his bald insistence "that theater songs were better than movie songs." Sheed, in fact, is fascinated by Hollywood—studio politics, the more or less free and easy life the songwriters enjoyed there in the thirties and forties, and the opportunities movie musicals gave them: a seemingly endless flood of films to supply songs for, and great performers to sing them, not just Astaire but Crosby and Chevalier, Judy Garland and Alice Faye, and on to Doris Day.

These lucky writers were both heroes and unknowns—heroes to the studios, unknowns to the public. Harry Warren, Richard Whiting, Ralph Rainger, Jimmy Van Heusen, Nacio Brown, Jimmy McHugh, Mack Gordon wrote hit after hit, even standard after standard, but they never achieved name recognition; you know their songs but you don't know who wrote them. (Frank Loesser was as anonymous as the rest until he broke for Broadway.) Sheed lingers lovingly on all their careers and achievements, even their persons: "In the few photos I have seen, Van Heusen looks something like Senator John McCain, which is to say a comfortable, good-natured fellow, somewhat prematurely bald in a friendly sort of way, as if hair was pretentious."

And La-la land itself?

I can verify that as late as 1950 . . . Los Angeles still seemed like a cow town to eastern eyes, with a defiantly antiquated-looking trolley clanking its way from a vestigial downtown to a string of minimalist beaches without a dune or an honest-to-God wave to be seen. The water moved just enough to prove it wasn't a lake, and it didn't so much invite you in as put up with you when you got there—if, that is, you were one of those eastern nerve-cases keen on swimming. For everyone else, the beach was just another place to have one's picture taken and to be discovered by a famous producer.

As for "that most sundering of places, Hollywood," it's "the home of divorce, where business partners break up even quicker than married ones and where even Siamese twins are likely to wind up just good friends." Even so: "Hooray for Hollywood," as the famous Whiting-Mercer song has it—"that screwy bally-hooey Hollywood," which proved to be an Eden for so many songwriters until musicals as they knew them went under, and they were left high and dry by television, teenagers, and rock and roll.

Like all love letters, Sheed's book is personal and immoderate—that's what makes it so much fun; that, plus its pitch-perfect style and humor. Why, then, quarrel with it? Only because of some peculiarities that need addressing. Why, for instance, is the vastly talented (and highly dislikable) Vincent Youmans—"Tea for Two," "Hallelujah!," "I Want to Be Happy"— only dealt with in a coda? Is he really less important than friends of Sheed's like Burton Lane and Cy Coleman who are awarded full chapters of their own? It's graceful of Sheed to say that in the case of Jule Styne, he felt that Max Wilk, in his admirable book *They're Playing Our Song*, "had done such a splendid job that there was no point doing another one." But how to explain the absence, except for a couple of almost glancing mentions, of Leonard Bernstein, who doesn't even get a look-in on a supplementary list of more than fifty names which appears in an appendix—a list that runs from Youmans and Sondheim and Fats Waller to such complete unknowns as María Grever, Brooks Bowman, and Kerry Mills?

I can only assume that Sheed can't forgive Bernstein for selling out, if not in the usual direction. How could the man who wrote such terrific songs for *On the Town, Wonderful Town,* and *West Side Story* have wasted his time on pretentious, boring stuff like the *Jeremiah* Symphony? (I'm in agreement with him there!) Gershwin, the closest parallel to Bernstein, may have dabbled in concertos and rhapsodies, but essentially he stuck to his real business, jazz, whereas Bernstein's real business was classical music. And even though he produced a semi-operatic *Candide* in counterpoint to Gershwin's *Porgy*, he more or less abandoned Broadway for the satisfactions of becoming one of the most famous conductors of our time. How could you, Lennie?

In the same spirit, "Austrian" Frederick Loewe is dismissed with two put-downs (and is also excluded from the supplementary list). His unworthy contribution: "scores set in Paris, London, and Scotland"—as if it's the scores rather than the books of musicals which determine their settings. (So much for *Gigi, My Fair Lady,* and *Brigadoon*.) And then there's Loewe's partner, Alan Jay Lerner, who "for most of his firecracker prime . . . had been tied to Fritz Loewe." Poor Alan.

We're back to the beginning, with Sheed's unyielding defense of his jazzy turf against Europe, classicists, operetta, rock, folk, country, and the rest. He's done a wonderful job with the material that calls to him, but I can't help feeling his turf is over-defended, and I wish his passions were more inclusive—for his own sake, not ours. How regrettable, it seems to me, that a man with such generous, perceptive love for George's and Irving's and Cole's house should miss out on the pleasures to be had from the house of Motown, for instance, or from Hank Williams, or Bob Dylan, or Carole King and Gerry Goffin, or for all I know, from rap.

On the other hand, it's gratifying—it's moving—to discover that this brilliantly acerb novelist and critic has had so much joy for so many years from the music he does love and from the men who created it.

August 16, 2007

Max and Marjorie:
An Editorial Love Story

Nov. 19, 1930

Dear Mrs. Rawlings:

We are very much inclined to publish your novel, "High Winds," in the magazine, but would you consider certain suggestions for the revision of it, to that end, which we think might very much improve it, excellent as we think it is as it stands.

So begins *Max and Marjorie*, a remarkable correspondence—and what one might call a remarkable love story (never an affair)—between two remarkable people. Mrs. Rawlings was Marjorie Kinnan Rawlings, who was to triumph within the decade as the author of *The Yearling* and, later, of *Cross Creek*. Her correspondent was Scribner's Maxwell E. Perkins— seventy years ago, and still, the most respected and honored editor in American publishing history.

They were an unlikely pair. She had been a feminist journalist and poet, something of a good old gal, who, unhappily married, found herself raising oranges in remote inland Florida and turning her hand to fiction. He was a mild-mannered, conservative Yankee raised on trust funds— one grandfather was both a senator and secretary of state; the other has been called America's first art critic. Also unhappily married, and the father of five daughters (when the fourth was born he sent a one-word telegram to his mother: "GIRL"), Perkins was not really at ease with women except when editing them. His early fame came from his having discovered F. Scott Fitzgerald and steered Ernest Hemingway through all but his first book, but he was to become most widely known as the editor who wrestled the larger-than-life Thomas Wolfe to the ground, carving from his larger-than-plausible manuscripts both *Look Homeward, Angel* and *Of*

Time and the River. Throughout the thirties and forties his reputation grew—for his diffidence and insistence on privacy as well as for his extraordinary string of successes. When he died, in 1947, he was working on his final discovery, James Jones's *From Here to Eternity.*

The first exchange with Mrs. Rawlings presages the tone of their professional relationship. Perkins jumps immediately to several pages of specifics: structure, characterization, motivation. "One expects at the start that Florry at least, will more completely transcend typicality, that her individuality would make her more of a character in her own right than she is, apart from her value as a representative of the Florida Cracker." "On Page 7 the first paragraph seems to us an intrusion of the writer." Etc., etc. And then a windup paragraph emphasizing that "we should like to arrange to publish" the revised manuscript. Of course, that "we" was he,

but it was less an editorial we than a determined de-emphasizing of self. The letter reaches Rawlings at home in Cross Creek, Florida, and she replies with a courtesy and diffidence equal to his: "It is extremely considerate of Scribner's to give me an opportunity to improve my story of the Cracker interior of Florida, 'High Winds.' I appreciate your painstaking criticism and the story can only profit by your editorial suggestions."

Two complicated people, moved by a common goal—to produce the best possible writing—had found each other, and apart from the minor irritations that inevitably arise between author and publisher over a long collaboration, they progressed through the next seventeen years from a gratifying and productive professional relationship to a true meeting of minds. There was in Rawlings none of the ego-need so many writers are shackled with. She didn't require cosseting and worrying over like Fitzgerald, careful handling like Hem, titanic effort and emotional asbestos like Wolfe. Her talent was smaller than theirs, no doubt, but it was individual and real, and she was rock solid—sensible, with excellent judgment, an obsessive worker never satisfied, and full of feeling. She saw life much as Perkins did; in a way, they came to act as moral touchstones for each other. Most of all, they trusted each other. And, of course, she was a tremendous success: *The Yearling*—to us a boys' book and a vehicle for Gregory Peck—was the number-one bestselling novel of 1938, a Pulitzer Prize winner, and admired by everyone from Fitzgerald to Margaret Mitchell to Ellen Glasgow ("It . . . tempts me to use the word 'genius.' And genius as a term in literary criticism does not often appeal to me").

The editorial relationship between Marjorie and Max goes on as it began. For her early novel *South Moon Under*, he again suggests cuts, structural changes, strengthening of certain characters. "At the end of this chapter would it be out of place to have old Lantry dance with Piety, as he did with the older girl, or instead of with Sarah?" (He knows that editing lies in the details.) She replies with characteristic modesty to his model editorial letter: "Your diagnosis and prescription are so specific, that I think between us we can have the patient on his feet in no great while. You have a truly amazing genius for taking the product of another's imagination in the hollow of your hand. It is the height, I suppose, of critical sympathy and understanding." But even before her letter reaches him, he is writing again—drawing back from seeming to impose or demand: "Ever since I wrote you I have been worried for fear what I suggested might seem to you to be asking a great deal. . . . What I suggested was perhaps more by way of example, to show what it seemed to us was required." (Note the "perhaps" and the "us.")

He also knows that editing lies in another, larger kind of sympathy— the sympathy that can intuit the kind of book a given writer may have it in him or her to write. *The Yearling* was his idea: "I was simply going to suggest that you do a book about a child in the scrub." Rawlings: "Such a book had never occurred to me. My first reaction was one of sheer distress, and then on second thought I was quite intrigued." His further reflections on this project reveal him in two lights. Referring to *Huckleberry Finn*, *Kim*, *Treasure Island*, and others, he says: "All these books are primarily for boys. All of them are read by men, and they are the favorite books of some men. The truth is the best part of a man is a boy." This is his romantic and innocent side. His sharp and humorous side comes out in the same letter: "The sales department always wants a novel. They want to turn everything into a novel. They would have turned the New Testament into one if it had come to us for publication."

It would be more than four years of constant communication before Mrs. Rawlings and Mr. Perkins became Marjorie and Max. Occasionally there were flare-ups: "Scribner proofreading is the worst of any publishing house in the country." "The jacket design of course is your affair and not mine, but when 'South Moon Under' meant that the moon was invisible under the earth, it was very silly to have a large quarter-moon behind some pine trees." Max rises to the defense in a flap over British rights, but only to defend the owner: "What happened was wholly my fault. . . . What I am concerned about is that you should get so totally wrong an impression of Mr. Scribner who is quixotically, almost, fair and true and considerate. You would know it if you saw him." (Later, Rawlings was to become so close to the entire family that she made a Scribner daughter her literary executor.) But such agitations are momentary and of no importance. By 1933, she has enough confidence in their shared approach to life to be able to write him, about a proposed public dinner in New York, "Can you imagine anything more revolting than a large room crawling with authors?"

His belief in her soundness is most clearly expressed in his eagerness to have her know his other writers. In 1936, he writes: "I should like to have Scott Fitzgerald see you, for I think you would do him a great deal of good. He is in a very defeatist state of mind, has been for years. . . . If you are near Asheville and tell me so, and are willing to see Scott, and perhaps be somewhat depressed by it first, I'll send him." The meeting takes place, and she reports:

> Max, we had a perfectly delightful time. Far from being depressing, I enjoyed him thoroughly, and I'm sure he enjoyed it as much. He was as nervous as a cat, but had not been drinking. . . . I do not think you need to worry about him, physically or psychologically. He has thrown himself on the floor and shrieked himself black in the face and pounded his heels—as lots of us do in one way or another—but when it's over, he'll go back to his building blocks again.

A few months earlier, Perkins had brought her together with Hemingway:

> The man astonished me. I should have known, from your affection for him, that he was not a fire-spitting ogre. . . . Instead, a most lov-able, nervous and sensitive person took my hand in a big gentle paw

and remarked that he was a great admirer of my work. . . . There is, obviously, some inner conflict in Hemingway which makes him go about his work with a chip on his shoulder, and which makes him want to knock people down. He is so great an artist that he does not need to be ever on the defensive. He is so vast, so virile, that he does not need ever to hit anybody. Yet he is constantly defending something that he, at least, must consider vulnerable.

Often Max writes her about Wolfe. In 1935 he even urges her to "write to Tom about his book and put a little hell into the letter. . . . It might be very effective. But there must be no collusion between us." This is an extraordinary gesture of trust, for Wolfe was Perkins's greatest worry as well as the writer he loved the most. Some time later, the three of them are out together for an unlikely night on the tiles, and she writes to Perkins afterward, recalling

Tom Wolfe plowing his way among the vegetables in a drizzle of rain at four o'clock in the morning, while you and I followed like pieces broken off from a meteor in transit. I shouldn't have started the argument about suicide in the Chinese dive if I'd known he would take it so personally! I have always found suicide a delightful abstraction for discussion, but when I found that he thought I was urging him to do it, and refused at the top of his lungs, "even to satisfy his publishers," I wished I had argued about something simple, like transcendentalism.

Her outrage when Wolfe breaks away from Scribner's for another publisher evokes a characteristic response from Max, focusing on what he sees in Wolfe as "a kind of desperate tearing himself loose in order to stand up alone. And of course that is what he ought to do, in fact, and must do, if he is to become a really great writer."

The tragic Oedipal drama of Perkins and Wolfe played itself out all too quickly, and when Tom died in 1938, having sent from his deathbed a moving and loving letter to Max, Rawlings wrote with her characteristic understanding and sympathy:

I have grieved for you ever since I heard of Tom's death. I grieve, too, for the certain loss of the work he would unquestionably have done, for his very touching letter to you shows a chastening and mellowing of that great half-mad diffusive ego, that would have been a guarantee of the literary self-discipline we all so wanted for him. . . . I know how glad you must be that you never withdrew your personal goodness from Tom, even when others were bitter for you.

In fact, 1938 was a climactic year in many ways—not only Wolfe's death and *The Yearling* but a dangerous illness and operation confronting Rawlings. By this time, writer and editor are so in tune that she can comment on his personal life in ways that few others would have dared. His wife, Louise, whom he had foolishly prevented from pursuing an acting career, has grown increasingly restive, and has moved toward a romantic Catholicism that severely tested the patience of the not very ardently Episcopal Perkins. Rawlings writes of her: "She is very sweet and a little pathetic, and I understand her. You are so much wiser than she—you must not be intolerant. The Catholic matter will probably fade away. I don't mean to be presumptuous in speaking so. But you know that." That he could break through his reticence to raise so personal a subject indicates both how troubled his feelings about Louise were and how much confidence he placed in Marjorie.

Only weeks later, before going into the hospital, she wrote to him, "If by chance I should not come out of it, I do wish I could make it clear to you and to everyone else interested in me for whatever reason, that it would be the sort of death that would not matter. . . . I have lived so full and rich a life, with so much more than my share of everything, that I feel indebted to life, instead of life's still being indebted to me." Perkins reacted with two uncharacteristic letters. One was to the man Rawlings was planning to marry, begging him to "inform me as soon as you possibly can. We here are her publishers, but that has nothing to do with it. It is for personal reasons that I am concerned and I hope you will wire me as soon as you can after you hear the result of the operation and all. . . . I do not know to whom else I could turn, and I shall feel most anxious until I hear." To Marjorie herself, on the same day, he writes by hand, "Even if I had never seen you, & we had done everything by letter I should be profoundly concerned because the privilege—which is what it was—of cooperating with you as an Editor has been one of the happiest & most satisfying experiences I have ever had,—or ever shall—& I am most grateful for it."

If that is Max's most fervent moment with Marjorie, perhaps hers with him comes a year later, and can serve as an epitaph to their friendship:

> I think you must know how conscious I am of the special quality of our relationship. It existed from the beginning, in my recognition and appreciation of your great critical gift, and I cannot conceive of its being changed by anything. I should expect you to have the same patience with me, the same understanding of what I try to do, if the results were completely unsalable. And you must surely know that no material returns from my work could possibly be as important to me as the doing of the work; and that there is more satisfaction in your verdict of approval than in that of any best-seller list. When I have done the best I can with any piece of writing, and you say it is all right, then I am done with it. What happens in the way of money and awards and what not, is remote, and has no more connection with the work itself than would an inheritance from someone I had never heard of. My mental contact with you is a basic thing. I shall need it and want it and feel free to ask for it as long as I write. I could not imagine your withholding it, and you must not ever imagine for one moment that I could put other things ahead of it, or fail to appreciate it.

(Max in reply: "Being a Yankee, I am not very expressive, but I am mighty glad that you do value my opinions.")

Max and Marjorie is a revelation of two extraordinary—even noble— characters, as well as something rarely found in books: a convincing account of an evolving friendship. The letters between Perkins and Fitzgerald are very different—permeated by Scott's unfailing sweetness and generosity and acuity and by Max's unending concern for him, shoring him up psychologically, emotionally, and financially, even lending him money. Fitzgerald discovers Hemingway and steers him to Perkins, and indeed is consistently perceptive on other writers—from Sherwood Anderson to Raymond Radiguet. (In 1940, in his very last letter to Max, he writes, "No one points out how Saroyan has been influenced by Franz Kafka. Kafka was an extraordinary Czechoslovakian Jew who died in '36. He will never have a wide public but 'The Trial' and 'America' are two books that writers are never able to forget.") He also understands the role Max plays in the lives of his writers (this is in 1938): "What a time you've had with your sons, Max—Ernest gone to Spain, me gone to Hollywood, Tom Wolfe reverting to an artistic hill-billy."

The correspondence with Hemingway is compelling in other ways—and a corrective to the current view of Hem. He generally comes across as manly rather than macho, intuitive rather than insensitive, explosive but quietly repentant—a man strung out by the tension of trying to be a great writer. These letters are far more concerned with publishing matters than editorial ones. Max is at his most gingerly with editorial suggestions, and those he actually makes are, even more than usual, cloaked in hesitations and qualifications: "I do think that bringing in a speech, just because it is one, does tend to make the book seem too miscellaneous perhaps. I would rather favor leaving it out." His prose is punctuated with quaint, almost fussy locutions: Heaven Knows; I hope to thunder; I would like to do it mighty well. What amounts to his passive aggression is nailed by Hemingway: "I have to have some one I can trust and can write frankly to and that person has always been you Max only now I can't write frankly about anything without fear of offending you." Yet on Max's death, Hemingway writes to Charles Scribner: "We don't need to talk wet about Max to each other. . . . If it would do any good you might let it be known that while Max was my best and oldest friend at Scribner's and a great, great editor he never cut a paragraph of my stuff nor asked me to change one. One of my best and most loyal friends and wisest counselors in life as well as in writing is dead."

In the last half century, publishing has drastically changed. To a great degree, the loyalties, decencies, and courtesies of Perkins's day are gone. It is hardly true today that, as Max wrote to Marjorie in 1932, "these times are very adverse to advances, and generally speaking, there is no occasion to pay one on a first novel." (Needless to say, literary agents were less active then.) Communication has speeded up—when one of Marjorie's books is taken by the Book-of-the-Month Club, Max writes her the news, instead of telephoning—but book production has slowed down; in the thirties, books were routinely published three or four months after a manuscript was completed. Finally, alas, a book like *Max and Marjorie* can never happen again—extended letter writing is more or less a thing of the past. The one constant is editing: Not just old-timers but ardent young men and women, in love with publishing, are still going home every night toting manuscripts—and pencils. Even if they don't know it, they are acting in a tradition exemplified and strengthened by Maxwell Evarts Perkins.

Max's effect on his writers, and on American letters, is amply illustrated not only in *Max and Marjorie* and the collections of correspondence with Fitzgerald, Hemingway, and Wolfe, but also in A. Scott Berg's esteemed biography; in an early collection of letters, *Editor to Author*; and in the reminiscences of various colleagues and writers. But his effect on the generation of editors who followed him is less well understood. Certainly when I entered publishing, in 1955—eight years after his death—Perkins was the great legend, given his unique combination of shrewdness, humility, and editorial genius. How were young editors to measure up to this paragon? (Talk about the anxiety of influence!) Well, of course we couldn't, and then it stopped mattering. But there are still twinges. Rereading Scott Berg, I was foolishly pleased to realize that I live on the same enclosed garden in the East Forties where Perkins lived, and I was tickled at learning of Max's culinary arrangements. Apparently, Erskine Caldwell, then an unsuccessful Scribner writer, was being wooed by another publisher, who treated him to a sumptuous lunch. Caldwell, Berg writes, could not help silently comparing this reception with the one and only time Maxwell Perkins had bought him a meal. It was at a lunch counter. Max had ordered for both of them—orange juice and peanut-butter-and-jelly sandwiches. I was reminded that after I had worked on a number of books with John le Carré, he had it inserted into a contract that I was to take him out at least once for a decent meal. Unknowingly, in this regard at least I had lived up to Maxwell Perkins.

July 2, 2000

Becky in the Movies: Vanity Fair

No major nineteenth-century novel—unless you count *Dracula*—has been filmed as often as Thackeray's *Vanity Fair*. There have been five versions since sound came in, the first released in 1932, the latest just now, and yet the book consistently eludes filmmakers. Not one of them catches its essence, which has less to do with the plot or the characters than with the author/narrator's voice. The novel has frequently been seen as the model for *Gone with the Wind* (no one believes Margaret Mitchell's claim that she never read it), but although there are obvious similarities, the two books are utterly unalike in intention and result. *Gone with the Wind* is feverishly romantic, despite its famously antiromantic heroine; it's a passionate celebration of the Old South, soaked in nostalgia and regret—it's a novel with a fierce private agenda. *Vanity Fair* is the most antiromantic of nineteenth-century novels, and *its* famously antiromantic heroine is the real thing. Nobody sweeps Becky Sharp up the stairs, à la Clark Gable, and crushes her into submission (and orgasm), and she wouldn't be interested if somebody did. Becky is interested in money and social status, not love, although she's casually fond of Rawdon Crawley, her husband, and "was always perfectly good-humored and kind to him." Indeed, "If he had but a little more brains, I might make something of him."

Scarlett has Tara and the O'Haras and the myth of the Old South; her society is collapsing, but she knows where she belongs in it. Becky has no family, and her background is the opposite of respectable, her father an alcoholic artist, her mother a French opera dancer. In fact, she has no social standing at all except whatever she can manufacture for herself. But she's clever, and ambitious, and as unanchored morally as socially, and when she fails to snare a rich husband, her only way upward is that of an adventuress, as the cynical and observant Aunt Crawley quickly perceives. Scarlett

O'Hara learns the hard way—through war and devastation and the loss of Rhett Butler—but she learns. There's nothing for Becky Sharp to learn: She's known it all from the beginning. She's had to, to survive.

Although Becky is only one element of Thackeray's novel, it's the shape of her career and the ambiguities of her nature that first grip you. The alternate heroine—pretty, cosseted, foolish Amelia Sedley—is only interesting in regard to what happens to her; she herself is a shallow nonentity: used by Becky, abused by her selfish, narcissistic husband, overvalued by her maddeningly loyal admirer Dobbin, overprotective as a mother, and eternally having "recourse to the waterworks," as Thackeray unkindly points out. When she very occasionally flares up, you want to applaud. Throughout, she's merely acted upon, whereas Becky steers her own course, rampaging through society and basking in her successes while vigorously rebounding from the disasters that overtake her, most of which she's brought on herself.

Amelia is a nineteenth-century doll-heroine; Becky is an eighteenth-century picaresque hero, not a naïve one like Tom Jones but a knowing one like Moll Flanders. Does Thackeray approve of her? Does he like her? He shows her lying and cheating, malicious and cruel, yet he clearly admires her buoyancy and her resourcefulness. And his narrator is always telling us how good-natured she is, no matter how badly she may behave. He allows her to make her case: "'It isn't difficult to be a country gentleman's wife,' Rebecca thought. 'I think I could be a good woman if I had five thousand a year.'" And the narrator comments, "And who knows but Rebecca was right in her speculations—and that it was only a question of money and fortune which made the difference between her and an honest woman?" Although Thackeray was criticized by the self-righteous for this passage, it's much quoted in the film versions, since, even though it underlines Becky's sardonic cast of mind, it amounts to an argument in her favor.

But Becky's story, and Amelia's, are only two of the major elements of Thackeray's novel. The third—and to Thackeray the crucial one—is its unblinking vision of the great world of English society, in other words, of "Vanity Fair." In her recent excellent critical biography, *Thackeray: A Writer's Life*, Catherine Peters puts it this way: "The mixture of motives in the human mind, and the stratagems that men and women adopted to get their own way in the world, were his themes. He said of *Vanity Fair* that his aim had been to show a society of people 'living without God in the world.'"

And she quotes a letter in which he describes to a friend his excitement when he suddenly thought up his title: "I jumped out of bed, and ran three times round my room, uttering as I went, 'Vanity Fair,' 'Vanity Fair,' 'Vanity Fair.'" To a readership familiar with John Bunyan's *Pilgrim's Progress*, the most influential and widely read book in English after the King James Version, the concept of "Vanity Fair" was a completely familiar one and acted as an immediate signal of the book's intentions.

Certain great novels lend themselves easily to being filmed, even if the results aren't necessarily satisfying. Some have been made more than once: *Anna Karenina, Madame Bovary.* You can see why—each has a strong story line and, even more important for Hollywood, the kind of tragic leading role that movie divas appreciate. (Garbo, remember, made *Anna Karenina* twice, once as a silent, once in sound.) Dickens, too, lends himself to film—each book projects a particular atmosphere that is transferable to the screen as well as being filled with filmable quaint characters. The movie that David O. Selznick put together from *David Copperfield*—George Cukor directing, W. C. Fields as Mr. Micawber, Basil Rathbone as Mr. Murdstone, Freddie Bartholomew as the young David—is still completely satisfying. David Lean's versions of *Great Expectations* and *Oliver Twist* are also highly effective.

But *Vanity Fair* is a different kind of book. As John Carey wrote in *Thackeray: Prodigal Genius*, Thackeray's "most trenchant writing comes when he shows selfishness, allied to want and the souring power of time, gathering like poison in the soul." So mordant a vision of the human condition isn't exactly comfortable material for a Hollywood movie. And there's nothing quaint about it. Nor is Becky Sharp a diva role; she's a greedy, manipulative, unscrupulous piece of work whose life trajectory peters out undramatically. That is not a Hollywood story, yet Hollywood has told it three times and, unsurprisingly, each time as a vehicle for a star. Whereas the two BBC versions, which don't depend on a star, take the Masterpiece Theatre route: They're large-scale and multicharactered, with lots of period detail—essentially, they're Napoleonic-period sagas—with Becky front and center but by no means the whole story.

The strangest by far of the Hollywood versions, made in the early thirties, features Myrna Loy, before MGM had figured out what to do with her. They loaned her out to the poverty-row Allied studio where, according to her autobiography, the movie was made in about ten days, and looks it. Weirdly, it's set in the late twenties (that's the *nineteen*-twenties), and Loy swaggers around in scoop-back evening gowns, supported by the veteran actor Conway Tearle as Rawdon Crawley. (Tearle was fifty-four at the time, and looks older—this was desperation casting.) No other actor of the slightest consequence is involved, the entire Amelia–George–Dobbin story is barely hinted at, and nothing much happens until Becky gets caught in a compromising situation with Lord Steyne, upon which she's immediately reduced to disgrace and penury. The whole thing lasts not much longer than an hour, and *that's* too long. Don't be surprised if you've never heard of this throwaway—no one else has, either.

Three years later, in 1935, Miriam Hopkins (so glorious in Lubitsch's *Trouble in Paradise*) grabbed the role and took it for a real ride. This time the movie is forthrightly called *Becky Sharp*, and it's famous for being the first three-strip Technicolor film. When it was restored some years ago, it was ravishing to look at, despite its palette being exaggeratedly vibrant. But even in its washed-out version, one could see how fascinating Hopkins was and how effectively it was directed by the talented if erratic Rouben Mamoulian. "Operatic" is an apt word for Mamoulian's ripe directorial style—David Thomson, in his *Biographical Dictionary of Film*, remarks approvingly on how Mamoulian's films "rustle with sound and shimmer with the movement of light on faces, color, and decoration. More than any other director—more than Lubitsch, even—he should be known for his touch."

In *Becky Sharp* his touch manifests itself in the draconian decisions he makes about the script—ruthlessly jettisoning whole elements of the story, and then lingering voluptuously on certain dramatic moments. For instance, the famous Duchess of Richmond's ball on the eve of Waterloo, when far-off cannon fire interrupts the festivities, becomes an extended seething spectacle of billowing cloaks, charging horses, blaring bugles. Then, as the delirium dies down, Becky remarks, "They'll be dying for their country. Well, I'm dying for my breakfast." None of this is in the novel, but it's *cinema*—and altogether true to Thackeray's Becky.

As for Hopkins, she's wild with energy and opportunism—voracious, sexy, and satirical; here's a Becky Sharp who's really sharp. The Amelia story barely exists. Neither heroine becomes a mother. There are lines like "My love for you is the only real thing in my life," and Becky really is crazy about Rawdon, planting passionate kisses on him at every possible opportunity, so that the punishment for her sins is that she loses him—like Scarlett with Rhett. (*Gone with the Wind*, note, wasn't published until a year later.) Miriam Hopkins, with her bobbing curls and gleaming teeth and unappeasable avidity, is hard to take at times, but her Becky is alive—a cheat, a liar, but gay and gallant. It's a valid approach, even if it isn't Thackeray's.

In fact, the closest representation of the novel's surface is to be found in the 1998 BBC five-hour version. It's telling that its DVD package names no actors, not even Natasha Little, who plays Becky (and very ably). This is a careful and respectful reconstruction, extremely well cast—there are no false notes. Is it Thackeray? No, because it doesn't comment on the action, it just lets it unroll. But it's relatively true to the situations and the characters, and it's fun to watch—a definite improvement on a four-hour 1967 version, in which Susan Hampshire does a no more than respectable job as Becky. (She was a lot righter as *The Forsyte Saga*'s Fleur.)

And now we come to Reese Witherspoon, and the revisionist version the born-in-India (like Thackeray) filmmaker Mira Nair has concocted for her. Myrna Loy was a star in the making when she played Becky; Miriam Hopkins was already a second-tier star. But Witherspoon is at the top of the heap, apparently commanding $15 million a movie after her smash hits *Legally Blonde*, its sequel, and *Sweet Home Alabama*. Which means that she isn't being squeezed into *Vanity Fair*; it's being molded to her. Nair's revisionism is most blatant in her perverse deployment in the film of Bollywood elements, including a sexy nautch dance put on for the Prince Regent at the mansion of Lord Steyne, who takes up Becky and introduces her to high society. She also transports us to India itself, although the book never travels beyond Germany. But Nair's most grating liberties involve the ending, as Becky and her early conquest, Joseph Sedley, Amelia's preposterous brother, sway atop an elephant while the locals grin and wave. This happy ending runs completely counter to Thackeray's intentions. He allows Becky to survive in relative, and unexotic, comfort, but makes it clear that there *are* no happy endings, for anybody. Life just doesn't allow them.

It's particularly disconcerting that Nair's ending gives us a jolly old Jos Sedley, since *Vanity Fair* the novel, as opposed to *Vanity Fair* the vehi-

Becky's second appearance in
the character of Clytemnestra

cle, concludes with Jos dead, possibly murdered by Becky. This is the
most ambiguous event in Thackeray's book. Two pages before the end, he
gives us Joseph begging Dobbin to rescue him from Becky: "He would do
anything; only he must have time: they mustn't say anything to Mrs.
Crawley:—she'd—she'd kill me if she knew it. You don't know what a terrible woman she is." Three months later Joseph is dead, leaving some
money to Becky, and "the solicitor of the Insurance Company swore it

was the blackest case that ever had come before him" and "talked of send-ing a commission to Aix to examine into the death."

But Becky prevails, as usual, and the money is paid. If you read the novel in most available editions, that's all you know. But if you read it with the illustrations Thackeray drew to accompany his text, you come upon a full-page picture captioned "Becky's second appearance in the character of Clytemnestra." (Years before, she'd given a terrifying impersonation of that avenging queen in a charade at Lord Steyne's.) In the picture, Becky—her hair hanging loose and lank, malevolence deforming her face, a knife clutched in her hand—is hiding behind a curtain, eavesdrop-ping on Joseph's appeal to Dobbin. This can't be intended literally—it's three months later, after all, that Jos dies—but if it isn't telling us that Becky was a murderess, what is it telling us?

After acting as prosecutor, John Sutherland, in his thoughtful essay "Does Becky Kill Jos?," concludes that she's innocent—at least of mur-der—on the grounds that while she may be "an adventuress who might well stoop to some well-paid adultery," she's a woman for whom murder is entirely out of character, a conclusion with which I agree. Perhaps the Clytemnestra drawing exists to illustrate Joseph's feverish delusions; per-haps it's there to tease and puzzle us, as Sutherland suggests. We can't know. Yet we continue to feel that there must be a documentable truth here. Becky Sharp is so vivid a character that we forgot she's an invention, not a case history. Our knowledge of her can't go beyond that of the man who invented her, and Thackeray himself, being questioned about her culpability, only smiled and responded, "I don't know."

But playing a possible murderess was never in the cards for the eter-nally adorable Reese Witherspoon. Indeed, every aspect of Becky Sharp's nature is softened for her by Nair. Even her cold rejection of her only child, young Rawdy, is prettied up. In the movie, it's Lord Steyne who sends him out of the drawing room; in the novel, his mother "struck him violently a couple of blows on the ear," and "after this incident, [her] dis-like increased to hatred." The *Legally Blonde* girl hating her child? You must be thinking of Joan Crawford. In fact, Witherspoon's Becky does nothing really nasty—an indiscretion or two, of course, a touch of greed, but all because she's had such a hard time. We're even given an opening scene showing her as a child cleverly managing her drunken father's af-fairs and winning our sympathy by being sentimental over the sale of a portrait of her dead mother.

As for Becky giving up her chance to flee Brussels when it appears that Napoleon has prevailed at Waterloo, so that she can watch over helpless, pregnant Amelia, this is pure invention—Margaret Mitchell's invention (think Scarlett and Melanie). And Rawdon? On the eve of battle, he tells Becky, "If you should wake to find me dead, you must be sure of this—that you are a woman who has been truly loved." Has he been watching daytime soaps? Imagine the skeptical Thackeray tuning in on dialogue like this!

So Witherspoon is presented as a saucy, racy, piquant redhead, who triumphs over adversity through her courage, charm, and generosity. She's barely raffish, let alone tawdry (Thackeray's illustrations make it clear just how debased Becky becomes). But though it's a wrong-minded performance, it isn't a bad one. She's a good mimic, and in the one scene in which Thackeray shows Becky committing a truly generous act— bringing Amelia and Dobbin together—she's convincing. Witherspoon could have made something of *Vanity Fair* if Nair had reinvented the novel the way the makers of *Clueless* reinvented *Emma*. Instead, she exploited it.

The movie's most insidious flaw lies in its pretensions to feminism. Witherspoon is quoted in an interview in *Vanity Fair* (Graydon Carter's, not Thackeray's) as saying, "I saw Becky as a kind of early feminist— wanting more. Attributes like ambition or desire were perceived as wicked then; now they're not." And Nair adds, "She got her comeuppance; they put her in her place, made her stand in the corner and face the wall. I have no time for that." But star and director have got it backward. Thackeray gives us a complicated, compromised character, a tough woman who goes wrong yet prevails and whom he can admire despite her profound moral failings. That was a startling approach for mid-nineteenth-century England. Nair and Witherspoon give us the traditional Hollywood tale of a basically decent, life-loving woman whom life has wronged and who is granted a traditional Hollywood happy ending. Their Becky has to be essentially innocent to be rewarded. Who's the real feminist here?

November 18, 2004

Parsing the Thirties:
Nearly Anything Goes

I t didn't take long for us to become nostalgic for the thirties, when we hadn't even been born." So wrote Morris Dickstein toward the close of *Gates of Eden*, his passionate account of the 1960s, speaking for himself and his group of fellow undergraduate intellectuals at Columbia College. He published *Gates of Eden* in 1977, in the immediate wake of the period he was celebrating, but it's taken him all this time to turn to the prehistoric (for him) Golden Age of the Thirties. He and his friends, he tells us, "looked back wistfully at the excited ideological climate of the thirties, about which we knew next to nothing," and *Dancing in the Dark* is essentially an expedition into this unfamiliar territory with the goal of pinning down its political, cultural—and somewhat schizophrenic—climate.

Dickstein was at home in the sixties: It's all real and immediate to him; he knows it inside out. Now he's mostly relying on research, and because he's thorough, he's been able to assemble and transmit an immense amount of information about a wide range of subjects, not only in his own fields, literature and film, but stretched (thinly at times) across music, art, dance, and design. Much of what he's come up with will be fresh and instructive to readers who are only casually familiar with the period; much of it is fun to read even when you know the material well—who can resist yet another smart take on Cole Porter or Frank Capra? But of necessity his grasp is far more secure in some areas than in others, the trap for any such omnium-gatherum. Thin ice is always dangerous.

In this book, as in *Gates of Eden* and *Leopards in the Temple* (2002), his superb exegesis of the post-war novel, Dickstein is at his best when considering texts. He's first and foremost a teacher: The sound of a professor's voice is everywhere in evidence, occasionally, even, by direct personal reference, as when he says of James Agee and Walker Evans's *Let Us Now*

Praise Famous Men, "When I've assigned it to undergraduates, the results have been disastrous." Sometimes the tone is strictly academic:

> From what we've said so far, it would seem that the language of social awareness in the 1930s is at least two different languages: a language of naturalism concerned with documenting social fact, and a language of modernism that plumbs the mind of the observer, translating complex states of consciousness into new narrative modes.

You have the sense here and elsewhere that his most reasoned arguments are reconstituted lectures or expanded lecture notes, his conclusions sharpened by years of teaching this material to avid (we hope) students.

The scholarly impulse, as apart from the pedagogic impulse, is at its most pronounced when he devotes five pages to scrutinizing the obscure *Hungry Men,* a 1935 proletarian road novel by Edward Anderson, of which he shrewdly remarks, "Out of some fear of reading like a novel, *Hungry Men* doesn't allow itself the indulgence of a plot, as if the mechanics of narrative closure would undermine the authenticity of its social observation." His close study of proletarian fiction suggests a long and close familiarity with it, almost as if it had been the subject of a Ph.D. thesis. (His actual thesis was on Keats.) And his command of the material relaxes his tone.

There's nothing overextended or over-academic when, for instance, he's expounding on the historical importance (and literary collapse) of Michael Gold, author of the famous 1930 fictionalized autobiography *Jews Without Money,* or when he's providing a salutary reminder of the virtues of Erskine Caldwell, whose place in history has been tainted by association with the coarse dramatization of *Tobacco Road* and by the steamy covers of the very popular paperback editions of his novels back in the 1940s and 1950s. The comparison he draws between *Let Us Now Praise Famous Men* and Caldwell and Margaret Bourke-White's documentary book about sharecroppers, *You Have Seen Their Faces,* is particularly instructive as he turns his gift for exegesis not only to the very different writing styles of Caldwell and Agee but to the very different photographic styles of Bourke-White and Evans.

Famous Men, as he refers to it, is one of Dickstein's principal texts, and in his attempt to sort it out—and sort out his own reactions to it—he overenthuses, even while acknowledging the confusion in Agee between the documentary impulse and "autobiographical meditation" (or, as I tend to think of it, spiritual masturbation). Quoting an extended passage of what some might label "literary" and others "fancy" writing, he remarks, "Were I not so moved by it, I'd be tempted to dismiss this as self-indulgent prose-poetry, spirituality heightened into resonant vagueness, or as material for a psychoanalytic biography." That rings true: *Let Us Now Praise Famous Men* is a book that's hard to take—unless you're in love with it.

Another example both of Dickstein's talent for probing complicated texts and of his inflating the value of what he sees as the signature works of the period is his heated embrace of Henry Roth's *Call It Sleep.* Dickstein was in his impressionable early twenties in 1964 when this tormented, powerful, flawed novel from 1934 was rediscovered, and it obviously resonates deeply, and personally, with him. If you're searching for an important proletarian novel of the period, *Call It Sleep* is a feasible candidate, but is it "one of the great novels of the century"? ("Great" is a word that in his enthusiasm Dickstein devalues. If two of Zora Neale Hurston's early stories are "great," and Porgy's love duet is "great" and *Let 'Em Eat Cake* is a "great" musical achievement, what words of praise are left for *King Lear* or *The Marriage of Figaro*?)

Since his proclaimed subject is the effect of the Depression on the culture of the thirties, Dickstein appropriately walks us through James T. Farrell's coming-of-age novel *Studs Lonigan*, although I suspect he isn't aware that for a generation older than his, *Studs* was more of a forbidden "dirty book" than a political statement. On the other hand, his determined attempt to squeeze *Tender Is the Night* into his canon is far from convincing. (And why is *The Great Gatsby*, that quintessential novel of the twenties, brought back for a guest appearance in the thirties? I guess Dickstein simply can't resist it, and as he did with Agee, he shows himself here to be susceptible to florid writing, singling out as "gorgeous prose" a passage about Gatsby's need to "suck on the pap of life, gulp down the incomparable milk of wonder.")

What's most telling is his choice of which writers to treat in depth. Appropriately, there are the mordantly provocative Nathanael West, the politically correct Zora Neale Hurston and Richard Wright, the notable but ultimately disappointing Clifford Odets. Why, however, is John Dos Passos treated so cursorily? Isn't *U.S.A.* one of the few genuinely major works of the decade? It's at least as significant as any of the above—and more directly relevant to Dickstein's avowed subject.

You have to feel sympathy for Dickstein when he has to address the one unquestionably major novelist of the period. He's too honest and too good a reader not to acknowledge that the decade's "best writer" is Faulkner, but how to work this modernist-cum-Southern-gothic anomaly into his thesis? He writes perceptively and persuasively about *As I Lay Dying*, but he can't make a case for including Faulkner in his armory. "Faulkner's career," he acknowledges, "sits oddly in our study, since he was by no means a 'Depression author.'" And there goes the ball game.

He has no need to apologize, however, for his focus on the novel that dominates his discussion of Depression literature—*The Grapes of Wrath*. As with Agee and Fitzgerald (but not Dos Passos and Hemingway), he takes Steinbeck personally, telling us of his formative encounters with the writer's work when he was young and susceptible, and then of his nostalgia for him when "I lived in Northern California with my wife and kids in the summer of 1973, when we visited Monterey and Cannery Row." And personally, rather than politically, is indeed the way to take Steinbeck, since despite *In Dubious Battle*, his bleak account of a Communist labor leader, Steinbeck was in no way an ideologue—his political position was essentially a middle-of-the-road liberalism.

And it was no ideology that led him to *The Grapes of Wrath*; as Dickstein rightly remarks, Steinbeck "was anything but a rigorous or systematic thinker." Rather, his burning sympathy for the victims of an outrageous and failed system was the direct result of his firsthand observations as a journalist. In this, he can be compared to Dickens, whose ardent political protests were also based on direct observation and personal sympathy, not theory. It's not much of a stretch to see *The Grapes of Wrath* as a descendant of *The Old Curiosity Shop*, with the Joads' desperate progress through the Dust Bowl as a parallel to Little Nell and her grandfather's terrible pilgrimage through the dark Satanic mills of England's industrial midlands. (*Les Misérables* is another passionate and personal, rather than ideological, outcry against the injustices of a deeply defective polity. *Uncle Tom's Cabin* is yet another.)

I'm sure Dickstein would agree that Steinbeck, despite his real talent, didn't possess the genius of Dickens or Hugo. He's very aware of the pretentiousness of much of Steinbeck's writing and the confusion of much of his thinking. Yet his *own* sympathies lead him to deal with Steinbeck's flaws defensively, adopting an unattractive anti-elitist tone. Steinbeck's novels are "scorned by highbrow critics" (what does he think he himself is?). And if Scott Fitzgerald was dismissive of Steinbeck, he "had his reasons: Steinbeck was the kind of socially committed writer who had displaced him in the 1930s and made his own work seem like a back number." This is atypically ungenerous, and suggests the powerful tug of Dickstein's reflexive preference for writing that is socially committed.

For all that *Dancing in the Dark* seems so inclusive in its reach, one of its problems is that it's actually disturbingly exclusive. The fiction of the thirties is far more various than Dickstein suggests, and much of what he omits bears on his subject, even if indirectly.

There is no mention, for instance, of Thornton Wilder's chronicle of a modern Candide, *Heaven's My Destination*, one of the ten top bestsellers of 1935. An earnest, good-natured, puritanical young man, a traveling textbook salesman in the Midwest—Joad country—undergoes a series of comic disillusionments, discovers some unpalatable realities about America and religion, and loses his spiritual certainties along with his rose-colored glasses. As a comment on the America of the Depression years it's remarkable, but Wilder is too literary, too elitist, to qualify for Dickstein's approbation. (*Our Town* is mentioned only in passing.) And what does it tell us that in 1936, the year of the unprecedented success of *Gone with the Wind*, the number-two bestselling novel was George Santayana's philosophical *The Last Puritan*, about as far as a novel can get from *Jews Without Money*? Wilder, Santayana, and other decorous writers have something to suggest about the period—so does *The New Yorker,* particularly in its cartoons—but they're off the radar for someone born in the forties and conclusively shaped by the sixties.

The Faulkner problem arises again when Dickstein turns to poetry. The era's leading poet, Robert Frost, made his position clear in a famous letter to a younger poet: "I wouldn't give a cent to see the world, the United States or even New York made better. I want them left just as they are for me to make poetical on paper." (You can't get less political than that.) Dickstein doesn't fare much better with Wallace Stevens and William Carlos Williams, but he lucks out with his fourth poet, Langston Hughes, "certainly one of the best young poets who became radicals and firebrands in the early thirties." That's about as far as he can make his case in this area, and he backs off from poetry fairly quickly.

In the field of fine arts, Dickstein's lack of interest is undisguised. Ben

Shahn, for instance, to cite the most blatant example, goes unacknowledged except for three passing references to him as a photographer. The famous "Passion of Sacco and Vanzetti" paintings and the Jersey Homesteads Mural go unmentioned, as does Shahn's collaboration with Diego Rivera on the famously aborted Rockefeller Center mural.

When it comes to classical music, Dickstein is similarly narrow. There is Aaron Copland—and Aaron Copland. (With a perfunctory nod to Virgil Thomson.) He overrates Copland's talent and overstates Copland's status: "Beloved by audiences, echoed by the younger composers he helped nurture, [his key works] became an intrinsic part of the nation's cultural life." Again, Copland is "a permanent classic and a perpetual audience favorite." Not that Copland is a negligible figure, but he's nowhere near as central a figure as Dickstein believes him to be. Perhaps that doesn't matter, though, because Dickstein is less interested in Copland as a composer than as musical America's leading exemplar of populism, as manifested in his scores for film and dance—although his most famous dance work, *Appalachian Spring*, doesn't come along until 1944 and has nothing to do with either the thirties or the Depression.

Populism, then, it becomes increasingly clear, is the key to Dickstein's take on the thirties. Populism is neither genteel nor ideological; it's the *real* America. At one point he presents a list of admired figures: "Copland, [Thomas Hart] Benton, Steinbeck, Capra, John Ford, Walker Evans, James Agee, Marc Blitzstein, Woody Guthrie, and even Virgil Thomson" constitute a lineup of artists whose work is "refreshing." (As it happens, he barely refers to Blitzstein elsewhere in his book, and his account of Benton is perfunctory.)

Woody Guthrie, on the other hand, is one of his great heroes, who became "such a figure in American legend that it's hard to believe the person really existed." This is the romantic reaction to Guthrie that inspired so many young people in the sixties, and Guthrie's grip on Dickstein also makes sense in light of his account of himself as coming from a politicized, union-centric immigrant family. As with Henry Roth and Steinbeck, his strong personal interest in Guthrie is very much a reflection of his background and his moment.

As for modern dance, one of the most complicated and suggestive cultural phenomena of the thirties, Dickstein has no context whatsoever. His very few mentions of Martha Graham are pro forma; he knows that she's considered a major figure but is only really aware of her as a minor appendage to Copland, rather than as a genius more important and influential than Copland himself, or for that matter than any of the thirties novelists other than Faulkner whom he takes seriously. But Graham, unlike Faulkner and Frost, was caught up in the political and populist ferment of the decade and should have been a central player in his narrative.

The title of the essential book on dance and politics during this period tells the story: *Of, By, and For the People: Dancing on the Left in the 1930s*, a collection of essays edited by Lynn Garafola. As is true of so much else involving revolutionary politics, modern dance was a hotbed of sectarian conflict. To some (like Michael Gold, writing in the *Daily Worker*), Martha Graham was "revolutionary in name only." Yet Ellen Graff, in her article "Dancing Red: Art and Politics?," points out that "in 1934 dancers could march from the Workers Bookstore to the Martha Graham Studio in no time at all, a fact that made it possible to fight the spiritual wars of revolutionary politics and modern dance almost simultaneously."

An essay by Barbara Stratyner tells us that "Communist Party pageants . . . were all-star extravaganzas, featuring the best-known and most innovative composers [like Marc Blitzstein], choreographers, and directors." Stacey Prickett describes events like Edith Segal's *The Belt Goes Red*, performed at Madison Square Garden in 1930, which "took as its theme the assembly line, the ultimate symbol of mechanized, alienating labor." She also points to the role of unions, revitalized by the disastrous effects of the Depression, within the modern dance movement.

The omission of this rich history from Dickstein's overview is not only unfortunate in itself but a symptom of how his range is narrower than it should be: This is material you can't afford to ignore in a serious meditation on Depression realities and the culture.

One of the strong features of Dickstein's approach is his sense of what might appear to be the bipolar nature of the thirties—the apparent clash between the frightening social realities and the ritzy glamour of so much of the entertainment of the period. (The cover of his handsomely designed and illustrated book makes the point dramatically: on top, a row of leggy chorines; below, a row of grim, seedy, unemployed men.) The Okies, yes, but also Astaire and Rogers, screwball comedy, deco. Movie audiences, severely shrunk in the early thirties, wanted to be cheered up, distracted. "Brother, Can You Spare a Dime?," yes, but also:

> *We're in the money, we're in the money,*
> *We've got a lot of what it takes to get along.*
> *We're in the money, the sky is sunny,*
> *Old Man Depression you are through, you done us wrong.*

Here, Dickstein's stars are not only Astaire and Rogers, but also the Gershwins, Cole Porter, and Busby Berkeley (to whom he gives a little too much credit when he states that he "single-handedly created the 1930s Hollywood musical"). It's a pleasure to be exposed to his happy enthusiasm for these masters. (Informed enthusiasm is, in fact, Dickstein's most appealing quality as a teacher and critic.) Yet again and again he reveals how shallowly immersed he is in thirties popular (as opposed to populist) culture.

He barely acknowledges radio, the defining new medium of the decade—the essential mode of entertainment for Depression listeners because once they'd acquired their radio, it was free. There's the usual nod to *Amos 'n' Andy*, a bare mention of *The Goldbergs*, and not much more, beyond the many obligatory references to FDR's "fireside chats." Yet radio was a tremendous democratizing and uniting force in this period, with a lot to be learned about the Depression even from its soap operas, just as the "shop-girl" romance novels and short stories of the period both reflect social realities and provide fantasies of escape from them. Joan Crawford's ruthless up-from-poverty saga *Possessed* (1931) has just as much to tell us about the seamy side of Depression life as Dickstein's preferred gangster and road films.

He's obviously far more at home in the early thirties urban film world, both gritty and deluxe, than in the more pastoral, kindly world of great stars like Janet Gaynor or Will Rogers, whose movies also respond, if in a different key, to the Depression-era need for escape and reassurance. In fact, the two most blatant omissions from his book are Walt Disney and Shirley Temple. (She at least is acknowledged—disparagingly; he, the most revolutionary film talent of his time, doesn't rate a single mention.) If Dickstein had stopped to examine these two most popular film phenomena of the decade, it might have occurred to him that Shirley and Mickey (Mouse, that is) share a crucial trait—their indefatigable, cheerful pluck in the face of adversity. That's what Depression-era Americans needed to be reassured of: their ability to bounce back from the harrowing circumstances of their lives. There's no better example of the public's unconscious wisdom in finding what it needs in the culture. But Disney and Temple are apparently beneath Dickstein's notice; his eye is on the sophisticated or the brutal, rather than the guileless escapist fantasies of the time.

He's particularly impassioned about Cole Porter (five "great"s are sprinkled over the page about Porter's *Anything Goes*), and writes discerningly about him: "Porter's songs were exceptionally daring for the 1930s: sex gave them their pulsing vitality, an image of high society gave them their brightness and buoyancy, and a certain self-loathing grounded in sexual unhappiness gave them heft and shading." The pages on Porter are among the most satisfying in his book. So what if Porter was a product of the twenties, not the thirties? Songs like "Let's Do It," "The Laziest Gal in Town," and "What Is This Thing Called Love?" were written well before Black Tuesday hit America.

The same is true of Astaire and Gershwin. They certainly helped assuage anxieties through the thirties, but "Swanee," Gershwin's first big hit, goes back as far as 1919 and *Rhapsody in Blue* dates from 1924, while Astaire was a favorite on Broadway and in the West End throughout the twenties. But why quibble? Dickstein loves and appreciates them—particularly the populist *Porgy and Bess*—although the existing literature on Astaire in particular is so formidable that Dickstein doesn't have much original to say about him.

When it comes to jazz and popular singing, he's ingested the obvious books and delivers adroit accounts of what was happening. Benny Goodman, Bing, Ella, Louis, et al. are all on hand. Reading Dickstein on them, you may feel that he was learning on the job, but that's not necessarily a bad thing. It means he's coming to them fresh. On the other hand, you can't help feeling that while he's mapped the surface of the subject, what lies beneath is terra incognita. He dips in and out of these matters smartly, but there's no sense of his having fully absorbed them.

Unsurprisingly, then, Dickstein is at his best when a passion for his subject is fueled by a long history of studying and teaching it. His greatest strengths, apart from literature, lie in film, and his confidence in this field gives him an authority that's lacking when he deals with other subjects. He's obviously thought long and hard about Frank Capra, for instance, the most populist (and popular) of the top directors of the time, shrewdly concluding:

> Capra's populist simplicity showed up in the way he personalized social problems into Boy Scouts and bosses, heroes and villains. But the same approach enabled him to transform America into a vivid personal myth of archetypal simplicity, affecting humor, and elemental emotional power. Like Chaplin, like Dickens, Capra remained in touch with something raw and vulnerable in himself and his audience, a memory of humiliation, struggle, and inner resolution. The coming of the Depression gave it a more than personal meaning, and helped turn it into a not always comforting social vision.

This may sound high-flown, but it also makes good sense. You may not agree with everything Dickstein says about the movies, but you can tell that his views reflect close knowledge and long consideration.

The fact that in *Dancing in the Dark* Dickstein proceeds on such different levels of intimacy with its subjects gives it a curiously unstable quality: Sometimes there's too much, sometimes there's too little, and the terms of his responses keep shifting. There's also the problem of his lack of interest in both the more conservative aspects of the art of the period and the down-and-dirty of pop culture—the ubiquitous comic book, for instance. Can it be accidental, for example, that Superman comes along at the end of the decade to rescue us all from disaster? Or to put it another way, isn't "Clark Kent," at bottom, an action-figure embodiment of FDR?

Dickstein maintains that he's under no obligation to be all-inclusive— that his announced theme, the explicit relationship between the Depression and thirties culture—releases him from the obligation to approach the culture comprehensively. But so prodigious a trawl through a cultural era sets up the largest expectations, leaving the relatively knowledgeable reader discomforted by the absence of what's been left out. That's why, despite the book's often original thinking and many felicities of expression, it's hard to accept it as a whole. It just isn't whole enough.

Dickstein's fullest justification for his approach comes at the beginning of his *Gates of Eden*: "Unlike those historians who try to catalogue everything, I've slighted cultural phenomena for which I felt little affinity, as well as others that were more conservative than innovative, and therefore tell us little about cultural change." But *Gates of Eden* doesn't promise more than it delivers. And it's personal in a very different way from the new book. About his teacher Paul Goodman, for instance, he tells us:

> I . . . was disappointed that I couldn't get him more interested in some of the clever and brilliant things I was saying. My bright-young-man's ego was bruised. I wasn't used to it. Later when he published his journal *Five Years* to show the world that he was not a good man but one driven and debased by sexual hungers and humiliations, I was able to guess at what happened: I simply hadn't turned him on.

(Bad luck, Morris.) *Dancing in the Dark* is a book about the thirties. *Gates of Eden* is not only a book about the sixties, it's an expression of the sixties.

It would seem that although Dickstein's mind is today fully concentrated on the thirties, his heart and soul still reverberate to the gods of his youth. A characteristic case in point: Someone of his generation would naturally consider Woody Guthrie's assertive "This Land Is Your Land" to be an alternative national anthem, whereas anyone really at home in the thirties would realize that, for better or for worse, the true alternative was Irving Berlin's consoling "God Bless America"—as sung by chubby, upbeat Kate Smith, in those years America's best-loved singer, who goes unmentioned in *Dancing in the Dark*.

December 3, 2009

Analyze That: H.D., Bryher, and Freud

Kat darling, Love and barks, Fido." "Hallo Mog, Love, Rover." It's hard to follow at first, but you get used to it. Kat (also Mog, Hyacinth, Lynx, Dryad, and just plain Cat) is Hilda Doolittle—H.D. to you—the celebrated Imagist poet (so christened by her onetime fiancé Ezra Pound) and, for a long stretch, Mrs. Richard Aldington. Fido (also Br, griffon, F.D., Dolly, small dog, Fitho, and Chang) is the novelist Bryher, née Annie Winifred Ellerman, and also—through a couple of odd marriages of convenience—Mrs. Robert McAlmon and Mrs. Kenneth Macpherson. Rover (also Dog, Dawg, Kex, K., Kay, Bloodhound, and Big Dog) is Macpherson himself, novelist and artist, who had an extended affair with H.D. and then married Bryher so that they could adopt the child H.D. had by Cecil Gray while she was married to Aldington. Rover himself was on the whole gay, but then so was Fido, and so was Kat once in a while. Got it?

Around this core of unconventional and talented people circled a pack of other unconventional and talented people. There was Pound (H.D. got cross with him over his rabid anti-Semitism, but their friendship resumed after the war, when he was incarcerated at St. Elizabeths); D. H. Lawrence (he and H.D. were so close that they traded manuscripts until in 1918, shocked by her loose behavior, he decided never to see her again); the friends of her youth William Carlos Williams and Marianne Moore; and many more, whose once-imposing names have receded into footnote material. And then there is Sigmund Freud—"Papa" and "the Professor" in private correspondence, but never to his face.

Analyzing Freud, edited by Susan Stanford Friedman, presents the correspondence among H.D., Bryher, and their circle during the two short periods, in 1933 and 1934, that Kat spent in Vienna, being analyzed by Papa with Fido paying the bills. It's a fascinating production. The letters reveal two complicated, appealing, highly intelligent women; give us a sense of Vienna at a time of tremendous political upheaval and danger; and present Freud in close-up, as observed by the awed yet canny H.D. (Much later she was to write more formally about her experience with him in the moving *Tribute to Freud.*)

H.D.'s road to Vienna had been a rocky one. Raised in Pennsylvania by a severe astronomer father and a warm but repressed mother, she went to Bryn Mawr, then left for Europe in 1911. During World War I a beloved brother was killed, and her father died of the shock; she herself lost a baby and then almost died of double pneumonia. There were dangerous breakdowns. It was Bryher who rescued her, tenderly seeing her back to health. They are assumed to have had a brief affair, but that quickly turned into a loving domestic relationship that stretched out through the decades. The two women shared their lives, although each of them shared with others, too. And they shared H.D.'s daughter, Perdita, who grew up with two mothers.

By the thirties, H.D. had long been established as a poet of consequence, but she was eager to break away from the "Imagist" label Pound had pasted on her. She grew grander in her ambitions; invested herself in Greek drama, which she translated and recast; wrote overwrought autobiographical fiction. But her emotional condition was fragile, and Bryher—who was obsessed with psychoanalysis, and indeed became something of a lay analyst herself—was determined that she should be treated by Freud. Since Bryher was rich, she could afford to pay for the treatments and the expense of Vienna. (Her father, a shipping magnate, was one of the richest men in England.) In late February 1933, H.D. left Perdita in Switzerland with Fido, Rover, and Quex (Dorothy Hull, a semi-psychotic housekeeper), and bravely set out for Vienna to expose herself to the unsparing insights of the founder of psychoanalysis.

Luckily for us, H.D. was a fluent, unguarded, honest—you could say indiscreet—letter writer. Her almost daily missives to Bryher reveal her in all her charm and impossibility. ("Do, do forgive me when I am a snarly cat. I will bite out the burrs and be a good cat-on-the-mat for ever and ever amen, after this.") She's funny and perceptive about her temporary new home: "I like this part of Vienna so much. . . . It's all artz, artz and student with smart university ladies in various degrees of having-arrived, and bows and scrapes and gnadidges." (You have to accustom yourself to her unlikely stabs at spelling and punctuation; these letters were written at top speed, meant only for her nearest and dearest.) She's endlessly gossipy, even bitchy, and Bryher matches her, gossip for gossip and bitch for bitch. And they're both excellent writers: One could argue that H.D.—like Byron, like Wilde—is at her freest and best in her letters. Wouldn't you rather overhear her giggling over Rebecca West or the Sitwells than, say, cope with a passage like this from her unpublished autobiographical novel, "The Gift": "Under every shrine to Zeus, to Jupiter, to Zeus-pater or Theus-pater or God-the-father, there is an earlier altar. There is, beneath the carved superstructure of every temple to God-the-father, the dark cave or grotto or inner hall or cellar to Mary, Mere, mut, mutter, pray for us."

Besides the incidental pleasures—the gossip (H.D. calls it "sending you the dirt"), the sense of a generously shared life, the up-close view of Europe possibly on the brink of war—what makes the correspondence especially valuable is H.D.'s observation of Freud, both as a writer taking him in and as a patient grappling with him. From the first visit to the famous office in Freud's home at Berggasse 19, she is both overwhelmed and confrontational: The transference and the countertransference go into immediate high gear. For a while she reports to Bryher on the analysis itself, until Freud, following standard analytic method, warns her against talking about it. But there is no ban on talking about Freud himself: "He is like an old, old bird, he jerks out his arm, commandingly like a terrific old hibou sacré, it scared me to death. He is so old and so majic and so sweet." He's also a "little old mummy of an Oedipus-Rex" and "an exquisite old fish-papa" and an "old, old, old, thousand-year old Tom-cat!"

As the analysis takes hold, H.D. becomes more descriptive, more serious, more genuine. "He is a rare, exquisite being, small, very fragile looking but one does not notice his 'infirmity' as he calls it, the thing I much feared." (An allusion to the prosthesis in his mouth, which he wore as a result of his cancer of the jaw.) "He speaks such lovely English in a slightly timid manner with such a mellow Austrian intonation." "He has that wistful ghost look of someone who has been right past the door of the tomb, and such tenderness with such humor. . . . He is the real, the final healer." And, to Havelock Ellis, another close friend: "He is as always, fine, remote, spiritual yet so warm and near and sweet. He has of course a god-like, saint-like, imp-like quivering sense of humor, which alone should put him among the immortels."

And we do get a sense of what the analysis was like, since on occasion H.D. breaks silence and recounts her dreams, and describes how she and

Freud dealt with them. She also reveals the emotional texture of their relationship: On the one hand, "he has made me cry so terribly"; on the other, "we are terribly en rapport and happy together." There are also delicious bypaths down which the correspondence wanders. The constant concern for the well-being of Pussy (Perdita); the continuing melodrama of the housekeeper Quex, also known as Dragon and Queen, who, the analyst Hanns Sachs warned, was potentially dangerous; and Bryher's courtship of the famous actress (and tease) Elizabeth Bergner, who in 1933 fled Hitler for England. (You can experience her relentless charm in the 1936 film of *As You Like It*, in which she is a simpering Rosalind to Laurence Olivier's Orlando.) Bergner led Bryher a merry chase. Loyal as always, H.D. finds a tacky little shop in Vienna where "an old bitch" sells her, at inflated prices, pictures of La Bergner that she sends on to Bryher. Even Freud is impressed by the connection to this huge star of stage and screen. "He was simply floored," H.D. reports.

The most unlikely drama that unfolds in the letters might be titled "A Comedy of Chows." At H.D.'s very first session with Freud, he warns that it would be unwise for her to approach his favorite, Yo-fi. H.D. knows better, and Yo-fi falls under her spell. Round one to H.D.! (Bryher is all ears: "What I must know is—does the chow share the analysis hour?") Soon two puppies are born to Yo-fi, and on April 26, 1933, H.D. writes: "I had a terrible ¼ hour yesterday, as papa wants to get rid of two chows . . . they have now 5 dogs. . . . He asked me most pointedly what kind of a garden we had, and how many dogs 'already.' . . . I may be mewing up the wrong tree, but I have a vague hunch, he is sentimentally inclined to offer us the unwanted male twin." And that very evening, in another letter, "The worst has happened. . . . I feel like the Virgin Mary at the entrance of the dove. Pa-pa has offered us one of Yo-fi's pups. What will we do about it?"

H.D. and Bryher do not want this puppy, but they're too polite, or scared, to say so. What they do is stall. On May 3, Kat writes: "I think, Fido, the only thing to do . . . is to hold it over very tentatively, as I am doing." It holds over (and over) until, in September, Anna Freud steps in, writing to Bryher about the dogs: "My father never wanted them to be a worry to you and you should have no feeling of obligation about them. They were just meant as a pleasure; there are too many worries around anyway, not counting the dogs."

Before this welcome rescue, however, the comedy of manners has been punctuated by a scene of pure farce:

Had a terrible time yesterday. Yo-fi is back and doesn't like Lun, and flew at her in the room. We had been to the kitchen to see the pups. Freud ran like lightening and flung himself on the floor and pulled them apart, all his money fell out and Anna and the maid rushed in, Anna screaming in German of course, "Pappachen beloved you shouldn't have done that," and the maid taking off Yo-fi in her arms like Jesus with a lamb.

But all was not fun and games in Vienna. One serious side of Bryher revealed itself in the financial help she funneled through Freud to endangered Jews, mostly from analytic circles. And we follow H.D.'s bold actions on a day when most of Vienna is shut down by demonstrations and Fascist activities. (She's the only one of Freud's patients to turn up for her session that day, and she braves the troopers to go to the opera—it's *Götterdämmerung*.) We also begin to sense how deep her problems go. Freud recognizes, and she acknowledges, that she has a strong, almost megalomaniac impulse. Analyzing a dream about a baby in a basket in a river (linked to the Doré illustration of Moses in the bulrushes), she speculates (in *Tribute to Freud*), "Do I wish myself, in the deepest unconscious or subconscious layers of my being, to be the founder of a new religion?" And there are delusions of grandeur: "My work is creative and reconstructive, war or no war, if I can get across the Greek spirit at its highest I am helping the world, and the future. It is the highest spiritual neutrality."

Ironically, H.D. has indeed emerged as the founder of a new religion. Susan Stanford Friedman has been studying her, writing about her, and, it would seem, attempting to canonize her for well over a quarter of a century. In *Analyzing Freud*, she proves herself to be an excellent editor—scrupulous and thorough—but her convictions about H.D.'s importance as an artist and a thinker are so unmediated, so impervious to question, that they distort her view of what was taking place between the poet and the analyst during those intense months in the early thirties. The very first lines of her introduction reveal her agenda: "Imagine the drama. The performance. The play of two great minds. Two supple phrasemakers in the wordshop of the dim Viennese study dotted with antiquities from around the world." (To be fair, Friedman's prose calms down after a few pages.) Her view, in other words, is that Freud and H.D. are equal masters, equivalent geniuses, who are involved together not in therapy but in a "collaboration." I suspect that this reading of what took place in Freud's study would have come as a surprise to H.D. herself. She might frequently and forcefully disagree with the Master but, as she writes in *Tribute to Freud*, "I was a student, working under the direction of the greatest mind of this and of perhaps many succeeding generations." And she quotes him as chastising her: "I keep an eye on the time—I will tell you when the session is over. You need not keep looking at the time, as if you were in a hurry to get away." Does this have the ring of two geniuses engaged in a joint adventure?

For Friedman, though, it is H.D., not Freud, who is the main event. In the past she has edited, with a colleague, a collection called *Signets: Reading H.D.*, which includes articles with titles like "Fishing the Murex Up: Sense and Resonance in H.D.'s *Palimpsest*." She is also the author of the 1981 critical study *Psyche Reborn*, in which she speaks of the poet's "lifelong revolt against a traditional feminine destiny," which "set her apart from the literary mainstream and led her ultimately to a woman-centered mythmaking and radical re-vision of the patriarchal foundation of Western culture." This, then, is why H.D.'s proper place in the literary pantheon has been denied her: It is the "distortions of a phallic criticism" that have insisted on seeing her as a "feminine" lyrical Imagist, dismissing her later "adaptation of the 'masculine' modes of epic quest and philosophic symbolism." I've tried to forget my own phallus while searching for signs of genius in H.D.'s immense body of published poetry and prose, but although I discern a large intelligence, a high level of craft, and a vast ambition, I can identify only an intermittently interesting talent.

Freud clearly admired and liked H.D., and he was polite and encouraging about her writing. But even in that area he is by any standard her superior. Consider a brief letter he wrote to her in May 1936, acknowledging a gift of flowers: "I had imagined I had become insensitive to praise and blame. Reading your kind lines and getting aware of how I enjoyed them I first thought I had been mistaken about my firmness. Yet on second thoughts I concluded I was not. What you gave me, was not praise, was affection and I need not be ashamed of my satisfaction. Life at my age is not easy, but spring is beautiful and so is love."

December 22, 2002

Astaire to Zopy-Zopy:
The International Encyclopedia of Dance

In 1974, at a meeting of the Dance Critics Association, the idea of a
full-scale encyclopedia of dance was proposed. Ballet was enjoying its
famous "boom." Modern dance had escaped from its arty and/or earnest associations and become mainstream. Even popular dance—made
newly respectable by the canonization of Fred Astaire—was under academic consideration. The time was ripe for a major gesture, both as a
catalyst for scholarship yet to be undertaken and as a statement to the
world that dance had arrived as an art to be taken seriously, just like
painting and music. Earlier critical and historical writing in the field,
however capable, had been sporadic and uncodified; here was the opportunity to give dance its due. So, under the leadership of the dance historian Selma Jeanne Cohen, the *International Encyclopedia of Dance* was
launched. And only twenty-four years later, here it is—six extra-large,
double-column volumes, a total of nearly four thousand pages, available
to the public at $1,250.

The career of this venture, begun almost casually, was to become
something of an epic struggle as the encyclopedia staggered from one publisher to another—from Scribner to the University of California Press to
the Oxford University Press, where it was finally readied for publication.
(Scribner was meant to bring it out in 1983.) Along the way it escalated in
both size and cost, but it remained true to its original idea: Well before the
culture wars broke out in the academic world, the encyclopedia was pro-
grammed to be both multicultural and multidisciplinary. "Dance" was no
longer to refer merely to theatrical performance; what had once been the
province of ethnology and anthropology was now to assume equal—even
primary—status in relation to ballet and its theatrical siblings.

In one of the encyclopedia's blessedly few entries written in academic-speak, the gauntlet is thrown down. William C. Reynolds, in his twenty-five-page essay on European traditional dance, asserts:

> Much dance has become the sole prerogative of elite professional performers, presenting it to a mass of passive consumers. . . . Marginalized traditional dance deserves preservation, if only as a genetic time capsule, openable at some future time of return to humanized society, capable of contributing to revived respect for individual creativity, free from the dominance of supplied culture, as a revival of natural human esthetics built on empowered bodily experience.

This is polemical, not scholarly or critical, writing, and, alas, its message to a large extent governs the encyclopedia.

I don't argue the importance of "marginalized traditional dance"; indeed, the ethnological material here appears to me impressive in its breadth and depth, and I have no reason to doubt its thoroughness or accuracy. But for whom is it written? Surely any intellectually curious reader should be able to browse with pleasure and profit through an encyclopedia. I find it difficult to imagine someone without a predisposition to read about such matters as Azerbaijani folk dance ("One type of yally has various forms known as kochari, uchayag, tello, and galadangalaya; another type is a dance mixed with games called gazy-gazy, zopy-zopy, and chopu-chopu") browsing profitably through Oxford's many hundreds of pages of such information. This is writing by specialists for specialists, and is all too likely to confuse, if not intimidate, the general reader. Perhaps more important, the only principles that apply to this kind of scholarship are those of accuracy (of course) and inclusivity: Everything is by definition as important as everything else. But this is not true of art, and the encyclopedia falters where judgment is required. Here, multicultural and multinational inclusivity at the expense of common sense undermines the encyclopedia's credibility.

Luckily, a great proportion of the entries on Western theatrical dance are both responsible and readable. There are useful essays on general topics ranging from photography (by Mindy Aloff), documenting dance through film and video (by Virginia Loring Brooks), and lighting (by Jennifer Tipton) to dance libraries and museums (by Mary R. Strow), post-1960 social dancing (by Sally R. Sommer), and the avant-garde (by

Sally Banes). A number of the articles on individuals or institutions are equally good: Dale Harris on Diaghilev's Ballets Russes and on Margot Fonteyn is superb; so are Lynn Garafola on Diaghilev himself and Robert Garis on the New York City Ballet. Robert Greskovic on Peter Martins and Edward Villella (and on various technical ballet matters) is very fine. So, too, are Vera Krasovskaya (the dean of Russia's ballet historians) on Petipa, Ivanov, and the Maryinsky style; David Vaughan on Frederick Ashton and Merce Cunningham (though a full column listing Cunningham's awards and honors could be considered overkill); David Daniel on Rudolf Nureyev and Suzanne Farrell; Nancy Reynolds on Maria Tallchief; Angela Kane on Paul Taylor; David Hamilton on Stravinsky; Joan Acocella on Nijinsky and Mark Morris. The quality of the entries on early ballet history is consistently high. And I am particularly grateful for the ample documentation of early social dancing (the gaillard, the quadrille, etc.); this is material not easily available elsewhere.

Most of our leading dance writers and scholars—or those active twenty or so years ago, when the bulk of the encyclopedia was commissioned and written—are generously represented. Recognizing the importance of the undertaking, they produced first-rate work for little money, often on tight deadlines. (Those deadlines were for the presumed 1983 publication, of course. Alas, thirty-eight of the writers have not lived to see their contributions in print.) Unfortunately, a last-minute effort to update articles written all those years ago is a failure; the new material is generally thin and hurried.

Also unsatisfactory are many of the entries on popular dance. Camille Hardy's article on American musical theater, for instance, is both too long and too plodding, and she gets too many specifics wrong. What does she mean by saying that "Eddie Cantor pranced his way to stardom" in *Whoopee!* in 1928, when he had already been a star for at least a decade, and was famous for his singing and comedy, not his dancing? Similarly, the 1934 *Anything Goes* was hardly Cole Porter's first hit show. And it's Frederick Loewe, not Lowe. (As for her prose: "Visually, audiences at the Metropolitan Opera House were taken by storm by the 1916 appearance of the Ballets Russes de Sergei Diaghilev.") There are no pieces on James Cagney or George M. Cohan—so much for *Yankee Doodle Dandy*. And what is the point of a piece on Ginger Rogers that doesn't list her dance films, or a reference to Rita Hayworth that names one of the two films she made with Astaire but not the other? The entries covering this entire area of dance history have a perfunctory feel to them. (Conspicuous exceptions are John Mueller on Astaire and Nancy Becker Schwartz on Busby Berkeley.)

There are several decidedly odd aspects to the encyclopedia. I don't understand why almost all the many entries on national dance are introduced with lengthy geographical-historical descriptions. Nothing about dance is illuminated by the knowledge that "by 6000 B.C.E., the Anatolian plateau and Armenian highlands were a neolithic farming center, one of those that led to the rise of civilization in the ancient Near East about 3500 B.C.E." or that "Senegal has 15 to 17 language groups, with the Wolof (30 percent), Serers (17 percent), and Peuls (12 percent) constituting the majority." Puzzling in a different way is a peculiar prudishness—so consistent that I have to assume it was deliberate policy. Constant Lambert—Margot Fonteyn's lover and, more important, her greatest intellectual influence—is not even mentioned in the Fonteyn article. Nureyev and Erik Bruhn "formed a friendship that lasted throughout their lives." Hugh Laing's relationship with Antony Tudor was apparently merely collegial—"a lifelong creative association and friendship." Merce Cunningham and John Cage share "a collaboration," "an esthetic," "a working alliance," but not a life. Even Isadora Duncan's startling personal history is barely touched on. But the central emotional relationships of such artists are not matters of gossip; they bear directly on the art and careers of these people. And this prudishness extends to ballets themselves—the article on Nijinska's *Les Biches* manages to sidestep its sexual ambiguities, probably the most famous thing about it.

The most ludicrous example of the absence of personal history is the treatment of George Balanchine. Without question, the finest piece of writing in these four thousand pages is Arlene Croce's magisterial, profound meditation on Balanchine's art. But it is pure criticism (the only example in the entire encyclopedia). There is no chronology, no history, no life, no account of the professional career of the most significant figure in twentieth-century dance. Who can guess why no supplementary article was commissioned? The result is that whereas the very full (and welcome) accounts of the careers of, say, Ashton and Fokine amount to miniature catalogues raisonnés, a reader in search of the Balanchine story will not find it here.

This is an extreme example of the failure of editorial focus that detracts from the overall reliability of the encyclopedia. On the very first page of the foreword, Lincoln Kirstein, prescient as always, is quoted as warning against basing the project "either on the rarefied euphoria of dance buffs and balletomanes or on the amateurism of critics whose overly specialized monologues speak mainly to themselves." Nobody listened. Boosterism and fandom run rampant, a telltale signal being the boasts of international acclaim and worldwide impact, etc., that punctuate the text. "A whole new generation of Australian dancers good enough to take New York and London by storm . . ." (I must have been in London when they were storming New York and in New York when they were storming London.) Christopher House helped win Toronto Dance Theatre "unprecedented international acclaim." Everybody you ever heard of is "incomparable." Barbara Newman is breathless over all her subjects—Anthony Dowell, for instance, is "peerless," "great," "legendary," but we get no suggestion of his less than legendary career as head of the Royal Ballet. And are we really to take seriously Horst Koegler's labeling as "important" such Johann Kresnik ballets as *Sylvia Plath*, *Pasolini*, *King Lear*, *Frida Kahlo*, and *Susi Creemcheese*? (I think I'd rather take my chances with Chen Weiya's "notable" *Miners and Sunlight, Hua Mu-Lan Coming Home from the Frontline*, and *Single-plank Bridge*.)

Again and again I found myself wondering whether anyone at Oxford University Press had actually read the articles for content—in fact, acted as an editor, as distinct from a copy editor. I would like to know by whom Alvin Ailey's *Revelations* is "estimated" to have been performed more often than *Swan Lake*. Why discuss the five surviving portraits of Claude Ballon and not show any of them? (And why in the entry on photography describe in detail a particular photograph of Emma Livry and display a slightly different one?) Why not prod the Russian commentator on *La Bayadère* to discuss its importance to Pavlova's career and the influence the Nureyev and Makarova revivals had on the West? (Of course, way back when this piece was written, the defectors Nureyev and Makarova were taboo in the Soviet Union.)

Did we really need to know that Maggie Gripenberg—the first Finnish dancer to dance barefoot "as far as is known," renowned for "bringing rhythm to Finland"—was buried at the Artists Knoll of the Old Cemetery in Helsinki? How not mention, in the article on *Fancy Free*, that it was Jerome Robbins's first ballet? Why does the article on *The New York Times*'s critic John Martin—in his day America's most influential writer on dance—fail to mention that for years he fulminated against Balanchine's "plotless ballets"? What can it possibly mean to say that Kenneth Mac-

Millan's work "has established ballet as one of the most expressive forms of the theater"? Why, in a lengthy article on Erik Satie, not refer to the pieces Mark Morris choreographed to his music? (In fact, why lengthy articles on so many composers only peripherally connected to dance?) How badly does the world need five columns on Korean dance research and publications, or eight columns (one column?) on televised dance in Canada? Why does the extensive article on the waltz say almost nothing about its history in this century and nothing at all of its crucial place in ballet?

I can only assume that the contributors either created their own guidelines or were allowed to ignore any that were laid down—nothing else could explain the disparity in length, tone, and approach to the various subjects. For example, no one can have tried to rationalize the difference between the compact and businesslike Russian contributors and the overlong, overwrought, overhyped, and overrepresented Canadians. (But then Oxford University Press can look forward to more sales in Canada than in Russia.) Nor did anyone, presumably, question all the back-scratching—the articles in praise of certain contributors, for instance; or the article on Valeria Dienes—who "developed her symbolics into a communication theory called evologic (consisting of time synthesis, irreversibility, emergence, and samelessness)"—written by Gedeon P. Dienes, her son; or, in a breathtaking stroke of auto-nepotism, Henrik Neubauer assuring us that in Slovenia "most dance research is still done by Henrik Neubauer." Then there is Selma Jeanne Cohen herself, who "has served as a catalyst in dance criticism, history, and esthetics, stimulating philosophers and others to explore in greater depth questions concerning the identity of the dance work, expression and style." Actually, her account in the preface of how the encyclopedia was born is charmingly girlish for a catalyst and stimulator: "Then one day, at a meeting of dance writers, Arlene Croce, editor of *Ballet Review*, remarked that what dance really needed was a thorough, scholarly encyclopedia. And—horrors—everyone in the room looked at me."

Even the technical editing is unsteady. Most obvious is the sloppiness of the fact-checking and the proofreading, inexcusable in a scholarly reference book. One glaring error can stand for many: A coryphée is far from being a principal dancer. The index is peppered with omissions and mistakes—including a mystifying reference to George M. Cohan in Volume 7 of this six-volume work. Typographical errors abound, the most dazzling being, "That the lyrical and plotless 'Aureole' ... was created for the 1962 American Dance Festival was itself risque because, at that time, the festival was predominantly a platform for America's more expressionist modern dance choreographers." Oh, that naughty Paul Taylor! (And let's hope that Lynn Seymour danced the fiancée, not the fiancé, in *Le Baiser de la Fée.*)

Serious errors of judgment were made in deciding whom to include. The editors seem to believe that anyone who ever ran a minor company or choreographed, however badly, is by definition more important than just another major dancer. There is no Marie-Jeanne, for instance— surely a little space stolen from the scores of pages on Kabuki family genealogies or the columns on Cape Breton step dancing might have been devoted to this paragon of classic technique on whom Balanchine created *Concerto Barocco* and *Ballet Imperial.* And a policy boasted of in the introduction turns out to be a disaster. Elizabeth Aldrich, the project's managing editor, tries a preemptive strike in explaining why so few new subjects and "biographees" have been added since the aborted publication of 1983, but her excuses are unconvincing, a sacrifice of common sense to expediency and methodology. There is no excuse for omitting the Miami City Ballet, the most celebrated new ballet company of the past fifteen years. And here are three dancers who go without entries in the encyclopedia: Darci Kistler, Darcey Bussell, and Sylvie Guillem—in other words, the three dominant younger ballerinas of our time. Such omissions add to the overall impression the encyclopedia gives of premature obsolescence.

For a comprehensive account of the ballet dancers of the past century one would be better advised to acquire the recent two-volume *International Encyclopedia of Ballet* published by the St. James Press. It includes full chronological lists of dancers' repertories (the Oxford volumes don't) and seems responsible in its judgments (although it, too, ignores Marie-Jeanne). It does not, however, echo the absurd omission of Merrill Ashley and Patricia McBride. If dancing triumphantly for Balanchine for decades, sustaining a tremendous part of the New York City Ballet's repertory, and stimulating him to new explorations of syncopation (McBride in "Rubies") and allegro technique (Ashley in *Ballo della Regina*) doesn't qualify a dancer for inclusion in a dance encyclopedia, I can't imagine what would, particularly when so many marginal figures from marginal venues are being imposed on our credulity.

People in the dance world have been rooting for Selma Jeanne Cohen for almost twenty-five years, and she has held on with remarkable tenacity to her project. Because of her, and despite extraordinary obstacles, the encyclopedia now exists, and the fact of its existence is the most important thing about it. It will serve as a basis for all future endeavors; no one will ever have to start from scratch again. But the very size of the accomplishment and the many years spent on it underscore one's distress at what has gone wrong. I can only speculate that at some point between 1983 and now, Cohen and her chief collaborators lost control or energy. The torch was passed to Aldrich—a respected dance scholar, whose demanding job at Oxford was to undo much of the unsatisfactory copyediting that had previously been done, gather new material, and prepare the gigantic text (much of it written in ragged translaterese) and the profuse, well-chosen, but, alas, poorly reproduced illustrations for the press. She has done a heroic job of organization and administration. But something beyond copyediting and pro forma updating was required, and it was not provided. As a result, a thorough job of cleaning up and cleaning out remains to be done.

I urge Oxford University Press to issue a revised, affordable paperback edition in a few years, structured not simply alphabetically but by subject matter (as Grove separates jazz from classical music). Properly updated volumes devoted to historical and recent ballet, others on ethnic dance, modern dance, and popular dance—each sold individually and, most important, with the entire revision under the editorial guidance of an enlightened and judicious generalist—will make the *International Encyclopedia of Dance* everything it ought to be: the authoritative reference work on dance for decades to come.

July 26, 1998

Fast-Talking Dames

The screwball comedy of the thirties has been lucky in its interpreters. Stanley Cavell, Elizabeth Kendall, James Harvey have written illuminating books about it; Pauline Kael, Parker Tyler, Manny Farber, James Agee have shed light. Is it really surprising that this most verbal of film genres should have compelled the interest of our most sophisticated film critics? Besides, these movies are so much fun to think about, to write about—to watch!

The iconic movies of the genre—*It Happened One Night, The Awful Truth, The Lady Eve, His Girl Friday, Bringing Up Baby, My Man Godfrey, The Thin Man, Ninotchka* among them—form a particularly loved and admired pantheon. But what do they have in common? No two of them star the same actress—they feature Claudette Colbert, Irene Dunne, Barbara Stanwyck, Rosalind Russell, Katharine Hepburn, Carole Lombard, Myrna Loy, and Greta Garbo—and only Howard Hawks directed more than one of them. True, three of the heroines are heiresses (the Depression was big on heiresses), but of the others, one is an adventuress, two are already married, one is a reporter, one a Communist apparatchik.

What these films have in common, naturally, is satisfied romance—the right woman ends up with the right man. But that's true, too, of other forms of comedy, as well as of weepers and musicals, even Westerns. The thesis of Maria DiBattista's *Fast-Talking Dames* is that the special invention of thirties comedy is the verbal sass of its female characters. In other words, it's the wit, the speed, the freedom peculiar to the way these women talk that set them apart from the vamps and victims and hoydens of the silent period, that reflect the new economic and social realities of the era, and that—most important of all—lead to generous and happy unions within marriage. Good talk, in other words, leads to good sex—in fact, is a requisite for it. (This is a lesson we've already been taught by Shakespeare's romantic comedies. It is his Rosalind and Viola and Beatrice—as well as Congreve's Millamant and Austen's Elizabeth Bennet—who are the original fast-talking dames.)

Indeed, DiBattista cleverly suggests:

> We can confirm the Shakespearean lineage of the fast-talking dame's rhetorical virtuosity by remarking her skill in the "seven degrees" of dramatic reply cataloged by Touchstone in *As You Like It*. . . . Retort courteous—Myrna Loy; quip modest, Irene Dunne and Claudette Colbert; reply churlish, Ginger Rogers, who also scores with reply valiant; counterattack quarrelsome, Katharine Hepburn . . . lie circumstantial, Carole Lombard . . . and lie direct, the specialty of the great female con artist, Barbara Stanwyck.

The strongest sections of *Fast-Talking Dames* are those that anatomize these beautiful and charming—and voluble—women, and their equals in looks and spirit, Jean Harlow and Jean Arthur.

It's particularly gratifying to see justice done to Harlow, "so explosive yet disarming in her sexual candor that the only way to restrain her is to yoke her to a sentimental myth that she is at heart a one-woman man whose greatest desire is to get married and stay married. . . . Wisecracks are her sexual armor, but they are open to counterattack." And to follow the subtle comparisons to Lombard, whose "comic response to her predicaments is more rambunctious than raffish." Lombard herself is "the great pretender," whose characters "flourish in that most hilarious but difficult of dramatic forms perfected by Wilde—the trivial comedy for serious people." Ginger Rogers? Her "purity is less sexual than existential. It's her independence, hard-won, more than her chastity, easily defended after all, that she fights ardently to preserve." Myrna Loy? "The most companionable of modern women—witty, unaffectedly but unmistakably intelligent and reliably good-humored." Jean Arthur, mentor to both Mr. Deeds and Mr. Smith? "With her proletarian savvy and wry, throaty humor," she "makes a sympathetic heroine for comedies with class politics on their mind." Brief quotation can do only partial justice to the loving shrewdness with which DiBattista considers this band of admirable women who give as good as they get, if not a great deal more.

It is the triumph of confident articulation that sets these comedies and their heroines apart and turns them into a genre. And this is true even of an anomalous movie like *Stage Door,* which has no Mr. Right (and therefore no Clark Gable, Cary Grant, Gary Cooper, or William Powell) to engage with its two heroines. *Stage Door* is in essence a female buddy film, whose resolution gives us Katharine Hepburn and Ginger Rogers falling not in love but into friendship—after a class war (and a war of words) as sharp as that in any of the more conventional comedies about heiresses being taught basic values by working men, or rich guys falling for working girls, or rocky marriages straightening themselves out. You could say that Hepburn gives Rogers class and Rogers gives Hepburn heart, but neither of them has to learn how to give lip. In one of our own day's most successful romantic comedies, *Pretty Woman,* Richard Gere gives Julia Roberts all that money can buy and she teaches him how to feel, but does either of them say anything you can remember?

Maria DiBattista is a professor of English and comparative literature at Princeton, and heads its film studies committee. Her literary background enriches her view of film, with its apt references to Tocqueville, Calvino, James, Kundera, Baudelaire, Congreve, Barthes, et al., and on the whole she can be congratulated on avoiding academic-speak. She's also persuasive in her contention—not, I'm relieved to say, presented polemically—that "when film found its human voice, it simultaneously gave to the American woman, as performer and heroine, a chance to speak her mind, to have a real, not just a presumptive, say in her own destiny." But when her book veers from its announced topic, the dame herself, into extended analysis of certain key films, one can't help hearing the voice of the professor. Are these later chapters—on *Bringing Up Baby, The Awful Truth, Ninotchka, His Girl Friday,* and *The Lady Eve*—reworked lectures or a reworked Ph.D. thesis? It wouldn't be a crime if they were, but there's a noticeable change of tone. The earlier sections of the book are written in a voice far closer to the voices in *Baby, Friday,* and *Eve* than the one that tells us: "*The Awful Truth* gives one last glimpse of sexual desire in which the aroused human being, through a process of comic displacement and diminishment, is reduced to a clockwork mechanism, disappearing into the entrails of time. Henri Bergson's philosophical view of comedy as one response to the spectacle of human automatism has never been so vividly 'demonstrated.'" The focus changes, too: The discussion of *Bringing Up Baby,* for instance, is centered on Hawks, the director, and Grant, the hero, far more than on fast-talking Hepburn, who is hardly characterized here.

As for *Ninotchka,* DiBattista is well aware of the incongruity of placing

Garbo—"There was nothing hurried in her speech," which is putting it mildly—among the fast-talking dames. Yet the clever analysis of the film justifies her inclusion. And remember: Her delayed debut in sound, *Anna Christie*, was brilliantly promoted with the phrase "Garbo talks"; from the beginning, the question of Garbo's speech was vital. In the course of *Ninotchka*, her speech, at first flat and dry, subtly modulates, warms, sexualizes. She may never talk fast, but it is through her talk, as much as by her iconic face, that we discover her. And then, famously, "Garbo laughs." Most thirties heroines have to learn what, or whom, they really want, and the back-and-forth of conversation helps them learn it. But Ninotchka has to learn who she really is, and it's laughter, more basic even than speech, that reveals her to herself and to us.

Fast-Talking Dames is filled with insights into films and actors, although in its eagerness to elaborate its thesis it overrates such films as the limp *It's a Wonderful World* (Colbert and James Stewart) and the ghastly *The Bride Came C.O.D.* (James Cagney and Bette Davis; you can't get a whole lot less funny than Bette Davis falling into a cactus). It is also valuable as an example of the kind of professional criticism we can now begin to take for granted as distinguished members of the academy address movies with a seriousness previously reserved for literature.

But this raises the question of just how much seriousness these movies can actually support. Can *Bringing Up Baby* sustain the weight of attention we bring to *Middlemarch*, say, or to *The Winter's Tale*? Occasionally, DiBattista slides into overinterpretation—you sense that there's less here than meets her eye. Yet movies have become our basic cultural coin—the one subject everyone can talk to everyone else about, regardless of age or circumstance. Fifty years ago, conversational chasms could be bridged by the question—it became a cliché—"Read any good books lately?" Today's "Seen any good movies lately?" is the no-fail equivalent: Everyone either has or hasn't, and is happy to tell you about it. We shouldn't be surprised, then, that movies have found their way into the curriculum, just as fiction did during the last century. And we shouldn't be surprised when professors of literature choose to anatomize a *Bringing Up Baby*. They may at times overthink, but at least they're thinking hard, and—as critics are meant to do—they're showing us things we didn't see for ourselves.

Artists in Exile

Joseph Horowitz's *Artists in Exile* is very ambitious, very stimulating, and very confused. Much of the confusion comes from the disparity between what the book says it's going to be about—in the words of its subtitle, *How Refugees from Twentieth-Century War and Revolution Transformed the American Performing Arts*—and what it actually turns out to be: the stories of scores of European artists who happened to come to America in the twentieth century. Almost none of them "transformed" the American performing arts, and many of them weren't refugees at all but immigrants in the great American tradition. After all, we all came from somewhere else.

Who is an "exile"? Someone who's been compelled, by fiat or circumstance, to abandon his native land and reside elsewhere—and who would rather be back where he came from. Napoleon: The moment he could escape from Elba he was on his way home to Paris (and Waterloo). Ovid: banished in disgrace to the shores of the faraway Black Sea and forever pining to return to Rome. There are true exiles in Horowitz's book, most of them Jews or Gentile anti-Nazis who fled Europe to find sanctuary in America. But all but a few of these were content to stay on after the war, claiming the possibilities of the New World and embracing their new life; in other words, ceasing to be refugees and becoming immigrants and, usually, citizens.

Take the two most famous movie stars Horowitz summons up to support his points: Garbo and Dietrich. He gives us potted versions of their hardly obscure life stories and not very illuminating commentary on their work, but sidesteps the fact that neither of them was either an exile or a refugee. Garbo arrived in America from Sweden in 1925 to work for MGM; she had almost stayed on in Germany, where she had just filmed

Pabst's *The Joyless Street*. And although she made trips home to see family and friends, and claimed to hate Hollywood, she chose to go on living in America, spending her final decades in famous seclusion in the East Fifties in Manhattan. There was never a moment when she couldn't have repatriated herself.

Dietrich got to America in 1930, well before the Nazis took power in Germany, and although they were eager to lure her home, she stayed on, as an American citizen, until she moved to Paris a decade before her death. Horowitz acknowledges that "the United States, clearly, was more to Dietrich than refuge from the storm," and he's certainly right in stating that "her identification with the language and culture of Germany was permanent." But that's true of just about all immigrants and the cultures they come from: It's their children (like Dietrich's daughter) who morph from immigrant mentality to American mentality.

To a certain extent Garbo and Dietrich were what Horowitz calls "agents of cultural change," but they had never been on the run, and the impact they had on American culture was no greater than the impact American culture had on them. The movies would have been the movies, however sadly diminished, without them; they wouldn't have been "Garbo" and "Dietrich" without America. Horowitz asks, about Garbo, "Would she have prospered better had she not been so closely bound to the United States?" But as what? A stage actress in Stockholm? A film star under Goebbels? Would this strange, unmoored narcissist really have been happier if MGM hadn't helped her become the most striking of all screen presences?

Again and again Horowitz focuses on famous figures who were here because they chose to be—starting with his first extended example, George Balanchine, who got out of Russia in 1924 when he was twenty. In Europe, Diaghilev gave him the opportunity he needed, and later Lincoln Kirstein offered him America, with which he fell in love. Balanchine, as Horowitz understands, had the greatest impact on an American art form of any of the twentieth-century émigré geniuses, but although he had come to something of a dead end in Europe, in transplanting himself to America in 1933 he was moving *toward* something, not away from something.

Balanchine remained Russian Orthodox in his religion, retaining his affection for his Russian friends, for Russian food and drink, for Glinka, Tchaikovsky, Glazounov, and Stravinsky (though not Prokofiev and Rachmaninoff, who had offended him), but he had no nostalgia for Russia itself. When he finally returned there, in 1962, he hated it. He was fervent about his adopted country and proud of his American citizenship. In other words, his American years were not an exile but a fulfillment. Horowitz has done his homework, absorbing and quoting the work of various commentators on Balanchine (I'm one of them), but no one who really understands Balanchine could remark, as he does in his introduction, that Balanchine "shed" Petipa, who was his lifelong artistic lodestar. It's all there in the ballets. Although Horowitz knows *about* them, he doesn't really know them. That's why he can also say that Balanchine created "an American ballet tradition utterly distinct from Petipa and Diaghilev." Rather than reject the past, Balanchine absorbed it and built on it.

Fortunately, Horowitz's knowledge of music gives him something insightful to tell us about Balanchine:

> The evidence of his musical sophistication marks his ballets in ways obvious and hidden, general and specific. His *Scotch Symphony* solves the problems of Mendelssohn's *Scotch* Symphony—a work undone by a long coda whose cheerful note of triumph is (at least for post-Victorian ears) impossibly thin. Balanchine's ballet omits all but a few introductory measures of the symphony's long A minor first movement. As a result, the entire work begins and ends in the major. With its most turbulent music left out, with the finale the only sonata form, the center of gravity is shifted toward the fortified close. This recomposition is clinched by the choreography, which (in addition to turning the repetitive Adagio into a pas de deux both central and sublime) achieves closure by pairing the dancers as "wedded" couples—a Shakespearean ending. No other choreographer could stage and "correct" a Mendelssohn symphony this persuasively, but there is a cost: the Scherzo must be slowed down for dancing.

This and other such telling passages, however, have nothing to do with Balanchine's being a refugee, an immigrant, or in exile; they have to do with the specifics of his genius, which were just as evident in early works like *Apollo*, created in 1928, five years before he arrived in America.

By far the most interesting parts of *Artists in Exile* are those dealing with musicians, because this is material Horowitz knows in depth. He can't stop returning to the years that Antonín Dvořák spent here (1892–1895), and about which he's written an entire book, *Dvořák in America*, but he also gives us a useful series of biographical essays on the lives and achievements of many of the composers, conductors, and instrumentalists who came here in the following century for one reason or another—by no means all political.

Some stories are tragic, others triumphant. Some composers embraced America and flourished; others—Krenek, Dohnanyi, Toch—either resisted their new home or were rejected by it. Stravinsky, Schoenberg, and Hindemith survived with varying degrees of success and comfort; all of them chose to become American citizens. Before he died in 1945, Bartók lived unhappily for a few years on West Fifty-seventh Street in Manhattan, but although he did important work here, he was one of those who were unable to accommodate themselves to their new circumstances—"one of those émigrés," as Horowitz tellingly says of him, "whose United States residence was an irreducible, implausible quirk of fate."

Kurt Weill and Erich Korngold had big careers here, the first on Broadway, the second in Hollywood: Too bad that they had to "go commercial" to do it. Horowitz is ambivalent about this. He goes on and on about Weill: Did he, in his eagerness to succeed, betray his real talent? Who can say? Yes, he never wrote another *Threepenny Opera*, but not necessarily because he emigrated; some artists never surpass or even equal their early successes. A perfect example is Michel Fokine, the most important choreographer of the first years of the twentieth century, whose career never recovered from his break with Diaghilev. His disappointing American sojourn, which lasted until his death, in 1942, is the obverse of Balanchine's, but you wouldn't know it from this book. Inexplicably, Horowitz barely touches on him.

One unsurprising phenomenon that emerges from all these stories is that those immigrants who were relatively young when they arrived— among them, Balanchine at twenty-nine, Weill at thirty-five, Korngold at thirty-seven—fitted into their new lives more easily and readily than those who were older and more settled in the world they came from (Fokine, for instance). No one, it would seem, planted himself more firmly than Edgard Varèse, who arrived here in 1915 at the age of thirty-two: Neither a refugee nor a political exile, he became wholeheartedly American (above all, like Balanchine, he loved New York). There's no way Horowitz can shoehorn Varèse into his refugee-exile concept, but if you don't know his story, this is a happy way to learn it.

Likewise, Horowitz's account of the life of that imposter-cum-genius Leopold Stokowski, the grandson of an Anglo-Irish boot-maker, is riveting—I wish he'd give us a complete biography—but the only thing about Stokowski's life and achievement that reflects his having emigrated here is that America gave him tremendous opportunities, and he grabbed them. Born in London, he became the organist at Saint Bartholomew's Church in New York at the age of twenty-three, and he wasn't yet thirty when he took over the Philadelphia Orchestra in 1912; by 1915 he was an American citizen. I can't take seriously Horowitz's argument that "though he had lived in the United States since 1905, Stokowski was essentially exiled in America because of World War I." Stokowski's brand of self-dramatizing populism could only have thrived here, and he knew it.

Stokowski is a Horowitz favorite, partly because—unlike many of the other European conductors who succeeded here—he performed a lot of new American music. This is one of the author's hobbyhorses, but I don't see why just because America gave them sanctuary, great musicians raised in the European tradition owed it to modern American composers to play their music. Horowitz's truculent bias in this regard—his disapproval of what he terms "the incurable Eurocentrism of classical music as imported to the United States"—seems to me to reflect an unfortunate streak of provincialism. Surely we were lucky to have these gifted men offering us the music they knew best.

Yet his regard for, and understanding of, the musical émigrés—again, by no means all of them refugees—makes a worthy contribution to our understanding of the history of music in this country. The noble Adolf Busch, the mandarin Serge Koussevitzky, the difficult Otto Klemperer, and the tragic Dimitri Mitropoulos are portrayed with sensitive discrimination. About the uniquely triumphalist Arturo Toscanini, Horowitz has already written in depth in *Understanding Toscanini*, but it's useful to have his viewpoint recapitulated here, even though Toscanini—that fiercely anti-Fascist and almost godlike symbolic figure to Americans of the 1930s and 1940s—is an exception to every rule.

Artists in Exile also provides a valuable reminder that many of the important institutions that have formed our musical experience were the brainchildren of émigrés—the Marlboro festival (the Busch family, including Adolf's son-in-law, Rudolf Serkin); the Tanglewood festival (Koussevitzky)—while the influential Leventritt piano competition was greatly shaped by the Hungarian conductor George Szell and the

Bohemian-born pianist Serkin. Serkin, in fact, is a central figure in Horowitz's account—of all the émigré pianists, he was the one who most easily accommodated himself to his adopted country. Returning to Europe for a visit in 1947, he wrote: "When the first excitement of recognition is over, what is left is a terrible homesickness. I feel like an American tourist here. . . . I didn't realize how deeply I have already taken root in America." Yet Serkin is one of the performers Horowitz chides for essentially ignoring American music. But was it really misguided or ungrateful of a European artist to find Beethoven, Mozart, and Brahms more congenial to his talent than Aaron Copland and Roy Harris?

As for the three most celebrated instrumentalists in America in the 1930s and 1940s, all of whom came from Eastern Europe and became American citizens, Arthur Rubinstein is barely mentioned and Jascha Heifetz and Vladimir Horowitz are marginalized—as if they were outside the scope of this book. They just don't fit its arguments. These artists may have been beneficiaries of America's "insatiable New World musical marketplace that propelled them toward maximum fame, fortune, and instrumental display," but, according to the author, without an institutional base they were denied the creative and collaborative opportunities they might have found in Europe. "One may reasonably inquire whether their astounding instrumental gifts were to any degree squandered in the United States," the implication being that, like Weill and Korngold and—as we shall see—like Lubitsch and Garbo, they were just too commercially successful on American terms. If only they hadn't chosen, long before the war, to make the most of what America offered them!

Of the arts dealt with by Horowitz, perhaps we know least about early-to-mid-twentieth-century theater. It's also the area about which he's least convincing on the subject of émigré cultural impact. Yes, the exotic and talented Alla Nazimova had a splashy career after she arrived here from Russia in 1905, specializing in, and helping to popularize, Ibsen and originating the role of Christine in *Mourning Becomes Electra.* What was she like as a stage actress? Many found her magnificent, others over the top. What's left to us of the years of her career that mattered are a few of her silent-screen melodramas, including her demented *Salomé* (you can find her "Dance of the Seven Veils" on YouTube—be prepared) and her ultra-deco *Camille* opposite an effective Valentino, in which she's maddeningly stylized.

Essentially she changed nothing, although her example may have helped inspire Eva Le Gallienne and Stella Adler. But European stage actresses had been impressing (and/or scandalizing) Americans since the mid-1800s, and Rachel, Bernhardt (nine American tours), Duse (she even died in Pittsburgh), and Modjeska were far bigger sensations than Nazimova, as Garbo and Dietrich would be after her. Nor does Nazimova fit the pattern of refugee or exile. She quickly learned English—by 1907 she was appearing on Broadway in something called *Madame Coquette*—and after her silent-screen moment of notoriety, went on to a long though spotty career on the stage and in Hollywood, her name still honored, but a has-been. She had been an interesting sideshow but in no way a catalytic presence.

The saddest story is that of Max Reinhardt, a genuine refugee, who had been the emperor of German-language theater—one of the greatest and most powerful of all director/impresarios. His *The Miracle* had successfully toured America in the 1920s, but after he filmed *A Midsummer Night's Dream* in Hollywood in 1935 (he was sixty-two), things went downhill, and though he was well regarded as a teacher in Los Angeles, by 1943, when he died, he was a relic of a distant and mostly forgotten past, unable to transplant his huge-scale vision of theater to the world of Broadway. No other theater really mattered in America, and the great Reinhardt was too much of an institution, too planted in his formidable history, to fit comfortably among us.

A very different story is that of the talented stage designer Boris Aronson, to which Horowitz devotes well over twenty pages. But what does it prove? Aronson was very young—about twenty-three—when he arrived in New York in 1923, and although his aesthetic preferences may have been formed in Europe, he developed his style here, his chosen home. All in all, his work is no more "European" than that of his famous predecessor Robert Edmund Jones, who in his youth spent a year in Germany observing Reinhardt's theater but was as American as one can be: New Hampshire, Harvard, the Provincetown Playhouse. (Among his great successes were *The Green Pastures*, *The Philadelphia Story*, and a number of plays by O'Neill, including *Mourning Becomes Electra*, *Ah! Wilderness*, and *The Iceman Cometh*.) According to Frank Rich in his magisterial *The Theatre Art of Boris Aronson*, Jones was "the American designer Aronson most admired."

But the person Horowitz most admires of the transplanted European theatrical figures is Rouben Mamoulian, who in 1923, at the age of twenty-six—neither a refugee nor in exile—arrived here via Paris, Moscow, and London. He was clearly a real talent, working in opera, operetta, and dance as well as theater, breaking through on Broadway with the original play of *Porgy*. (He would later direct—thrillingly—Gershwin's *Porgy and Bess*.) After enjoying a significant if hardly central early career in sound films—the Fredric March *Dr. Jekyll and Mr. Hyde*, Garbo's *Queen Christina*, *Becky Sharp*—he triumphed yet again on Broadway with Rodgers and Hammerstein's *Oklahoma!* and *Carousel* before, in the late 1940s, it all began to peter out. Of Mamoulian's films, Horowitz most appreciates the novel and sparkling *Love Me Tonight*, with Jeanette MacDonald and Maurice Chevalier, and in fact indulges himself by using up five pages to walk us through it.

Unfortunately, he also uses it as a stick with which to beat Ernst Lubitsch, whom he consistently disparages. Mamoulian, you see, "eschewed nostalgic regard for Old World sentiment and locales. With no anchored 'past,' he enthusiastically lived in the present." On the other hand, "Lubitsch's adaptability—to sound, to Hollywood, to America generally—may be read as a lack of depth." Poor Lubitsch—he can't do anything right. "An undeniable defect of Lubitsch's films is the absence of memorable star turns by Americans." Even when he uses James Stewart and Carole Lombard and Claudette Colbert and Gary Cooper, "these powerful screen icons are more powerful in the films of other directors." (Lombard in *To Be or Not to Be*? Stewart in *The Shop Around the Corner*?) That masterpiece *Trouble in Paradise*? Not only is it "synthetic" but "there is no emotional tension between the three principal players." Besides, it has the temerity to employ a European locale, which "has a distancing effect: these shenanigans would play out differently in 'Boston.'" So true—that's why it *has* a European locale: It's about Europe.

Not only that, but Lubitsch wasn't an intellectual: "He was not at ease in the presence of a Thomas Mann or Max Reinhardt." In fact, "like Korngold, he was a clever middlebrow craftsman mistaken for a highbrow genius." Another strike against him: Lubitsch, according to Samson Raphaelson, had "a wretched, meaningless home life." Of Lubitsch's films, only *Ninotchka* comes up to Horowitz's standards. Even so, the fact "that *Ninotchka* is Garbo's most enduring film must be considered a disappointment. She deserved to attempt Hamlet or Joan of Arc." Does Horowitz have any sense of humor at all? Anyone who so totally fails to appreciate

Lubitsch simply has no business writing about the movies, since he so obviously fails to understand what a movie is.

Artists in Exile anatomizes many of the important European directors who came to Hollywood and either succeeded there (that is, Americanized themselves), or couldn't or wouldn't forget their European roots and after the war went home. Not surprisingly, the ones who stayed and became recognizably American directors—including Otto Preminger, Billy Wilder, Fred Zinnemann, Douglas Sirk, William Wyler, and (exceptions to the rule) Lubitsch and Michael Curtiz—were younger than the ones who departed: Fritz Lang, Jean Renoir, Max Ophuls, Victor Sjöström, all of whom had had important careers in Europe and so had major reputations to return to. F. W. Murnau, alas, died in California in a car crash, leaving behind two masterpieces—*Sunrise* and *Tabu*—but he was essentially peripheral to Hollywood, and knew it. To get the full flavor of what the exiles experienced, one should read Ophuls's wonderful memoir, *Souvenirs*, with commentaries in which his son, Marcel, and his widow describe how he was taken up in Hollywood—and let down—by Preston Sturges.

Horowitz industriously sketches all these careers, giving us his (somewhat naïve) take on their accomplishments and failures. But although he writes feelingly of a few individual films—*Sunrise*, *The Wind*—the movies come across as new territory for him; he seems to be learning on the job. What can we make of someone who cites Hollywood's "dual German-American beginnings"? What German-American beginnings are those? Edison? Griffith? DeMille?

In a footnote early in his book, Horowitz acknowledges the ambiguous nature of his project: "In my title, I use the terms *exile* and *refugee* loosely." But this title has set up expectations that not only go unfulfilled but baffle the reader as he tries to follow the book's argument. At other points Horowitz says that his book is really about the impact of immigrant artists on our culture. No foreign movie star, however, had a more sensational impact on America than Rudolf Valentino, who is barely mentioned. (Even his sometime lover, the Polish silent star Pola Negri, is given a few paragraphs, and she was no more a refugee than he was.) Don't Italians count—unless they're Toscanini?

No one could expect Horowitz to be all-inclusive, but glaring omissions like Valentino throw the reader off-balance. The author declares that he's concentrating on émigrés who resided here a long time (as Valentino did, until his death), even if they eventually went home or chose not to become citizens. Which is fair enough if "exile" is really his subject. But if it's "impact," who, say, had more of it than Enrico Caruso, who dominated opera in America for close to twenty years and, indeed, married an American? (He's mentioned several times, but only in passing.) A number of great opera singers, in fact, settled here permanently: Ezio Pinza and Lauritz Melchior, two of the very greatest and neither a political exile, were here before the war, stayed through the war, and remained after the war, going on to successful careers on Broadway and in Hollywood. Don't *singers* count?

Despite its claim to a coherent large idea, what, finally, we have in *Artists in Exile* is a highly arbitrary catchall of mini-biographies, plus perceptions and analyses of widely disparate originality and merit. Perhaps we should just relax and salute Horowitz for the brave effort that's gone into piecing together an account of so many different disciplines and packing in so much information. But the difference between his solid grasp of musical history and his fragile hold on dance, theater, and the movies exposes the pitfalls of amateur interdisciplinary scholarship. A hot track in today's academy, this approach to cultural history generally adds up to knowing a little bit about a lot of things, and—without solid underpinnings—forcing shaky connections in order to fit a concept. Horowitz just doesn't know how much he doesn't know, and by stretching himself so widely and arbitrarily, he's built his edifice on treacherous ground.

May 15, 2008

The Hitmaker: George S. Kaufman

George S. Kaufman, a founding wit of the Algonquin Round Table and probably the greatest hitmaker in Broadway history—*You Can't Take It with You, The Man Who Came to Dinner, Of Thee I Sing*, and a score more—is currently being celebrated, or, you might say, exhumed, by the Library of America, in a volume of nine plays called *Kaufman & Co.*. Why "& Co."? Because Kaufman (he pronounced it "Koffman") was the American theater's busiest collaborator: Of the dozens of straight plays he wrote, only one, *The Butter and Egg Man*, was by him solo. Presumably, he did it to show that he could, but, despite its success, he went right back to working with others. To Howard Teichmann, the co-author of his last hit play, *The Solid Gold Cadillac*, he wrote, "A thought on collaboration. It is marriage without sex, and subject to many vexations. But pay no attention to them, because in one respect at least it is wonderful. The total result is frequently far more than the combined abilities of two people might give you. . . . And if I don't know about collaboration who the hell does?"

There had been many collaborators before Teichmann. The first, when Kaufman was fourteen and growing up in Pittsburgh, was Irving Pichel, who was to become a Hollywood director; the play was a father-son melodrama called *The Failure*. Needless to say, nothing came of it. Kaufman's first significant partner was Marc Connelly, with whom, in 1921, he wrote his first hit, *Dulcy* (the play that made Lynn Fontanne a star), and two other hits, *Merton of the Movies* and *Beggar on Horseback*. But the work habits of the two men were different, their ambitions were different, and they agreed to part company—Connelly to write *The Green Pastures*, a Pulitzer Prize–winning all-black fantasy featuring "De Lawd." None of the Connelly collaborations are included in the Library of

America volume, probably because none are really known today. The movies made of them, both silent and in sound, are obscure, and so the plays, rarely revived, have no recognition value for us. But *Merton* might well have been squeezed in, to flesh out the concept of "Co." And *Beggar on Horseback*, a somewhat odd adaptation of a German Expressionist romance, if that isn't a contradiction in terms, was considered adventurous and literary in its day, and has novelty value, at least.

In 1924, Kaufman began his long working relationship with the bestselling novelist Edna Ferber (*Show Boat, So Big, Giant*). Theirs was a fraught friendship and collaboration. Many people thought she was in love with him, but she was physically unattractive, demanding, and aggressive—not qualities that appealed to him in women. They had three great successes together, spread out over ten years—*The Royal Family, Dinner at Eight*, and *Stage Door*—all of which we know best today through the movie versions. The latter two are considerably superior to the plays they're based on: Not only does film tone down their staginess, but wouldn't you rather see Hollywood's *Dinner at Eight* cast—Jean Harlow, John and Lionel Barrymore, Wallace Beery, Billie Burke, and the sublime Marie Dressler—than the cast of some pallid revival? Ferber, caustic as usual, resented the fuss made about David O. Selznick's all-star spectacular. "Very good," she commented. "I wonder who wrote it."

As for *Stage Door*, the wonderful Gregory La Cava film doesn't have the luminous Margaret Sullavan repeating her stage triumph, but it does have Katharine Hepburn and Ginger Rogers in brilliant contrast, and far sharper and more amusing dialogue, a lot of it improvised. Too bad the Library of America couldn't have given us the movie script instead of, or in addition to, the more sentimental stage version. (Ferber was incorrigibly romantic about the theater; Kaufman was more skeptical.)

In her autobiography, *A Peculiar Treasure*, Ferber downplays the tensions between the two partners, but in later years (and after two flops) Kaufman refused to have anything more to do with her. "I am an old man and not well," he wrote to her. "I have had two or three strokes already and I cannot afford another argument with you to finish my life. So I simply wish to end our friendship." Eventually they made up, and, shortly before he died, she visited his sickbed. He barely responded to her presence, but as she left the apartment she heard him calling, "Edna! Edna, come back here." When she rushed into the bedroom, he was sitting up and alert. "Edna," he asked, "are you going to the funeral?" "What funeral?" "Yours. You're dead, Edna, dead!" And fell back onto his pillows. This macabre incident hardly suggests that Kaufman was deeply invested in their reconciliation.

And then there were the Marx Brothers. *The Cocoanuts* and *Animal Crackers* were the only two shows that Kaufman wrote specifically for stars, and, since the boys were constantly changing lines and stage business, they amounted to (unwelcome) collaborators. As Alexander Woollcott put it, the Marxes were "inclined to get out of any vehicle and carry it instead." Backstage at *The Cocoanuts* one night, Kaufman irritated his pal Heywood Broun by interrupting him in the middle of a story. "Well, I had to," Kaufman apologized. "I thought I heard one of the original lines of the show." Working with the Marxes was hell all the way—at the first reading of the *Cocoanuts* script, Harpo and Chico fell asleep. Besides, Kaufman said, "how can you write for Harpo? What do you put down on paper? All you can say is 'Harpo enters,' and then he's on his own."

Oddly, though, the work he did for the Brothers holds up better than some of his more highly praised, conventional comedies. He doesn't fight their anarchic spirit but reaches out to it. The stage business is appropriately demented, the dialogue for Groucho is echt Groucho. "You want ice water in Room 202? I'll send up an onion. That'll make your ice water." And Groucho's ad-libs became an added attraction—playgoers kept coming back to see what he'd pull next. One night, with President Coolidge in the audience, he stopped the show: "Isn't it a little bit past your bedtime, Cal?" But, despite the liberties he took with the script, Groucho knew what he had in Kaufman. "Kaufman molded me," he said. "Kaufman gave me the walk and the talk." You could make a case for Groucho being George S. Kaufman's most lasting contribution to posterity.

Kaufman's assistant on *The Cocoanuts* was Morrie Ryskind, who was also involved in his other Marx Brothers projects, including the script for *A Night at the Opera*. More important, he was the co-author of *Of Thee I Sing*, the 1931 satirical musical about politics that not only became a smash hit but was the first musical to be awarded a Pulitzer Prize. Produced at the height of the Depression, *Of Thee I Sing*, with a gleeful score by the Gershwins, was something totally new on Broadway, unless you count its obvious debt to Gilbert and Sullivan. The hero is John P. Wintergreen— "Wintergreen for President! / Wintergreen for President! / He's the man the people choose; / Loves the Irish and the Jews"—who gets elected on a platform of Love: "Love is sweeping the country; / Waves are hugging the shore; / All the sexes / From Maine to Texas / Have never known such love before." It's all breezy fun, with Kaufman's chief target the utter pointlessness of America's vice president, in this case the bumbling but adorable Alexander Throttlebottom. The Supreme Court, beauty contests, and "Ze French" also come in for gentle ribbing, but the satire, like all of Kaufman's, is good-natured: It's not that he pulls his punches but that there *are* no punches, just featherweight jabs. The ferocious bite of a true satirist—a Molière, a Swift, a Twain (Kaufman's hero)—is absent from his work, reserved for his famous put-downs at the expense of private victims.

The most important collaboration was that with Moss Hart, which began, in 1930, with *Once in a Lifetime*—a satirical take on Hollywood—and went on to the two biggest hits of Kaufman's career, *You Can't Take It with You*, which ran for two years and won him a second Pulitzer, and *The Man Who Came to Dinner*, based on the shenanigans of his great pal Woollcott. *You Can't Take It with You* is deservedly the best known of Kaufman's plays, frequently revived and still enjoyable. What sets it apart is that the characters, however calculated their zaniness, seem human, not stick figures cracking wise. Frank Capra's film version (which won the Best Picture Oscar for 1938) is how we know it best, and, unless you're irredeemably anti-Capra, you can't help falling for Jean Arthur, James Stewart, Edward Arnold, Spring Byington, Ann Miller, and the other residents and visitors at the house of Grandpa Vanderhof—Lionel Barrymore, in one of his typical smarmy-gnarly impersonations. The message is pure Capra, but it's also pure Kaufman: Naïve goofballs outfox greedy business types; money is the root of all evil; don't waste your life on uncongenial hard work. Instead, take up the xylophone, make fireworks (or fudge), take ballet lessons from impoverished comic Russians, write silly plays. It's the theme of a lot of Depression-era movies: Perhaps it provided comfort to people who had already stopped doing uncongenial hard work because they'd lost their jobs.

The Man Who Came to Dinner is closer to the typical Kaufman farce, but it stands out because of the fun of its awful hero, Sheridan Whiteside, who not only was based on the famous Woollcott but was played by him for a few weeks in a West Coast production. The idea is simple but immediately engaging. The great Whiteside, lecturing in a small Ohio town, fractures his hip and is laid up for weeks in the home of the despairing couple who have had him to dinner, and whose crime is that they're ordinary middle-class Midwesterners. Indulging himself in every petty tyranny, Whiteside disrupts their lives—undermining their authority with their children, tormenting his nurse and doctor, commandeering the phone, offending anyone in earshot with a barrage of insults. Celebrity friends turn up to amuse him—barely disguised replicas of Harpo ("Banjo"), Gertrude Lawrence, Noël Coward. And then he reveals his good heart by promoting the romance of his acerbic secretary with an idealistic young journalist, after having done his selfish best to gum it up. As usual, Kaufman draws back from the kill. (Try to avoid the disastrous Warner Bros. version, which gives us Bette Davis bravely coping with finding herself in a comedy.)

Kaufman and Hart had another hit with *I'd Rather Be Right*, in which the incomparable George M. Cohan returned to the stage to play FDR (whom he loathed) in a fanciful romance set in Central Park and featuring the usual Kaufman bland young couple and, again, the Supreme Court—apparently an irresistible target in the New Deal era. The Library of America editors don't make the mistake of including it in their collection.

Hart went his own way after a perfunctory 1940 farce called *George Washington Slept Here* failed to do particularly well, but the two men remained intimate friends for life—the much younger Hart the closest thing to a son the older man ever had. Kaufman, who had enjoyed more than a score of hits in a score of years, now experienced an almost unbroken series of failures. In the next twenty years, the only successful shows he wrote were an adaptation of John P. Marquand's *The Late George Apley*, *The Solid Gold Cadillac*, and the Cole Porter musical *Silk Stockings*. Hart's career accelerated: *Lady in the Dark*, *Winged Victory*, the scripts for *Gentleman's Agreement* and the Judy Garland *A Star Is Born*, and the direction of both *My Fair Lady* and *Camelot*. But his most lasting work is the memoir *Act One*, a tremendous bestseller in 1959, which recounts his long and painful apprenticeship in the theater, climaxed by the triumph of that first collaboration with Kaufman, *Once in a Lifetime*. Hart had written a promising play, but the amount of work needed to turn it into a success was staggering, and more than once the venture nearly foundered. Hart, the ardent neophyte, was in awe of his new partner, the most successful man on Broadway, and he provides us with our closest look at the way Kaufman approached his work:

> There was an element of the demoniacal in his tireless search for
> just the right word to round a sentence into its proper unity, for the

exact juxtaposition of words and movement that would slyly lead the audience along the periphery of a scene to its turning point and then propel them effortlessly to its climax. . . . No moment, however small, seemed unimportant enough to escape his almost fierce attention, and his grasp of the play's latent values was immediate and complete. My eyes and ears were opened anew each day to the thousand-and-one endless details that go to make up the subtle and infinitely fragile clockwork of a play's interior mechanism, and to the slow cultivation of its subsoil that gradually makes it blossom into something vital and alive. I watched and listened with the consecration of a yogi.

"Clockwork," "mechanism"—the words can be applied to the entire Kaufman oeuvre. But these are not the inexorable, subversive mechanisms of the farces of Feydeau, whose riotous chain reactions lead to berserk confusions that turn the bourgeois world upside down; they're maneuvers calculated to please and, finally, comfort a very different bourgeois world, the world of Broadway. Kaufman's ruling impulse, always, is to succeed, to win, not to impose his mordant view of life.

Winning was crucial to Kaufman not only in the theater but at croquet, his one sport, and bridge, his chief hobby, which he played at a near-expert level. "I'd rather be a poor winner than any kind of loser," he once acknowledged—or boasted. And he always had to be in control, which is no doubt why, starting in 1929, with *June Moon*, the one play he wrote with Ring Lardner, he preferred to direct his own work. (He had already started directing the work of other playwrights: The string of hit shows he staged runs from *The Front Page*, in 1928, to *Romanoff and Juliet*, in 1957, by way of *My Sister Eileen* and *Guys and Dolls*.)

The seeds of his compulsion to control and to succeed, and of others of his more disturbing characteristics, lie in a difficult childhood. The Kaufmans were relatively well-off German Jews in the Pittsburgh of 1889, the year George was born. His father was a good-natured businessman who kept changing businesses—whenever something was panning out, he got bored and moved on. His mother was both arrogant and severely neurotic. For most of her adult life, she was beset by frenzied jealousies and imaginary illnesses leading to dramatic deathbed scenes; nurses—eventually, psychiatric ones—were kept on hand to deal with her. Her husband responded by just leaving the house when things got bad: "Nettie, I'm going out for a walk. I'll be home when you get back to your senses." George had an older and a younger sister, but the sibling who affected him most powerfully was an older brother who had died as a baby. It was this tragic death, exacerbating her intense hypochondria, that led Mrs. Kaufman to the extreme measures she took to protect little Georgie. No milk—milk could make children sick. All water to be boiled. No rough games. And, especially, no close contact with others, since others could transmit disease. Georgie grew up painfully thin, painfully shy, and painfully unconfident of his abilities.

By the time he was an adult, he had become the victim of numerous phobias—constantly washing his hands, compulsively picking up real or imagined lint from the floor, and so frightened of death that sometimes he wouldn't go to bed for fear of dying in his sleep. As for contact with others, he couldn't bear to be touched: no handshakes, even. A famous story involves one of his innumerable girlfriends, who made the mistake at dinner one night of tasting his soup with her spoon, at which he immediately sent for a new bowl. Later, when he was kissing her, she remarked, "I see. You're not so worried about my germs now." "I've been looking at you all evening," he replied, "and I've decided it's worth the risk."

His sexual history was peculiar from the start. In 1905, when he was sixteen, he and six other boys signed a pact to remain pure until they married—they called it the Black and White Club, because they had set down their vow in black-and-white. It seems that they all kept their word: Certainly, Kaufman was a virgin when, at the age of twenty-seven, he married Beatrice Bakrow. And when, the next year, Beatrice had a stillborn child, Kaufman was so disturbed that he was never able to resume sexual relations with her. In due course, although they remained dependent on each other, adopted a baby, and obviously cared for each other, they went their separate sexual ways.

Kaufman, in fact, became known for the number of women he took to bed, with some of whom he maintained affairs for years while enjoying other adventures and with all of whom he remained on good terms. For a man who abhorred physical contact, he managed to rack up a good deal of it. In 1936, to his horror—and to the amazement, and relish, of the general public—he became notorious as a lover when the diaries of the beautiful movie star Mary Astor became public during an acrimonious divorce proceeding. We'll never know whether some of the entries that were printed were forged, whether they were really written in purple ink (or was it lavender? or violet?), whether there were really "many exquisite moments . . . twenty—count them, diary, twenty. . . . I don't see how he does it." We do know that it all exploded into scandal, and that Kaufman had to slip out of Los Angeles to avoid having to appear in court. The two top headlines in *The New York Times* of August 11, 1936, were CORN CROP WORST SINCE '81 and WARRANT OUT FOR KAUFMAN. The staunch Beatrice stood by him: "We have been married twenty years. We are adults, leading our lives in adult fashion. George is a good husband. I love him very much. He is in love with me despite the things that may have happened. . . . She kept a diary. Very stupid, that."

Beatrice Kaufman was as formidable a figure as her husband. She had done clever work as a press agent, a script reader, a book editor, but it was her style, her intelligence, her judgment that drew people to her. In 1928, *The New Yorker* published a hilarious Profile of her by Ring Lardner. ("It is her modest boast that she is never seen in the same costume twice and generally not even once.") This ran almost a year before the magazine got around to her husband, with Woollcott doing the honors. By then, the Round Table at the Algonquin had secured its relentless grip on the public imagination, and Kaufman, Woollcott, Robert Benchley, Dorothy Parker, Harpo, the Lunts, Harold Ross, and other current demigods were indulging themselves at lunch while slicing one another up. Typical: Kaufman, responding to a mock-anti-Semitic remark that the half Jewish Parker was studiously ignoring, stood up and announced, "I've had enough slurs on my race. I am now leaving this table, this dining room, and this hotel. And I trust that Mrs. Parker will walk out with me—halfway."

Humor had been Kaufman's entrée into the great world. After a half-baked education and some stabs at ordinary jobs (ribbon salesman was one), he began sending comments to the highly popular column put together for the *Evening Mail* by Franklin Pierce Adams—F.P.A. to the world. Adams was impressed, and found young Kaufman a column of his own, at *The Washington Times*, which lasted until the owner spotted him one day and demanded to know "What is that Jew doing in my city room?" With that, Kaufman's career in Washington was over, but, with the help of fairy godfather F.P.A., he was absorbed into the world of New York journalism, and ended up running the theater desk at the *Times*, a job he clung to for years after he became a successful playwright. It was a safety blanket—security against the disaster he was always certain was about to strike. His opening-night anxieties went well beyond the norm. After the curtain came down on one rollickingly triumphant premiere, the leading actor found him slumped against a wall "looking a little like the late Marie Antoinette in the tumbril."

This difficult, complicated man, who talked aloud to himself in the street, was generally silent in company until, suddenly, he would spring one of those famous put-downs. In Palm Springs one day, Moss Hart turned up in ludicrously elaborate Western garb, from expensive Texas boots to twenty-gallon Stetson. One look was all Kaufman needed to greet him with "Hi-yo, Platinum." When Hart bought a country estate in Bucks County, near the Kaufmans', and rebuilt and reforested it, Kaufman remarked, "This is what God could have done if He'd had money." When an inept bridge partner got up to go to the men's room, Kaufman snapped, "Fine. This is the first time this afternoon I'll know what you have in your hand." And so on. These quips, in the heyday of the Round Table, were passed around and savored, like Dorothy Parker's. They're still funny, but they lack the pure brilliance of Oscar Wilde's; and, unlike Wilde's, they were often meant to wound.

But if Kaufman could, on occasion, be brutal, he was consistently warm and attentive to his family, to Bea's family, to his (adopted) daughter, Anne. And though he rarely allowed familiarities, and fled from any kind of sentimental gesture or utterance, he was secretly generous to friends and acquaintances down on their luck. Similarly, although he constantly fretted about money and knew how to cut a deal, he was known in the business for his absolute integrity and fairness, both in financial matters and in matters of billing. His policy was simple: Whichever collaborator came up with the idea for the play was billed first. Thus, *Dinner at Eight* is by Kaufman and Ferber, while *Stage Door* is by Ferber and Kaufman. On the opening night of *Once in a Lifetime*, as the applause rolled in, he stepped forward during the curtain calls—he was appearing in the play—and, breaking an iron-clad rule of his, made an opening-night speech. It wasn't long: "I would like the audience to know that eighty percent of this play is Moss Hart."

When Beatrice suddenly died, in 1945, Kaufman was undone. "I'm through," he said. "I'll never work again. I'm through." But he did work again, and he married again, too, four years later. She was Leueen Mac-Grath, a beautiful and successful English actress many years his junior. At first, they were extremely happy—his daughter later said that these were the happiest years of his life—but the usual problems developed, and they were divorced in 1957. The divorce left them good friends, and they went on collaborating on plays, despite the fact that they had given birth to a couple of Broadway flops. But even being married to two women he loved didn't help Kaufman express feelings in his work. As he himself acknowledged, he simply could not write a love scene—if a plot required anything resembling one, it was left to the collaborator of the moment. And he was weak on characterization. Hart humanizes him, Ferber supplies sentiment, and in *June Moon* it is clearly Ring Lardner who provides the hint of disagreeable reality that is generally absent from the other comedies.

June Moon gives us Fred, the typical Kaufman young rube headed for the big city with stars in his eyes and cotton between his ears. Once he hits New York as an aspiring songwriter, he encounters not only the usual Kaufman phonies who try to take him for a ride but a pair of conniving sisters, one after his money and the other cheating on her husband. This is close-to-the-bone realism for Kaufman. Of course, the sisters are eventually outmatched, Fred strikes gold with "June Moon, shining above, / Will my true love come soon? / June Moon, I am so blue; / I know that you long for her, too," and sweet young love prevails. This is Broadway, after all.

You will encounter the equivalent of young Fred in the young George of *Once in a Lifetime,* who blunders into a triumph over the caricaturized moguls of Hollywood, and whose only discernible feature, apart from stupidity, is that he never stops cracking Indian nuts. You'll meet up with him again in *The Butter and Egg Man,* Kaufman's solo effort about the theater; this time around, he's young Peter, the wide-eyed sucker who learns fast and ends up out-suckering the sharpies. And here he comes again, as young Merton in *Merton of the Movies,* another swipe at Hollywood, in which a total naïf (he starts out as a clerk in Gashwiler's General Store in Simsbury, Illinois) stumbles his way to stardom. Needless to say, in all these plays boy meets girl, boy loses girl, boy gets girl—in other words, they're romantic comedies masquerading as satires.

When, in the more spacious collaborations with Ferber and Hart, Kaufman strays from this formula, his sure command of structure, dialogue, and pace holds everything together. But when he strikes out into serious territory, as in the 1939 patriotic pageant *The American Way,* written with Hart and starring Fredric March, the results are unfortunate. We follow through the decades the lives of the Gunthers, a German immigrant couple who succeed in America and love their adopted country. At a rabble-rousing Fascist meeting, Martin Gunther as an old man

356

speaks up ("Do not bring this madness over here! . . . Democracy is *not* finished") and is beaten to death by local goons. His funeral oration:

> To Martin Gunther we pay a just homage. For it may be truly said that he was an American. He lived as an American; he died as an American. I can think of no finer epitaph. I see in the life of Martin Gunther, and even in his death, high hope for America. It will go on, this country, so long as we keep alive the thing that Martin Gunther died for. Let us keep this land of ours, which we love so dearly, a land of hope and freedom.
> (*A single voice starts "The Star-spangled Banner." Another joins in, then more and more, until every voice in the Square is uplifted in the national anthem. Men, women, children—their voices mount to a fervid finish.*)
> CURTAIN.

I'll say.

Kaufman died in 1961. In the seventies, three long biographies were published—by Howard Teichmann, Scott Meredith, and Malcolm Goldstein—on which I have drawn for the facts of his life. These books differ in approach and tone, but they share the assumption that Kaufman was an important figure, whose work mattered. A quarter of a century later, the Library of America is making the same claim. But then the Library of America is, as its publisher, Max Rudin, recently stated in *Publishers Weekly*, "expanding what the notion of great American literature is." Is this code for dumbing down? Or are we really meant to believe that *The Royal Family* and *Animal Crackers* fulfill *anybody's* notion of what great literature is?

When I was a kid, and theater-mad, I not only spent all my allowance on Broadway matinees but avidly read plays of the past. One of my favorites was *The Man Who Came to Dinner*; I couldn't get over the hilarity of Sheridan Whiteside's first line—"I may vomit"—or his comeback to a nervous neighbor who has brought him a jar of calf's-foot jelly: "Made from your own foot, I have no doubt." This play, unlike most of the others by "Kaufman & Co.," still has some vitality, but I no longer find myself laughing. Either I've lost my sense of humor or it has evolved. Or the world has moved on.

The easy laugh, the insistent cleverness of the plot mechanisms—the very qualities that delighted pre-war Broadway—may explain why today, with the well-made play a thing of the past, Kaufman's work seems for the most part so bloodless and predictable. Even at the height of his fame, the danger was clear to some observers. In a 1939 *Time* cover story, Louis Kronenberger wrote of Kaufman's career,

> It proclaims an amazing foresight in always taking the pulse of Broadway as the clue to its heart, a habit of always writing fashionable plays and never revolutionary ones. It proclaims a playwright who has made sport of everything while never giving offense to anybody. It proclaims a really great practical theatre mind, with no philosophy except that the theatre is entertainment and that good entertainment pays.

Great literature endures, but even first-rate entertainments fade. It doesn't take away from Kaufman's genius for success or from the pleasure he provided audiences for so long that today his work reads like a footnote to literature, rather than the thing itself.

November 29, 2004

The Storyteller: Rudyard Kipling

Everything about Kipling is extreme—the abundance of his talent, his precocity, his early fame and success, the variety of literary forms he mastered, the passionate admiration and loathing he evoked in critics and readers, the contradictions within him, the contradictions in the way he has been perceived, both during his life and since his death.

About his precocity, there are no contradictions. Born on December 30, 1865, he had seen his early "Schoolboy Lyrics" printed (privately, by his mother) by the time he was sixteen. By the time he was twenty-one, poems and stories were appearing in profusion in both India and England. By the time he was twenty-five, he had published the stories collected in *Plain Tales from the Hills, Soldiers Three, The Story of the Gadsbys, In Black and White, Under the Deodars, The Phantom Rickshaw,* and *Wee Willie Winkie*; had completed his famous, if flawed, novel *The Light That Failed*; and had suffered a breakdown. By thirty he had published his *Barrack-Room Ballads* and the two volumes of *The Jungle Book*, and was completing *Captains Courageous*. At thirty-five, he had *Stalky & Co.* and *Kim* behind him. At forty, he had written the *Just So Stories* and had twice refused a knighthood. (Later, he was twice to refuse the Order of Merit.) At forty-one he won the Nobel Prize. Not even Dickens, the writer he in so many ways resembles, got off to a faster start. Yet despite this extraordinary level of early performance and success, and although his output after forty was to be smaller in quantity and less to the pubic taste than what preceded it, his finest work was still to come.

Kipling's most ardent admirers would not suggest that he is a writer on the level of Shakespeare and Dickens, yet he shares with them—and with no other major English writer of fiction or drama—this thrilling, prolific beginning. His limitless facility, combined with his uncanny powers of observation and an unabashed passion for the very act of writing, propelled him through scores of stories and a vast amount of poetry in half a dozen years. Reading this early work—all of it polished and professional, even those stories that are slight or formulaic—one senses a young man's sheer joy in having so great a subject, India, to grapple with, and his absolute confidence that he can master it. At this point, he is (again, like Dickens) working as a journalist, devouring the world around him and rushing to report everything he sees. He had spent his early childhood in India and had returned there as a very young man, and he knew it inside out—the British sahibs and memsahibs, of course, but also the enlisted men, both English and "native"; the Sikhs, the Pathans, the Afghans; the water boys and the elephant drivers; the half-castes and priests and merchants and lepers; even the dogs and the snakes and the polo ponies. He knew how the government administered and how the bureaucracy stifled. He recognized the thrills of colonial ambition and the perils of colonial isolation. He realized what England had done for and to India, and what India had done for and to the English. And his great luck was that this knowledge, in tandem with his formidable gifts, gave him an exotic and fascinating world with which to attract a large public; he was like a traveler returning from outer space with the first solid news about Mars. Almost overnight, Kipling captured the attention of English-speaking readers everywhere with his revelations of the India that was the heart of Victoria's empire.

India, then, is almost exclusively the subject of Kipling's early career. But there is one significant exception, and that is "Baa Baa, Black Sheep," the famous account of his anguished years as a small boy in England, to which his parents had exiled him and his even younger sister (he was six, she was only three) to be educated and, as it were, Englished in the care of foster parents. This story (to the extent that it *is* a story and not a superficially altered burst of autobiography) of the child Rudyard's six years of torment in what he calls the House of Desolation is an isolated, and therefore especially unsettling, account of the great trauma of his life—what he clearly felt to be an abandonment into misery and degradation. We cannot know how literally accurate the details of his humiliation at the hands of the "Holloways" are—he more or less corroborated them many years later in his formal autobiography, and his sister, in her old age, further confirmed them—but we certainly sense that this is an accurate account of his feelings; feelings that until much later in his life are almost totally missing from his work. Dickens, suffering a comparable if less severe trauma in his months in the blacking factory, did not write about it directly until *David Copperfield*, when he was nearly forty, but his emotions about that time permeate *Oliver Twist*, *Nicholas Nickleby*, *The Old Curiosity Shop*, and *Dombey and Son*, all of which involve tormented and endangered children. Kipling appears to have lived in a peculiar state of denial: Not only does the central event of his young life go unrecorded except in this one story, but his profound sense of the blackness of life is suppressed for many years.

One can, however, infer the severity of the trauma from the insistence of two themes in his work, one reflecting the idea of who he was before he was damaged, the other reflecting his unquenchable rage at what had been done to him, yet neither acknowledging, even obliquely, the event itself. In a series of somewhat cloying stories, Kipling presents a little boy who not only lives in a paradise of adoring parents and servants (the idealized India of his earliest youth) but has total power over his environment. In "Tod's Amendment," "Wee Willie Winkie," "Son of his Father," and others—all of them both fantasies of unrestricted power and elegies for a lost kingdom—the little boy easily and gaily dominates his world, and woe to them who try to frustrate him. And then, in literally dozens of stories dealing with childhood, adolescence, and adulthood, emerges the theme of revenge. It's as if Dumas had gone on writing *The Count of Monte Cristo* over and over again. Most blatantly, almost all the episodes in *Stalky & Co.*, Kipling's romanticized reinvention of his school days, involve the success of the three young heroes at getting their own back (and then some) at schoolmates or masters who have displeased them—in one story, "The Moral Reformers," revenge takes the form of physical abuse amounting to sadism. It isn't mere late-Victorian squeamishness that prompted a reviewer, in 1899, to refer to *Stalky*'s "piling on of youthful brutality beyond all need."

Revenge is by far the most frequent hinge to Kipling's stories: Husbands kill unfaithful wives; obnoxious officials are taught lessons; downtrodden employees punish employers; boors are humiliated (sadistically, again, in "A Friend's Friend"); uppity young subalterns are put in their place. Hoaxes, elaborate practical jokes, physical punishment, public disgraces—all these provide the mechanisms by which Kipling's anger is compulsively rekindled and assuaged. But were it not for "Baa Baa, Black Sheep" and corroborating biographical data, we would find it impossible to understand Kipling's violent swings between idyllic happiness and savage resentment. Reticent in life, silent in his fiction, he gives us only two clues to the intensity of his suppressed suffering: this one story, and the nervous breakdown of 1890 (of "overwork"). There are many instances of tragedy punctuating the Indian stories, but these are observed, impersonal tragedies. George Moore put it succinctly: "Mr. Kipling has seen much more than he has felt." This freeze on emotion and self-examination left him most at ease in the world of boys and boy-men whose strongest bonds are with one another, in school or as comrades-in-arms. (Or with animals: David Malouf, in his libretto for Michael Berkeley's opera *Baa Baa, Black Sheep*, makes a powerful case for considering Mowgli, living among the creatures of *The Jungle Book*, to be a mirror image or projection of the boy Punch among the Holloways.)

One psychological peculiarity that strikes the reader is that the people whose actions led to the trauma—the mother and father who, for whatever well-meaning reasons, dispatched Kipling to the House of Desolation—are not punished or even reprimanded in his fiction. (Or in life: Kipling was always touchingly devoted to both his parents.) Perhaps if he could have brought himself to blame he would have found it easier to forgive. As it is, his fathers and mothers are usually idealized, offstage, or dead: Kim is not the only orphan in his fiction.

Strangely, movingly, it is only when Kipling himself is punished as a parent—by the loss of his beloved daughter Josephine at the age of six (in 1899) and, more decisively, by the loss of his son, John, in the war in 1915—that he begins to expose his feelings to himself and deal with them in fiction. So that, emerging from this second House of Desolation by confronting it, he begins to evolve from his compulsive need for revenge to a new embrace of healing. His most complex and profound stories come toward the end, one of them—"Dayspring Mishandled," written in 1928—a long, convoluted work in which a lifelong and diabolical plan for revenge gives way at last to pity and regret. Bruised by the torrent of Kipling's revenge tragedies and comedies, we come away from this story uncertain who is most relieved by its therapeutic resolution its central character, Kipling, or ourselves.

Acts of healing are to be found throughout these later stories—from the healing of a house seemingly inhabited by ghosts ("The House Surgeon"), to the healing of breakdown ("An Habitation Enforced"), to the healing of shell-shock in a surprising number of post-war works. In fact, and significantly, whereas Kipling's interest in the wars of his youth lay in the way soldiers lived and fought, and in the adventure of battle, the First World War stories are almost entirely concerned with the effect of war on people, combatants and noncombatants alike. These stories—even the notoriously violent "Mary Postgate"—are about pain endured rather than pain inflicted.

If we can now readily isolate the themes of Paradise Lost and revenge in Kipling's early stories, at the time they were written what would have registered most was their actual material—the specifics. Kipling's love of detail, his descriptive powers, and his dogged insistence on understanding how everything works remain consistent over forty years. In the beginning, it is the workings of India—*everything* about India—that grips him; that is why the hundred or so Indian tales are even more impressive taken together than read singly: They add up to an immense and convincing record of a way of life. It is only when India recedes and other subjects catch his attention that one comes to realize that the question of how things work—*any* things—is as important to Kipling as India itself. He wants to know, and to dramatize, not only how wars are fought and countries governed but how ships are sailed and hedges are trimmed; how inanimate objects operate and how animals think. He digs into the technicalities of cars, radios, airplanes, as they emerge into general use. (Sometimes these stories are pure exercises in scientific popularization, yet in "Wireless" the excitements of early radio are made the basis, or background, of serious fiction.) Since most readers' first impressions of Kipling are of nineteenth-century India and of the children's books, and because his early start as a writer, in the 1880s, places him for us as late Victorian, it is startling to find references throughout the later work to such phenomena as Hollywood and "Kodaking," and to come upon a line like this one from "Dayspring Mishandled": "This was before the days of Freud." But these oddities do not strike one as modern touches worked up by Kipling to demonstrate that he is still on top of things; rather, they are further reflections of his ceaseless curiosity about the world and its workings.

This curiosity extended to the future and how *it* would work—as in "With the Night Mail," a powerful and original piece of science fiction. And, more and more, he tried to explain the past—not only in the *Puck of Pook's Hill* stories, in which England's history is anatomized for young readers through the magic of Puck, but in the late historical/religious stories, in which he approaches the narratives of early Christianity and the rituals of Heaven and Hell with the same vigorous need to explicate them that he felt for the mechanics of the Indian bureaucracy and the mysteries of the steam engine.

His very virtuosity often led him into exaggeration and self-parody in this kind of story. Much of the collection *The Day's Work* is uncomfortable to read—especially the coyness of having locomotives and ship engines and folksy Vermont horses (one named Tedda Gabler!) think aloud. Yet even in this questionable genre the reader can be amused and convinced, as by "The Maltese Cat," about a polo match seen from the point of view of the ponies, in which ingenuity and exciting action blunt the cuteness. It was this direction in Kipling's fiction that Henry James deplored in an often-cited letter of 1897: "In his earliest time I thought he perhaps contained the seeds of an English Balzac; but I have quite given up in proportion as he has come steadily from the less simple in subject to the more simple—from the Anglo-Indians to the natives, from the natives to the Tommies, from the Tommies to the quadrupeds, from the quadrupeds to the fish, and from the fish to the engines and screws." But James balances this justified disparagement in a letter written a year earlier ("I am laid low by the absolute uncanny talent—the prodigious special faculty of it. . . . He's a rum 'un—one of the very few first *talents* of the time"), and in another letter two years later, in which after expressing his disgust at Kipling's "loud brazen verse" he goes on to say, "His talent I think quite diabolically great." (James Joyce, too, as Norman Page points out in his invaluable *A Kipling Companion*, cited Kipling—along with D'Annunzio and Tolstoy—as one of the nineteenth century's "greatest natural talents.") Alas, James didn't live to read those stories in which Kipling's talent was to be applied to material that James would certainly have found more congenial than talking locomotives—in fact, on occasion, to semi-Jamesian données, as in "Dayspring Mishandled."

James's ambivalence about Kipling is particularly worth noting because it presages the ambivalence of so much of the criticism and comment to come. No writer of the period—except perhaps James himself—has been so worried over, so condemned and reclaimed. Certainly no writer of the period has had so many remarkable explicators, among them T. S. Eliot, W. H. Auden, C. S. Lewis, George Orwell, Edmund Wilson, Lionel Trilling, Randall Jarrell, Angus Wilson, Kingsley Amis. And there is important work being done on Kipling today—by dueling biographers and by outstanding critics like J.M.S. Tompkins and Craig Raine. Eliot was primarily concerned with reconsidering the poetry, but he shares with his fellow critics the urge to rescue Kipling—or to place him, their efforts underlining the fact that, given his "diabolically great" talent, he has to be acknowledged and dealt with. However difficult a specimen he is to pin down, and however much one may dislike aspects of his mind and manner, he cannot be ignored.

Much of the problem has been political. Because India shifted so abruptly from being Britain's great colonial achievement to being Britain's great colonial shame, and because of the strident jingoism of many of Kipling's poems and pronouncements, by the First World War he had become identified as the foremost spokesman for British imperialism—as politically incorrect as a writer can be. Although the India tales are far more ambivalent about Britain's role in the subcontinent than might at first appear, and although Kipling in the 1920s wrote with anguish about the recent war, he was labeled then and thereafter as a reactionary, a glorifier of war, and an imperialist. (Shakespeare has suffered similar accusations in regard to the shamelessly propagandistic and Tudor-flattering history plays.) Norman Page quotes that canny belletrist Bonamy Dobrée as saying, as early as 1929, "It will only be possible to give him his rightful place when the political heats of his day have become coldly historical." That moment may have come: Surely we can now read and judge the stories as fiction, and the poems as poetry, without feeling apologetic about responding to their genius. But with the cooling of political heat comes the responsibility to identify the nature of that genius.

Some of the difficulty in doing so lies in the multiplicity of Kipling's interests, in his uncanny aptitude for impersonating other writers, and in the nature of his growth as an artist. In his early work he can remind us of near-contemporaries like Mark Twain (the two writers admired each other); Robert Louis Stevenson (in 1889, Henry James writes to Stevenson, "We'll tell you all about Rudyard Kipling—your nascent rival; he has killed one immortal—Rider Haggard; the star of the hour, aged 24"); Conan Doyle; H. G. Wells; Jules Verne; even Wilde and Pinero. Here is a typical exchange of dialogue from "A Second-Rate Woman," one of the Mrs. Hauksbee stories of Anglo-Indian social life:

Mrs. Mallowe—"I always prefer to believe the best of everybody. It saves so much trouble."

Mrs. Hauksbee—"Very good. I prefer to believe the worst. It saves useless expenditure of sympathy."

Kipling wasn't really interested in tossing off epigrams à la Wilde; he was echoing the kind of hard chatter he heard from his mother and other clever women of her kind. But he was also tapping into a literary vein of the moment, unable to resist his talent for mimicry.

And just as he couldn't help testing diverse literary styles and genres, he couldn't dampen his enthusiasm for dialect—as with Mulvaney's Irish speech throughout the *Soldiers Three* stories; or a Pathan's, as in "Dray Wara Yow Dee"; or a Sikh's, in "A Sahibs' War"; or a Frenchman's turn of phrase in "The Bull That Thought." His descriptive power—his eye—was as acute as that of any English writer, and his ear was equally acute. Dickens indulged his love of melodrama in his famous readings and theatricals; the more timid Kipling becomes instead a ventriloquist, performing on the page in a series of monologues whose content often matters less to him (and to us) than the verisimilitude of the narrator's voice.

Another kind of story is set within a formal frame, with an anonymous "I" introducing the action and commenting on it (and sometimes subtly undermining it). In this, Kipling suggests Conrad, that other great documenter of imperialism. But the trajectories of the two careers are almost diametrically opposite. Conrad, born eight years before Kipling but not publishing his first book until 1895, moves from the ornamental and literary *Almayer's Folly* and *An Outcast of the Islands*, to the profound intuition and despair of his middle period, to the potboilers of the years before his death, in 1924. Kipling begins with all the easy brio of an indefatigable born journalist and moves through a somewhat confused and self-conscious middle period, when his first great subject has dried up for him, into a final period that reveals a new depth of feeling and understanding.

In the best of these latter stories—undoubtedly evoked by the death of his children and the devastation of war—Kipling is a changed man, although we still note his insatiable curiosity about how things work and his extraordinary facility; there are stories of this period that could easily have been written thirty years earlier. But there are also superb war stories—in particular, the implacable "Mary Postgate" and the mystical "The Gardener." And there are stories—the above-mentioned included—in which women are no longer either the clever and manipulating matrons of Simla or the foolish (or worse) young girls who trap or undo wholesome young men but are formidable protagonists. (One of these, "The Wish House," with its grim awareness of old age and approaching death, its evocation of passion and sacrifice, its supernatural ambiguities, and the sheer genius of its dialogue, dialect, and detail, can make a solid claim to be considered Kipling's finest story.) And there are the religious stories. All of this later work may or may not appear to us more valuable than the best of the early work, but it unquestionably helps us chart a progression that would have surprised Henry James, from the brilliantly simple to the brilliantly complex, and from a focus on the external world to a probing of the interior—a progression that no one could have imagined in the early years and that reminds us of how hard a worker and how complicated a man Kipling was. Ironically, by the time he was producing his most intricate and charged work, the literary world had left him far behind. When he died, in 1936, he must have seemed as ancient and irrelevant as a dinosaur to readers of Lawrence, Joyce, Woolf, Forster, Hemingway, Faulkner, Waugh. Not only was he a political throwback but his defining qualities of observation, curiosity, and energy—his very facility—would have seemed hopelessly out of date. Though not to the young. The children's books, at least, have remained staples from the time of their writing until now.

In general, there is comforting agreement among the various anthologizers and commentators as to which are the best of Kipling's stories, though there is occasional disagreement, too. For instance, Angus Wilson, in his perceptive book *The Strange Ride of Rudyard Kipling*, cannot embrace "Mrs. Bathurst," a story that others, myself among them, find powerful and moving. (Craig Raine is particularly helpful on this impacted and ambiguous story.) But almost all critics would include on their list of Kipling's best "Baa Baa, Black Sheep," "The Man Who Would Be King," "The Wish House," "The Gardener," "On Greenlow Hill," "The Bridge-Builders," and "Mary Postgate." Yet even these masterpieces hardly demonstrate the wide scope of Kipling's interests and techniques. "Mrs. Hauksbee Sits Out" is representative of the amusing playlets he enjoyed composing; "The City of Dreadful Night" is a virtuoso display of descriptive writing; "Jew in Shushan" is a surprising expression of Kipling's sympathies; "A Bank Fraud" shows the attractive side of his sentimentality; "The Strange Ride of Morrowbie Jukes" has a powerful allegorical quality; "A Wayside Comedy" is startlingly explicit about sexual relationships. "The Mark of the Beast" is a horror story, "With the Night

Mail" is science fiction, "The House Surgeon" has ghosts. "The Drums of the Fore and Aft" is an extraordinary depiction of battle. "The Head of the District" displays Kipling's consummate grasp of how Victoria's India *worked*. "Love-o'-Women" confronts passion, "Without Benefit of Clergy" confronts love. "The Man Who Would Be King" is a superb adventure (and was made into a superb John Huston movie, Michael Caine and Sean Connery joining Ronald Colman, Victor McLaglen, Lionel Barrymore, Walter Huston, Stewart Granger, David Niven, Errol Flynn, Cary Grant, Douglas Fairbanks Jr., Spencer Tracy, and Sabu in a long line of Kipling film heroes). And "The Bridge-Builders" is both a lesson in engineering and a compelling religious phantasmagoria.

Of course, each of these stories is other things, too—Kipling would not be the finest writer of short stories in English if his work could be so easily reduced and pigeonholed. That he was far less successful as a novelist suggests his limitations but does not detract from his achievement: Reading the entire body of his stories only confirms James's recognition of his prodigious talent. In fact, there has been no writer since Dickens whose talent was so immediately apparent to readers and critics alike; no talent so lavish and fluent. If through most of his life Kipling used this fluency, or facility, to hide behind, the mask itself is never less than spellbinding.

October 1994

Lit-Flicks

Question: What do Shakespeare, Molière, Jane Austen, and the Brontës have in common other than genius?
Answer: They've all been the subject of movies that aim to show us how great writers do the thing they do—that is, write.

We're not talking about movies that recapitulate a highly dramatic event in the writer's life: the Dreyfus affair in *The Life of Emile Zola*; Oscar Wilde's trial in a scattering of Wilde movies. Or a special case like the film of *The Hours*, Michael Cunningham's highfalutin novel that glossed the life of Virginia Woolf and provided Nicole Kidman with an Oscar-winning nose. We're talking about movies that think they can convey something about "the creative process" by dishing up conventional plots for their heroes against lots of period decor: Boy meets girl, boy loses girl, we get *Hamlet*.

Actually, in *Shakespeare in Love* we get *Romeo and Juliet*. Joseph Fiennes is darting around Olde London hoping to scrounge up an idea for a new play, and then he encounters Viola (Gwyneth Paltrow), the young heiress who's madly stagestruck and far more interested in the young Bard than in the powerful aristocrat she's duty-bound to marry. The Queen herself—Judi Dench in her own Oscar mode—has okayed the marriage, though she has her doubts. (No fool, she.)

Forget the cuckoo tongue-in-cheek plot, along with the doublets and the candelabra and the cleavage; forget the Will-Viola kiss-fest that quickly turns into a fuck-fest (oh, those lusty Elizabethans!); forget the dedicated-to-the-theater yet comical antics of the Players. And listen to the message on the current *Shakespeare in Love* DVD package: "When Will Shakespeare needs passionate inspiration to break a bad case of writer's block, a secret romance with the beautiful Lady Viola starts the words flowing like never before!"

The key word is "inspiration," and the message of all these lit-flicks (as well as film bios of the more flamboyant painters and composers) is that to get the job done—to write the great play, compose the great symphony, paint the Sistine Chapel or the bridge at Arles—you need to Experience Life. Which means you need to fall in love—and then lose the loved one. And suffer. Yes, young Will Shakespeare may have done some effective work before *Romeo*—that's why theater managers are hounding him to come up with something new—but it's only when sparks start to fly between him and Lady V. that the poetry perks up. Pre-Viola we see the quill faltering in his ink-stained hand, blotched and incomplete pages flung to the floor. (His more personal tool has lost its touch, too.) Post-Viola, the quill flies across the foolscap—whole acts are tossed off in mere hours—though where he finds even the odd moment in which to wright his play is hard to determine, since he's rehearsing all day and tooling all night. But that's what inspiration will do for you.

When he actually gets going, the play he's writing comes easily, because it just mirrors what's going on in his life. Juliet's nurse? Viola has one, too, and her ambitious parents are Capulet clones. Mercutio killed? Will's rival and friend, Chris Marlowe, is conveniently offed. The balcony scene? It's a convenient balcony that grants Will access to Viola's bed. And though unlike Romeo and Juliet the lovers don't die, they're cruelly torn apart—Viola, with her earl, to the Virginia colonies; Will to his commission from the Queen. A comedy next, she commands—"for Twelfth Night." Sadder, wiser, but permanently inspired, Will picks up his quill and we see that his new heroine's name will be . . . Viola! As his lost love heads for the ship that will bear her away forever, he assures her that she'll always be his muse—though how she'll provide the inspiration for, say, *Timon of Athens* or *Coriolanus* is not made clear.

In brief: A fantasy Shakespeare has been used as a pretext to concoct an upmarket romantic comedy and, in passing, to demonstrate how, even for the greatest of geniuses, Art imitates Life.

So much of this view of creativity is paralleled in the movie *Becoming Jane* that if its costumes weren't late-eighteenth-century rather than Elizabethan, and if the gender of the great writers involved weren't reversed, it might not be so easy to tell the two movies apart. "Jane" is Jane Austen, and although for years she's been scribbling away for the amusement of her family, it's only when handsome daredevil Tom Lefroy, fresh from the fleshpots of London, turns up in the neighborhood that she finds the real-life experience that leads eventually to *Pride and Prejudice*. Again, the events of Jane's romance closely anticipate the action of her novel. Tom is at first boorishly dismissive, then comes to appreciate her; Jane, once her dignity is restored, falls deeply in love. They part, yet they can't resist each other and come together again. Unlike Mr. Darcy, however, Tom is poor and the sole support of his family back in Ireland, so finally they must go their separate ways. But Jane has now known love and suffering, and so is primed to give us Elizabeth Bennet, Marianne Dashwood, Anne Elliot, et al.

All that we know of the relationship between Jane Austen and the real Tom Lefroy comes from a few lines in a few of her letters. They meet during the end-of-the-year holidays of 1795, and in a letter to her sister, Cassandra, dated January 9, 1796, Jane refers to him as "a very gentleman-like, good-looking, pleasant young man, I assure you. But as to our having ever met, except at the three last balls, I cannot say much; for he is so excessively laughed at about me at Ashe, that he is ashamed of coming to Steventon, and ran away when we called on Mrs. Lefroy a few days ago." (They had been observed dancing together more than the conventional two times.) Later in the same letter, after a good deal of lighthearted gossip, much of it about other young men (including one "whose eyes are as handsome as ever"), she goes on: "After I had written the above, we received a visit from Mr. Tom Lefroy and his cousin George." The former "has but *one* fault, which time will, I trust, entirely remove—it is that his morning coat is a great deal too light. He is a very great admirer of *Tom Jones*, and therefore wears the same coloured clothes, I imagine, which *he* did when he was wounded."

A few days later, the day before a party at the house where Tom is staying, she writes: "I rather expect to receive an offer from my friend in the course of the evening. I shall refuse him, however, unless he promises to give away his white coat." She then instructs Cassandra to make over to a friend all her previous admirers, "even the kiss which C. Powlett wanted to give me, as I mean to confine myself in future to Mr. Tom Lefroy, for whom I don't care sixpence." And the following day: "At last the day is come on which I am to flirt my last with Tom Lefroy, and when you receive this it will be over. My tears flow as I write at the melancholy idea. Wm. Chute called here yesterday, I wonder what he means by being so civil." A day or so later, Lefroy is off to his law studies in London, and that's it, apart from a reference in a letter three years later to his being in the neighborhood, Jane being "too proud to make any enquiries." She, as we know, never married, though there was a moment years later when she almost did. Tom went on to marry, father a large brood, and become the Lord Chief Justice of Ireland (and live to be ninety-three).

So what happened during those three or so weeks? A (very) brief flirtation? A quickly doused romance? A bruised ego? An occasion for sardonic joking? A permanently wounded heart? Since Cassandra destroyed so many letters after Jane's death, we can't ever know. And since Austen's antiromantic stance is so basic to her mode of thinking and writing, we can't tell from these few remarks whether she's just having her usual fun or whether she's deploying her habitual irony to mask real feelings. The tone is very much the tone of her brilliantly parodic juvenilia, and certainly in no way suggests the anguish of Marianne or the melancholy regret of Anne.

Does it matter? Do we care how strictly the plot of the movie adheres to the few known facts? Indeed, what are we hoping to find in *Becoming Jane*? If we're looking for a convincing notion of what Jane Austen was really like—that is, if we're looking to identify this "Jane" with the author of the books we love—we can take a deep breath and acknowledge that the combination of a literate script and Anne Hathaway's committed and expert performance allows us to suspend disbelief, at least for the duration of the movie. This, despite the fact that from what we actually know, Hathaway is too good-looking, too unfettered, too *modern*: making little speeches about the value of fiction and the nature of irony; sliding too easily into a fuzzy feminism. Austen certainly held strong views, and no doubt asserted them with authority, but not in the spirit of a Gwyneth Paltrow or a Julia Roberts—or an Anne Hathaway. Like all of us, she was a product of, and an expression of, her own time, and we can sense the difference: This movie is the twenty-first century speaking. Even so, its surface is plausible enough, and Hathaway's performance is persuasive enough, for us to indulge in the delusion that we're actually encountering the famously elusive Jane Austen.

If, however, we're looking to *Becoming Jane* for an understanding of how this particular late-eighteenth-century young lady became "Jane Austen," we can only be disappointed. Jane Austen was Jane Austen from the moment her consciousness formed: The wit, the relentless powers of observation, the trenchant moral vision, the sense of the ridiculous are all evident in her adolescent writings; it didn't take a Tom Lefroy to unleash them. Certainly the circumstances of her life informed the novels—she wasn't a fantasist—but it's her unique mind that animates them, and that draws us to her; that makes us want to know her (and so makes possible a film like this one). That she loved, that she suffered, may or not be true, but these things can't begin to explain her. The movie's title is a misnomer: You can't *become* what you already *are*.

What Austen *has* become in recent years is a brand name. Thanks to the endless flow of movies and TV dramatizations, the six novels are practically household names. And they're only the beginning. At least a dozen attempts at sequels to *Pride and Prejudice* are available today on Amazon. *Emma* has been retold from the point of view of Jane Fairfax. Austen herself is the heroine of a series of detective novels. (The ninth and latest is *Jane and the Barque of Frailty*: "Jane Austen arrives in London to watch over the printing of her first novel, and finds herself involved in a crime that could end more than her career.") Not to be left out, Mr. Darcy has his own literature, as well as co-starring in a Mr. and Mrs. Darcy crime series (*Suspense and Sensibility*, *Pride and Prescience*). There's the movie version of the bestseller *The Jane Austen Book Club* and a new book called *Just Jane: A Novel of Jane Austen's Life*. There's a *Pride and Prejudice* board game ("Marriage is the object"), a Jane Austen action figure....

Can any of this commerce, however sincere, help us understand the unique genius it purports to elucidate? Alas, no. "Understanding" Jane is no more a possibility than "becoming" Jane. There are the Jane Austen novels; the Jane Austen industry, including this perfectly respectable movie, is irrelevant.

And then there's *Molière*, a new French film, in which the previously interesting Romain Duris (*The Beat That My Heart Skipped*) impersonates the young and very hirsute playwright, who learns a thing or two when, to escape debtors' prison, he lends his talents to a very rich gentleman and so discovers the material for his great comedy *Le Bourgeois Gentilhomme*. Oh yes—he also falls madly in love with the Gentilhomme's aristocratic Lady, from whom fate and the exigencies of the plot separate him: She must stay in her dreary marriage for the sake of her vulnerable daughter. Besides, what could the future hold for a scruffy traveling player and the elegant, and older, Mme. Jourdain? He suffers, she suffers. Still, like Will and Viola, they have their fun, and plenty of it, before they must part. (*Shakespeare in Love* has a lot to answer for.)

The Brontës: Nancy Coleman, Olivia de Havilland, and Ida Lupino in *Devotion*

It's déjà vu all over again: Boy gets girl, boy loses girl, we get *Tartuffe*—the name our hero assumes when in residence at the château Jourdain. Meanwhile, we've watched *his* ink-blotched hand gripping his quill as it races along, no doubt composing masterpieces inspired by Madame's cleavage. Luckily for the young scamp, Mme. Jourdain is not only muse, she's instructress. The silly boy wants to be a tragedian, but she sets him straight: Tragedy is not for him. "Make them laugh." (Fast-forward to Preston Sturges's *Sullivan's Travels*.)

Unlike *Shakespeare in Love* and *Becoming Jane*, *Molière* has no redeeming qualities. But it offers the same message they do: Genius can only be explained through biographical anecdote; if you haven't lived it, you can't write it.

This, apparently, is also the story of the Brontës, as reconstructed in a deservedly forgotten 1946 movie called *Devotion*. Ida Lupino is Emily, Olivia de Havilland is Charlotte, and you may be startled to learn that they're both in love with the same man: Paul Henreid. Emily sees him first and pines for him, but he can't love her "that way." It's Charlotte who snags him in the end, though not until she's experienced unrequited infatuation for Monsieur Heger, the proprietor of the school in Brussels where the two girls go to teach. (See *Villette.*) So both girls suffer, which is why we have *Wuthering Heights* and *Jane Eyre*. Their sister Anne is given no love interest, which presumably is why she can do no better as a novelist than *Agnes Grey* and *The Tenant of Wildfell Hall*.

The horrifying story of the Brontës is known to the world, four of the five girls dying young of consumption, Emily among them. In *Devotion*, though, she doesn't cough once; she doesn't even clear her throat. She simply fades away through Henreid-deprivation, her spirit joining Heathcliff on the moors.

Even in the mid-forties this movie was greeted with derision, although Lupino makes a game try at Emily. Its only interest today is to demonstrate that the Love + Suffering = Art equation was alive and flourishing in Hollywood sixty years ago. Its roots, of course, lie further back, in the Romantic movement of the nineteenth century—the idea of a pre-Romantic Haydn or Fielding (or Shakespeare or Austen) subscribing to it is preposterous. But Hollywood has to adhere to this approach if it's going to make this kind of movie. You can't have a successful period piece without love and sex, so if you pin your story on a great writer, he/she has to be in love/sex. No one's going to pay money to see Shakespeare, retired, performing civic duties back in Stratford, or Jane Austen sitting at her desk in her early forties writing *Persuasion*.

Some years ago Hollywood put a more contemporary writer up on the screen: Lillian Hellman. She's not a genius like the others—far from it—and she already has her man (poor Dash), but *Julia*, based on Hellman's barefaced fabrications in *Pentimento*, gives us several of the essential conceits of the lit-flick genre. To begin with, she too has writer's block. There's no ink-stained hand clutching a quill, because Lillian types, but as she's struggling to finish her first play, *The Children's Hour*, we see her tossing wads of crumpled paper to the floor. And then, to show just how blocked she is (and how cranky), she flings the bloody typewriter out the window. Luckily, Hammett is on hand to encourage her, drive her to do her best, and eventually assure her that she's written the best play of the decade.

Most of the movie is not about Lillian the writer but about Lillian the loyal friend of the heroic Julia. (They're Jane Fonda and Vanessa Redgrave, in case you've forgotten.) Along the way, however, we get a version of that obligatory rite of passage for famous writers in the movies: the scene of public triumph. It's opening night of *The Children's Hour*, and as Hellman enters the restaurant where the celebratory party is being held, the entire

Broadway first-night crowd rises to its feet to acclaim her. She's famous—just the way, as she's confessed to Dash, she's always wanted to be!

Flash back more than three hundred years. It's the first performance of *Romeo*, and, yes, this crowd too rises to its feet. Standing ovations weren't invented yesterday.

Jane? Years after her thwarted romance, she uncharacteristically agrees to read aloud from *P and P* at a public occasion—because Tom Lefroy has happened to turn up in town with his young daughter. Forget that Austen published anonymously and remained private about her work all her life: Here's an occasion for her to lock eyes with her lost love *and* to receive the sweet applause of the assembly.

Charlotte? With *Jane Eyre* a huge success, she's off to London to be feted by all, and be squired around London by none other than Thackeray (Sydney Greenstreet), who tactlessly points out that Emily's novel is greater than hers. No matter: Charlotte has the fame and the applause and the contracts, and Emily is still a nobody—and about to be a dead one.

Molière? Thirteen years have gone by since his encounter with the Jourdain household, and just as Will Shakespeare obliges Queen Bess with the comedy *Twelfth Night*, Molière obliges Louis XIV's brother, Monsieur, with the comedy *he's* insisted on: the *Gentilhomme*. Applause? Laugh till they cry? You guessed it.

So you love and you sacrifice and you suffer, but it's all worthwhile, because sooner or later the world is at your feet. Forget genius—you're box office. Coming next week to theaters everywhere: *Ibsen in Love. Becoming Willa. Emerson.*

September 27, 2007

The Case of John Steinbeck

The extraordinary thing about John Steinbeck is how good he can be when so much of the time he's so bad. There are talented writers who grow into their full maturity and then decline, slowly or precipitously. But that isn't Steinbeck. You can divide his work up into coherent periods, but there's no coherent trajectory of quality.

The publication of the fourth (and, blessedly, final) volume of his fiction by the Library of America makes it easy to track the entire writing career, apart from some journalism and the two weakest of his novels: his first—a puerile potboiler, *Cup of Gold* (pirates!)—and the late *The Short Reign of Pippin IV*, a limp, petulant social satire. In fact, just about everything he wrote is in print, not only in these four volumes but in handsome Penguin paperbacks, which sell well over a million copies a year, with *Of Mice and Men* accounting for more than half of them. (It's short, it's easy to follow, and it's full of feeling—a perfect assignment for junior-high readers.) Two other short books are assigned to younger kids: the affecting *Red Pony* stories (why are so many horse books so sad?) and a faux-primitive parable, *The Pearl*, that makes *The Old Man and the Sea* read like Flaubert. *The Grapes of Wrath* also sells well, of course, and so does *East of Eden*, which a few years ago had a tsunami moment when Oprah "picked" it. (No doubt the Elia Kazan movie featuring James Dean attracts readers—little do they suspect that it tackles only the final segment of the novel.)

So if all of Steinbeck is in print forty years after his death (in 1968), and despite the force-feeding of hundreds of thousands of schoolkids with his work—and official canonization by the Library of America—why is he so decisively off the literary map? Other than Brad Leithauser, who in 1989 published a perceptive fiftieth-anniversary homage to *The Grapes of*

Wrath, who in America considers him seriously today, apart from a handful of Steinbeck academics and some local enthusiasts in Monterey?

Nor is dismissal of his work by the literary establishment anything new. When to everyone's surprise, including his own, he won the 1962 Nobel Prize, the reaction was startlingly hostile. "Without detracting in the least from Mr. Steinbeck's accomplishments," ran a *New York Times* editorial, "we think it interesting that the laurel was not awarded to a writer . . . whose significance, influence and sheer body of work had already made a more profound impression on the literature of our age." And on the eve of the award ceremony in Stockholm, Arthur Mizener, again in the *Times*, questioned why the Nobel committee would reward a writer whose "limited talent is, in his best books, watered down by tenth-rate philosophizing." It's a question difficult to answer. (Steinbeck himself had doubts. When asked by a reporter whether he believed he deserved the prize, he responded, "Frankly, no.")

This philosophizing—his compulsion to hector us with heavy-handed opinions and ideas—remains one of the chief obstacles to reading Steinbeck with pleasure today. Like so many other writers of his time, he's disgusted with capitalism, yet he's not really a revolutionary—he comes across more as a disaffected adolescent, dishing out a kind of callow cynicism. Although he's constantly laying down the moral law and grappling with the larger issues, he's not an abstract thinker or theorist. Instead, he's got a chip on his soul—a suspicion of formal education, a resentment of authority and institutions. (It's that resentment which undoubtedly kept him from joining the Party, even at the peak of his radicalism in the thirties.) In other words, he has the ardor and sincerity—and the confused notions—typical of so many intelligent autodidacts.

His rebelliousness doesn't seem to have been triggered by reaction to a constricting upbringing. The Steinbecks were genteel middle-class, although John's low-key father suffered the failure of his modest business in Salinas. Mrs. Steinbeck was a cultured schoolteacher who came from a large Irish clan, the Hamiltons, whom John would later dramatize—and romanticize—in *East of Eden*. When his parents grew old and ill, he looked after them devotedly, but his family situation doesn't appear to have imposed greatly on his psychic life. In fact, although he had many male friends to whom he was unswervingly loyal, a wide assortment of girls, and a handful of encouraging and influential teachers, individuals don't seem to have meant as much to him as The People—or as animals. You could say, in fact, that he tended to regard human beings primarily as a species of animal: there to be studied.

The young John actually was an autodidact of sorts. He sporadically attended Stanford, dropping in on it for a term or two of courses, retreating, returning, never graduating. He wasn't denied an education; he chose to educate himself. In his early twenties he spent two fierce winters in almost total isolation, alone with his dogs, his books, and his typewriter, caretaking a summer house on Lake Tahoe. Big, burly, and awkward, he was an imposing physical presence, and he did long stretches of physical labor to support himself. He came close to starving during a miserable sojourn in New York when he was twenty-four, working as a laborer on the construction of Madison Square Garden and failing as a reporter for a New York paper. Through all of this he never doubted his vocation as a writer. And he wasn't shy about what he wrote. When friends, girls, former teachers weren't being bombarded with his early stories and sketches, they were held prisoner as he read aloud to them for hours at a time.

Early in 1930, just short of twenty-eight, he married bright, capable Carol Henning. They more or less lived on love—his parents were able to give him a bare-bones place to live and an allowance of $50 a month. Food was basic, possessions spare. But their happy-go-lucky penury didn't last long. Steinbeck's fumbling apprenticeship and erratic early publishing career were over by the early 1930s, when he began attracting critical appreciation and a readership.

The earliest books are hard to take, straining for meaning and literary effect. His third published work, *To a God Unknown* (1933), displays many of his worst qualities. Its protagonist, Joseph Wayne, leads his family of farmers from desiccated New England to lush California, where his empathic relationship with the land eventually explodes into what we, if not Steinbeck, recognize as a feverish psychopathology: "He stamped his feet into the soft earth. Then the exultance grew to be a sharp pain of desire that ran through his body in a hot river. . . . His fingers gripped the wet grass and tore it out, and gripped again. His thighs beat heavily on the earth. . . . For a moment the land had been his wife." (He arrived at this febrile style mainly on his own—Jack London, among others, had more influence on him than D. H. Lawrence, the more obvious source.)

There's a vast disparity in tone and content between this overwrought literary exercise and his next novel (and first bestseller), *Tortilla Flat* (1935), that rompy account of salt-of-the-earth down-and-outers in Monterey.

They drink, they brawl, they fornicate, they steal—oh, those happy simple paisanos! And what about their dialogue? Danny: "I looked for thee, dearest of little angelic friends, for see, I have here two steaks from God's own pig, and a sack of sweet white bread. Share my bounty, Pilon, little dumpling."

But through all this "undiluted cuteness," as Alfred Kazin called it in *On Native Grounds* (1942), Steinbeck's lifelong themes begin to emerge, first among them the idea of community. Danny's house, we're told in a preface, "was not unlike the Round Table, and Danny's friends were not unlike the knights of it." They're innocents, and they're all for one and one for all. Most important, they're "clean of commercialism, free of the complicated systems of American business." Far better to be a bum with a heart of gold than a solid citizen.

By the mid-1930s the crucial events of Steinbeck's youth were behind him. He was married. His parents had died. He was a name to be reckoned with. And he'd met the man who would prove to be the most important friend of his life—Ed Ricketts, a marine biologist in Monterey, who for eighteen years, even after John moved east and until Ed's untimely death, in 1948, would be his philosophical and moral touchstone. Ricketts appears and reappears in Steinbeck's work in various inspirational guises, an idealized figure, a counterbalance to all the demonized figures—the greedy, the small-minded, the hypocritical—at whom Steinbeck endlessly rails. He is also the central figure in *The Log from the Sea of Cortez* (1951), a chronicle of a Ricketts-led marine biology expedition to Mexico that Steinbeck introduced with a moving and perceptive tribute to his late mentor. *The Log* shows Steinbeck at his best—he's active, he's outdoors, he's focused on the natural world, and of course he's with Ricketts. The prose is uncluttered and unfancy, the observation acute. Tellingly, although Carol was along for the ride, her presence is unacknowledged in Steinbeck's account: It's all guys on his Sea of Cortez.

In 1934 Steinbeck befriended several labor organizers and was immediately engrossed by their stories of the cotton workers' strike of the previous year. Within months he began work on *In Dubious Battle* (1936). The California of *To a God Unknown* and *Tortilla Flat* was a convenience—a place he knew and could plunder for material. The plight of the dispossessed and the exploitation of the poor during the Depression years was a calling, a crusade, that led to his most important work.

In Dubious Battle centers on Jim, an alienated and angry young loner who joins the Party in San Francisco. The strike begins: vigilantes, scabs, gunfire. Jim is wounded, and grows more and more fanatical. "I'm stronger than anything in the world, because I'm going in a straight line." The straight line leads to his being killed.

The style of *In Dubious Battle* is radically new. Description, action, dialogue are straightforward and gritty. Still, Steinbeck can't resist injecting an idealized guru figure into this realistic world—a kind of fellow-traveling doctor who lends the strikers a hand. "Doc": "Man has met and defeated every obstacle, every enemy except one. He cannot win over himself. How mankind hates itself." Jim: "We don't hate ourselves, we hate the invested capital that keeps us down." One suspects that this is what the endless bull sessions between Steinbeck and Ricketts must have sounded like. Even so, *In Dubious Battle* is an impressive step forward.

The second of Steinbeck's populist novels, *Of Mice and Men* (1937), is written in the same direct and effective manner. It begins, as so many Steinbeck novels do, with a loving evocation of its natural setting: "A few miles south of Soledad, the Salinas River drops in close to the hillside bank and runs deep and green. . . . On the valley side the water is lined with trees—willows fresh and green with every spring."

And he loves his central characters, too, the pair of itinerant ranch hands—"bindlestiffs"—named George and Lennie. George is the smart one, the leader; Lennie is the massive semi-idiot, worshipping George, dreaming of the little bit of land they might one day own, and—his most powerful fantasy—the rabbits he might one day be able to tend and caress.

We know that this isn't going to happen, and on some level George knows it, too, but he needs to believe in it as strongly as Lennie does: It's the illusion they live by. And then, catastrophe. Yes, the pathos is laid on thick; yes, everything is foreshadowed and manipulated. (Edmund Wilson called it "contrived with almost too much cleverness.") But Steinbeck's sympathy for these decent, forlorn men is so intense that it carries us along with it. Uninfected by moralizing, ingeniously if stagily constructed, and credibly populated, *Of Mice and Men*, far from Steinbeck's most ambitious book, is the closest he came to a fully satisfying work of art. (It also provided his entrée to the world of Broadway. The play version, cannily crafted by George S. Kaufman, was not only a hit but won the New York Drama Critics' Circle Award. Alas, this easy success encouraged what was to become a lifelong infatuation with, and failure in, the theater, a form essentially alien to Steinbeck's talents. His finest work is almost always reportorial.)

Although he didn't, as was frequently misreported, go to Oklahoma to observe the migrant Okies as they set out on their hegira to the West, Steinbeck did spend weeks with them in California—on the road, in their camps. At first he was working as a journalist to air their desperate situation, but quickly he realized that here was the material for the major novel he felt ready to write.

The motor of *The Grapes of Wrath* (1939) is his compassion for—his ready identification with—these people. Yet even here, his characters are somehow generalized, more real as a group force than as individuals. Ma Joad is too good to be true. ("Her hazel eyes seemed to have experienced all possible tragedy and to have mounted pain and suffering like steps into a high calm and a superhuman understanding.") Tom is the strong, basically virtuous young man trapped by fate and history. Rose of Sharon (that name!) is more a symptom than a real young woman. This is the crucial flaw in Steinbeck's fiction, pinpointed by both Kazin and Wilson in the early 1940s and even more glaring in the light of what was to come. As Kazin put it, "Steinbeck's people are always on the verge of becoming human, but never do." Wilson: "The characters of *The Grapes of Wrath* are animated and put through their paces rather than brought to life. . . . It is as if human sentiments and speeches had been assigned to a flock of lemmings on their way to throw themselves into the sea."

Still, *The Grapes of Wrath* is unquestionably a major achievement. The question is, is it a good book? Steinbeck drove himself to write it in a mere five months, but it was already all worked out in his head, as we learn from *Working Days*, the fascinating journal of its composition that remained unpublished until 1999. The chapters alternate between straightforward, powerful storytelling and authorial commentary, just as the dialogue alternates between sharply observed speech and preposterous hot air. How can the writer who reports a dying old woman saying "I'm jus' pain covered with skin" also have his Ed Ricketts substitute, the itinerant preacher Casy, spout things like "Listen to people a-talkin', an' purty soon I hear the way folks are feelin'. . . . I hear 'em an' feel 'em; an' they're beating their wings like a bird in a attic"?

In the chapters of commentary the migrants are seen as bugs, as ants. Early on, there's an extended description of a land turtle crawling along—

indomitable, symbolic. Mechanized farming has broken the bond between man and the earth: "Tractors don't love the land." And then there's the Manself: "Fear the time when Manself will not suffer and die for a concept, for this one quality is the foundation of Manself, and this one quality is man, distinctive in the universe."

The Grapes of Wrath is a vertiginous conjunction of sweeping, irresistible narrative and highfalutin theorizing. That readers in 1939 tolerated the latter is testimony to the power of the former—and to the readiness of America to be affected by the terrible story of the Joads. With the book's overwhelming success—it was the bestselling novel of the year, won the Pulitzer Prize, etc.—and the further impact of John Ford's impressive film version, which appeared in movie houses only months after the book's publication, Steinbeck graduated from being an admired young writer to worldwide acceptance as a major figure in American literature.

We can see in hindsight that with *The Grapes of Wrath*, the most significant arc of Steinbeck's career came to an end—the impassioned reporting of large-scale human tragedy, the Zola-esque attacks on injustice. Indeed, an entire cultural era was coming to an end: the populism that broadly ranged from *Waiting for Lefty* to early Frank Capra movies and documentaries like *The Plow That Broke the Plains*. At the close of *The Grapes of Wrath*, Tom Joad, on the lam, slips away into the dark to join the good fight for The People. A year or two later, with the war upon us, he would have been heading for the nearest draft board.

Meanwhile, Steinbeck's life was disintegrating. He was depleted, resentful of attacks from the left and the right, aggrieved by the negative response of critics like Wilson and Kazin, and facing the fact that his marriage was coming to an end. Carol had been a real collaborator, serving as a sounding board and editor, coming up with the titles for *Of Mice and Men* (from Robert Burns) and *The Grapes of Wrath* (from "The Battle Hymn of the Republic"). But now she was feeling trapped and unfulfilled. And he had embarked on an intense affair with an aspiring band-singer, "Gwyn" Conger, that would lead to another failed marriage. The war came to his rescue, giving him the subject of his next novel, *The Moon Is Down* (1942), as well as an excuse to get out of America and the doldrums (leaving Gwyn resentfully behind) by hiring himself out as a war correspondent.

The Moon Is Down is set in a small town in one of the German-occupied countries—presumably Norway, though unnamed. The occupying soldiers are not all bad, the locals are not all good, and the book was angrily attacked for comforting the enemy by, among others, James Thurber. But its real flaws are not political. It's a play masquerading as a novel (Steinbeck thought he was inventing a new art form—the narrative play), and it's excruciatingly creaky and stagy. It's also unbearably preachy. As the noble mayor of the town is led off to be executed, we're treated to Socrates' final speech from the *Apology*.

On the other hand, Steinbeck's war reportage is fresh and strong—England under the blitz, North Africa, Italy. He was several times in the heat of battle, most dangerously at Salerno. He's the kind of reporter who turns events into human-interest stories and creates "characters," but his eye is keen and persuasive. You can tell that he's still happier looking outward than inward, and more at ease as a man among men—or a boy among boys—than in more emotionally challenging relationships. (Although he had a busy sexual life and was married three times, Steinbeck was never at ease with his female characters: They tend to be either saints or whores, or they're symbolic, except for those who are pure evil.)

You see his ease as a reporter again in the *Russian Journal* he published in 1948, after spending six weeks with the photographer Robert Capa exploring the post-war Soviet Union. Capa serves the same function here as the poodle will in *Travels with Charley*—he's chum, ally, and comic relief. Steinbeck understands the telling detail, as when his hosts in Stalingrad troop into his hotel to show him with pride "a red velvet shield, covered with a lace of gold filigree from the King of Ethiopia" and "a tablecloth with the embroidered names of fifteen hundred women in a small British town." This is more appealing stuff than anything in his two most recent novels.

In these, he's clearly scrambling for material. *Cannery Row* (1945) is a dip back into *Tortilla Flat*, "born out of homesickness," as he acknowledged—homesickness not only for Monterey but for Ed Ricketts, who is sanctified as "Doc." *The Wayward Bus* (1947) presents a bunch of disparate characters artificially thrown together under difficult circumstances—*The Bridge of San Luis Rey* with a bus instead of a bridge. It's not only artificial, it's sour and unconvincing, its people specimens Steinbeck has collected and studied the way he helped Ed collect and study marine animals.

Meanwhile, he was turning over in his mind the novel that "may be my swan song, but . . . certainly will be the largest and most important work I have or maybe will do."

East of Eden (1952) was intended both to tell the epic story of the Salinas valley and to stage the eternal struggle between good and evil in terms of the original family: Adam and Eve and their two sons. It's a perplexing book—melodramatic, self-indulgent, even trashy; yet at last you feel you're reading a real novel rather than fictionalized reportage—a novel with strong characters, large-scale story development, a central idea holding it together. And in the first-person passages, which lovingly reimagine his mother's family, the Hamiltons, Steinbeck was able to move beyond the impersonality of his earlier work.

The fulcrum of the book is the tragic story of the fictional Trasks: Adam, the good man; Cathy (Eve), his evil wife; Adam's brother, Charles; and a second pair of brothers, Adam's sons, Cal and Aron (Cain and Abel, in case you missed the connection). To an impressive degree Steinbeck succeeds in turning this ambitious metaphor into a moving human drama, and it can be gripping when it isn't maddening. Unfortunately, it's disfigured by the most intrusive of all his guru figures, who stains the narrative with his relentless wisdom. This is Lee, Adam's Chinese "houseboy," who discards his faux pidgin in order to speak profound things in impeccable English (he's been to college and, as a hobby, translates classic Chinese poetry into English). It's Lee who introduces to Adam (and to us) the ultimate message of *East of Eden* and the heart of Steinbeck's philosophy: the Hebrew concept of *timshel*, which Lee happens to have picked up from a learned old rabbi. *Timshel*, we're told, means "thou mayest"; in other words, thou hast a choice. "I have a new love for that glittering instrument, the human soul. It is a lovely and unique thing in the universe. It is always attacked and never destroyed—because 'Thou mayest.'" And he can cook, too!

On the positive side, Steinbeck's descriptive style is by now highly fluent and convincing. How surely, for instance, he evokes the town's brothels:

They seemed very small, and they tried to efface themselves in outside neglect, and the wild overgrown front yards tried to hide them from the street. Remember how the shades were always drawn with little lines of yellow light around their edges? You could hear only a murmur from within. Then the front door would open to admit a country boy, and you'd hear laughter and perhaps the soft sentimental tone of an open-face piano with a piece of toilet chain across the strings, and then the door would close it off again.

In *East of Eden* the reporter Steinbeck is often effectively at the service of the novelist Steinbeck. Yes, the book is highly overheated, its febrile drama uninflected by humor or irony, but it's a large achievement and it's hard to forget.

The personal aspects of *Eden* are painful to relate. By the late 1940s, Steinbeck's second marriage had shattered. (Domestic life and giving birth to two boys, Thom and John, had kept Gwyn from the "creative" life she felt entitled to.) Late one night in 1948, Ed Ricketts's car was struck by a train. "The greatest man in the world is dying," Steinbeck told his pal Nathaniel Benchley. In despair he rushed to Monterey—arriving too late to see his friend alive—and, as Jackson J. Benson puts it in his monumental biography, *John Steinbeck, Writer* (1984), "With that sense of timing that only someone with show-business experience could have developed, Gwyn confronted John upon his return from California and told him that she wanted a divorce."

She also told him that she hadn't loved him for years and had been abundantly unfaithful to him. Benson circles around the real point—the Steinbeck family was up in arms to keep it quiet—but Gwyn also tortured John with the "confession" that he was not the father of their second son.

In his book *The Other Side of Eden* (2001), the younger John dismisses this notion as preposterous, and indeed father and son were far too physically alike for it to be true. Gwyn was lying to hurt her husband. But Steinbeck had no way of knowing that at the time, and the hatred he came to feel for her saturates *East of Eden*. Adam Trask's wife, the sadistic, murderous, brothel-keeper Cathy (later Kate), torments him with the story that their twin boys are actually the sons of Adam's brother, Charles.

Young John's book is an ugly portrait of dysfunction, his father alternately overprotective and indifferent, his mother alcoholic and violent. On his sixteenth birthday, he tells us, she became so drunkenly abusive that he threw a TV set out of the window of her twelfth-story apartment and then "punched her in the mouth as hard as I could, and hammered at her body for God knows how long." Therapist: "Why didn't you go to your father for protection after you beat your mother?" Young John: "I'd already given up thinking he would protect me from her insanity. He was into his Great Writer Bubble, so it wasn't like having a dad around, but instead having the Great Writer present. By the age of thirteen, I realized my father was an asshole."

Nevertheless, in interviews over the years both sons spoke affectionately and admiringly of their father, if not of his fathering.

Steinbeck was only fifty when *East of Eden* was published, but very little of merit was to follow. Most disappointing to him was the failure of his years-long struggle to retell his beloved *Morte d'Arthur* for contemporary readers. (To get closer to the source he transplanted himself and his third wife, Elaine, to Arthur country for a year.) This effort was never completed and is of little value except as a reminder of Steinbeck's lifelong romance with the nobility of individual heroic effort. (His favorite book was *Don Quixote*.)

As had happened after *The Grapes of Wrath*, after *East of Eden* he was a writer without a subject, by now decisively cut off from his roots. For his first forty years, his worldview had been dominated by California, and when he abandoned it, he was deracinated. Hemingway, you feel, never looked back; Faulkner never left home. Steinbeck did leave home, choosing to live in New York, but he remained at heart a small-town guy, an outdoorsman, a fisherman, a handyman, not an urban sophisticate. His life in the big city was populated by well-known New Yorkers–about-town: Abe Burrows, John O'Hara, Fred Allen, the Benchleys, Burgess Meredith, the Frank Loessers. When Joshua Logan invited him to a party for Princess Margaret, he told Elaine, "That's not the way I live." But it *was* the way he lived.

Still, he could never have written about Manhattan. What eventually gave him a new fictional world was the old whaling port of Sag Harbor on Long Island, in which he and Elaine (a happy marriage at last) settled down for much of his final fifteen years—a kind of Monterey with a down-east accent. He could slop around, gossip with the locals, enjoy the waterfront—and observe. The result was his last novel, *The Winter of Our Discontent* (1961), which, although hardly a masterpiece, was Steinbeck's best work since *East of Eden*.

This book is not only a geographical and sociological world away from everything that preceded it, it's also a new kind of novel for Steinbeck—a novel of moral crisis, told entirely in the first person, very much in the spirit if not the tone of East Coast novelists like his friend John O'Hara, James Gould Cozzens, John P. Marquand, Hamilton Basso (*The View from Pompey's Head*), and Sloan Wilson (*The Man in the Gray Flannel Suit*). Its protagonist, who presents himself as a decent man and law-abiding citizen, is confronted with temptation and succumbs, almost committing a serious crime and betraying both his employer and a childhood friend—in effect, everything he believes in. At the end, he's a demoralized man, forced to acknowledge to himself exactly what he has become.

The Winter of Our Discontent, however, is not only about a personal crisis but about a greater one as well: "Readers seeking to identify the fictional people and places here described would do better to inspect their own communities and search their own hearts, for this book is about a large part of America today."

Steinbeck had found his last big subject—the moral deterioration of the times. *The Winter of Our Discontent* pits honest work against new, get-rich-quick money; decency against slickness and trickiness. Ethan Hawley's moments of weakness and the dishonesty of his adolescent son, reflecting the contemporary Charles Van Doren scandal, are deliberately projected as symptoms of a national collapse.

It's not, then, by accident that Steinbeck's last ambitious project is called *Travels with Charley in Search of America* (1962). On his cross-continent trip in the camper he's named Rocinante, after Don Quixote's horse, he finds the old-fashioned virtues of independence and community more or less vanished. Everyone's on the move: "You got roots you sit and starve," a woman living in a mobile home tells him. In Monterey, his fantasy paradise, he's faced with the painful truth that "Doc," "Danny," and the Round Table of good-natured bums and big-hearted whores no longer exist—if they ever did. The horrible racism he encounters in New Orleans when a group of white women—"The Cheerleaders"—scream obscene and violent words at a tiny black girl being ushered into a newly desegregated school propels him back home, sickened for his country.

Steinbeck's heart, as always, is in the right place, but there's something artificial about *Charley*. Many of the encounters he reports sound like pure inventions. His son John put it bluntly: "Thom and I are convinced that he never talked to any of those people. . . . He just sat in his camper and wrote all that shit."

During the sixties he had become a kind of cultural ambassador for the United States, close to people like Yevgeny Yevtushenko and Dag Hammarsjköld. He had always been less radical than people thought he was—again, the outrage over injustice and poverty in *The Grapes of Wrath* and *In Dubious Battle* was personal, not ideological. He was, in fact, a liberal, middle-of-the-road Democrat—hero-worshipping FDR, an ardent campaigner for Adlai Stevenson, and eventually close to Lyndon Johnson, whom he liked and vigorously supported, particularly on the Vietnam War.

This position did nothing to improve his standing with intellectuals, but it was sincere. He believed the Vietcong were murderers, despised the draft-card burners back home, and admired the American troops he encountered as a war reporter on a trip to Southeast Asia in 1966, only two years before his death. Young John was in Vietnam, and Steinbeck managed to get himself helicoptered to an exposed hill outpost where John was fighting. In a surreal moment, the mutually antagonistic father and son found themselves under fire together. The son was to write, "I saw my father behind some sandbags overlooking my position with his M-60 at the ready. . . . I mean, who, in God's name, was producing this movie?"

Steinbeck's final work years were spent on journalism, and his subject was almost inevitably America. A collection of think pieces and nostalgia called *America and Americans* (1966) reveals him at his most characteristic. He's moralizing, he's didactic, he's searching for big answers to big questions. He's generous and vulnerable and touchy. And he's more and more dismayed by what he sees around him: "I have named the destroyers of nations: comfort, plenty, and security—out of which grow a bored and slothful cynicism." You could say that by the end he had evolved into a kind of minor and irrelevant prophet, both disillusioned and irredeemably optimistic.

And he's become that unfashionable and embarrassing thing, a patriot. "I believe," he wrote at the end of his life, "that out of the whole body of our past, out of our differences, our quarrels, our many interests and directions, something has emerged that is itself unique in the world: America—complicated, paradoxical, bullheaded, shy, cruel, boisterous, unspeakably dear, and very beautiful."

Somewhere along the way, "The Battle Hymn of the Republic" had turned into "My Country, 'Tis of Thee."

April 17, 2008

White House Whodunits

Heck!—to use Eve Cooper's favorite expletive—there's a new First Daughter at large in Detectivesville. Eve is the creation of Susan Ford, a First Daughter in her own right: Remember Gerald Ford and his four kids? Teenager Susan was the youngest—she had three big brothers—and, she tells us in a preface, she enjoyed her several teen years in the White House despite the lack of privacy (all those Secret Service guys never out of sight) and the formalities of presidential life. The Fords moved out early in 1977, and a quarter of a century later—after the Carters, the Reagans, the first Bushes, the Clintons, the second Bushes— Susan is staking her insider's claim to the old homestead with her first novel, *Double Exposure: A First Daughter Mystery* (written with Laura Hayden). She's working in an honorable tradition: First Daughter Margaret Truman has turned out a slew of successful thrillers, and let's not forget the run of First Mom mysteries by Elliott Roosevelt. (Mom, of course, is detective Eleanor Roosevelt.)

So meet Eve Cooper, whose really nice dad has just been elected president (unlike poor Gerald Ford, who was thrust into the job as a result of the Nixon-Agnew disasters). She's twenty-five, a professional photographer temporarily unemployed and living in the White House with President Dad, kid brother Drew, and official First Lady, Aunt Patsy. (Mother is dead, and another brother, a computer nerd, is doing his thing in Vermont.) One winter's day, Eve and her sometimes rival, sometimes boyfriend, the official White House photographer, stumble on a body in the Rose Garden. You don't need to know whose, or why it's there, or even who the murderer is—you don't read First Daughter mysteries for the plot. You read them for the fun of picking up clues of a different kind, clues to the private life of a real presidential family, the author's own.

And what do we think we learn about the Fords, who weren't around long enough to do much more than give us a desperately needed breather after the Nixon agonies? We learn what we always knew, or thought we knew: that they were just plain folks. Eve/Susan likes the White House, but, she says, "I'm not used to living in such overwhelming splendor . . . I've never even stayed in a hotel this nice. I was brought up in a middle-class neighborhood. Our idea of elegance was using matching place mats at Thanksgiving." I believe it of the Fords, although this leaves out the complicated and appealing Betty Ford, with her modern-dance background and her problems with alcohol. I mean, didn't you always feel that she was for real, as opposed, say, to Barbara Bush, that tough pol, with her suburban hair and her public agenda of dogs and kids and values? But there's no place for "real" in White House entertainments, so it's no wonder Eve's mom has been airbrushed from the picture.

Having no mom means that Eve is kept busy being Big Sister to supernormal Drew, who eats like a starving man, oversleeps on school days, has trouble with his new schoolmates as the First Son, and would fit right in with the Brady Bunch. The Cooper Bunch gets to have breakfast together, "pretending for a half hour or so each day that we all live a normal life. Dad, in particular, needs that sense of normality before heading to the Oval Office each morning to assume his role as the Leader of the Free World." Let's listen in to the president's breakfast chat: "If I start hearing anything about my autograph on a school absence excuse slip going up for sale on eBay, you're going to be so grounded." By the way, Dad secretly prefers hot chocolate to coffee at breakfast. Is this a revelation about the thirty-eighth president?

Eve has been a successful crime-scene photographer back in Denver, and the photography stuff in the book is convincing, but if she's twenty-five and has been exposed to violent crime, you'd never know it. From the start, it's clear that she's a sentimentalized echo of the teenage Susan Ford, not a grown woman. (Her closest literary ancestor is Nancy Drew, who even gets a mention.) When she's on a tear, Eve may down a beer or two, but her only real vice is recklessness, so that in the time-honored tradition of girl detectives, she walks right into the killer's web and shows her pluck. And when the chips are down, Dad is there to back her up. He doesn't give her a roadster, the way Nancy's father did, but he gives her his vote of confidence: "My daughter understands and appreciates the gravity of this situation as well or better than anyone here, and I think she may have given us our best chance to clear up this mess." Eve's reaction? "As I stood there, I realized for the first time that I wasn't asking simply for my father's support in my decision, but asking for the support of the President of the United States. A shiver slithered up my spine at the thought." Forget the prose: This is a sensible response to being the child of a president. Nancy/Eve/Susan has produced an honorable if dopey book.

Margaret Truman, gone from the White House for almost fifty years, writes not as an insider but as an observer; her impersonal novels take us all over Washington—murder strikes at the Smithsonian, the CIA, the Supreme Court, in Georgetown (I would think so); on the Potomac, Embassy Row, Capitol Hill; at the Library of Congress, the National Gallery, the Watergate, and just across the street at the Kennedy Center; even at the National Cathedral. Tourists beware: Apparently, you're not safe anywhere at all in the nation's capital.

The title of the first Truman bestseller, *Murder in the White House*, published in 1980, promises more than it delivers. Yes, a murder takes place in the White House, but it's not the one Margaret grew up in. The only sly reference to her own situation as the beloved daughter of Harry S. is also the only witty device I've come across in my sweep through half a dozen of her books. I don't think it's unfair to reveal, twenty-two years after its publication, that the murder in the White House is committed by none other than . . . the First Daughter herself! When she confesses, "The President held his daughter in his arms, an island of humanity, abruptly cut off from all trapping of office, from all others except themselves." There it is again: the conflict between being human and living the presidential life. The one recognizable Trumanesque note in this book is the closeness of the presidential family, even after First Daughter Lynne has admitted offing the evil secretary of state (in the Lincoln Bedroom—where else?).

The Truman Capital Crimes novels are carefully plotted conventional mysteries held together by their political background. No excitements, no revelations, no style, but they're professional. The personality of the author is reflected in only two ways: In the dedications, which are family all the way—husband, kids, grandkids ("with love from Gammy"). And in a lavish supply of details about decor, food, and culture: In *Murder on Capitol Hill*, for instance, "Lydia James was grateful the performance was over. She'd never particularly appreciated Haydn, though she did admire some of his symphonic works like 'London' symphony Number 101 that mixed a rondo with a variation form." And, "For most of the meal—a fillet for Clarence that had been dry-hung to age for four weeks, according to the restaurant owner Douglas McNeill, and a terrine of baby coho salmon with truffles and pistachios for her—they avoided discussing Lydia's committee work." Ms. Truman and her editors don't grasp the distinction between "imply" and "infer," or between "disinterested" and "uninterested," and occasionally an arty word clashes with the workaday prose—"His thick sandy hair hung errant across his forehead"—but through hard work and reliability, she has earned herself a wide readership. Her strategy works: Though she uses the family name, she omits anything reflecting on the family. This is what's called having it both ways.

The wild card in the presidential pack is Elliott Roosevelt. Let's face it: These books are bizarre. First of all, of his twenty or so Eleanor Roosevelt mysteries, at least half have been written since his death, in 1990. Not that you can tell: The books he's written since he died are no better or worse than those he was around for. The secret ingredient is finally acknowledged, as follows, on the title page (but not the dust jacket) of what its publisher, Thomas Dunne, tells me is the final installment of the great First Lady's career as a shamus: "Elliott Roosevelt's™ *Murder at the President's Door*, An Eleanor Roosevelt Mystery, by William Harrington for the Estate of Elliott Roosevelt." Mr. Harrington is thanked in earlier books, and Mr. Dunne explains that he was a longtime collaborator, but that Elliott "was deeply involved" and left behind him enough plot ideas and circumstantial detail to make possible the entire posthumous oeuvre.

If the Trumans are absent from their daughter's fictions, the Roosevelts are front and center in their son's. Elliott keeps himself strictly offstage, though in *Murder in Georgetown* we learn that in the judgment of Alice Roosevelt Longworth, "Elliott is a naughty boy." The president, however, is very much a presence, with his sense of humor and his carefully concealed disability and his famous martinis and his faithful advisers, Harry Hopkins and Louis Howe. We get the notoriously inadequate White House housekeeper, Henrietta Nesbitt, and, always, FDR's secretary and comforter, Marguerite (Missy) LeHand, who with Eleanor's apparent sympathy and approval spends evenings with the president perched on his bed in her trademark peignoir, listening to classical music and eating takeout. (Anything to avoid Mrs. Nesbitt's bland diet. As Mrs. R. remarks, "The president despises tuna salad. But it is nutritious and economical, so I am afraid he gets it a great deal more often than he could wish.") Eleanor always tactfully knocks on her husband's bedroom door before entering (my already huge admiration for the lady has shot up still further). What did she feel about Missy? In *Murder in the Chateau*, we get a clue: One morning, "She knocked, then walked in. Occasionally she would find his secretary Missy LeHand already there—or Missy still there; she was never sure which—but that was no longer an issue." Missy's peignoirs, by the way, turn up in just about every book: They're yellow, they're pink, they're "sheer white," covering a "royal-blue silk nightgown," whereas Eleanor herself, her son informs us, "had utterly excruciating taste in clothes . . . she seemed to have a talent for choosing the most unflattering things she could find."

Before we move on from the sex life of the Roosevelts, let's look in on Eleanor and her great friend Lorena Hickock. There's that letter to Hick quoted in *Murder in Georgetown*: "Dearest, dearest Hick, How I miss you! How bleak life is without you! How I long to hold you in my arms and plant kisses on you! On your eyes, dear Hick. On your mouth. On you everywhere!" FDR makes it clear that he knows this kind of talk is merely "a way of expressing yourself. . . . All I ask is that you and Hick kiss and caress in private to your hearts' content. But not where others can see and hear." The president was famous for his practicality.

And then there's the other side of Eleanor's love life. In at least two books—don't be shocked—Eleanor is kissed. In *Murder in the Chateau*, Irish adventurer Kevin O'Neil tells her, "'I have never heard any but good of you. I hold you in my arms, and I'm going to kiss you, Mrs. Roosevelt. For now, and for the last time . . . I promise you I will never offer to kiss you again—assumin', that is, you do not come to my room and my bed some night. Is it agreed?' A woman of fifty-seven was not ready to refuse what he offered. She had never been kissed, more than cousinly, by any man but Franklin. On the terms he stated, she did not refuse Kevin O'Neil." And it's not only the romance of wartime France that quickens Eleanor's blood. In *Murder in the Executive Mansion*, "She stood, and for a minute they stood facing each other, wordless. Then both of them moved on the same impulse, and Detective Captain Edward Kennelly kissed Mrs. Eleanor Roosevelt. They separated, smiling at each other, their hands lingering together, then dropping apart. Nothing was possible."

Almost all the Roosevelt mysteries I've read begin with a murder in the White House. (Mrs. R.: "We cannot imagine, for this moment, what consequences might follow a public announcement that a mysterious corpse has been found in a White House refrigerator.") The exception—

and a front-runner in any crackpot-plot competition—is *Murder in the Chateau*, in which Eleanor is sent on a top-secret mission, via seaplane, submarine, fishing smack, and truck, deep into Vichy France to conspire with General Rommel, Sarah Churchill, and various other luminaries to unseat Hitler and stop the war. She knows she's heading into danger, but "I . . . have always been ready to serve my country." Indeed, as it turns out, "The First Lady had never faced so grave a peril." Yet she solves a murder or two, gets kissed, and it's only because Germany invades Russia that her mission aborts. And as a side benefit, her old acquaintance Gertrude Stein comes calling at the château, as does Josephine Baker, who sings and dances for the assembled guests.

Mrs. R., we're told, "could not imagine why Josephine Baker was here," but we who have witnessed the flood of celebrities whom Eleanor encounters in her role as First Lady are not in the least surprised. In one book or another, we come upon Babe Ruth and Lou Gehrig; W. C. Fields ("'It is a pleasure to meet you, Mr. Dukenfield.' She rarely addressed anyone by a nickname or pseudonym, and she knew that Fields' real name was William Claude Dukenfield. 'I once saw you juggle'"); Shirley Temple; George Gershwin; Louis Armstrong ("'I'm honored, honored,' said Armstrong. . . . 'The honor is mine, Mr. Armstrong,' she said"); Kate Smith, singing "God Bless America"; H. L. Mencken; Major Dwight Eisenhower; Joe Kennedy (she serves him coffee and "a small assortment of vanilla wafers and crisp little cookies"); and, in *Murder at Midnight*, our old friend from the château: "'Lovey works very hard,' said Alice B. Toklas ingenuously, nodding toward Gertrude Stein. Gertrude Stein laughed. 'Thank you, Pussy,' she said." (Stein's own account of this meeting, in *Everybody's Autobiography*, is less intimate: "Mrs. Roosevelt was there and gave us tea, she talked about something and we sat next to someone.")

Most exciting of all is Eleanor's brush with Ernest Hemingway: "'I've read two or three of your books, Mr. Hemingway,' she said. 'I've read one of yours, Mrs. Roosevelt,' he said. 'I understand your next novel will be about the civil war in Spain,' she said. 'What will it be called, have you decided yet?' 'I want to call it *For Whom the Bell Tolls*.'" And then who comes along? "'Have you met Bill Faulkner?' Hemingway asked, nodding toward a rather vacant-looking dishevelled man who was approaching them. 'I don't believe I've had the honor,' she said. Hemingway introduced them. William Faulkner squinted at her and blinked. 'Shuh pleasure,' he muttered. He was very drunk. 'Give my best wishes . . . to the Pres . . . dunt.'"

Please don't think that Eleanor is so busy hobnobbing with Nobel Prize authors that she neglects her responsibilities as detective. In fact, FDR is always cautioning her to be discreet: "I believe you are inter-meddling in police business, Babs. Please leave the Hawkshawing to the Hawkshaws." But what's a First Lady to do when corpses keep turning up outside the president's door? Babs interviews suspects, dons disguises, defends the innocent, draws up lists of clues. She even goes incognito to the district jail to interrogate a striptease dancer named Blaze Flame, who suddenly catches on: "Wait a minute. . . . You're not some woman cop. You're . . . Jesus Christ, you're Mrs. Roosevelt!" But Eleanor's true indignation is reserved not for the criminals, whom she inevitably unmasks, but for two offstage figures who are anathematized in almost every book: Douglas MacArthur, who has a beauteous mistress stashed away in a hotel because he's afraid to tell his mother about her, and J. Edgar Hoover. "'There is a rumor . . . that he is secretly an ardent sodomite,' she said. 'It is whispered that he is "married" to his assistant, Clyde Tolson.' 'I don't like that,' said the President."

It's sad news indeed that the Eleanor Roosevelt Mystery series has apparently run its course. No offense, Margaret T. and Susan F., but you both lack that certain demented something that Elliott R. brings (brought?) to the business. What a shame that the most famous and formidable of all First Children never gave it a try. Alice Roosevelt Longworth, known fondly as "Washington's Other Monument," queened it over the capital for well over half a century. Teddy's oldest child, wife of Speaker of the House Nick Longworth, cousin of Franklin (whom she liked) and Eleanor (whom she didn't), she was charismatic, ultra-political, frivolous, charming, and, most of all, informed. She wrote her memoirs, and they're wonderfully amusing, but think what she could have done with the mystery genre! After all, more than anyone else in Washington, she knew where the bodies were buried.

August 25, 2002

Scrutiny *Bound*

The magazine *Scrutiny* appeared first in 1932 and published its last issue in 1953. Four times a year for just over twenty years, always under F. R. Leavis's direction, it went about its chief business— the reevaluation of the classics of English literature, the judging of serious contemporary literature, the establishment of standards. Now, in 1963, the Cambridge University Press is reissuing all of *Scrutiny* in twenty bound volumes—a unique and immensely valuable publishing feat, for the complete *Scrutiny* contains the most remarkable continuity of literary criticism in our time, a vast bulk of brilliant and useful work. In addition, it stands as an important historical record. Nowhere else can we follow with such immediacy and completeness the revolution in literary opinion that has taken place since 1930—a revolution *Scrutiny* greatly helped to bring about.

Its aims were announced in its manifesto. It was to take up the work of the *Calendar of Letters* and *Criterion*, but to be more than "a purely literary review"; to print serious literary criticism, but also to be "seriously preoccupied with the movement of modern civilization"—somewhat in the manner of the American magazines it admired (in particular, *The New Republic*). It was to review a few carefully selected new books, and publish original compositions (only a limited amount of poetry actually got printed, plus one weak piece of fiction). Most important, it was to provide and maintain "standards"—its contention was that "the general dissolution of standards is a commonplace." It welcomed articles from its readers, but could not pay for them. And it printed about 750 copies of every issue.

Immediately *Scrutiny* engaged the respect of many serious readers—

and infuriated many others. Its range was wide, so that individuals and organs of many different interests reacted strongly to it. The first issue, for instance, saw the start of *Scrutiny*'s twenty-year war on the cheapening standards of the English literary establishment, in this case represented by the Sunday papers and weekly magazines. This steady, vigorous attack did not win for *Scrutiny* the support of the organs it was attacking. The same can be said of *Scrutiny*'s feud with many of the literary scholars of the period. The "academics" responded to the magazine with the pique that generally results when a vigorous and rigorous no-nonsense voice assaults what has been more or less a preserve of politeness.

T. S. Eliot had led the way, but not in the pugnacious spirit *Scrutiny* was to display, and Eliot himself had been both ignored and derided. *Scrutiny*'s attack was more widely applied, more barbed in tone, and far more often directed against current writers and critics. ("Yet Mr. Quennell is not being perverse or wilfully stupid; he is merely what nature and environment and the habit of unchallenged complacency have made him and most of his colleagues in the literary reviewing line. . . .") These writers reacted accordingly.

But to emphasize the contentious side of *Scrutiny*'s early years is to lessen its positive achievements. Dr. Leavis, in his retrospect for this republication, unabashedly lists those achievements, and to read through the eighty or so issues of his magazine bears out his claims. Here is what *Scrutiny* did:

Following the lead of Eliot, but with greater specificity, it reconsidered the mainstreams of English poetry, tracing out the dominant traditions and vital interrelationships of the major and minor poets, ignoring reputation and returning again and again to the text for new judgment, carefully but passionately elucidating a new view of the poetry of the past. This view aroused the wrath of the Miltonians and Shelleyites (it still does; last month in the *New Statesman* William Empson was once again quarreling with Leavis's famous Milton essay of 1933), but on the whole the major judgments of Dr. Leavis and his colleagues still stand; they have been disputed but not refuted, since no one of a comparable authority and experience has come along to do a re-revaluation. Eliot and Pound, I. A. Richards and G. Wilson Knight, had started providing readers with new tools for judging, new ways to read. It was *Scrutiny*, with its careful analysis of the texts themselves combined with a broad cultural understanding—practical criticism combined with scholarship—that did the job of applying these tools to the entire literature. What resulted was a truly New Criticism, and those results are now generally (if grudgingly) accepted.

The same can be said of *Scrutiny*'s revaluation of the English novel, and in this case there was far less of a body of serious criticism to set out from. There was the "great characters" view of fiction, and a considerable amount of sensitive but scattered and impressionistic writing of the Woolf-Forster variety. Dr. Leavis both found a new way to read the novel—as "dramatic poem"—and isolated what he termed the Great Tradition of Austen, George Eliot, James, Conrad, and Lawrence. The work his wife (Q. D. Leavis) did on Jane Austen is possibly the most famous and decisive criticism of a novelist to emerge from *Scrutiny* (or anywhere else through these two decades). He himself really rediscovered George Eliot for our generation; did the same for Conrad; and through his long and zealous championship of Lawrence, finally disentangled the Lawrence myth from the Lawrence genius. He and his colleagues re-saw the novel; and we read and judge differently now because they did.

As for *Scrutiny*'s running judgment of the writers of the thirties and forties, those judgments were usually severe, were violently resented at the time, and have generally come to be accepted. What gave the reviewers their strength was that most often they were the same critics who, in the front of the magazine, were examining the major works of English literature. They brought the same standards and methods to bear, and the result was that current books were neither puffed nor made the objects of personal spleen. The tacit assumption was that any book with pretensions to being reviewed in *Scrutiny* should be treated with total seriousness, despite fashion or reputation. When Dr. Leavis attacked the *Work in Progress* (it was progressing toward *Finnegans Wake*) in 1933, it was with this entire critical apparatus and a deep sense of what art should be:

> Mr. Joyce's liberties with English are essentially unlike Shakespeare's. Shakespeare's were not the product of a desire to "develop his medium to the fullest" but of a pressure of something to be conveyed. . . . Conscious management in the *Work in Progress* is not the agent of a deeply serious purpose; it serves in general an inveterate solemn ingenuity, and it is often the very willing pimp to poor wit.

The Joyce mills of our graduate schools would not agree, but they could hardly pretend that their book was not being taken seriously.

The same can be said for the treatment Mrs. Leavis accorded Hemingway in 1936: "Hemingway, with whom [Dos Passos] is often compared to his disadvantage, and whose technique is at least as much derivative, would not be worth interesting oneself in even if he had been original, so cheap are his emotional formulae, so second-rate his attitudes, and so limited and monotonous his structural patterns." I have deliberately chosen examples that may infuriate still, in order to suggest the emotional aura which *Scrutiny* reviews projected. To balance them, here is Mrs. Leavis again, this time at considerable length, in a 1940 review of Orwell's *Inside the Whale*, a book whose political bias was hardly calculated to win *Scrutiny*'s admiration.

He is evidently a live mind working through literature, life and ideas. He knows what he is interested in and has something original to say about it. His criticism is convincing because his local criticisms are sound (always a test), and though his is not primarily a literary approach he is that rare thing, a non-literary writer who is also sensitive to literature. He is not sufficiently disciplined to be a considerable literary critic, he is and probably always will be a critic of literature who, while not a Communist, has nevertheless corresponding preoccupations, but the great thing is, he has a special kind of honesty, he corrects any astigmatic tendency in himself because in literature as in politics he has taken up a stand which gives him freedom. . . . Even his enthusiasms—another test—turn out to be sound criticism. Thus, you may think that the only thing wrong with the title-essay of this book is that he seems to think Henry Miller a great novelist, but it turns out after all that he doesn't. He claims for *Tropic of Cancer* no more than that it is an example of the only kind of tolerably good novel that can be written now ("a completely negative, unconstructive, amoral writer, a passive accepter of evil")—and expects as you and I do, that Miller will "descend into unintelligibility, or into charlatanism" next. . . . But one thing above all there is to his credit. If the revolution here were to happen that he wants and prophecies, the advent of real Socialism, he would be the only man of letters we have whom we can imagine surviving the flood undisturbed.

Here, it seems to me, are intelligence, fineness of judgment, and generosity combined—as they always ought to be in serious reviewing.

The catalog of *Scrutiny*'s successes and importances might be prolonged considerably, and the temptation to prolong it is also considerable, even if only to list and applaud its many major writers: L. C. Knights; James Smith; D. J. Enright; W. H. Mellers, the very able music critic (though it is hard to match his passionate concern for the English composers of the period); D. A. Traversi; John Speirs, who applied the *Scrutiny* method to Chaucer and other medieval writers; Martin Turnell, who attempted the French classic plays; Denys Thompson, who, with several others, made a searching study of English education. The major *Scrutiny* names read like an honor roll—and there are many more—to say nothing of the occasional contributors who come somewhat as a surprise: Auden, for instance, and Santayana; and the single odd appearance of Norman Podhoretz, praising (not so oddly) *The Liberal Imagination.*

Why, one might ask, did the regular *Scrutiny* writers come together, and what held them together for so long? Was it simply that the magazine had such high standards—or did it have an underlying rationale or philosophy that specifically attracted them? It seems to me that the latter is true. The magazine reflects a peculiar combination of humanism and puritanism, welded together by fervor. From the start, in the early thirties, when Marxist criticism was extremely fashionable, *Scrutiny* was solidly anti-Marxist—and for reasons it took many liberals until the last decade or so to discover. It was equally anti-chic, or anti-camp (Bloomsbury cliquery and Sitwell-dom were among the archenemies). Its values were solid human values, *moral* values; it looked back with regret to a time when the people had their own idiosyncrasies of speech, played music in their homes, had a vital popular literature, lived wholesome and creative lives on farms and in towns. The key word is "moral"—Dr. Leavis's Great Tradition is the great tradition of moral examination, and it is not irrelevant that one of his favorite books is *The Pilgrim's Progress.*

These general attitudes gave great strength and intensity to *Scrutiny*'s vision of literature; they also limited it. Much of English fiction simply didn't interest *Scrutiny*—Fielding, Sterne, even Richardson are never treated in depth. And Dickens remains, to my mind, the single large failure of the magazine. Again and again various of the *Scrutiny* critics returned to the problem of Dickens, but none of them dealt with it successfully. Their failure ranges from such a silly remark as Frank Chapman's "But, on occasions, Dickens rises superior to Smollett" to the tortured clash in Dr. Leavis between "In ease and range there is surely no greater master of English except Shakespeare" and his insistence on finding *Hard Times* the one successful Dickens novel. In *Hard Times*, Dickens is "for once possessed by a comprehensive vision, one in which the inhumanities of Victorian civilization are seen as fostered and sanctioned by a hard philosophy, the aggressive formulation of an inhuman spirit." That "for once" indicates Leavis's impatience with Dickens for wasting his genius on the kind of books he wrote, for being the kind of genius he was. And yet, in his analysis of *Hard Times*, Leavis's inexorably fine eye leads him again and again to praise the book most highly for the very qualities that are stronger in so much of Dickens's other work. Not even Dr. Leavis could transform Dickens into D. H. Lawrence; Dickens was both great and frivolous, and *Scrutiny* could not forgive him.

Again, the irritation of *Scrutiny* critics toward all of Restoration comedy (it seems almost personal pique at times), their refusal to see anything good in the entire body of work, is an indication of how unequipped the *Scrutiny* sensibility was to deal positively with what seemed to it frivolous and/or immoral. Bunyan *or* Congreve; not both. At one point, Dr Leavis actually applauds George Eliot for beating Congreve at his own game. In Eliot "we are not offered wit and phrasing for our admiration and the delight of our palates." Or as he suggests elsewhere, "Certainly charm is overrated when it is preferred to maturity."

This earnestness, which so often reinforces and strengthens *Scrutiny* judgment, also results, unfortunately, in the acceptance into the canon of certain contemporary works of high moral purpose but less striking literary merit. T. F. Powys's *Mr. Weston's Good Wine* is one case in point. Another is L. H. Myers's *The Root and the Flower*, a general *Scrutiny* favorite that many *Scrutiny* admirers (like myself) have struggled through on orders from above. How this moral zeal occasionally led to the judging of literature in an extra-literary way—something utterly at odds with *Scrutiny*'s basic ambitions—can be seen at its baldest in an early article on Myers by D. W. Harding:

> The worth of Myers' work ought perhaps to be regarded as largely
> independent of one's opinion of the novels as works of art, where

judgments may differ widely; essentially they are means of communicating, and they would still be of remarkable value if you
concluded that they were scientific essays of an unusual kind.
Their first value lies in the fact that they do succeed—by whatever
means—in conveying extremely clear and sensitive insight into
the conditions of adult and self-responsible lives in a civilized
society.

This kind of criticism has nothing whatever to do with the *Scrutiny*
method, but it has everything to do with the *Scrutiny* ideal.

But as I have said, these are the incidental failures of a strength that is
responsible for much of *Scrutiny*'s success. When that strength attached
itself to writers worthy of it, and related to it, it assisted at prodigies
of interpretation and revelation. The obvious example is Lawrence, for
whom Leavis performed a service few critics have been able to render a
great writer; he was able to do so not only because he recognized Lawrence's genius but because it was so sympathetic to him. So was George
Eliot's; so was Conrad's; so also were Samuel Johnson's, Pope's, Hopkins's.
He was less sympathetic to T. S. Eliot, so much of whose work he greatly
admired (and fought for), and from whom he so benefited. The poet and
early critic he always praised, but the *figure* he turned violently away from,
until at last Eliot takes on an obsessive role in the pages of *Scrutiny*, turns
into an anti-Lawrence—the un-Lawrence, as it were: a force Leavis found
both dangerous and fascinating. In fact, Leavis's ambivalent and changing
attitude toward Eliot is one of the most gripping dramatic threads of these
volumes—*criticism* as dramatic poem.

Indeed, it is difficult to avoid discussing Dr. Leavis as a dramatic
character—not that he wants to be discussed, but that his energy and
power, his personality, constantly compel our strong emotional response.
He was always a passionate adherent and a passionate enemy; quarrels
pepper the pages of the magazine, and their tone was rough. ("Everybody
must feel unwilling to enter the feverish spirit of Dr. Leavis' quarrels,"
wrote Empson in a 1935 letter to the editors.) When they center on literary differences of opinion, they can be interesting and fruitful. They
seem less so when Dr. Leavis's embattled voice is describing *Scrutiny*'s
position at bay in the inimical world of *The Times Literary Supplement*, the
BBC, Bloomsbury, Oxbridge, and the *New Statesman*. In his current retrospect he appears more willing than he has been before to acknowledge

Scrutiny's decisive triumphs. But the energy he still puts into pursuing old battles—and his extremely emotional and dramatic view of those battles—is very disturbing. "I will record here, as a relevant and representative datum, this: we had a great influence—and not the less because *Scrutiny* was known to be an outlaw enterprise—on generations of Cambridge students from the Indian subcontinent who now form key *elites* in India and Pakistan." This talk of outlaws and *elites* (and there is much more of it) is not only disturbing, it is uninteresting (except, perhaps, clinically). It is particularly disturbing when one is on Dr. Leavis's side—as in the famous feud with C. P. Snow. And yet it would be a mistake to brush aside Leavis's and *Scrutiny*'s argument with the literary establishment because it is sometimes expressed hysterically. *Scrutiny* attempted to erect a dam of standards against what it recognized as a flood of self-serving mediocrity in the literary and educational circles of England, circles that had cast out England's one contemporary genius, Lawrence, and were clearly not prepared to reform at *Scrutiny*'s insistence. The magazine succeeded in reorganizing literary opinion; it could hardly have expected to change all England—Leavis was not Cromwell. Perhaps his own knowledge that he could not achieve what had to be achieved is what makes him at times so angry, so desperate, so fanatical. One's only quarrel is with that extreme note in his voice: It makes him so vulnerable to attack by his inferiors.

Besides, there is a real drama or heroism about *Scrutiny*. The very conditions under which it published were so difficult—the few copies printed and sold, the absence of any paid advertising, the inability to pay either writers or editors. Under war conditions the magazine almost went down, and its most touching moment came in 1941, when—in the superb issue that contains the first of Mrs. Leavis's articles on Jane Austen and Dr. Leavis's on Conrad—the editors announced that they thought they could keep going if they could only find another hundred subscribers. (After the war, the printing rose to fifteen hundred, and presumably this solved the financial problem.) It is exciting just to think of so valuable and influential a magazine maintaining itself this way for twenty years. Even the end was dramatic—Dr. Leavis's sudden decision to stop since he could not find enough young talent to help put together a satisfactory issue four times a year. He was right. By the end, *Scrutiny* had become less interesting. Not only were the newer contributors not very original but the major job of revaluation had been done. And as for contemporary writers, although

Scrutiny eventually savaged Graham Greene and Dylan Thomas and a few others, its heart wasn't in it. Dr. Leavis was really still occupied with the inferior writers of his youth.

For years now, old copies of *Scrutiny*, their pale blue covers growing grimy and ragged, have been hoarded, bought, borrowed, and occasionally stolen by teachers and students here and in England. Now the entire two decades' worth is available, and we can only be grateful to the publisher and to Dr. Leavis for making it so. The Collected Works of famous novelists are no longer issued in elegant uniform sets; the Collected *Scrutiny* is. Is this a further proof that we are living in an Age of Criticism? I prefer to think of it as a tribute to one of our times' significant creative achievements.

December 7, 1963

Am I Judith Krantz?

Am I Judith Krantz?

This is a question that haunted me through the first hundred or so pages of *Sex and Shopping*, Ms. Krantz's "confessions." You may say that the disparity in gender makes the question look frivolous— I've certainly never felt that "Maybe I *will* get to heaven and discover that there I have a penis!" or that "If I could be sure of this, I'd die happy." And it might seem that I'm skating too blithely over the difference in our ages. (Precocious Judith Krantz, née Judy Tarcher, graduated from Birch Wathen, a small Manhattan private school, a few years before I did.) But fans of *The Twilight Zone* or *The X-Files* know that there are sound explanations for such phenomena.

Instead of carping, consider the similarities: Little Judy Tarcher and little Bobby Gottlieb were both overachieving, unhappy kids, unpopular and solitary in school until ninth grade; obsessive readers; brought up "without a single trace of religious observance" and a minimum of family ties. We were both bruised by Birch Wathen with its cliques of spoiled girls and its jumble of ill-assorted boys and its pretense that it was a gentile school—hymns, Christmas—when it was at least 90 percent Jewish. (A spy among the teachers told me that every Yom Kippur, Miss Birch would ask why the school was so empty. "It's Yom Kippur, Miss Birch." "Nonsense! This isn't a Jewish school.")

And what about our lawyer-parents—Judy's mother, my father—both of whom were masters at withholding desperately sought approval? Judy's father was less censorious than impersonal and distanced: "I remember having only one single private conversation with him during my entire childhood. I was frightened by noises in the night, and Daddy sat by my bed and explained why wood makes sounds as it expands and contracts over a twenty-four-hour period.... The only words of parental advice my father ever gave me were 'Nothing is ever lost. Look under things.'" (Actually, that's good advice, considerably more useful than the two bits of counsel Judy received from her mother: "Never marry a man who smokes a cigar" and "All greens go together in decorating, but never, ever use turquoise anywhere.")

Like me, Baby Judy was raised on the draconian four-hour feeding schedule that was standard in the thirties, grew up hating gym (and, later, flying), lost the only grandparent she knew when she was nine, and (a typical post-Lindbergh anxiety) was terrified of being kidnapped—"I tried to reason with myself. We lived on the sixth floor of a twelve-story building, and it seemed impossible for the kidnappers to come down from the roof or up from the street. But I had no success." You needn't have worried, Judy: The kidnappers were fully occupied scaling the walls of 27 West Ninety-sixth Street to my *ninth*-floor apartment.

Were we the same person? Twins separated at birth? Is this a mere accident of geography and sociology? And if we're not the same person, did we ever meet? I don't mean in the glamorous world of publishing (we never did), but in the far more glamorous world of high school? It's certainly possible: One of Judy's three best friends turns out to have been Barbara Bluestein, whose younger sister, Marion, was one of *my* best friends, and I was often in the Bluesteins' Central Park West apartment.

Only after college did our paths significantly diverge. Judy went to Paris determined to become as French as possible and to lose her virginity, whereas I went to Cambridge determined to become as English as possible. And I was already married. But to this day we have shopping in common, though I don't necessarily agree that "I know what I'd do when faced with possible cancer. Shop!"

If you've read the first Krantz bestseller, *Scruples*, you know that young Judith Tarcher—sorry, young Billy Ikehorn—finds herself living in Paris with a down-on-her-luck French countess and, after various French mortifications, is thinned down, dressed up, and initiated into both *l'amour* and the Higher Taste, all of which will serve her well when, eventually, she opens her famous store on Rodeo Drive, Scruples itself. Sex and shopping! It's a Cinderella story, though Billy doesn't need a prince to raise her up from drudgery; she becomes a (metaphorical) princess all on her own. As for the second Krantz blockbuster, *Princess Daisy*, it was inspired "in the middle of the night, sometime in the winter of 1978" by an irresistible line that popped into her head: "She was born Princess Marguerite Alexandrovna Valensky, but everyone always called her Daisy."

Krantz's own progress toward princessdom (in her case, bestseller-dom) was less certain: She didn't begin publishing fiction until she was fifty. But she had served a long, honorable apprenticeship in journalism, writing top-level feature stories for women's magazines. Not only did this experience strengthen her writing, it educated the writer in the ways of commerce; at the crucial moment, she was ready to absorb the advice on how to deal with publishers given her by Sylvia (Mrs. Irving) Wallace: "Remember, you travel only by limo."

Overall, Krantz's account of her career is sensible and instructive. She has a healthy respect for her accomplishments in the pages of *Cosmopolitan* and its cousins: "If I've ever contributed something solid to women feeling at peace with their own sexuality, it's that article ['The Myth of the Multiple Orgasm']. Nor are there multiple orgasms in any of my novels." Yet as someone engaged in her fourth traversal of Proust, she has a healthy take on the limits of her talent. Her poise slips only once—when her first book is climbing the bestseller lists, she's convulsed with the desire, the *need*, to reach the top. In her journal of those frenzied days, she wrote, "I will do *anything* to become number one." And when the impossible dream is realized, "I felt as if a soft, powdery, powerful, white explosion had lifted me into the air and was holding me there." At this moment of climax, her saintly husband, Steve, phones Van Cleef and Arpels in New York and tells them to send along the diamond earrings they've been holding. It's all come together—success, ecstasy, shopping.

But the greatest reward—her mother's approval—is still withheld. Two weeks after receiving *Scruples*, Mrs. Tarcher calls to say, "It was a difficult book for a mother to read." A few weeks later, she softens: *Scruples*, she informs her daughter, isn't "really pornography but sociology." Mature Judith Krantz's sardonic response to this hurt is to remark, "I'd rather hoped it was fiction." But it's clear that, however mediated by time and psychoanalysis, little Judy Tarcher's pain at her mother's coldness has never left her.

Mrs. Tarcher is superbly rendered—the most successful Krantz characterization by far. All her steeliness is there—this mother explaining to her grown daughters why Judy, her eldest, had always been her favorite ("When you've seen one child learn to walk and talk, how interesting can it be to watch another do the same thing?") or angrily reacting to a phone call from her daughter Mimi announcing her divorce ("It's so typical of you to call at this time of night.... You should have known you'd ruin my dinner.") What makes this portrait moving as well as horrifying is the somewhat baffled sympathy with which the author can finally accept and even admire her mother, the victim of a grim childhood and a clearly disastrous marriage. (Only on Mr. Tarcher's death does it emerge that he had had many lengthy affairs and, it would seem, a child by a woman to whom he left a quarter of a million dollars.)

Judith Krantz's truce with her parents and her past can be attributed partly to her success—as a writer, as a woman, and as a social being, moving easily and happily among her version of the crème de la crème in Paris, New York, and Los Angeles; partly to a naturally buoyant and practical temperament; and partly to her analysts, although she convincingly skewers two of them. She enjoys her looks, her husband and children and friends, and her *things*—her three sable coats, for instance: She simply wore out the first two, and why not? "An unworn sable sulks in the closet." At the 1939 World's Fair (she's eleven), she flings herself "on the deliciously rich-smelling carpet of the backseat of a Rolls-Royce. Home! Home at last!" And as for accessories, "In a changing world, for a woman who loves handbags, Hermès is a rock in a raging storm."

Finally, if we read *Sex and Shopping* carefully enough, we can pick up valuable tips for dealing with crises. Arriving at her analyst's office one afternoon, she finds a publicist barring her way: In only two hours, she's to appear on *The Merv Griffin Show*! Luckily, she's already had her hair done and picked up her new dress. "I went home and considered my moves. First I took a Miltown.... Then I tried on the dress to make sure it looked okay, accessorized it, *washed my turquoise earrings . . .*" Okay, the emphasis is mine, but at such a moment would you or I have remembered to wash our earrings? We would not. And that's why we're not number one.

May 17, 2000

My New York City Ballet

In the spring of 1948, a few weeks after my seventeenth birthday, the only teacher in my not overly distinguished New York private school whom I really liked (and who actually liked me) invited me and a class-mate to a matinee of Ballet Society at the City Center. Why she thought of taking us I don't know—she didn't explain and I didn't ask. It was enough to have been singled out this way, and by someone so *sophisticated*. (Sophistication was a key concept in post-war New York.) My ballet background was meager (this was pre-*Nutcracker*): My mother had taken me, when I was about twelve, to see Alicia Markova in *Giselle*, and I remember my bewilderment at all those girls in white gauze hopping around the stage. Then she took me to the "boys' program" at Ballet Theatre: *Fancy Free* (sailors) and *Rodeo* and *Billy the Kid* (cowboys). They made more sense than *Giselle*'s Wilis, but not much more. And I had seen the current Broadway musicals with "ballets" in them—*On the Town*, the Agnes de Mille shows such as *Oklahoma!* and *One Touch of Venus*, and Balanchine's *Song of Norway* and *Where's Charley?* But they were a far cry from the austerities of Ballet Society, of which I retain only a few strong impressions: a girl covered in what seemed to be gold leaf in *The Triumph of Bacchus and Ariadne* (she had been touched by King Midas), and the exhilarating outpouring of music and dance that was *Symphony in C*. It was just enough so that by the fall of that year, when Ballet Society morphed into the New York City Ballet I was ready to try it. Instantly, I fell in love, and since I was now an undergradu-ate at Columbia, only a quick subway ride from the City Center, I was able to pursue this new passion for four uninterrupted years.

New York then was in the first flush of having become the capital of the world. In the late thirties the city had filled up with refugees from Nazi Germany—an immigration that drastically altered its cultural tone. New

Yorkers became more cosmopolitan, more international, more . . . sophisticated. Touchstones for young intellectuals (or bohemians, as the braver among them saw themselves) were the Museum of Modern Art of Picasso's *Guernica* and its film department's screenings of such masterpieces as Carl Dreyer's *The Passion of Joan of Arc*—and in fact all of what we then called "foreign film." These were the pre-Fellini, pre-Bergman days of French movies like *La Symphonie Pastorale* and of the Italian neorealists Rossellini and De Sica. Revival houses—the decrepit Thalia up on Ninety-fifth Street in particular—showed endless reruns of Pagnol's *The Baker's Wife* and Harry Baur in *Crime and Punishment*. Martha Graham embodied the height of the seriousness of "modern dance." And of course there was Greenwich Village, with its world of louche bars and their promise (or threat) of casual sexual encounters. This was the background we brought to Balanchine, this plus whatever reading we were deeply engaged in—in my case, typically for the times, Henry James. In other words, we were earnest, and dedicated to High Art. Balanchine fit us like a glove.

Going to the New York City Ballet in those days, with the City Center half empty and the *Times* less than enthusiastic, had a satisfyingly conspiratorial feeling to it. But far more important, at least for me, was the way Balanchine's dances and dancers made me feel. Whether I was watching *Orpheus*, with its ultra-modern Noguchi artifacts (we used to call them the divine toilet seat and the sacred catcher's mask), its beautiful Stravinsky score, and its wrenching story, or the ecstatically uplifting *Symphony in C*, or the rigorous, black-and-white Hindemith *Four Temperaments*, which seemed to carry the concept of "modern" as far as it could go, I was released from the tyranny of words and filled with joy. I can remember rushing out of the City Center after countless performances and clunkily jeté-ing up Sixth Avenue, to the tolerant amusement of my not-yet first wife and my closest friend, Richard Howard. They were in Balanchine's grip, too, but they also had a grip on themselves.

We would buy the cheapest tickets ($1.20, I think) for the cavernous second balcony and do what students always do—sneak down to the better seats during the first intermission. These years, with the steadily growing Balanchine repertory and the regular visits of Sadler's Wells with Margot Fonteyn and the classics, were the foundation of my ballet education and also my saturation in the Balanchine aesthetic. Watching him was how we learned to watch dance, and perhaps also how we learned to consider the world: Here was an art that emphasized speed and energy on the one hand, clarity, restraint, and strict obedience to classic ordinances on the other. There was a hierarchy on display, with the ballerina regnant; everyone onstage understood and accepted this arrangement. Very young dancers would arrive and slowly (or, if they were as talented as Allegra Kent or Suzanne Farrell, quickly) move up the hierarchy until they reached what Balanchine saw as their natural level. Virtue was always rewarded. At least to those of us who were observing, nothing but talent was involved—no vulgar considerations of commerce or publicity, which were anathema to young intellectuals in the early fifties. The Man in the Gray Flannel Suit had no place on the stage of the City Center.

From 1952 to 1954 I was at Cambridge in England, and when I got back, the company had reached one of its peaks, and then, after Tanaquil LeClercq was stricken by polio, it fell into one of its slumps—relieved by the arrival of a superb French dancer, Violette Verdy, who not only strengthened the ballerina ranks immeasurably but gave Balanchine the opportunity to make roles that demanded her Gallic elegance and her supreme musicality. Except for Karin von Aroldingen, Verdy remains the only European ballerina to have become an essential part of City Ballet, as opposed to the impressive series of leading male dancers who were imported from the Danish tradition—Erik Bruhn, Helgi Tomasson, Adam Lüders, Ib Anderson, Nikolaj Hübbe, and, of course, Peter Martins. Verdy and Melissa Hayden—a dynamo of confidence and assertion, and a tremendous audience favorite—anchored the repertory, along with Balanchine's first male American star, the boyishly charming yet serious and ambitious Jacques d'Amboise (né Joseph Jacques Ahearn), who as a virtuoso, a partner, and a mentor to young dancers played a central role in the company for more than three decades.

Throughout these years I was at the City Center, and then at the State Theater, after the company's move there, whenever possible. But it never occurred to me that I would ever meet a dancer, let alone have anything directly to do with George Balanchine or the New York City Ballet. Dancers were semi-divinities to me—I didn't think of them as people one might know; I don't think I thought of them as people at all. The fact that I was now older than many of the dancers was irrelevant: Allegra Kent at seventeen, Edward Villella at twenty-one, seemed to me as grand, as far above mortal life, as Pavlova and Nijinsky—and imagine knowing *them*.

Soon after I began working at the publishing house of Knopf, in 1968, Martha Swope—the official photographer of City Ballet, whom I had known in another connection—asked me if I would be interested in publishing a big, opulently illustrated book about the company with a text by its co-founder, Lincoln Kirstein. Naturally I said I would, and it was quickly arranged. Lincoln (and here I switch to first names, since that was the way I came to know him and his colleagues) was pleased with the results and asked me to work with him on a book about Nijinsky. By this time we had become good . . . what? I can't really say "friends," since I don't believe Lincoln saw relationships in terms of friendship. More than acquaintances, though. He was an easy writer to work with (although his prose wasn't easy) and a fascinating man to spend time with—certainly the finest mind I had ever encountered, and the strongest personality as well. His almost hulking size, his superb head, the splendor of his vision and his accomplishment, even the baroque magnificence of his town house with his collection of art and art objects, made a profound impression. But even more meaningful to me was his approach to life. All his energy went toward trying to make the right things happen by identifying what he hoped was ability and giving it full rein. But unlike anyone else I knew, he didn't seem to mind if his protégés or projects failed, and he didn't want credit if they succeeded. He wasn't waiting for a payoff; his impulse toward talent was disinterested.

At some point in the early seventies, Lincoln asked me to serve on a new board of directors he was establishing for City Ballet. I told him that I would always do anything I could for the company but didn't think I belonged on such a board since (a) I wasn't comfortable with the rich and (b) I would be unhappy as a money-raiser. He replied that money wouldn't be my concern; what he wanted was someone who understood the company and Balanchine. In fact, he was more explicit: "I want someone on the board who knows ballet and will understand what to do at the critical moment." (That moment, I understood, was the moment at which Balanchine would have to be replaced.) It seemed to me a tremendous compliment.

The new board was, needless to say, a rubber stamp for Balanchine: Who was going to deny him anything? In other words, it was a reflection of Lincoln, who saw his role as making possible anything Balanchine wanted to do. The board didn't need to exercise strict financial controls, since that role was filled by the company's formidable manager, Betty Cage, whose powerful personality and gimlet eye were directed at saving money, saying "no" whenever necessary and "yes" whenever possible. (Maria Tallchief refers to her as "a combination labor negotiator, certified public accountant, legal expert, Mother Superior, Father confessor, and psychiatrist.") It was through Betty that my involvement with the company grew more active. Every Monday she made dinner in her West Side brownstone for Lincoln and a few friends—Tanny LeClercq's mother, McNeil Lowry of the Ford Foundation and his wife, et al.—and I was often included. At dinner one night, when the talk came around to the weekend matinees, which were not attracting a family audience, I pointed out that these afternoon performances were often unsuitable for kids— not many parents would choose to take their children to the highly erotic *Bugaku*, for instance. Lincoln instantly said, "If you're interested in programming, why don't you help Betty with it?" Programming each season was yet another of Betty's responsibilities, and she generously accepted my participation; by this time it had become just another chore for her, but to me it was utterly absorbing.

The technical problems of putting together a nine-week subscription season, eight performances a week, were immense. First there was the nature of the subscription itself—four performances for each of the sixteen subscription series, with no repeats of ballets within a series, not only for the coming season but from the past two. Then there were the requirements of the stage manager, Ronnie Bates: what scenery could go up in a single performance, and in what order. Each performance demanded musical variety, and this involved our imperious musical director, Robert Irving. More complicated were the problems of the ballet mistress, Rosemary Dunleavy, who could prepare only a certain number of ballets for performance in any given week. There was the question of who danced what: You couldn't have three Patricia McBride or Kay Mazzo ballets on one program. And you didn't want more than one piano ballet, or one romp, or one black-and-white, or one ballet in which the girls at some point let their hair down. Balanchine liked a rousing closer, with the whole corps de ballet whipping up a storm. Jerry Robbins had very definite ideas about when and how often his ballets should be scheduled. But the technical difficulties were solvable if you laid out enough versions of a schedule and kept shifting ballets around. The more challenging part was creating programs that made aesthetic sense—juxtaposing ballets so that the program as a whole had variety, depth, and coherence. Perhaps it was easier for me to do this than for company stalwarts who rarely watched an entire program from the audience; in any case, when Betty decided I was doing it properly, she left me to my own devices.

Before every season I sat first with George (as I had started to call him before I realized that he was "Mr. B." to almost everybody, then didn't know how to backtrack), then with Jerry, to tell them which ballets I thought should be brought back or dropped. Balanchine—Mr. B.— George—hardly cared, except from a musical point of view. (His often-stated view was that even if the dancing was "lousy" the audience— particularly students—could sit back with their eyes closed and just listen.) Jerry, as I say, was more involved. And both of them had to let me know—if *they* knew at the time—what their new ballets were going to be, since one couldn't schedule "New Ballet No. 1" as a rip-roaring closer lasting twenty-five minutes if it was going to end up a simple pas de deux.

Eventually the programs were agreed upon and could be turned into brochures and ads. After a year or two I got involved in these marketing matters as well, and for ten years or more I supervised all of the company's sales efforts from my office at Knopf. As time went by, I came to realize what had happened: City Ballet had been to a great extent a mom-and-pop store, with a tiny administrative staff and a not very big budget. Now the company was growing, Mom and Pop were feeling overextended, and some outside energy was needed, or at least tolerated. I saw myself as a useful kind of glue, whether helping with union negotiations, lending a hand with mailings and the phones in the subscription department on weekends, occasionally acting as a spokesman for the company (as during a 1976 orchestra strike), serving as liaison between the management (of which I was an unofficial part) and the board, or carrying messages to and from the major figures in the company when they found it inconvenient or uncomfortable to communicate directly. In fact, I saw myself during this period as a part-time messenger of the gods, and I found this kind of uncomplicated service to two great men and a noble institution highly satisfying.

Through these years I spent a considerable amount of time with "George," since there were always issues to resolve. Sometimes I would stand with him in the wings watching performances, sometimes I would go to his office, and if there was a crisis I would call him at home. He was always calm, always courteous, always realistic, and always impersonal. I had understood that I was caught up in some kind of psychic drama with Lincoln: Was he the ideal father? (Hardly!) The ideal mentor? (Not if he could help it.) Perhaps the ideal citizen-patron. I understood that, whatever our relationship was, it would eventually and abruptly be broken off—that had happened with countless people who cared for him—and when it did happen, I was prepared if not consoled. With Balanchine, though, there was no relationship at all, nor could I imagine one or want one. I also couldn't imagine what he thought I was doing in his ballet company or even that he knew who I was. After several years, I asked his personal assistant, Barbara Horgan—who had become a close friend of mine, and who went on to head both the George Balanchine Trust and the George Balanchine Foundation—why he accepted me to the extent that he was aware of my existence. Barbara explained: It was my name. After all, "Gottlieb" is the German equivalent of "Amadeus," and the Mozart connection was good enough for Mr. B.

I have two memories of Balanchine during these years which emphasize one of his outstanding characteristics: his utter practicality. The Tchaikovsky Festival of 1981 was notable for an amazing backdrop that had been commissioned from Philip Johnson for the entire celebration. It was a gigantic assemblage of clear plastic tubes strung together and hung from the top to the bottom of the stage, and it was very beautiful when properly lit. But on the day it was being installed—which was the day the festival was to begin—everything was chaos. One of the very large tubes fell to the stage, narrowly missing a stagehand, who would have been seriously injured if it had struck him. And then as the tubes were exposed to the heat of the powerful stage lights they began to smell (actually, they began to stink). No one knew whether the stage would be ready by eight o'clock, or whether the theater would be inhabitable. Balanchine sat in the middle of the theater ignoring the hysteria surrounding him, totally focused on the way Merrill Ashley's tiara for *Swan Lake* sat on her head. That was the one thing he could do something about, and he was doing it.

Some time before that, a dispute between the company and the musicians had been submitted to arbitration, and negotiations had been moved to the World Trade Center. (We had been in discussion for almost six months.) The sessions were excruciatingly boring because one side would make a proposal and the other would caucus—sometimes for half a day or even longer. If you arrived at nine in the morning and finished with the paper and the crossword puzzle and the gossip and what work you had brought along, there was nothing left but the telephone. Late one morning we ran out of dimes but were afraid to leave the building to get more in case we were summoned to the bargaining table. Eddie Bigelow, one of the central figures of the administration, used his last dime to leave a message for George Michelmore, the company's orchestra contractor, to bring us more dimes, and plenty of them. An hour later Balanchine burst into the room with a bag of dimes, hoping he had arrived in time. They had given the message to the wrong George, but he was so happy to have been given a useful job to do that no one had the heart to disillusion him.

Early in the 1980s, Lincoln asked me to get to know Peter Martins. "I'm too old," he said. "He'll need someone when the time comes." Lincoln had made it abundantly clear to me over the past few years that he saw Peter as Balanchine's successor, but this was the first indication he had given that he felt his own powers diminishing. It was not a happy moment. But I did get to know Peter, and we got on well, possibly because we shared an insatiable appetite for talking about the company. At this time I often traveled with the ballet—to London several times, to Copenhagen, to Saratoga for its summer seasons—and it was mostly on these trips that I would go out after performances with Peter and his companion of many years, the principal dancer Heather Watts, for long dinners consisting of pasta, wine, Strindbergian contention, and ballet talk. By the time Balanchine was in his final decline and Peter and Jerry Robbins were overseeing the company jointly, I was in essence doing the same things for Peter that I had been doing for Balanchine—scheduling the season, overseeing the marketing, and being a general handyman. Ironically, when Balanchine died, the crisis Lincoln had foreseen never arose: The board understood that Peter was next in line, and in that sense the transition took place smoothly. Perhaps Balanchine's long illness and slow withdrawal from company matters made things easier; Peter just did more and more as George did less and less, and then he was doing everything, apart from what Jerry chose to do. The mainstays of the management—Betty Cage, Eddie Bigelow, Barbara Horgan—were firmly in place. And the dancers danced. Yet everything was different.

When I went to work at *The New Yorker* in 1987, four years after Balanchine's death, the dancers were still dancing, but a lot of people thought they were dancing less well. Prominent among them was the magazine's great dance critic, Arlene Croce, who wrote several fierce denunciations of Peter and the company. (She was not alone.) Since I was close to Arlene both personally and professionally, and indeed was now the person publishing these negative pieces, my situation at City Ballet was hopelessly compromised; Peter, who was both angry and hurt, felt I should withdraw from the board of directors, and sometime in the late eighties I did so. What saddened me most was not that after fifteen years of active participation I was cut off from the company, or the break in my friendship with Peter, but that I too was unhappy with what I saw taking place on the stage. As Peter said to me with more emotion than I had ever before heard from him, the problem wasn't just that I edited and published Arlene, but that I *agreed* with her. And this was not simply a matter of aesthetics; for people like me, it was a life-defining moment. Arlene had once said, "The New York City Ballet is our civilization," and that civilization had entered a worrying new stage.

In the time since then, my relation to the company has once again been that of an observer—more recently as a critic. But if I'm no longer part of the City Ballet, it remains part of me. The great spectacle of Balanchine's accomplishment—the high drama of his achievement, which it was New York's privilege to witness for so many years—is still at the heart of my emotional and moral life. As Ira Gershwin says, they can't take that away from me.

December 1998

My complete essay on the New York City Ballet, of which this is an excerpt, originally appeared in *Vanity Fair* and can be found in its entirety at www.fsgbooks.com/lives andletters.

Ms. *Adler*, The New Yorker, *and Me*

A few months ago, I reviewed a book of memoirs by my old friend and colleague Michael Korda, in which I turn up as a good guy. Now, Renata Adler has written a book—*Gone: The Last Days of "The New Yorker"*—in which I'm one of the bad guys. Renata's editor is Michael Korda, and her agent (and Michael's agent) is Lynn Nesbit, who's a close friend of mine. And some years ago, I edited a novel of Renata's at Knopf. Oh, yes, I worked with her when I was the editor of *The New Yorker*, too. Small world, isn't it?

Renata's book (and I'm in first-name mode because this is all very personal) centers on the moment when I replaced William Shawn as the editor of the magazine. S. I. (Si) Newhouse Jr. had bought *The New Yorker* several years earlier, promising to consult (though with whom?) on the matter of the succession. The manner in which the change actually came about was both abrupt and unclear, and people at the magazine were violently (and naturally) distressed. Under these highly charged circumstances, just about everyone behaved at his or her worst: Shawn obfuscated, Si kept silent, and the rest of us said and did things we would rather not recall. Renata, however, has now chosen to recall, or mis-recall, them—a dozen years after the event, when one would have hoped they could be seen in perspective. But polemicists are rarely interested in perspective, and in the course of her current tirade, Renata takes few prisoners and sees few people in three dimensions. One person who, oddly enough, gets off lightly is Si, the man who, after all, made the fateful decision. Perhaps one must take into account that he remains a powerful figure in Renata's world—and besides, his wife, Victoria, was at Bryn Mawr with Renata, who, during the Troubles, bravely admitted to her assembled co-workers, "She is my friend."

Gone sets out its thesis right away: *The New Yorker* ceased being *The New Yorker* the day William Shawn left it, early in 1987. "As I write this, *The New Yorker* is dead," she announces. That, of course, is a matter of opinion, and mine is hardly likely to echo Renata's. But it would have been interesting to watch her incisive critical mind analyze the contents of the magazine under the three very different editors who followed Mr. Shawn: me, Tina Brown, and David Remnick. That never happens; there is only generalized assertion of an absolute. In fact, since Renata was rarely around the magazine during these years, she all too often substitutes generalization and hearsay for firsthand knowledge. On one crucial point in the preface, for instance, she is seriously wrong. The magazine, she tells us, began "from almost the moment Mr. Shawn left it, for the first time since its earliest years, to lose money." I remember the numbers clearly: In the last year of Mr. Shawn's stewardship, the magazine lost $12 million. Toward the end of 1992, the losses were down to between $3 million and $4 million, and heading toward breakeven (later, they were to escalate). But the specific numbers aren't what matter here; I cite them only to demonstrate how an experienced but agenda-driven reporter like Renata allows herself to accept without evidence—and repeat as gospel—anything that supports her thesis.

Renata begins with reminiscence (bright young woman gets job at magazine), then quickly goes on the offensive. She writes, "I had hoped to finish this book without addressing either Ved Mehta's *Remembering Mr. Shawn's 'New Yorker'* or Lillian Ross's *Here but Not Here.*" Somehow her hopes are dashed. She confides that both writers—though Lillian "to a greater extent"—have been her friends, then closes in: Friend Ved's book she dismisses with a sideswipe of disdain—it's merely "self-serving and unpleasant"; closer friend Lillian is savaged. The battleground is Shawn. He's no longer here, so his admirers can no longer vie for his immediate favor; instead, they quarrel over whose view of him is to prevail. "Mr. Mehta's Shawn is something of an unctuous, pious, humorless creep, whose distinction lies in his esteem for Mr. Mehta's work. Ms. Ross's Shawn is an unctuous, pompous, humorless creep, whose greatness is revealed in his feeling for her—and his dislike and disdain for everybody else." In fact, Renata's reading of Lillian's book is that it is "an astonishing and fierce, unremitting, though apparently inadvertent, attack on Mr. Shawn, his magazine, and virtually everything he stood for and believed."

But what is Renata's own view of him? Equally harsh. She indicts Shawn for what she perceives to be the failings of *The New Yorker* during his later years: "A moral certitude, an absence of self-doubt—especially in political matters—that became a minor flaw and then a major flaw." And "What had been a place of originality and integrity began to publish, and defend, instances of false reporting and plagiarism. What had been a place of civility, tact, understatement, became a place of vulgarity, meanness, invasions of privacy." And "Mr. Shawn, it seemed obvious to some of us, never had the slightest intention of naming or making way for a successor." Three editors she rightly nominates as plausible successors—Gardner Botsford, William Whitworth, and John Bennet—"were driven out, cast as villains, or simply passed over in the periodic charade by which Mr. Shawn attempted to persuade others, and perhaps himself, that he had any intention of permitting the magazine to survive him." Finally, she blames Shawn for what she calls the magazine's "ethic of silence . . . There began to be a feeling that it was vulgar, perhaps morally wrong to write." When pieces were not scheduled, or were scheduled and then shelved, "It was unthinkable to inquire about this." She does notice, though, that "blunt people, and particularly screamers, got their way," and astutely she recognizes that "Certainly a source of [Shawn's] power was the determination of non-bullies to protect his delicacy of feeling." (We call this kind of behavior passive aggression.) What she doesn't recognize is that she has echoed—in fact, being much cleverer, surpassed—Lillian with her own "astonishing and fierce," though hardly inadvertent, attack on a man she claims to love and revere.

What's it all about—the rage, the resentment, the revenge? Renata gives us a clue: "I had in my mind, by now, what I thought of as an iconography or theology of *The New Yorker*. Mr. Shawn was the father; Lillian Ross, the mother. The son was Jonathan Schell; the spirit was J. D. Salinger." Theology, possibly, but that "father" is in lowercase. To a large extent this book is an explosion of pain and anger from someone caught up in the dynamic of a drastically dysfunctional family—what must have hurt most is that there was no place in it for a daughter. Jonathan Schell had been the best friend and roommate of Shawn's son Wally, and when Jonathan came to the magazine, he quickly became Shawn's closest associate, apart from Lillian. In Renata's account, family dysfunction and political dysfunction are linked: "[T]he magazine began to churn out volumes of what, even then, was politically correct propaganda and heavy preaching. Mr. Shawn and, to a lesser degree, Ms. Ross were spending more and more of their time with Mr. Schell." Jonathan's real crime, clearly, is that he had so much influence—influence that Renata demonstrates she had always hoped to attain.

She offers unsolicited advice, sees herself as a "hired gun," spanks her fellow writers, even protests to Shawn about material he is planning to run. In 1965—Renata is a young woman, at the magazine only two years—she goes to his office to denounce the publication of *In Cold Blood*. "I said I thought that the pieces violated certain fundamental principles of the magazine. They were lurid, I thought, and sensationalistic. Their structure was of only prurient interest," etc., etc. "Mr. Shawn listened . . . He did not appear to agree or disagree, or even to wish I would go away." (The man was a saint!) Undeterred, months later she and several colleagues once again set out to protect *The New Yorker* from William Shawn by protesting another piece he was about to run. When Shawn made it clear that he couldn't permit this kind of interference, they were "taken aback." How could he object, when "the whole purpose had been to spare the magazine the embarrassment" that publishing the piece would bring? But this time Renata had learned her lesson—"We never again, in his presence, criticized anything in the magazine." On the other hand, out of his presence, "One evening, Bill Whitworth, Jane Kramer, and I had gone to see Gardner Botsford at his house in Turtle Bay—to ask him to consider becoming Shawn's successor." If she can't be the Daughter Apparent, she can try to stage-manage the succession.

Her book reflects a dangerous arrogance. Whatever Renata says or does is, by definition, right. When she launches her notorious attack on Pauline Kael in *The New York Review of Books*, it presumably doesn't occur to her—or matter to her—that most of us don't trash our colleagues publicly, or that she might be embarrassing both the magazine and Shawn. ("Even Mr. Shawn took it hard," she acknowledges—or boasts.) Earlier, she had panned a collection of John Hersey's pieces, including "Hiroshima," a landmark in *The New Yorker*'s history. Too bad: "They did not seem to me to hold up very well." Nor does she have much positive to say about most of her living former colleagues, or about the many writers David, Tina, and I have brought to the magazine. (Her friend Lillian, however, has only the highest regard for Tina: "[S]urprising as it may seem on the surface," Lillian wrote, "William Shawn and Tina Brown, the current editor, are indeed similar," a notion that Renata quite properly guts; whatever Shawn's failings, she protests, "He did not deserve this." In fairness to Lillian, it should be pointed out that she produced this abominable passage while working at reinstating herself at Tina's *New Yorker*.)

But if there are no imaginable similarities between William Shawn and Tina Brown, there are surprising ones between Renata Adler and Lillian Ross—in their private lives (single parents of adopted sons, sporadic output), and in their methods, too. As we have seen, like Lillian, Renata undermines Shawn while ostensibly championing him. She exposes the vulgarity and mawkishness of Lillian's "revelations" about her long liaison with Shawn—the most original passage in *Gone* reflects Renata's intuition that Lillian is really addressing Shawn's children with these revelations; his sons "and any other competitors for his love, respect, and time." And of course she deplores Lillian's assault on Shawn's privacy. But then comes a six-page scene describing her own farewell to Shawn at the end of his editorship. "'First of all,' I rather muttered, 'it goes without saying, I love you and I hope to keep seeing you for the rest of our lives.' He had interrupted, saying 'I love you' quite firmly. When I said the words about seeing each other, he said, again firmly, 'We will keep seeing each other.' Then we were both in tears." They're in tears again later on, and finally, as she's leaving: "From behind his desk, he said again, in a tone of surprising firmness and, considering the distance, gentleness, 'I love you.' I said again that I loved him. We shared a sense, I think, that since the day I first walked in and through the years, we were by temperament, style, understanding—through Hannah [Arendt], Wally, Lillian, Mrs. Shawn, those birthday parties—family." We can imagine how Shawn would have enjoyed having these private moments dished up for us. No matter. Like Lillian, Renata is staking her claim—to being "family" (a daughter at last). Not only that: She and Shawn share temperament, style, understanding. So much for the competition!

But where Renata really trumps Lillian's ace is in the matter of inaccuracy. She gores Lillian's claims to plausibility, but her own book is riddled with errors, of varying degrees of importance and disingenuousness. (Not surprising: She was not known at *The New Yorker* for relishing the checking process, and there are no pesky fact-checkers in book publishing.) To begin with, many names are wrong—Phyllis Maginley for Phyllis McGinley, Wen Weshler for Ren (Lawrence) Weschler, Conrad Richler for Mordecai Richler (or could she be thinking of Conrad Richter?). Most peculiarly, the publisher of *The New Yorker*, Peter Fleischmann, is misidentified as Stephen Fleischmann, his son. This is the carelessness of someone who believes she doesn't need to check or be checked.

As for misstatements of fact, I'll stick to what I know about at first hand. I never fired the jazz writer Whitney Balliett, and neither, thank goodness, did anyone else. I didn't, "within weeks," name Adam Gopnik "culture editor" of the magazine—that required Tina, half a dozen years later. Shawn could not possibly have said he met me once when I was a child—my childhood was spent far from such glamorous encounters; he may have been referring to my wife, whose father was the *New Yorker* writer Niccolò Tucci. Renata couldn't have seen in my Knopf office "an immense white porcelain she-wolf with dugs"; perhaps her eye had been caught by an un-immense and genderless Styrofoam borzoi (the Knopf emblem)—the dugs were in the eye of the beholder. And if, during the traumatic and hectic time immediately following my arrival at the magazine, I made even a few of the fatuous and self-regarding remarks she credits me with, I apologize to one and all. I'm not really stupid enough, though, ever to have said—or to have thought—"People love me. I've already weaned them from Mr. Shawn."

But at least Renata throws me a few halfhearted compliments, topped by this one: "With time" my "style and manner at the magazine improved." The person who is shown no mercy is the writer Adam Gopnik, who had come with me to *The New Yorker* from Knopf, and who is relentlessly portrayed as an ingratiating, manipulating self-advancer. But even if this is an accurate portrayal, why should a Sherman tank like Renata be wasting its firepower on a gerbil? Why mock Adam's physical characteristics? Indeed, why the unmistakably personal edge to the assault? I believe it's once more a matter of family dysfunction: For decades, Richard Avedon has been among Renata's closest friends; then, some years back, he more or less adopted the Gopniks. Sibling rivalry strikes again! Following her practice of quoting (or misquoting) private conversations with people she has allowed to believe are her friends—"I kissed him on the cheek"—Renata has Adam saying many foolish and embarrassing things. I can only hope she's accurate when she quotes him as saying, "It's always been my dream to go to *The New Yorker.* You don't think, do you, that the staff will think I'm Bob's catamite?" (That's called protecting your ass.) Let me put everyone's mind at ease: If I had ever wanted a catamite, it wouldn't have been Adam.

Gone is part wacky, part unpleasant. Renata hauls up for airing countless slights and grudges; some of them have been festering for more than thirty years. Having trashed various *New Yorker* writers—the late Edith Oliver, the living John Newhouse—she proceeds to trash their editors.

(She fancies herself an editor, by the way; one of her old grudges is that the magazine's fiction department firmly vetoed the notion that she might join it.) She reveals: "Twice, at publications other than *The New Yorker*, I actually thought of going to the printer, armed with a rifle perhaps, and lying down, rather as political demonstrators used to do, and saying, They shall not print, in my name, this version of a piece." Mystifyingly, she takes issue with my habit of keeping my office door open: "Adult conversation, any real conversation," she asserts, "takes place behind closed doors." It all adds up: Closed doors, grudges, back-stabbings are standard components of a courtier society. No wonder they play so large a part in Renata's mental vocabulary.

As it happens, Renata suggests that there were courtiers at the magazine in my day. Doesn't she grasp that while under Shawn the magazine may have been some strange kind of family, it was also an extreme and destructive example of an office behaving like a royal court? There was *le roi soleil*; there was *la reine*, Mrs. Shawn, at home raising *les enfants*; there was *la maitresse en titre*, Lillian, swanning around and exerting influence; there was the favorite, Jonathan, resented by numberless courtiers; there was the exhausting jostling for position and trying to interpret the actions and words of *le roi*; and there was, inevitably, the resentful and clever chronicler—the Saint-Simon manqué—waiting to jump in with her self-aggrandizing account of everyone else.

But Renata Adler is no Saint-Simon. This book lacks the energy and bite even of her earlier work, let alone his; her intelligence has been undermined by her resentments and warped by her agenda. At least, though, *Gone* is friendly! I'm happy to report that not only are Lillian and Ved and half her other victims either friends or ex-friends but that, as she tells us, for the duration of my stay at *The New Yorker* "Mr. Gottlieb and I remained friends." Thank you for your friendship, Renata.

January 16, 2000

Acknowledgments

To my friend Bob Cornfield, who insisted that I could and should write—a hard concept for me to accept. To my wife, Maria Tucci, who believes in my writing as fervently as I believe in her acting. And to other close friends who have been supportive and/or inspiring, including Joan Acocella, Mindy Aloff, Alma Guillermoprieto, Richard Howard, Diane Johnson, Alastair Macaulay, Janet Malcolm, Daniel Mendelsohn, Claudia Ross Pierpont, Richard Overstreet. In one way or another, and in various combinations, we bring in each other's wash, as my great friend Irene Mayer Selznick used to say.

A number of editors have encouraged me and published my work:

Graydon Carter at *Vanity Fair* commissioned me to write about the first fifty years of the New York City Ballet and provided an immense amount of space in which to do it, and *Vanity Fair*'s Doug Stumpf cheerfully shepherded all those words into print.

Charles ("Chip") McGrath more or less gave me free rein when he was the editor of *The New York Times Book Review*. From our days together at *The New Yorker* we knew that we read alike, and whether he's editing me or I'm editing him, the process is gratifying and smooth.

First the late Barbara Epstein and then Robert Silvers opened the brilliant pages of *The New York Review of Books* to me and applied their formidable editorial talents to my work, while their squadron of sub-editors and assistants good-naturedly accommodated my obsessive need to fix and re-fix—the natural mode of someone who is himself first and foremost an editor.

At *The New Yorker*, David Remnick generously urged me to write for the magazine, and on one occasion persuaded himself to run an article I don't think he cared for as much as I did. I'm gratified to be able to acknowledge also my editor and friend there, Ann Goldstein.

At *The New York Observer*, Peter Kaplan, who for his own mysterious reasons was determined that I appear in his pages, allowed me to publish in them not only 150 or so reviews for my Dance column (none of which appear in this book) but dozens of book reviews, some of extraordinary length for a general newspaper. (His successors have been equally warm.) The person who has edited all this work, including everything I've written for the paper since he left it to pursue his own writing career, has been Adam Begley; we've had an amazingly happy relationship, both editorial and personal—for me, one of the most rewarding side effects of becoming a writer.

Jonathan Galassi and Jeff Seroy welcomed·me enthusiastically to Farrar, Straus and Giroux, and the publishing process there has been collegial and fun. I need to thank also Susan Mitchell for her elegant jacket design, Jesse Coleman, Brian Gittis, Debra Helfand, Jonathan Lippincott, Chris Peterson (whose patience for editorial detail is as boundless as mine), and Greg Wazowicz.